CHELSEA HOUSE PUBLISHERS

Modern Critical Views

HENRY ADAMS
EDWARD ALBEE
A. R. AMMONS
MATTHEW ARNOLD
JOHN ASHBERY
W. H. AUDEN
JANE AUSTEN
JAMES BALDWIN
CHARLES BAUDELAIRE
SAMUEL BECKETT
SAUL BELLOW
THE BIBLE
ELIZABETH BISHOP
WILLIAM BLAKE
JORGE LUIS BORGES
ELIZABETH BOWEN
BERTOLT BRECHT
THE BRONTËS
ROBERT BROWNING
ANTHONY BURGESS
GEORGE GORDON, LORD BYRON
THOMAS CARLYLE
LEWIS CARROLL
WILLA CATHER
CERVANTES
GEOFFREY CHAUCER
KATE CHOPIN
SAMUEL TAYLOR COLERIDGE
JOSEPH CONRAD
CONTEMPORARY POETS
HART CRANE
STEPHEN CRANE
DANTE
CHARLES DICKENS
EMILY DICKINSON
JOHN DONNE & THE 17th-CENTURY POETS
ELIZABETHAN DRAMATISTS
THEODORE DREISER
JOHN DRYDEN
GEORGE ELIOT
T. S. ELIOT
RALPH ELLISON
RALPH WALDO EMERSON
WILLIAM FAULKNER
HENRY FIELDING
F. SCOTT FITZGERALD
GUSTAVE FLAUBERT
E. M. FORSTER
SIGMUND FREUD
ROBERT FROST
ROBERT GRAVES
GRAHAM GREENE
THOMAS HARDY
NATHANIEL HAWTHORNE
WILLIAM HAZLITT
SEAMUS HEANEY
ERNEST HEMINGWAY
GEOFFREY HILL
FRIEDRICH HÖLDERLIN
HOMER
GERARD MANLEY HOPKINS
WILLIAM DEAN HOWELLS
ZORA NEALE HURSTON
HENRY JAMES
SAMUEL JOHNSON
BEN JONSON
JAMES JOYCE
FRANZ KAFKA
JOHN KEATS
RUDYARD KIPLING
D. H. LAWRENCE
JOHN LE CARRÉ
URSULA K. LE GUIN
DORIS LESSING
SINCLAIR LEWIS
ROBERT LOWELL
NORMAN MAILER
BERNARD MALAMUD
THOMAS MANN
CHRISTOPHER MARLOWE
CARSON MCCULLERS
HERMAN MELVILLE
JAMES MERRILL
ARTHUR MILLER
JOHN MILTON
EUGENIO MONTALE
MARIANNE MOORE
IRIS MURDOCH
VLADIMIR NABOKOV
JOYCE CAROL OATES
SEAN O'CASEY
FLANNERY O'CONNOR
EUGENE O'NEILL
GEORGE ORWELL
CYNTHIA OZICK
WALTER PATER
WALKER PERCY
HAROLD PINTER
PLATO
EDGAR ALLAN POE
POETS OF SENSIBILITY & THE SUBLIME
ALEXANDER POPE
KATHERINE ANNE PORTER
EZRA POUND
PRE-RAPHAELITE POETS
MARCEL PROUST
THOMAS PYNCHON
ARTHUR RIMBAUD
THEODORE ROETHKE
PHILIP ROTH
JOHN RUSKIN
J. D. SALINGER
GERSHOM SCHOLEM
WILLIAM SHAKESPEARE (3 vols.)
  HISTORIES & POEMS
  COMEDIES
  TRAGEDIES
GEORGE BERNARD SHAW
MARY WOLLSTONECRAFT SHELLEY
PERCY BYSSHE SHELLEY
EDMUND SPENSER
GERTRUDE STEIN
JOHN STEINBECK
LAURENCE STERNE
WALLACE STEVENS
TOM STOPPARD
JONATHAN SWIFT
ALFRED LORD TENNYSON
WILLIAM MAKEPEACE THACKERAY
HENRY DAVID THOREAU
LEO TOLSTOI
ANTHONY TROLLOPE
MARK TWAIN
JOHN UPDIKE
GORE VIDAL
VIRGIL
ROBERT PENN WARREN
EVELYN WAUGH
EUDORA WELTY
NATHANAEL WEST
EDITH WHARTON
WALT WHITMAN
OSCAR WILDE
TENNESSEE WILLIAMS
WILLIAM CARLOS WILLIAMS
THOMAS WOLFE
VIRGINIA WOOLF
WILLIAM WORDSWORTH
RICHARD WRIGHT
WILLIAM BUTLER YEATS

Further titles in preparation.

Modern Critical Views

D. H. LAWRENCE

Modern Critical Views

D. H. LAWRENCE

Edited with an introduction by

Harold Bloom

Sterling Professor of the Humanities
Yale University

CHELSEA HOUSE PUBLISHERS
New York
New Haven Philadelphia

PROJECT EDITORS: Emily Bestler, James Uebbing
ASSOCIATE EDITOR: Maria Behan
EDITORIAL COORDINATOR: Karyn Gullen Browne
EDITORIAL STAFF: Perry King, Bert Yaeger
DESIGN: Susan Lusk

Cover illustration by Peter McCaffrey

Printed and bound in the United States of America

Library of Congress Cataloging in Publication Data

D.H. Lawrence.
(Modern critical views)
Bibliography: p.
Includes index.
1. Lawrence, D. H. (David Herbert), 1885–1930—Criticism and interpretation—Addresses, essays, lectures. I. Bloom, Harold. II. Series.
PR6023.A93Z62337 1985 823′.912 85–17505
ISBN 0–87754–655–X

Chelsea House Publishers

3 5 7 9 8 6 4 2

Contents

Editor's Note

This volume gathers together a representative selection of the best literary criticism that has been devoted to the writings of D. H. Lawrence during the past twenty years. The editor's "Introduction" is in two parts, the first having been published originally in 1958 (with a coda from 1966), and the second written for this volume. I have combined them to suggest both a past moment in the history of Lawrence criticism, or a collision of Formalist attack and Romantic defense, and my own transition from a half-believer in Lawrentian myth to what I hope is a more mature critical perspective.

My introductory comments are followed by a selection of critical discussions, arranged in the chronological sequence of their publication. David J. Gordon's overview of Lawrence's own literary criticism emphasizes its balance between subjectivity and restraint. With Philip Rieff's analysis of Lawrence's polemic against Freud, we move to the center of Lawrence's concerns, a center so individual that it also contains Lawrence's apocalypticism, which is described in Frank Kermode's subsequent essay.

Lawrence's novels are the subject of the next sequence, with readings of *Sons and Lovers* by Louis L. Martz, *The Rainbow* by Colin Clarke, and *Aaron's Rod* and *The Plumed Serpent* by David Cavitch. With Sandra M. Gilbert's meditation upon Lawrence's death poems, the focus moves into an area that is significantly complemented by Barbara Hardy's consideration of the representation of women throughout Lawrence's works. F. R. Leavis follows, with his very influential reading of *The Rainbow*, which contrasts usefully with Clarke's more Romantic sense of tradition.

A thematic group comes next, starting with Garrett Stewart's tracing of the link between Lawrence's difficult ontology and a crucial aspect of his style. Leo Bersani, exploring the paradoxes of Lawrence's representations of "stillness" as a state beyond representation, in some sense handles the same link, but in a very different way. The problematic status of personal identity in Lawrence, discussed here by Elizabeth Brody Tenenbaum, is related to this difficult crux of Lawrence's originality in presenting his women and men.

A movement back to specific short stories and novels begins with

H. M. Daleski's account of *The Ladybird* tales, continues with an appreciation of *Women in Love* by the novelist Joyce Carol Oates, and culminates in George Levine's observations upon *Lady Chatterley's Lover.* We return to Lawrence's poetry with Ross C. Murfin's comparison between Shelley and Lawrence, after which the remainder of this volume deals with the major fiction. Martin Price's essay concentrates upon the play of consciousness in *The Rainbow* and *Women in Love*, while Daniel J. Schneider investigates the aesthetic psychology of two of the early novels, *The White Peacock* and *The Trespasser.* With the final essay, a reading by Margot Norris of the important novella *St. Mawr*, we return again to Lawrence's very original metaphysics of being, his ontological journey into an undiscovered country of our existence.

Introduction

Art was too long for Lawrence; life too close.
—R. P. BLACKMUR

As a judicial critic, R. P. Blackmur approximates the Arnold of our day. He *ranks* poets. His essay "Lord Tennyson's Scissors: 1912–1950" creates a new scriptural canon out of modern poetry in English. Class I: Yeats, Pound, and Eliot. Plenty of other classes, but all their members standing below Pound and Eliot. In a rather sad class, the violent school, lumped in with Lindsay, Jeffers, Roy Campbell, Sandburg, etc., are D. H. Lawrence and Hart Crane. Lawrence and Crane "were outside the tradition they enriched. They stood at the edge of the precipice which yawns to those who lift too hard at their bootstraps."

Presumably, Blackmur bases this judgment upon two of his own more influential essays: "D. H. Lawrence and Expressive Form" and "New Thresholds New Anatomies: Notes on a Text of Hart Crane." Both essays will be sizable relics when most specimens of currently fashionable analysis are lost. But because they attempt so little *description* and so much value judgment they will be relics at best. By their documentation we will remember what illusions were prevalent at a particular moment in the history of taste.

Blackmur is a critic of the rhetorical school of I. A. Richards. The school is spiritually middle-aged to old; it is in the autumn of its emblematic body. Soon it will be dead. "Lord Tennyson's Scissors" is only an episode in the school's dying. But, as criticisms die so grudgingly, the essay is worth clinical attention.

Northrop Frye has recently said that all selective approaches to tradition invariably have some ultracritical joker concealed in them. A few sentences from Frye's *Anatomy of Criticism* are enough to place Blackmur's pseudodialectics as false rhetoric:

> The dialectic axis of criticism, then, has as one pole the total acceptance of the data of literature, and as the other the total acceptance of the potential values of those data. This is the real level of culture and liberal education, the fertilizing of life by learning, in which the systematic progress of scholarship flows into a systematic progress of taste and understanding. On this level there is no itch to make weighty judgments,

> and none of the ill effects which follow the debauchery of judiciousness, and have made the word critic a synonym for an educated shrew. Comparative estimates of value are really inferences, most valid when silent ones, from critical practice, not expressed principles guiding its practice.

What I propose to do here is to examine Blackmur's "debauchery of judiciousness" in his criticism of Lawrence, and to suggest where it is inadequate to the poetry.

Poetry is the embodiment of a more than rational energy. This truth, basic to Coleridge and Blake, and to Lawrence as their romantic heir, is inimical to Blackmur's "rationally constructed imagination," which he posits throughout his criticism. Eliot's, we are to gather, is a rational imagination, Lawrence's is not. Eliot is orderly; the lines beginning "Lady of silences" in *Ash-Wednesday* convey a sense of controlled hysteria. Lawrence is merely hysterical: the concluding lines of *Tortoise Shout* are a "ritual frenzy." The great mystics, and Eliot as their poetic follower, saw their ultimate vision "within the terms of an orderly insight." But Lawrence did not. Result: "In them, reason was stretched to include disorder and achieved mystery. In Lawrence, the reader is left to supply the reason and the form; for Lawrence only expresses the substance."

The underlying dialectic here is a social one; Blackmur respects a codified vision, an institutionalized insight, more than the imaginative Word of an individual Romantic poet, be he Blake or Lawrence or Crane. In fairness to Blackmur one remembers his insistence that critics are *not* the fathers of a new church, as well as his quiet rejoinder to Eliot's *After Strange Gods:* "The hysteria of institutions is more dreadful than that of individuals." But why should the order of institutions be more valid for poetry than the order of a gifted individual? And why must order in poetry be "rational," in Blackmur's minimal sense of the word? Lawrence's poetry, like Blake's, is animate with mental energy: it does not lack *mind.* For it is precisely in a quality of mind, in imaginative invention, that Lawrence's poetry excels. Compared to it, the religious poetry of Eliot suggests everywhere an absence of mind, a poverty of invention, a reliance upon the ritual frenzy of others.

Blackmur, who is so patient an exegete of verse he admires, will not even grant that Lawrence's poetry is *worth* descriptive criticism:

> You cannot talk about the art of his poetry because it exists only at the minimum level of self-expression, as in the later, more important poems, or because, as in the earlier accentual rhymed pieces written while he was getting under way, its art is mostly attested by its badness.

Neither half of this confident judgment is true, but Blackmur has a thesis about Lawrence's poetry that he wants very much to prove. The poetry does not matter if the essay can be turned well to its despite. For Lawrence, according to this critic who denies his fatherhood in a new faith, is guilty of the "fallacy of expressive form." Blackmur's proof-of-guilt is to quote Lawrence external to his poetry, analyze the quotation, and then to quote without comment some fragments of Lawrence's verse ripped from context. But the fact is that Lawrence was a bad critic of his own poetry. Lawrence may have believed in "expressive form"; his poetry largely does not.

Blackmur quotes the final lines of *Medlars and Sorb Apples:*

> Orphic farewell, and farewell, and farewell
> And the *ego sum* of Dionysos
> The *sono io* of perfect drunkenness.
> Intoxication of final loneliness.

Here, for Blackmur, "the hysteria is increased and the observation becomes vision, and leaves, perhaps, the confines of poetry." We can begin by restoring the context, so as to get at an accurate description of these "hysterical" lines. For the tone of *Medlars and Sorb Apples* is very quiet, and those final lines that Blackmur would incant as "ritual frenzy" are slow with irony, if that word is still available in the discussion of poetry. The Orphic farewell is a leave-taking of a bride left in the earth, and no frenzy accompanies it here.

Medlars and Sorb Apples might be called a natural emblem poem, as are most of the *Birds, Beasts and Flowers* sequence; one of the signatures of all things. In the "brown morbidity" of the medlar, as it falls through its stages of decay, Lawrence tastes the "delicious rottenness" of Orphism, the worship of the "Dionysos of the Underworld," god of isolation and of poetry. For the retorts of medlars and sorb apples distill the exquisite odor of the autumnal leave-taking of the year, essence of the parting in Hades of Orpheus and Eurydice. The intoxication of this odor, mingled with Marsala, provides that gasp of further isolation that imaginatively completes the loneliness of the individual soul. The poem is an invocation of this ultimate loneliness as the best state of the soul. The four final lines are addressed directly to medlar and sorb apples as an Orphic farewell, but different in kind from the Eurydice-parting, because of Lawrence's identification of Orpheus with Dionysos. This Orphic farewell is a creative vivification, a declaration of Dionysiac being, a perfect lonely, intoxicated finality of the isolated self of the poet. What smells of death in the autumnal fruit is life to him. Spring will mean inevitable division, crucifixion into sex, a genuine Orphic farewell to solipsistic wholeness. The poem is resolved finally as two overlapping cycles, both ironically treated.

Tortoise Shout is Blackmur's prime example of "the hysteria of expression" in Lawrence, where "every notation and association, every symbolic suggestion" possible is brought to bear upon "the shrieking plasm of the self." In contrast, Eliot's Rose Garden with Virgin is our rational restorative to invocatory control.

Eliot's passage is a simple, quite mechanical catalogue of clean Catholic contradictions, very good for playing a bead-game but not much as imaginative meaning. The Virgin is calm and distressed, torn and most whole, exhausted and life-giving, etc. To Blackmur, these ritualistic paradoxes inform "nearly the same theme" as *Tortoise Shout.* Unless *Ash-Wednesday* takes all meaning as its province, I am at a loss to know what Blackmur thinks he means. He invites us to "examine the eighteen pages of the poems about tortoises" with him, but as he does not do any examining, we ought perhaps to read them for ourselves.

The Tortoise poems, a continuous sequence, communicate a homely and humorous, if despairing, love for the tortoise, in itself and as emblematic of man and all created nature involved in sexual division and strife. The Tortoise-Christ identifications have throughout them a grim unpretentious joy, which Blackmur, on defensive grounds, takes as hysteria.

Baby Tortoise, the first poem, celebrates the infant creature as Ulyssean atom, invincible and indomitable. The best parallel is Whitman, in his praise of animals who do not whine about their condition. "No one ever heard you complain." The baby tortoise is a life-bearer, a Titan against the inertia of the lifeless. But he is a Titan circumscribed by a demiurge like Blake's Urizen; this is the burden of the next poem, *Tortoise Shell*, which seems to me closer to Blake than anything else by Lawrence or by Yeats. Blake's Urizen, the Old Man of the Compasses, draws horizons (as his name and its derivation indicate). The Nobodaddy who made the Tortoise in its fallen condition circumscribes with the cross:

> The Cross, the Cross
> Goes deeper in than we know,
> Deeper into life;
> Right into the marrow
> And through the bone.

On the back of the baby tortoise Lawrence reads the terrible geometry of subjection to "the mystic mathematics of the city of heaven." Under all the eternal dome of mathematical law the tortoise is subjected to natural bondage; he exhibits the long cleavage of division. An arbitrary division, a Urizenic patterning, has been made, and the tortoise must bear it eternally. Lawrence's earlier tone of celebration is necessarily modulated into a Blakean and humanistic bitterness:

> The Lord wrote it all down on the little slate
> Of the baby tortoise.
> Outward and visible indication of the plan within,
> The complex, manifold involvedness of an individual creature
> Plotted out.

Against this natural binding the tortoise opposes his stoic individuality, his slow intensity. In *Tortoise Family Connections* his more-than-human independence is established, both as against Christ:

> He does not even trouble to answer: "Woman, what have I to do
> with thee?"
> He wearily looks the other way.

and against Adam:

> To be a tortoise!
> Think of it, in a garden of inert clods
> A brisk, brindled little tortoise, all to himself—
> Adam!

The gentle homeliness that follows, in *Lui Et Elle* and *Tortoise Gallantry*, is punctuated by a purely male bitterness, in preparation for the great and climactic poem of the series, *Tortoise Shout*.

This last poem is central in Romantic tradition, deriving ultimately as much from Wordsworth as from Whitman. Parallel to it is Melville's enigmatic and powerful *After The Pleasure Party:*

> For, Nature, in no shallow surge
> Against thee either sex may urge,
> Why hast thou made us but in halves—
> Co-relatives? This makes us slaves.
> If these co-relatives never meet
> Self-hood itself seems incomplete.
> And such the dicing of blind fate
> Few matching halves here meet and mate.
> What Cosmic jest or Anarch blunder
> The human integral clove asunder
> And shied the fractions through life's gate?

Lawrence also is not concerned with asking the question for the answer's sake:

Why were we crucified into sex?
Why were we not left rounded off, and finished in ourselves,
As we began,
As he certainly began, so perfectly alone?

The subject of *Tortoise Shout* is initially the waking of the tortoise into the agony of a fall into sexual division, a waking into life as the heretofore silent creature screams faintly in its arousal. The scream may be just audible, or it may sound "on the plasm direct." In the single scream Lawrence places all cries that are "half music, half horror," in an instructive ordering. The cry of the newborn, the sound of the veil being rent, the "screaming in Pentecost, receiving the ghost." The ultimate identity, achieved in an empathy dependent upon Wordsworthian recollection, is between the tortoise-cry in orgasm, and Christ's Passion on the Cross, the connecting reference being dependent upon the poem *Tortoise Shell.*

The violence of expression here, obscene blasphemy to the orthodox, has its parallels in Nietzsche and in Yeats when they treat the Passion. Lawrence structures this deliberate violence quite carefully. First, a close account of the tortoise in coition, emphasizing the aspects of the act beyond the tortoise's single control. Then a startling catalogue (the form from Whitman, the mode from Wordsworth) of memories of boyhood and youth, before the major incantation assigned by Blackmur to the realm of the hysterical.

The passage of reminiscence works by positing a series of similitudes that are finally seen as a composite identity. The cries of trapped animals, of animals in passion, of animals wounded, animals newborn, are all resolved on the human plane as the infant's birth pang, the mother singing to herself, the young collier finding his mature voice. For all of these represent:

The first elements of foreign speech
On wild dark lips.

The voice of the solitary consciousness is in each case modified, usually by pain, into the speech of what is divided, of what is made to know its own separateness. Here, as in Wordsworth's great *Ode*, the awareness of separateness is equated to the first intimations of mortality.

The last protesting cry of the male tortoise "at extremity" is "more than all these" in that it is more desperate, "less than all these" in that it is faintest. It is a cry of final defeat:

Tiny from under the very edge of the farthest far-off horizon of life.

One sees why Lawrence has chosen the tortoise; the horizon of separateness-in-sexual-division could not be extended further and still be manageable in a poem of this kind. From this extreme Lawrence carries us to the other pole of human similtude, Christ or Osiris being divided, undergoing ultimate dismemberment:

> The cross,
> The wheel on which our silence first is broken,
> Sex, which breaks up our integrity, our single inviolability, our
> deep silence,
> Tearing a cry from us.
>
> Sex, which breaks us into voice, sets us calling across the deeps,
> calling, calling for the complement,
> Singing, and calling, and singing again, being answered, having found.
>
> Torn, to become whole again, after long seeking for what is lost,
> The same cry from the tortoise as from Christ, the Osiris-cry of
> abandonment,
> That which is whole, torn asunder,
> That which is in part, finding its whole again throughout the universe.

Much of the meaning in this is conveyed through rhythmical mastery; the scattering and reuniting of the self is incanted successively, now widening, now narrowing.

The cross here is the mechanical and mathematical body, the fallen residue of Blake's Human Form Divine. It is also the circumscribed tortoise body, as adumbrated in *Tortoise Shell.* As such, the cross is a demonic image, symbolizing enforced division (into male and female, or *in* the self, or self kept from another self) and torture (tearing on the wheel, crucifixion). The tortoise, torn asunder in coming together, and perpetually caught in that cyclic paradox, utters the same cry as the perpetually sacrificed Osiris in his vegetative cycle. Christ's cry of forsakenness, to Lawrence, is one with these, as the divine nature is torn apart in the Passion. The sexual reduction in this last similitude is imaginatively unfortunate, but as interpretation does not issue from Lawrence alone.

Blackmur, defending Eliot as a dogmatic critic and poet, has written that "conviction in the end is opinion and personality, which however greatly valuable cannot satisfy those who wrongly expect more." The remark is sound, but Blackmur has been inconsistent in its application.

Lawrence, as a Romantic poet, was compelled by the conventions of his mode to present the conceptual aspect of his imagery as self-generated. I have borrowed most of this sentence from Frye's *Anatomy of Criticism*, where it refers to Blake, Shelley, Goethe, and Victor Hugo. What Frye calls a mode of literature, mythopoeia, is to Blackmur "that great race of English writers whose work totters precisely where it towers, collapses exactly in its strength: work written out of a tortured Protestant sensibility." We are back in a social dialectic external to criticism being applied to criticism. Writers who are Protestant, romantic, radical, exemplify "the deracinated, unsupported imagination, the mind for which, since it lacked rational structure sufficient to its burdens, experience was too much." This dialectic is out of Hulme, Pound, and Eliot, and at last we are weary of it. Under its influence Blackmur has tried to salvage Wallace Stevens as a late Augustan, while Allen Tate has asserted that Yeats's romanticism will be invented by his critics. That the imagination needs support can perhaps be argued; that a structure properly conservative, classical, and Catholic enough is its necessary support is simply a social polemic, and irrelevant to the criticism of poetry.

Lawrence himself, if we allow ourselves to quote him out of context, can be left to answer his judicious critic:

> What thing better are you, what worse?
> What have you to do with the mysteries
> Of this ancient place, of my ancient curse?
> What place have you in my histories?

Lawrence, whom the older Yeats so deeply and understandably admired, is in much of his poetry and many of his novels and polemical writings another prophet of irrationalism, but his central poems and novels are well within the most relevant aspects of the Romantic tradition, and make their own highly individual contribution to the Romantic vision of a later reason. The insights of his finest novels, *The Rainbow* and *Women in Love*, are condensed in the relatively early and very Blakean *Under the Oak*, while the blind vitalism and consequent irrationalism of the later novels like *Lady Chatterley's Lover* and *The Plumed Serpent* are compensated for by the sane and majestic death-poems, like *Bavarian Gentians* and *Ship of Death*, and particularly by the poem called *Shadows*, which moves me as much as any verse of our century.

The speaker of *Under the Oak* is experiencing a moment of vision, a moment so intense and privileged that the whole natural context in which he stands becomes a confinement set against him, a covering that must be ripped asunder though his life run out with it. He speaks to the reader, the "you" of the poem, his rational, his too-rational companion underneath the sacrificial Tree of Mystery, and his impatience chastises our rationalizations and hesitations, our troubled refusal to yield ourselves to a moment of vision. Like Balder slain by the mistletoe, the poet is sacrificed to the chthonic forces, and struggles against a Druidic adversary, as in Blake's tradition. We are excluded, unless we too can break the barrier of natural and rational confinement:

Above me springs the blood-born mistletoe
In the shady smoke.
But who are you, twittering to and fro
Beneath the oak?

What thing better are you, what worse?
What have you to do with the mysteries
Of this ancient place, of my ancient curse?
What place have you in my histories?

At the end, Lawrence felt the full strength of that ancient curse. The marvel of his death poems is that they raise the ancient blessing of the Romantic Later Reason against the curse, the triumph over it. So, in the sublime opening of *Shadows:*

And if tonight my soul may find her peace
in sleep, and sink in good oblivion,
and in the morning wake like a new-opened flower
then I have been dipped again in God, and new created.

The poem turns on an imagistic contrast between the new-opened flowers of a still-unfolding consciousness, and the lengthening and darkening shadows of mortality. The imagination's antagonist in the poem is not to be found in the actual shadows, but in a reasonable conception of mortality, a conception that would make what Lawrence calls "good oblivion" impossible. In a related death poem, *The End, The Beginning*, Lawrence writes:

If there were not an utter and absolute dark
of silence and sheer oblivion
at the core of everything,
how terrible the sun would be,
how ghastly it would be to strike a match, and make a light.

But the very sun himself is pivoted
upon a core of pure oblivion,
so is a candle, even as a match.

And if there were not an absolute, utter forgetting
and a ceasing to know, a perfect ceasing to know
and a silent, sheer cessation of all awareness
how terrible life would be!
how terrible it would be to think and know, to have consciousness!

But dipped, once dipped in dark oblivion
the soul has peace, inward and lovely peace.

Renewal depends upon the expunging of self-consciousness, as much as it did in *Resolution and Independence*. Lawrence's death poem, *Shadows*, is finally a hymn of renovation, of the privileged moments becoming "a new morning."

II

Returning, twenty-seven years later, to what is now most of the first half of this introduction, is partly a self-reminder that Lawrence no longer needs the kind of defense that he required in the 1950s, which was the age of critical formalism, when R. P. Blackmur, Allen Tate, and their precursor T. S. Eliot reigned over the world of letters. Partly the editor is also reminded that at fifty-five he is not capable of the polemical zeal he manifested at twenty-eight. The Romantic tradition has been reinstated, and has its own ironical triumph. The poet Eliot is widely recognized now as one of its monuments, akin to his actual precursors, Whitman and Tennyson. And more ironically still, when I compare Blackmur and Tate to nearly any current critics, I see that Blackmur and Tate are to be praised as having more in common with Walter Pater than with my brethren.

Blackmur and Tate do not confuse poets with slumlords, as neo-Marxists do. They do not confuse poetry with post-Hegelian philosophy, do not read codes instead of poems, and do not worship a Gallo-Germano Demiurge named or troped as "Language." Unfortunately, they did mix poetry up with Eliot's version of theology, but at least they never forgot the claims of experience and of the aesthetic in itself, even though they frequently forgot that these claims took precedence over what Eliot had taught them was "the tradition." Eliot expelled Lawrence as a modern heretic in *After Strange Gods*, while confidently declaring the eminent orthodoxy of James Joyce. Lawrence was a Protestant apocalyptic, as religious as Blake, but also a personal myth-maker like Blake. If the churches are Christian, then Blake and Lawrence are not, though they are altogether religious in their visions.

Joyce, like his truest precursors, Dante and Shakespeare, was a poet of the secular world. Eliot's malign critical influence has given us the Joyce of Hugh Kenner and his disciples, for whom Joyce might as well be St. Augustine, and for whom poor Poldy is a benighted Liberal Jew, bogged in Original Sin. This is hardly the Joyce or the Poldy of Richard Ellmann and William Empson, or of the common reader. Joyce was not religious, not a believer, nor particularly fond of the Roman Catholic

Church. As for Poldy, if you can still read, and still believe that writers can represent persons in their books, then Poldy—gently sinful, Jewish, liberal—remains the kindest, most humane, and altogether most lovable character in modern prose fiction.

Lawrence, hardly a libertine, had the radically Protestant sensibility of Milton, Shelley, Browning, Hardy—none of them Eliotic favorites. To say that Lawrence was more a Puritan than Milton is only to state what is now finely obvious. What Lawrence shares with Milton is an intense exaltation of unfallen human sexuality. With Blake, Lawrence shares the conviction that touch, the sexual sense proper, is the least fallen of the senses, which implies that redemption is most readily a sexual process. Freud and Lawrence, according to Lawrence, share little or nothing, which accounts for Lawrence's ill-informed but wonderfully vigorous polemic against Freud:

> This is the moral dilemma of psychoanalysis. The analyst set out to cure neurotic humanity by removing the cause of the neurosis. He finds that the cause of neurosis lies in some unadmitted sex desire. After all he has said about inhibition of normal sex, he is brought at last to realize that at the root of almost every neurosis lies some incest-craving, and that this incest-craving is *not the result of inhibition and normal sex-craving*. Now see the dilemma—it is a fearful one. If the incest-craving is not the outcome of any inhibition of normal desire, if it actually exists and refuses to give way before any criticism, what then? What remains but to accept it as part of the normal sex-manifestation?
>
> Here is an issue which analysis is perfectly willing to face. Among themselves the analysts are bound to accept the incest-craving as part of the normal sexuality of man, normal, but suppressed, because of moral and perhaps biological fear. Once, however, you accept the incest-craving as part of the normal sexuality of man, you must remove all repression of incest itself. In fact, you must admit incest as you now admit sexual marriage, as a duty even. Since at last it works out that neurosis is not the result of inhibition of so-called *normal* sex, but of inhibition of incest-craving. Any inhibition must be wrong, since inevitably in the end it causes neurosis and insanity. Therefore the inhibition of incest-craving is wrong, and this wrong is the cause of practically all modern neurosis and insanity.

To believe that Freud thought that "any inhibition must be wrong" is merely outrageous. Philip Rieff subtly defends Lawrence's weird accusation by remarking that: "As a concept, the incest taboo, like any other Freudian hypothesis, represents a scientific projection of the false standards governing erotic relations within the family." Lawrence surely sensed this, but chose to misunderstand Freud, for some of the same reasons he chose to misunderstand Walt Whitman. Whitman provoked in Lawrence an anxiety of influence in regard to stance and form. Freud, also too authentic a precursor, threatened Lawrence's therapeutic originality. Like Freud, Lawrence's ideas of drive or will stem from Schopenhauer and from Nietzsche, and again like Freud, Lawrence derived considerable stimulus from later nineteenth-century materialistic thought. It is difficult to remember that so flamboyant a mythmaker as Lawrence was also a de-idealizer with a reductionist aspect, but then we do not see that Freud was a great mythmaker only because we tend to believe in Freud's myths. When I was young, I knew many young women and young men who believed in Lawrence's myths, but they all have weathered the belief, and I do not encounter any Lawrentian believers among the young today.

Rereading *The Rainbow* and *Women in Love* after many years, I find them very different from what I had remembered. Decades ago I knew both books so thoroughly that I could anticipate most paragraphs, let alone chapters, but I too had half-believed in Lawrence, and had read as a half-believer. Now the books seem richer and stranger, clearly an audacious and relevant myth, and far more original than I had recalled. States of being, modes of consciousness, ambivalences of the will are represented with a clarity and vividness that are uncanny, because the ease of representation for such difficult apprehensions seems unprecedented in prose fiction. Lawrence at his strongest is an astonishing writer, adept at saying what cannot be said, showing what cannot be shown. *The Rainbow* and, even more, *Women in Love* are his triumphs, matched only by a few of his poems, though by many of his short stories. In the endless war between men and women, Lawrence fights on both sides. He is unmatched at rendering really murderous lovers' quarrels, as in chapter 23, "Excurse," of *Women in Love*, where Ursula and Birkin suffer one of their encounters upon what Lawrence calls "this memorable battlefield":

> "I jealous! *I*—jealous! You *are* mistaken if you think that. I'm not jealous in the least of Hermione, she is nothing to me, not *that*!" And Ursula snapped her fingers. "No, it's you who are a liar. It's you who must return, like a dog to his vomit. It is what Hermione *stands* for that I *hate*. I *hate* it. It is lies, it is false, it is death. But you want it, you can't help it, you can't help yourself. You belong to that old, deathly way of living—then go back to it. But don't come to me, for I've nothing to do with it."
>
> And in the stress of her violent emotion, she got down from the car and went to the hedgerow, picking unconsciously some flesh-pink spindleberries, some of which were burst, showing their orange seeds.
>
> "Ah, you are a fool," he cried bitterly, with some contempt.
>
> "Yes, I am. I *am* a fool. And thank God for it. I'm too big a fool

> to swallow your cleverness. God be praised. You go to your women—go to them—they are your sort—you've always had a string of them trailing after you—and you always will. Go to your spiritual brides—but don't come to me as well, because I'm not having any, thank you. You're not satisfied, are you? Your spiritual brides can't give you what you want, they aren't common and fleshy enough for you, aren't they? So you come to me, and keep them in the background! You will marry me for daily use. But you'll keep yourself well provided with spiritual brides in the background. I know your dirty little game." Suddenly a flame ran over her, and she stamped her foot madly on the road, and he winced, afraid that she would strike him. "And *I*, *I'm* not spiritual enough, *I'm* not as spiritual as that Hermione—!" Her brows knitted, her eyes blazed like a tiger's. "Then *go* to her, that's all I say, *go* to her, *go*. Ha, she spiritual—*spiritual*, she! A dirty materialist as she is. *She* spiritual? What does she care for, what is her spirituality? What *is* it?" Her fury seemed to blaze out and burn his face. He shrank a little. "I tell you, it's *dirt, dirt*, and nothing *but* dirt. And it's dirt you want, you crave for it. Spiritual! Is *that* spiritual, her bullying, her conceit, her sordid, materialism? She's a fishwife, a fishwife, she is such a materialist. And all so sordid. What does she work out to, in the end, with all her social passion, as you call it. Social passion—what social passion has she?—show it me!—where is it? She wants petty, immediate *power*, she wants the illusion that she is a great woman, that is all. In her soul she's a devilish unbeliever, common as dirt. That's what she is, at the bottom. And all the rest is pretence—but you love it. You love the sham spiritually, it's your food. And why? Because of the dirt underneath. Do you think I don't know the foulness of your sex life—and hers?—I do. And it's that foulness you want, you liar. Then have it, have it. You're such a liar."
>
> She turned away, spasmodically tearing the twigs of spindleberry from the hedge, and fastening them, with vibrating fingers, in the bosom of her coat.
>
> He stood watching in silence. A wonderful tenderness burned in him at the sight of her quivering, so sensitive fingers: and at the same time he was full of rage and callousness.

This passage-at-arms moves between Ursula's unconscious picking of the fleshly, burst spindleberries, open to their seeds, and her turning away, tearing the spindleberry twigs so as to fasten them in her coat. Birkin reads the spindleberries as the exposed flesh of what Freud called one's own bodily ego, suffering here a *sparagmos* by a maenad-like Ursula. It is as though Birkin himself, lashed by her language, becomes a frontier being, caught between psyche and body. Repelled yet simultaneously drawn by a sort of Orphic wonder, Birkin yields to her ferocity that is not so much jealousy as it is the woman's protest against Birkin's Lawrentian and male idealization of sexual love. What Ursula most deeply rejects is that the idealization is both flawed and ambivalent, because it is founded upon a displaced Protestantism that both craves total union and cannot abide such annihilation of individuality. Birkin-Lawrence has in him the taint of the Protestant God, and implicitly is always announcing to Ursula: "Be like me, but do not dare to be too like me!" an injunction that necessarily infuriates Ursula. Since Lawrence is both Birkin and Ursula, he has the curious trait, for a novelist, of perpetually infuriating himself.

III

Lawrence compares oddly with the other major British writers of fiction in this century: Hardy, Conrad, Kipling, Joyce, Forster, Woolf, Beckett. He is primarily a religious writer, precisely apocalyptic; they are not, unless you count Beckett, by negation. His last book, *Apocalypse*, written as he died slowly in the winter of 1929–30, begins with Lawrence remembering that his own first feeling about the Revelation of John, and indeed of the entire Bible, was negative:

> Perhaps the most detestable of all these books of the Bible, taken superficially, is Revelation. By the time I was ten, I am sure I had heard, and read, that book ten times over, even without knowing or take real heed. And without ever knowing or thinking about it, I am sure it always roused in me a real dislike. Without realising it, I must, from earliest childhood have detested the pie-pie, mouthing, solemn, portentous, loud way in which everybody read the Bible, whether it was parsons or teachers or ordinary persons. I dislike the "parson" voice through and through my bones. And this voice, I remember, was always at its worst when mouthing out some portion of Revelation. Even the phrases that still fascinate me I cannot recall without shuddering, because I can still hear the portentous declamation of a nonconformist clergyman: "And I saw heaven opened, and behold a white horse; and he that sat upon it was called"—there my memory suddenly stops, deliberately blotting out the next words: "Faithful and True." I hated, even as a child, allegory: people having the names of mere qualities, like this somebody on a white horse, called "Faithful and True." In the same way I could never read *Pilgrim's Progress*. When as a small boy I learnt from Euclid that: "The whole is greater than the part," I immediately knew that that solved the problem of allegory for me. A man is more than a Christian, a rider on a white horse must be more than mere Faithfulness and Truth, and when people are mere personifications of qualities they cease to be people for me. Though as a young man I almost loved Spenser and his *Faerie Queene*, I had to gulp at his allegory.

Yet by the end of his book, Lawrence has allegorized Revelation into "the dark side of Christianity, of individualism, and of democracy, the side the world at large now shows us." This side Lawrence simply calls "suicide":

> The Apocalypse shows us what we are resisting, unnaturally. We are unnaturally resisting our connection with the cosmos, with the world, with mankind, with the nation, with the family. All these connections are, in the Apocalypse, anathema, and they are anathema to us. We *cannot bear connection*. That is our malady. We *must* break away, and be isolate. We call that being free, being individual. Beyond a certain point, which we have reached, it is suicide. Perhaps we have chosen suicide. Well and good. The Apocalypse too chose suicide, with subsequent self-glorification.

This would seem to be no longer the voice of Birkin, who in effect said to Ursula: "We *must* break away, and be isolate," but who never learned how to stress properly his antithetical desire for connection. Lawrence, approaching his own end, is suddenly moved to what may be his single most powerful utterance, surpassing even the greatest passages in the fiction and the late poetry:

> But the Apocalypse shows, by its very resistance, the things that the human heart secretly yearns after. By the very frenzy with which the Apocalypse destroys the sun and the stars, the world, and all kings and all rulers, all scarlet and purple and cinnamon, all harlots, finally all men altogether who are not "sealed," we can see how deeply the apocalyptists are yearning for the sun and the stars and the earth and the waters of the earth, for nobility and lordship and might, and scarlet and gold, splendour, for passionate love, and a proper unison with men, apart from this sealing business. What man most passionately wants is his living wholeness and his living unison, not his own isolate salvation of his "soul." Man wants his physical fulfillment first and foremost, since now, once and once only, he is in the flesh and potent. For man, the vast marvel is to be alive. For man, as for flower and beast and bird, the supreme triumph is to be most vividly, most perfectly alive. Whatever the unborn and the dead may know, they cannot know the beauty, the marvel of being alive in the flesh. The dead may look after the afterwards. But the magnificent here and now of life in the flesh is ours, and ours alone, and ours only for a time. We ought to dance with rapture that we should be alive and in the flesh, and part of the living, incarnate cosmos. I am part of the sun as my eye is part of me. That I am part of the earth my feet know perfectly, and my blood is part of the sea. My soul knows that I am part of the human race, my soul is an organic part of the great human soul, as my spirit is part of my nation. In my own very self, I am part of my family. There is nothing of me that is

> alone and absolute except my mind, and we shall find that the mind has no existence by itself, it is only the glitter of the sun on the surface of the waters.

Starting with the shrewd realization that apocalyptic frenzy is a reaction-formation to a deep yearning for fulfillment, this celebratory passage moves rapidly into an ecstasy of heroic vitalism, transcending the Zarathustra of Nietzsche and the related reveries of Pater in the "Conclusion" to *The Renaissance*. Lawrence may not have known that these were his ancestral texts in this rhapsody, but I suspect that he deliberately transumes Pater's "we have an interval, and then our place knows us no more," in his own: "But the magnificent here and now of life in the flesh is ours, and ours alone, and ours only for a time." Pater, hesitant and elaborate, skeptical and masochistic, added: "For our one chance lies in expanding that interval, in getting as many pulsations as possible into the given time." Lawrence, truly apocalyptic only in his vitalism, aligns himself rather with Whitman and Blake in refusing that aesthetic one chance, in favor of the dream of becoming integral, rather than a fragment:

> What we want is to destroy our false, inorganic connections, especially those related to money, and re-establish the living organic connections, with the cosmos, the sun and earth, with mankind and nation and family. Start with the sun, and the rest will slowly, slowly happen.

IV

Lawrence died four months short of his forty-fifth birthday, with every evidence that he was making a fresh start as poet and as visionary polemicist. As a novelist, he had suffered a decline, in the movement from the eminence of *The Rainbow* (1915) and *Women in Love* (1920) through the very problematical *Aaron's Rod* (1922) and *Kangaroo* (1923) on to the spectacular disaster of *The Plumed Serpent* (1926) and the somewhat tendentious *Lady Chatterley's Lover* (1928). Lawrence's greatest pride was in his achievement as a novelist, but it is the short novels and tales of his last decade, rather than the longer fictions, that persuade us how much was lost by his early death.

Despite the intense arguments of Dr. F. R. Leavis, Lawrence is not quite at home in any canon of the great English novelists, particularly when compared to Conrad. Even *The Rainbow* and *Women in Love* share more with Blake and Shelley, Whitman and Nietzsche, than they do with *Middlemarch* and *The Portrait of a Lady*. Beneath their narrative procedures, Lawrence's two great novels essentially are visionary prose poems, inhabited by giant forms acting out the civil wars of the psyche. In the penultimate chapter of *The Rainbow*, aptly titled "The Bitterness of Ecstasy," Ursula and Skrebensky suffer their final embrace together:

> Then there in the great flare of light, she clinched hold of him, hard, as if suddenly she had the strength of destruction, she fastened her arms round him and tightened him in her grip, whilst her mouth sought his in a hard, rending, ever-increasing kiss, till his body was powerless in her grip, his heart melted in fear from the fierce, beaked, harpy's kiss. The water washed again over their feet, but she took no notice. She seemed unaware, she seemed to be pressing in her beaked mouth till she had the heart of him. Then, at last, she drew away and looked at him—looked at him. He knew what she wanted. He took her by the hand and led her across the foreshore, back to the sandhills. She went silently. He felt as if the ordeal of proof was upon him, for life or death. He led her to a dark hollow.
>
> "No, here," she said, going out to the slope full under the moonshine. She lay motionless, with wide-open eyes looking at the moon. He came direct to her, without preliminaries. She held him pinned down at the chest, awful. The fight, the struggle for consummation was terrible. It lasted till it was agony to his soul, till he succumbed, till he gave way as if dead, lay with his face buried, partly in her hair, partly in the sand, motionless, as if he would be motionless now for ever, hidden away in the dark, buried, only buried, he only wanted to be buried in the goodly darkness, only that, and no more.
>
> He seemed to swoon. It was a long time before he came to himself. He was aware of an unusual motion of her breast. He looked up. Her face lay like an image in the moonlight, the eyes wide open, rigid. But out of her eyes, slowly, there rolled a tear, that glittered in the moonlight as it ran down her cheek.
>
> He felt as if the knife were being pushed into his already dead body. With head strained back, he watched, drawn tense, for some minutes, watched the unaltering, rigid face like metal in the moonlight, the fixed, unseeing eye, in which slowly the water gathered, shook with glittering moonlight, then surcharged, brimmed over and ran trickling, a tear with its burden of moonlight, into the darkness, to fall in the sand.

Dreadfully impressive, this possesses both the force of an experiential representation, and the form of High Romantic mythology. It could be a warring coition of Blake's Los and Enitharmon, an instance of what Blake called a "Reasoning from the loins in the unreal forms of Beulah's night." Presumably Lawrence intended it as part of his prophecy against "sex in the head," but in this instance he wrought too much better, perhaps, than even he knew. The pathos of these paragraphs would be excessive, except for their mythic implications. Short as it was, life was too long for Lawrence, art too close.

DAVID J. GORDON

Lawrence as Literary Critic

Lawrence's reputation as a literary critic is still marginal, but his criticism, judged by its quantity, quality, and scope, must rank as a major area of his achievement. It is chiefly represented by *Studies in Classic American Literature*; by *Phoenix: The Posthumous Papers of D. H. Lawrence*, that extraordinary anthology of prefaces, reviews, and miscellaneous essays which provides a record of the critic at every stage of his career; and by the voluminous letters, themselves an anthology of vivid critical commentary. Noteworthy criticism can also be found in almost every one of the many books of nonfiction that Lawrence wrote, and in his fiction and verse as well. His primary interests as a critic were the literature of the nineteenth and early twentieth centuries (especially American, Russian, English, and Italian) and literary theory (especially the theory of the novel and the relation of art to morality), but the full scope of his criticism includes much more: the "Study of Thomas Hardy," for instance, is, among other things, a wide-ranging interpretation of Western literature and art.

The undervaluation of Lawrence as a critic may be due in part to the long inaccessibility of essential sources, for *Phoenix* has only recently been reissued and the scattered letters only recently collected. But I believe there are more basic causes, inherent in the criticism itself—namely, its peculiarities of form, of tone, and of style.

Lawrencean criticism proceeds quite deliberately beyond the bound which formal criticism usually sets for itself: the elucidation of text and the relation of text to literary tradition. A good deal of modern formal criticism is, we are beginning to realize, more ideological than it pretends to be, but seldom is it so directly harnessed to such an explicit and individual moral vision. In *Studies*, for instance, on which his reputation as a critic chiefly rests, Lawrence sets himself not only a literary task, "to save the tale from the artist who created it," but also a prophetic task, to be "midwife to the homunculus" of a new era; his only other critical work of book length which proposes a literary subject, the "Study of Thomas Hardy" (unless we include *Apocalypse*, which is in this respect similar), combines literary criticism with art criticism, social and political criticism, and metaphysics.

The flexible, freewheeling form of critical essay which Lawrence developed for himself enabled him to pass naturally beyond a concern for art proper and to emphasize its relation to the civilization of which it is a vital expression. He sometimes flouted distinctions between fiction and fact—linking, for example, Hamlet and Napoleon, *The Idiot* and President Wilson, using both terms as symbols in a vast and tendentious historical myth—but it is essential to understand that he was keenly sensitive to aesthetic values. Art was for him both text and pretext, but its moral usefulness depended on its first being art. It was to art that he so often turned in his search for values, because he had made an assumption that was as fundamentally aesthetic as moral—namely, that "Art-speech is the only truth." By this Lawrence meant, first, that genuine art represents the deepest penetration of the human consciousness into reality, and, second, that "if it be really a work of art it must contain the essential criticism on the morality to which it adheres," and is therefore truer than any discursive statement. Similarly, the distinction between art and artist, which he also sometimes flouted superficially, was in fact essential to his critical objective, which was "to save the tale from the artist who created it," to reveal deeper and truer implications of a work than the artist himself may have been conscious of. It must be added that in the process of this revelation the critic tried, often successfully, to identify the truth in the work with the truth of his own moral vision, to merge what the work *really* says with what it should say.

To conduct criticism of this kind, Lawrence required a standard of value. He most often called this standard "life" and identified it both with "true emotion" within the individual soul and "true relationship" between self and otherness. Both true emotion and true relationship are norms, but flexible rather than fixed. They may change within the wide limits of vital possibility, limits that are to be defined only by the points beyond which the soul and relationship lose their natural subtlety and fluidity. Such a collapse may be caused by the erection of some fixed and permanent standard, the idealization of one direction of consciousness. Lawrence scolded Plato and Jesus, for instance, for making one emotion supreme; balance could not so easily be restored, because idealization tended thereafter to predetermine the naturally indeterminate vital consciousness. A paradox essential to Lawrence's thought, then, and one by which he escapes total relativism as well as total absolutism, is that life is both incorruptible (thereby absolute) and vulnerable (thereby subject to perversion by the force in man and, ultimately, in civilization that seeks fixity, finality, and changelessness.)

This belief underlies his approach to art. On the one hand, no art can be wholly false because art *qua* art in some degree honors life—"in their passional inspiration, [artists] are all phallic worshippers" was one way Lawrence liked to express it—and to that degree partakes of absolute value. But, on the other hand, no art can be wholly true, because the artist's emphasis will be inescapably relative to his time and place; for the artist of the modern epoch especially, the influence of civilization is likely to be reflected in art not only as metaphysical imbalance but also as a fear of the unknown, of openness to possibility, which inhibits or perverts the artist's very capacity to honor life.

It was primarily the "errors" of art and artist that concerned Lawrence: their deviation from the norm of "life," sometimes conceived as the hidden numen behind phenomena, sometimes as the gamut of vital possibility, and even as the one thing needful for our time. He was too engaged a writer, too intent upon changing the world he lived in, to observe the oscillations and perversions of vital consciousness from a lofty metaphysical perch. At the risk of being misunderstood or subject to correction himself at the next turn of history, he wanted to find and declare "the truth that concerns us, whether it concerns our grandchildren or not." He read literature mainly as a diagnosis of our psychic illness. The necessary truth of art he sometimes took for granted, particularly in his less deliberate remarks; the falsehood provoked him to rage.

This peculiarity of tone may lead one to suppose, quite mistakenly, that Lawrence's criticism is merely negative and reductive. When he suppresses the positive value that is necessarily implied in his view of art, it is important to remember that the judgment is, so far as art and artist are concerned, partial. I do not wish to suggest that Lawrence's criticism is balanced and reasonable, for it is not, but only that it is more complex and less reductive than may be supposed.

In a sense, "reductive" is a particularly inappropriate description of Lawrence's criticism, despite its partisanship, for the critic's rage, oddly, enhances rather than diminishes the work being discussed. W. H. Auden perceived this when he wrote of Lawrence, "He is so passionately interested in the work he is talking about and so little interested in his reputation as a critic that, even when he is violently and quite unfairly attacking an author, he makes him sound far more exciting and worth reading than most critics make one sound whom they are professing to praise." Although I should think one would have to find the critic's assumptions interesting and provisionally valid, it is not their final truth that need concern us; rather, we want to know how good a criticism they make for. And the point to be made here is that Lawrence's partisanship does not in itself vitiate that criticism. The Baudelairean prescription which Martin Turnell uses as an epigraph in "An Essay on Criticism" applies perfectly, as Turnell intends it should, to Lawrence: "Criticism should be partial, passionate, and political, that is to say, it must be written from an exclusive point of view, but from a point of view which opens up the widest horizons." One of the most wholesome influences of Lawrence as a critic is that, for all his improprieties, he takes literature more seriously than do many of us; unhesitatingly, he sees it as intensely relevant to the human situation. It is this passionate and encompassing sense of life that explains why even his terse and angry squibs are often richly suggestive.

Lawrence's moral earnestness is rather different from that of most other critics. They assess the merit of an artist's intention along with the skill of his execution. Lawrence usually takes these for granted, saying little about artists he does not think important, for "only the best matters." He gauges instead their courage and sincerity, the human qualities he most admires and so markedly possesses: Courage is "the only thing worth having anyhow"; "Before everything I like sincerity, and a quickening spontaneous emotion." Implied in this attitude is a profound faith in what men could be at their best and a profound resistance to what they settle for from timidity and ignorance. Thus he criticizes a book on the basis of what it should mean, identified if possible with what it does mean when read in depth. He berates an author not so much for failing as an artist as for failing as a man to realize the full implications of his work. As Richard Rees put it, "Lawrence could hate, but I believe he was incapable of feeling contempt."

Lawrence's manner of confronting fellow artists has not been well understood. He was in a significant sense the least arrogant of critics. It was in fact because the usual critical stance seemed to him an affectation of superiority, an impertinence, that he dismounted and took up hand-to-hand combat. He scolded, ridiculed, and first-named his subjects, but not to reduce a reputation or indulge his angry wit. It was always the issue that engaged him. One critic describes the encounter as "a dynamic conflict of value systems in which Lawrence always seems to win, if only . . . because he rarely tackles any writer whose position he does not think he can improve upon." But Lawrence "improves" on writers not to win a personal combat but to declare, on behalf of all men subjected to the same ideological pressures, a certain vision of life. Graham Hough puts it more carefully: "He exposes the weaknesses of civilization, rather than of individual authors. He blames it, not them, that we are not phallic worshippers." Indeed, for Lawrence all genuine artists are culture *heroes*. And that fact should help us emend Leslie Fiedler's petulant criticism: "Only D. H. Lawrence has ever challenged Whitman's claim to this honor [celebrator of the body]. . . . But one can hardly expect Lawrence to be fair since he coveted for himself the title of the anti-Christian Christ." "Fair" he may not be (although, since according to the Lawrencean psychology the celebration of the body may derive either from blood *or* mental consciousness, the challenge to Whitman is not on the face of it merely perverse or spiteful), but the role in which he casts Whitman finally ("the one man breaking a way ahead") is hardly a secondary one.

It is partly true of course, as Fiedler implies, that Lawrence tends to make his heroes forerunners to his own gospel. But that contributes to the excitement of his criticism. It is synthetic as well as analytic. Watching Lawrence struggle with himself while he struggles with his subject, one senses a developing artistic structure, a myth in the process of being forged.

No doubt this raises a troublesome problem. At what point does the subject become irrelevant; at what point could the critic as well be discussing anything at all; or, to put it another way, at what point does either the subject or the critic's world view come to seem an intrusion? Martin Turnell, who values personal force above all else in the critic and who therefore has a very high opinion of Lawrence's criticism, feels that the critic is an artist expressing himself through other artists. "He must not distort their vision, but he must communicate *himself* to the reader." That Lawrence succeeds in the latter will not be doubted. The extent to which he distorts the vision of others is a problem that will be considered in the course of this study.

A tone of anger, in any case, is no reliable indication of Lawrence's estimate of particular authors or works. His anger may properly attach to the historical tendency reflected in the work; a work may even be denounced for its ideological one-sidedness, yet approved precisely for revealing that danger to us. Moreover, the critic may be most severe where he admires most (as with *Anna Karenina*), on the principle that great work is worth quarreling with while lesser work is not: as he once wrote of a minor Hardy novel, "The spirit being small, the complaint is narrow." Readers who are confused by such integration of censure and praise are, I suspect, adhering to the notion that criticism should give grades rather than explore the sometimes contrary implications of a work of art; the dialectical critic seems to them merely illogical. Confronted with Lawrence's vituperations, we should remember that he maintained the profoundest respect for literature, following his own precept: "To my thinking, the critic, like a good beadle, should rap the public on the knuckles and make it attend during divine service. And any good book is a divine service."

Lawrence's gift for animated and—despite repetitiveness—incisive discourse is obvious, yet, strangely, he does put a considerable burden on the reader who would follow his argument closely. I believe this is due to an essential peculiarity of his style, a peculiarity reflected in violations of logic and in shifting, inconsistent, and symbolic terminology. It is not, I think, sufficiently acknowledged or understood by his critics: F. R. Leavis hardly seems aware of it, Graham Hough considers it superficial, and T. S. Eliot describes it as Lawrence's "incapacity for what we ordinarily call thinking." Aldous Huxley, addressing himself to Eliot's charge, points out that Lawrence did not reject what we ordinarily call thinking because of incapacity but because "the methods of science and critical philosophy were incompatible with the exercise of his gift—the immediate perception and artistic rendering of divine otherness." Huxley presents Lawrence as a man who, even in critical discourse, must be an artist. There is in fact a certain subjective immediacy in his criticism as in his art, an attempt to render "the felt quality of experience," although we should understand that Lawrence's critical intelligence is manifest the way any good critical intelligence is manifest: in the penetration of the questions asked, in the subtlety and flexibility with which discriminations are made, and in the skill with which arguments are sustained.

Lawrence's subjectivity must be distinguished from what might be called "subjectivism," implying a personal or egoistic bias and permitting a fixed, consistent point of view. Subjectivity, or "true knowing," being rooted in the blood rather than the mind, is to be regarded as flexible rather than fixed, as impersonal rather than personal, and even, when opposed to subjectivism (an expression of the detested mental consciousness), as objective. Lawrence sometimes identifies it with the unconscious, but prefers to think of it positively as simply another kind of consciousness: hence his use of such terms as blood consciousness, physical consciousness, and phallic consciousness.

The effort to present the felt quality of thought leads naturally to metaphor, and Lawrence often employs metaphors as conceptual categories in his criticism. But, having turned to them for their greater emotional precision, he seems to resent their logical imprecision and to insist, in both art and criticism, that he is *not* using metaphor but expressing the literal truth. Mrs. Ruskin need not have said that her husband should have married his mother: "he *was* married to his mother." For Lawrence inner vision seemed truer than outer vision, and he resisted a mere equation of the two. Like his own Count Dionys in "The Ladybird," he seemed to look at life inside out, presenting noumenal events with the literalness we expect in a description of phenomenal events.

One could say, employing a distinction made by Charles Feidelson, that Lawrence resisted the structure of symbolism, which presents opposed elements in a unity, and preferred the structure of dialectic, which asserts the unity as a logical proposition. Skeptical of the result, he constantly shifted the term that was to serve him as a standard. Among his many normative terms were blood, sensual, passional, phallic, and human consciousness; intuitive, spontaneous, and naïve self; the quick, the soul, the Holy Ghost, and Life. One of his favorites was "Holy Ghost," which recommended itself because of its very elusiveness ("you can't lay salt on its tail"), and its progress in Lawrence's criticism is instructive. It reigns supreme in *Studies* of 1923. By 1925 its elevation has become precarious: "Only the Holy Ghost knows what righteousness is. And heaven only knows what the Holy Ghost is! But it sounds all right." A few years later it has fallen: "It is difficult to know what name to give to that most central and vital clue to the human being, which clinches him into integrity. The best is to call it his vital sanity. We thus escape the rather nauseating emotional suggestions of words like soul and spirit and holy ghost." Trying to write about the deep life of the spirit in a language used for other purposes and in an age in which mass communication rapidly caused fresh phraseology to become stale, Lawrence was struggling with language itself. His very aggressiveness hints at the magnitude of his effort.

Unlike Blake, however, he did not devise a private vocabulary, nor did he regularly avoid the given terms of conceptual discourse. Thus many terms which he does use throughout his work—e.g., consciousness, knowing, imagination, spirit, objectivity, subjectivity, and even mind—can be honorific or pejorative, depending on whether they are understood as referring to the true consciousness or the false. At times, such indicative adjectives as pure, real, true, or their opposites may precede these nouns, but often not.

What makes the problem more acute than it need be is that Lawrence sometimes expresses whatever part of the truth he happens to be discussing with such positiveness and finality that he implies an absolute truth where he intends a relative one. In short, he overstates, and he must retract a little if he would make his meaning clear. Whitman is at first simply a "post-mortem" poet, but some pages later a poet whose doctrine brought him "to the Edge of Death"; "Turner is a lie, and Raphael is a lie," but a few paragraphs later, "almost a lie, almost a blasphemy." The qualification is characteristically made reluctantly or parenthetically, and sometimes not at all. But it is necessarily implied whenever Lawrence categorically denounces any genuine art or, for that matter, any genuine passion of the human soul, which cannot in his view be utterly false or misguided.

Lawrence's criticism is not logically consistent, not even as consistent as it might be on its own premises, but if we understand its peculiarities, we will discover that it is fundamentally coherent.

Given the kind of writer Lawrence is—so much of a piece and yet so easily misleading in isolated remarks—it is clear that his literary criticism cannot satisfactorily be segregated from his work as a whole. In discussing earlier the possible misunderstanding of Lawrence's tone, I would have spoken of the danger of considering his critical opinions out of context, except that the proper context is often not simply the particular work in which the opinion is found but the various works in which the author or work in question is treated or in which aspects of the critical method or doctrine are clarified. I observed at the outset that literary criticism is a major *area* of Lawrence's achievement, but it would be more accurate to call it a major *expression* of his achievement, as his art is another expression of the same whole.

The studies that have thus far been made of Lawrence's criticism specifically are few and limited in scope, nor has any of the other studies of his art or thought dealt with it extensively. But because an understanding of the criticism depends very much on an understanding of Lawrence generally, I have been aided by a number of essays which do not demarcate the literary criticism specifically as a subject of study. For the same reason, what I take to be a proper view of the criticism is still much obstructed by the opposed formulations of T. S. Eliot and F. R. Leavis, and I would like briefly to discuss this difference in order to clarify the view of Lawrence which I shall take.

In *After Strange Gods* Eliot wrote:

> I have already touched upon the deplorable religious upbringing which gave Lawrence his lust for intellectual independence: like most people

> who do not know what orthodoxy is he hated it. And I have already mentioned the insensibility to ordinary social morality, which is so alien to my mind that I am completely baffled by it as a monstrosity. The point is that Lawrence started life wholly free from any restriction of tradition or institution, that he had no guidance except the Inner Light, the most untrustworthy and deceitful guide that ever offered itself to wandering humanity. It was peculiarly so of Lawrence, who does not seem to have been gifted with the faculty of self-criticism, except in flashes, even to the extent of ordinary worldly shrewdness. Of divine illumination, it may be said that any man is likely to think that he has it when he has it not; and even when he has it, the daily man that he is may draw the wrong conclusions from the enlightenment which the momentary man has received: no one, in short, can be the sole judge of whence his inspiration comes. A man like Lawrence, therefore, with his acute sensibility, violent prejudices and passions, and lack of intellectual and social training, is admirably fitted to be an instrument for the forces of good or for the forces of evil.

Eliot, one feels—apart simply from the prejudices of his position—was not patient enough to understand Lawrence fully, to understand chiefly that essential self-criticism which is so thoroughly implicit in both his criticism and his art. Had he been so, he might have granted Lawrence the respect he grants to Blake, for his approach is about the same in both cases, and we would have at least the Eliot who, in Alfred Kazin's words, "managed to say exactly the right things about Blake's imaginative independence, and to draw the wrong conclusions." Yet with his keen eye for heresy, Eliot has perceived more truly than many sympathetic critics the basic radicalism of Lawrence's thought, and has put the issue squarely in contrasting independence and the Inner Light to tradition and institution.

Almost everything Eliot has written of Lawrence has been rebutted point by point by Leavis. I am reluctant to quarrel with a man who has long maintained a high regard for Lawrence's criticism (and who can be very keen when he stops polemicizing), but Leavis, instead of questioning the very prejudice against individual authority, has tacitly accepted it, and with what Kingsley Widmer neatly termed "a moralistic righteousness which is simply an inversion of Eliot's," has tried to show that Lawrence is really a saner, sounder, fairer critic than anyone else in his day. Leavis speaks, for example, of Lawrence's "unfailing sense of difference between what makes for life and what doesn't, between what tends toward health, and what away from health." Very well, but it is not clear that what Leavis means by life is what Lawrence means by it. Does Leavis understand, for instance, that the path to Lawrencean life leads very often through death?

The distortion risked by this approach is perhaps more evident in the work of lesser critics, for Leavis' own rage preserves something of the Lawrencean spirit. G. S. Fraser notes "that the central standard by which Lawrence seems to judge [literature] is a classical one: 'Nothing too much.' " And Ralph Maud, also finding Lawrence a critic who shies from extremes, feels that he would have won the approval of Irving Babbitt! In this case as in others, a radical thinker seems to be better understood by his conservative counterpart than by his liberal sympathizers.

Lawrence did indeed attack one-sidedness, but not because he sought to refurbish the classical ideal of balance based on the concept of the mean and on the assumption of an order or authority external to the individual. He sought instead the Romantic ideal of a new center of consciousness which would transcend (or subtend) the dualism of mind and body and which would be the basis of a new idea of community. The balance that Lawrence wanted would permit all desires their full natural expression—i.e. their expression up to the point beyond which they ceased to be spontaneous and became mechanical, ceased to be actions and became reactions, ceased to derive from the unknown well of the creative unconscious and became repetitions of already known actions and utterances. Particularly in the modern age, the ideological climate of which, so Lawrence felt, was clogged with dead ideals, and particularly for the artist, whose business it was as the "growing tip" of the "living, extending consciousness" to find a new vital utterance, this meant turning not toward the mean but toward the extreme; it meant getting beyond the known (often with some destructive violence, since the dead ideals were so oppressive) to the unknown. But the extreme must not become another fixed idea, another idealism. Hence the principle stated in "Education of the People" and basic to his thinking: "One should go to the extremity of any experience. But that one should stay there, and make a habit of the extreme, is another matter." This required courage and disciple, courage to go to the extreme and discipline to maintain, in doing so, the integrity of one's vital being. Discipline is not a word we associate with Lawrence, but a principle of restraint is in fact necessary to any voluntarist position that does not ask us simply to embrace chaos. For Lawrence there *are* limits, but man too quickly decides what they are. And the institutionalization of any limit or form, no matter how generously conceived, causes it to degenerate into a mechanical principle.

In application this theory remains subtle and complex. In *Studies*, for example, Lawrence both berates and admires the Americans for their extremity of vision, verging on death. He does so because he perceives in their art the simultaneous activity of two modes of consciousness: the ego or mental consciousness and the living or blood consciousness. In the mind death is a fixed idea and hampers development. In the blood it is part of life, a step to something beyond, for in true life-development there is no end, no final word. Lawrence once remarked that the greatest men for him were Dante, Leonardo, Beethoven, and Whitman. The remark is interesting because it can hardly be explained by ideological congruity and because, Whitman excepted, these are not men whom he otherwise extols. I suspect that he linked them because he believed that they had achieved an extreme vision *without ceasing to be artists*, without forsaking the inherent subtlety of art-speech.

Lawrence's world view, then, is not simply a version or inversion of classical humanism or Judeo-Christianity, although comparisons of these are sometimes in order. It resembles perhaps more closely the cosmology of the early Greek philosophers, although its orientation is far more anthropocentric, and ancient Eastern thought, although it is far more empirical, activist, and utopian. For all his hearkening back to the wisdom of earlier ages, Lawrence's world view is essentially modern and, I think, essentially Romantic. He tried to synthesize the naturalism of a scientific age and the supernaturalism of a religious age. He both adhered to the immediate and actual and aspired to the ultimate and transcendent. One can only sum up his position in some paradoxical phrase such as Aldous Huxley's "mystical materialism" or Northrop Frye's "apocalyptic humanism." But probably too much has already been written about Lawrence's ideas in themselves, and I shall not expatiate upon them except to clarify some specifically literary problem.

The difficulty of segregating Lawrence's literary criticism from his general criticism, or even from his art, indicates the usefulness of a comprehensive study and, at the same time, the problems involved in organizing such a study. An arrangement by authors or groups of authors with whom he deals, by genres or periods, or by his own chronological development would be artificial and would not take us to the center of the subject. These schemes will be used now and then, but it seems best to proceed in the main by a different principle, to view the whole subject from a different perspective in each chapter, even at the risk of some overlapping.

Basically then, this is a study of Lawrence from the vantage of his literary criticism. The central focus is the critic's moral argument: its relation to aesthetic judgment and theory, its sensitivity to unconscious meanings, and its pervasive prophetic intention. The unifying theme, loosely woven throughout, may be described as Lawrence in the Romantic tradition.

PHILIP RIEFF

The Therapeutic as Mythmaker

David Herbert Lawrence spent much of his creative energies contriving a second faith, something to succeed what he considered false Christian philosophy and its successor, the sterile rationalism of science. In *Psychoanalysis and the Unconscious* and again in *Fantasia of the Unconscious*, Lawrence made his main efforts to explain that second faith, otherwise expressed in his art. As doctrinal counterpoints, these two books together take on the importance, if not the excellence, of his art. Each is a heaven of an idea, a vision . . . of man at last released from his inwardness.

When first proposed in 1921, Lawrence's doctrinal externalizations of man inside-out were laughed away by the reviewers, without exception; what scant notice *Psychoanalysis and the Unconscious* received was good-humored, treating it as a bizarre and often incomprehensible new testament in the religion of Sex, ardent to supersede the then not very old testament of psychoanalysis. In the first few pages it does appear that Freud is cast down quickly to the role of Judas, fingering the gentle Jesus of an Unconscious for the police forces of civilization, leaving Lawrence alone in his true discipleship. The attack on Freud is not incidental to the presentation of his own doctrine. Lawrence saw in psychoanalysis yet another turning of man in upon himself, worse than religiosity, precisely because it aspired to a scientific discipline of inwardness. Yet Lawrence failed to credit this discipline with the results for which it was practiced; the turning outward that signified freedom from inwardness, was defined by Freud as the resolution of neurosis. The quarrel Lawrence picked with

---

Freud was more on means than ends. Both sought the end of the division between inner and outer life from which derived the characteristic cultures of commitment with its attendant illnesses of inwardness, as men clung to some mean idea that would help them get out of themselves. For Lawrence, the first healthy step was to stop having so many "ideas," false escapes, by way of which the poor thinkers were driven further in upon themselves. The world of "ideas," Freud's included, was the symptom of the disease at the root of our culture—false efforts at self-cure.

After Lawrence found out how completely his presentation had been misunderstood, he immediately tried again—belligerently, even somewhat peevishly. . . . *Fantasia* is a restatement and elaboration of his doctrine as it was stated in *Psychoanalysis*: it had an equally bad press. To the evident pleasure of his meaner critics, Lawrence the artist had strayed too far from his art and had thus exposed the incompetence of the prophet who urged the artist on. The few critical friends Lawrence had at the time delicately ignored both books, preferring to avoid the embarrassment of defending the artist against his urges toward prophecy. The embarrassment lingers on; friendly readers generally assume that the artist in Lawrence can still be distinguished from the prophet, and that his fiction can be properly enjoyed as such, without submitting to the pathos of learning from it those lessons Lawrence considered uniquely true to life.

The critical enemies of Lawrence were never thus confused. T. S. Eliot and Wyndham Lewis, to name only two, attacked the lyric fiction of Lawrence precisely because of the moral polemic embodied in it. . . . He was essentially a bad writer, Eliot announced, and moreover, sexually morbid, a snob, boor, uneducated, wrong-headed—finally, worst of all, rather unintelligent. The name-calling in which Lewis indulged shows that writer in a more than customary bad temper. Lawrence is said to purvey "Freudian hot-sex-stuff," to write a prose that is little more than an "eloquent wallowing mass of mother-love and self-idolatry," to support the cults of "homo" and "child," to be a consummate "nigger-lover"; for relish, Lewis adds the silly judgment that "Mr. Lawrence is, in full hysterical flower, perhaps our most accomplished English communist." No other writer in the twentieth century, except Freud, has been subjected to so much abuse from so many otherwise intelligent people. That these two men of genius have been treated with such excited prejudice characterizes that protective value which Walter Bagehot claims is the essential cultural function of stupidity. Because each, in his own way, had reached down to fundamentals, each stood accused of being at once irrelevantly eccentric and outright dangerous to the public at large. . . .

For these hundred years there have been sporadic attempts to encompass within rational science the irrational, from which religious emotions grow. Freud proposed the containment of that emotion by a science of the irrational; on the contrary, Lawrence proposed the transformation of that emotion, toward an end remarkably like that of Freud: the abolition of internality. Quite apart from the anti-scientific line followed by Nietzsche and Schopenhauer in philosophy, and by Hamann in theology, the psychologist Carl-Gustav Carus pioneered in the scientific effort to limit the cost, in personal capacity, of an inwardness founded on Christian premises. Prosper Enfantin made the most strenuous efforts among the French scientists of moral life, aiming specifically at combining the rational and irrational in a scientific movement that would also be religious in character. In England, a book titled *Mental Physiology*, written by William Carpenter, made an original English approach to unconsciousness. At the apex of this approach to the irrational from the scientific side stood Freud. But the line to Freud was not continuous. Rather, Freud's predecessors were sports of a culture that could only tolerate the religious emotion at its foundation by trying to find a method of examining it. Freud went beyond examination to diagnosis. He does not spring up as yet another sport among sports. Although Freud had read Carus and other less well known authors, his debts are not so easily assigned.

From the other side, the approach to unconsciousness was in advocacy of it. As an advocate, Lawrence takes his origin from the powerful tradition of religious mysticism, both Christian and non-Christian, aiming at an integration of the inner and outer man. Despite the frequent violence of his literary voice, there is an interior tranquillity in Lawrence's prose, a confident walking in the darkness of understanding that will seem odd to those only who have no familiarity with the imagery of mysticism. Mystics have never suspected that the worst is in the dark, as rationalists always have. Nor have they avoided the use of sexual imagery. On the contrary, even in the Christian tradition, erotic language was freely used to represent a vivid imagery of ways in which the inward man reverses the object of his interest and reaches out toward God. Mysticism bred acceptance of what the more ascetic rationalist tradition called the "animal" in man; mystics of all schools often decried the isolate and manipulative view of life bred by intellectualizing about it. The oneness of all creation is perhaps the fundamental prehension of both Christian and non-Christian mysticism; to that prehension Lawrence held throughout his life and work. From its oneness with creation mankind has fallen by misattributing omnipotence to thought; Lawrence inveighs against all abstractions, including psychological ones. The original sin against life is abstract thought.

The contents of Lawrence's two main doctrinal works are rather unevenly divided between analyses of the effects of overrationalizing our lives and the advocacy of a religious mood which is specifically irrational and erotic. The object of Lawrence's polemic is Freud, precisely because he was the genius who took the longest step toward rationalizing our erotic lives. Lawrence's analytic powers were limited by the passion of his advocacy; Freud could remain supremely analytical because he sought to advocate nothing. His analysis of the erotic life is no more an advocacy than an attack. For this reason, as Lawrence says early in *Psychoanalysis and the Unconscious*, Freud can never "get down to the rock on which he must build his church." The psychoanalytic movement cannot develop a cultic, passional character. Being analytic, the movement can never become communal. This is, at once, its limit and its salvation. It must remain, even at best, something less than a movement. Because a rational religion is a contradiction in terms, to Freud no less than to Lawrence, the psychoanalytic movement has no potential as a therapy of commitment. It is this therapy for which Lawrence pleads, once he has done with his polemic against Freud and defines his own position. . . .

In those halcyon creative years, before the full impact of 1914 had registered on the nerves of the middle twenties, it appeared (as indeed it had to advanced minds since the Enlightenment) that a therapy of commitment could be divorced from theology. Lawrence went further. There are long paragraphs, especially in the *Fantasia*, in which he suggests what became, from the twenties to nowadays, the position of advanced sensibility: a private sense of well-being, divorced from an ethic of social responsibility based on the guilt feeling of the private man. Thus, in two books that were written soon after the war that shattered the liberal, post-Christian moral frame, Lawrence gave a lead that is still being followed by our unchurched virtuosi of remissive cultural motifs. Lawrence's indignation against Freud reflected his impatience at the fact that, by accepting the cultural controls as fundamentally unalterable, Freud supported, with new techniques of mitigation, the type of man produced by this very system of controls and remissions. By appearing to confirm the inwardness of the dominant type rather than stimulate a cleaner break away from inwardness, Freud stood condemned, in Lawrence's mind, as a powerful new apologist of the old culture, which had so perverted the "moral faculty" in man.

"First and foremost," wrote Lawrence of his disagreement with Freud, "the issue is a moral issue. It is not a matter here of reform, new moral values. It is the life and death of all morality." Freud knew what he was doing, even if his followers did not. "Psychoanalysis is out, under a therapeutic disguise, to do away entirely with the moral faculty in man." By "moral faculty" Lawrence meant the capacity, built into culture, to make therapeutically useful commitments. But, according to Freud, this capacity was now being lost in the culture, and therefore to the human product of this culture. Freud sought a therapeutic mode beyond commitment, separated at last from what Lawrence defended as the "old religious faculty." Both men had been widely censured for the immorality of their therapeutic interpretations of that same religious faculty at the end of its tether. The difference between them was that Lawrence staked his case on a revival of the erotic mode, as a therapeutic release from inwardness, whereas Freud hoped that the rational analytic mode would achieve the same end. Here if anywhere, it would appear, is a perfect case of the pot calling the kettle black. Both men opposed the decayed internality of the post-Christian man. Each preached a doctrine of externalizaton, although Freud did it more obliquely. Lawrence accused the psychoanalytic discipline of being yet another style of inwardness—a danger Freud admitted in his pronounced fears about the Americanization of psychoanlysis. Nevertheless, the therapeutic mode developed by Freud is essentially alloplastic and aims far more systematically at an externalization of human vitality than any mode that Lawrence was ever capable of putting into words. For the limit set to the revolutionary reach of Lawrence's lyric vision of the inner man turned out of himself is Lawrence's postulate that this could only happen in religious terms, necessitated by the internal pressures of some new therapy of commitment. Freud, however, in his tentative way, was the more profoundly revolutionary figure, although it is admittedly difficult to image the Jewish clinician as the real revolutionary, clothed in his professional rectitude as he was and anchored besides in an orthodox bourgeois family. On the other hand, Lawrence lived so completely the romantic idea of the literary man that the imagination leaps to conclusions about the revolutionary character of his message without stopping to consider it contradictory elements.

"We are in for a debacle," Lawrence announced, rather too happily. It is an announcement in which Freud could have believed, given the clinical evidence he had collected from private sources and had noticed all around him in public relations as well. The "old world" of Reason was indeed "yielding under us," its thin dried crust of moral demands cracking up. But it was precisely a debacle that Freud strove to help this culture avoid, by shoring up Reason against further perverse outbreaks by post-Christian inwardness.

Coming to this ill-disciplined inwardness armed with his rationalist suspicions of it, Freud found there none of the "wonder of wonders" for which, Lawrence believed, men always wait. Rather, when Freud came back from his journey he brought with him, Lawrence writes, "sweet heaven, what merchandise! What dreams, dear heart! What was there in the case? Alas, that we ever looked! Nothing but a huge slimy serpent of sex, and heaps of excrement, and a myriad of repulsive little horrors spawned between sex and excrement. Is it true?"

Lawrence offers his beautiful incantatory "No" for an answer. Of course, these "gagged, bound, maniacal repressions, sexual complexes, faecal inhibitions, dream monsters" that "ate our souls and caused our helpless neuroses" were there. But we have planted them there. As itself a secular support of the inherited culture, psychoanalytic rationalism found what it was trained to suspect in the dark corners (inhabited by the dark gods), of which it is afraid.

To achieve knowledge of a "true unconscious," from which all life-giving commitments derive, science would have to abandon its "intellectualist position" and embrace the "old religious faculty," becoming thereby not less scientific but at last "complete in knowledge." Here is revived the ancient self-confidence of the mystic. Knowledge, in the mystical sense, is primarily unconscious self-knowledge and is non-rational. It is acquired by impulse rather than by the process that creates the repressed contents which latter, in the Freudian sense, complicate impulse. Lawrence advocated therefore half the Freudian definition of the Unconscious, while fulminating against the other half.

Rationalists had learned something essential about the complex nature of knowing a century before Lawrence accused them of ignorance, taking Freud as a representative figure. In the nineteenth century, rationalism lost its naïve intellectual arrogance precisely by making sense of the apparent insanities that eighteenth-century rationalism had taken for a folly characteristic of religious beliefs. The Resurrection, for example, was no longer dismissed simply as a deliberate fraud. Such an old rationalist wives' tale as the one about Christ recovering from a coma, after which he could not convince his disciples that he was still a natural man, did not survive later rationalist sophistication. The shift in the style of rationalist argumentation from that of Voltaire or Gibbon, on the one hand, to that of Strauss or Renan, on the other, corresponds to a transition from an outright hostility toward revealed religion, on the one hand, to a general sympathy toward the need of mythic explanations, on the other. This need had found in Jung the most sympathetic response, for his archetypes are myths that explain themselves. Jung's analytic psychology aspired to become revelation merged with science—each man's revelation therapeutically viable.

Lawrence's sympathy for the religious need was not really different from that of Jung. His departure from the rationalist tradition lies in a reversal of the direction of his suspicions. It is Lawrence's suspicions of the universal claims of Reason, in contrast to the suspicions of eighteenth-century rationalists against the universal claims of Faith, that mark the difference between the hope of that century and the experience of our own.

That Lawrence, like Jung, took no specific religious statement seriously, except insofar as it was a symbol of something else, brings him uncomfortably close to their common opponent, Freud, who had not taken a religious statement seriously either—save as a symptom. The only difference between symbol and symptom is that between advocacy and analysis. In Lawrence, the compassionate nineteenth-century science of religion was transformed into the characteristic religiously intimate poetry of the twentieth. Our lyric, with its tendency to evoke private worlds without end, has gone creedal at the same time that our prose has gone anti-creedal. Tapping the intimate pneuma of life, Lawrence is the purest of modern poetic talents, even in his novels, and certainly in his short stories. Probing the same nagging intensities of personal concern, Freud is the most significant of modern prose talents, anti-creedal in his very intention.

Whenever science refuses to maintain creative contact with the irrational, it grows even colder and more remote from "life" as Lawrence understood it. At least those rationalists who, with Freud, returned to a therapeutic examination of the committed consciousness that held their fathers, admit that their own scientific instruments derive from therapies of commitment. As rationalists, obsessed with the idea of examining the refuse of moribund and corrupt religiosities, our epigonal Freuds are really engaged in fighting one mode of internality with another. Because psychoanalysis is a secular paradigm of religious self-knowledge, it aims at abolishing itself. The logic of abolition is in the psychoanalytic effort itself, and in the next culture. As the ideal type of psychological man there is the therapeutic. Now the psychological man of this post-religious century is struggling to make his deeper and more subjective processes clearer as neuroses, rather than as gods, as his ancestors had done. Later, probably, the therapeutic will have externalized his emotional life successfully, and psychology will then cease to be a post-religious discipline; rather it will probably supply the language of cultural controls by which the new man will organize his social relations and self-conceptions.

Lawrence admits that such objectifications must differ from one historic period to another. He has no more faith in the Christian God who died finally in 1914 than in any of the Aztec gods dead far longer, which he tried to revive, experimentally, in his novel, *The Plumed Serpent*. Gods have lived, but their particular life histories are invariably conditioned by the different projections of the human self-conception out of which they are worshiped. What Lawrence really disliked were the religious conventions of our times; he could not rightly claim that we have no god-terms. Our Holy Ghost, as Lawrence knew, is now in the machine, where it took refuge after its home in the soul was condemned by modern scientific housing ordinances as too ancient and rundown.

The way the Ghost got into the machine is remarkably similar to the way God got into heaven. Whatever the differences between the therapeutic and the scientific man, they cannot become so great as Lawrence believed. The therapeutic will make a dynamic technology of the emotions, but not yet another divine mystery setting limits to the dynamics of the "inner" life. As a scientist, Freud was already aware how little the differences mattered; that his own science ultimately must amount to an interminable therapeutic process or it would not be a science in the strict, modern sense he intended. Yet such a process seemed culturally impracticable. For this reason, Freud did not mind admitting, as he did, that his science, too, like any other worth the title, included hypotheses that could be judged "myths"—"Just-So" stories—in a pejorative sense.

Now, two therapies may oppose each other, one claiming to be more scientific, but the scientific therapy arises less from within the Unconscious than does the unscientific one. Of course, Reality Principle notwithstanding, the *esse* of the external world remains its *percepi*. But the critical difference between religious and scientific therapies is in the locus of control and in the criterion of assessment. In religious therapies, the sense of well-being is measured against the commitment, which is said to "transcend" it. In scientific therapies, the commitment is measured against the sense of well-being, which is said to be "immanent" in the commitment. Finally, all commitments are alterable by therapeutic criteria. In this way, rationalism came to abolish any particular content by which a commitment was justified. All that remained was the form of internalization, which likewise had to be seriously modified, according to psychoanalytic theory.

Just what will replace the irrationalist form and creedal content is not yet clear. Nor did Freud, as a rationalist, pretend that the functional equivalent of religion as the predicate of culture could be discerned merely by turning up the volume of the "still small voice" of Reason. On the contrary, Freud was anything but sanguine about the future. The rationalist tradition experienced a chastened culmination in Freud. Freud's rationalism is the exact reverse of its crude counterpart of the eighteenth century, which had rejected all psychic products as somehow fraudulent. Understanding his patient's perceptual and social world as expressions of the percipient's intelligence and emotions, Freud erased the gap between therapeutic rationalism and self-assertive romanticism. Lawrence did not understand this subtle reconciliation. The condescension in Lawrence's criticism of Freud's "idealism" shows up Lawrence's impatience as a critic. A less polemical approach to Freud would indicate with what care he carried rationalism to its self-transformative reconciliation with romanticism. Lawrence suffers from the fundamentalism of his faith in the irrational; so strict is his advocacy that he fails to appreciate the final sinuous turn that Freud gave rationalism, separating therapy from commitment without thereby converting rationalism into yet another religious content. Freud did not preach a rationalist faith for the future; the weakness of Lawrence is that he felt compelled to preach an irrationalist one.

On the other hand, the fundamentalists of rationalism with their ignorant irreligions are still with us; they are to be met specially among the most highly trained and culturally emancipated people. Despite the cruel failure which their counter-dogma of technological determinism has suffered, they refuse to realize that everything great and good springs, as Lawrence believed, from a new fusing of man's inner and outer life, not simply from further changes in social and technological arrangements. The product of such rearrangements will serve only to distract men temporarily from the prison of their inwardness. This faith in the externals of things, rather than in the externalization of feeling, has had the effect of making man think less and less highly of himself rather than more and more so. This effect was attained although the faith was coated with the religion of humanity, which Lawrence despised as a rank sentimentalism no less profoundly than Freud. Pride of place was not missing in all the religious epochs of the Western psychohistorical process. That pride is now in danger of being abandoned. Compare Lawrence's daring to put the self at the center of the universe, imagining it also as the hot creative stuff from which even the remotest cold stars derive, with Russell's characterization of man as a passing and miserable accident in an indifferently creative universe. On the contrary, Lawrence proclaims, "it is the [life of the] universe which has resulted from the death of the individuals." In its anthropomorphic sense of the oneness of things, this therapeutic effort is breath-taking in its challenge to the scientific relocation of man in a more modest place in the universe. The myths here presented, as the doctrinal intuitions animating Lawrence's art, are sometimes carried along by a high good humor; but even when he is frolicsome Lawrence never loses his essential lyric seriousness of purpose—unless the accolade "serious" be denied to every poet by the predominantly prosaic mind of the emergent culture.

As to the fundamentals of social theory, Lawrence stands near Freud, although in the ardor of his polemics he himself remained unaware of their agreement. As a literary man, Lawrence cannot be expected to contribute anything more fundamental than intuitive agreement with that complete and erroneous reversal of the trend of social theory with which Freud has confused the scientific temper of our century; but such agreement is remarkable enough for its very rarity. Consider the theory that has dominated our understanding of relations between man and society since at least the second quarter of the nineteenth century. In the sociological tradition, the self is society individualized. The smallest unit of scientific analysis is the individualized social self. Freud did not abandon this position, which dominates all the social sciences. Nevertheless, by concentrating on all the painful vicissitudes of socialization, which begins for every human being by virtue of his birth into a family, Freud has opened the way to a revival of romantic theorizing about that polite fiction of our historic Western binge of inwardness, the socialized individual self. This dichotomy between inner man and his outer conduct is precisely the point of modern neuroses (in contrast to primitive culture) that Freud attacks. The romantic pre-social component in his theory, instinctualism, is not Freud at his best or most relevant. Lawrence mounts his own attack against what he thought to be a Freudian version of dichotomous inwardness—"mental consciousness," he calls it. The attack was gratuitous, although understandable. Misled by the vulgarizations of psychoanalysis when it first became fashionable in the twenties, Lawrence marked Freud down as the new leader of the old individualist camp. Aiming as he did to liberate the religious impulse in readers he considered miseducated by rationalist dogma, Lawrence failed to understand how undogmatic was his chosen rationalist opponent. Deliberately taunting his readers with examples of their own rigid dichotomizing of the categories of life, Lawrence commits what should be to him the sin of dichotomizing; Freud is put too strictly in that rationalist and "scientific" movement which, in confirming the sick internality of the Western personality, was giving yet another gasp of life to a dead religion. It is as if Freud were another churchman, engaged in nothing more than the construction of a new confessional box, rather than the most ingenious anti-churchman of the age.

In advocating the irrational during a time he considered fatally rationalist, Lawrence carried his understanding of the modern artist's alienation from the inherited culture too far. For he expressed thus his uncertainty about the quality and worth of his own participation in the unconscious. Like Walt Whitman, in whom he was greatly interested, Lawrence was not a direct expressionist of remissive unconsciousness but a painfully self-conscious protagonist of what Hegel first called "mansoul." It is questionable, however, whether any great modern artist can escape the double burden of having to relate himself analytically as well as expressively to his culture, no matter how profoundly he himself may manage to remain on intimate terms with it as a participant observer of its unconscious life. The modern artist cannot belong where there are no communities in which membership can be taken for granted. . . .

Without pretending to be writing history in any historian's meaning of the art, Lawrence, with his imagery of blood, sun, and earth, came closer than any other modern artist to a rueful sense of what the simplicity of passion might be, were it possible, in a culture rid of a dominating self-consciousness. "Blood" is perhaps the most common metaphor for passion in our literary language. The rhetoric of Shakespeare runs with a unifying consciousness of blood against a disuniting consciousness of mind. Having to be didactic, Lawrence writes awkwardly of "blood consciousness." But the time needed a teacher desperately, as he knew. Lawrence is the lesser artist because of his pedagogic inclinations. But his blood metaphors remain traditional, expressing for him, as for Shakespeare and others between, the possibility of leading the impassioned and yet social life. There is nothing sinister (or proto-Fascist) in Lawrence's use of ancient blood metaphors. Pathetically, he raised them from long disuse to compete against the contemporary machine metaphors of human passion, which, according to Lawrence, emptied passion of its social content. What is sinister, as a symptom, is our revulsion against blood metaphors when not kept under glass, as approved musuem pieces—or, what is worse, as laboratory specimens. Such metaphors have been dismissed as dirty or reactionary—even Fascist. Thus, manipulative self-consciousness has progressed to that stage of moral sickness which is confronted by Freud. For this progress of the disease, Lawrence blames the rationalized machine civilization into which he was born. But alienation, as he sensed elsewhere, was characteristic of the human condition long before the rationalizing of life by technological science. The blame is upon our ideas, not upon our things.

Alienation was originally neither a Marxist nor a psychiatric tool of understanding the human condition, but theological and specifically Christian. In the act of cognition—of desiring to become something more or other than what one might merely continue to be—the old Adam disobeyed God and thereby became estranged from the divine in himself. That unchanging inner part of life thus became unknown to him, repressed by his new commitment to the changing outer part. In the original version of the doctrine of alienation, man may cure himself only by accepting God's forgiveness, through Christ, and thus, in imitation of the divine mood, love not only his neighbors but also himself—in the discovery of his incapacity to change himself. When Catholic institutional theology made this self-reconcilation a routine, the early Luther tried to recall Western man to the necessity of leading an inner life at one with the outer; the doctrine of justification by faith alone drives from Luther's effort to correct the individualist turn of Catholic theology, and from his sensitivity to the overwhelming need of man to love himself in the world, as God had loved him. Lutheran doctrine was misused, to support the inner man rather than to render life more catholic. When Luther saw what violence his liberation of the inner man from his inwardness had let loose, he hedged in remorse against the consequences of his own position. The later Luther became far more the institutional Catholic than the revolutionary Protestant. Lawrence, however, polemical enthusiast for the same liberation, but without that experience of organizational responsibility which is thrust like an object lesson upon every revolutionary, rejects all hedgings. Welcoming as he did the imminent end of a culture created out of the divine ordering word (*logos*), he is not appalled by the "scream of violence," which to him expresses not death but the birth, in "pain and splendor," of true individuality.

The freedom for which Lawrence argues, especially in the later parts of *Fantasia*, is not the civil liberty considered by political philosophers; rather, Lawrence returns to the more traditional, religious conception of freedom as a condition of reconciliation between the inner and the outer life. The "bread question," as Lawrence mocks both Marxist class politics and liberal welfare politics, is not the essential one. In his advocacy of the impulsive Unconscious—the essential unique nature of every "individual creature," which appears in "defiance of all scientific law, in defiance even of reason"—Lawrence renders a modern version of the religious sense of freedom. On the "soul question," in its intuitions of what freedom really is, "religion was right and science is wrong." According to this "fearfully religious" man, as Lawrence once described himself, we moderns are captives not of regimes but of our own lust for reasoning from the outside in. His science of the soul is a form of "idealism," writes Lawrence—the most terrible default of a sick internality growing ever more dependent on an ever more alien outer technological order.

The politics of Lawrence resembles in remarkable ways that of

Prosper Enfantin and other Saint-Simonians about whom Lawrence apparently knew nothing. In a letter of July 26, 1915, to Russell, Lawrence writes out his sketch of a new hierarchal organic society that would permit communal passion. This society would culminate, as for Enfantin, in "one real head, as every organic thing must—no foolish republics with foolish presidents, but an elected King, something like Julius Caesar. And as the men elect and govern the industrial side of life, so the women must elect and govern the domestic side. And there must be a rising rank of women governors, as of man, culminating in a woman Dictator, of equal authority with the supreme Man." Of this hierarchy, Lawrence, again like Enfantin, at times imagined himself the head. Lawrence thus fits into that underground tradition of speculation about the religious rehabilitation of modern society which motivated significant political as well as literary movements in nineteenth-century Europe. Note that a woman governor of the "inner half of life" gives woman really the lesser say: over private life. That inner half is dominated anyway by the masculine thrust, from the outer half. There is a tremendous aggressiveness against women in Lawrence—an aggressiveness which psychoanalysis has explained superbly in case histories of religiously burdened men.

In the course of his correspondence with Russell, Lawrence declared himself unequivocally on the relation between culture and a therapy of commitment. "There is no living society possible but one which is held together by a great religious idea." Rid as Lawrence thought he was of Christian moral demands, he argued gratuitously with the anti-Christian Russell for just the "opposite principle to Christianity: self-fulfillment and social destruction, instead of self-love and self-sacrifice."

That opposite principle of Lawrence would admit, for the sake of immediacy in the externalization of the inner self, the scream of violence, as natural to man as the arched and stiffened back is to a baby having a temper tantrum and the showing of teeth is to animals. Our culture has established the pretense that a show of teeth means a smile and that love is benevolent in character. The less pretense, the less man would be trapped by internalities that were the moral residues of a Christian belief system. There was a period in Lawrence's life when he felt messianic enough to hope for an assembly of men and women who would form the "nucleus of a new belief," launching a "new center of attack" far removed from politics. In this respect, Lawrence shows himself as the most genuine of modern heresiarchs, chief and father of all the little heresiarchs—father-killers, ambivalent mother-lovers, professional immoralists, prematurely beaten generations of men who can conceive of no more creative acts than projecting their own dispirited inwardness upon the world and imagining that thus they may escape themselves. In his criticism of the rationalized organization of the inward life that is modern culture, Lawrence is truly revolutionary. He suggests a break away from psychologizing, not an extension of it. To him, psychologizing is a late variety of decrepit Christian culture, with sex in the head as the functional equivalent of intellectualizing about God.

Perhaps Lawrence would have been a less happy auditor of the scream of violence had he lived a little longer. He missed the noises from Nuremberg; he could not hear the screams in the neighborhood from which Freud was extricated, despite his reluctance to leave for Lawrence's still "idealist" England. Rationalist distrust of the irrational finds good cause in the bloody history of mankind. Lawrence read more than enough history to know better.

As it has turned out, no age has been more horrific than this remissive period in the psychohistorical process. As Jung believed, neglected elements of the Unconscious have revenged themselves for the ignorance of rationalist science. Repressed as theology, the Unconscious has manifested itself in all sorts of perverse religions; witness twentieth-century Germany, the great center of rationalism in the nineteenth century. We have paid dearly for the victory of rationalism—a victory that Freud, in his wisdom, wished to meliorate if only for the sake of preserving the weak hold over life that secular, uncommitted Reason had achieved in the course of fairly recent maneuvering. With his tremendous intuition into a historical development of which he had little grasp in any detailed or documentable way, Lawrence knew that Reason contends mainly with impulse, and with what he considered to be the legitimate and undeniable power of love. An argument, as he rightly sensed, is rationalist, or "ideal," when it is pressed against the possibility of some religious affirmation of living in the here and now. . . .

Lawrence was, after all, the most talented believer in the irrational yet to protest against that manipulative Reason born of the wedlock of power with profit that characterizes rationalist culture in contemporary Europe and America. This culture has barely survived its own remissive intellectualism, mainly by taking up those remissions into the larger system of religiously expressed controls. Reason itself became a prime article of faith. It is time again for the thoughtful of the culture to realize that creative remissions are basically religious in character and serve the superordinate controls. In our time, not science but religion must carry once again the power of criticism, if not that of love. Being religious, Lawrence's criticism goes at least to fundamentals, however little it may appear to justify its own eroticism except as a protest against the hegemony of Reason. It is inevitable that Lawrence's criticisms, encaged as they are in a network of affirmative myths, should be disputed; but they cannot be entirely rejected, except at our peril, let alone ignored.

. . . The religious problem is identical with the moral and the moral with the cultural. As systems of moral demands, every culture produces its communication modes, its aesthetic. In his two doctrinal works, Lawrence strives to preserve on the religious and moral level what elsewhere he protects on the aesthetic level: that aura of divinity around the person which Christianity has left behind. Lawrence follows the ancient theologically rooted distinction between person and personality; the latter, in its usage by the scientific and the liberal of our culture, is in process of destroying the former by pulling it to pieces and showing it to be composed of nothing except social parts. The person has been diagnosed as a kind of intersection of environments and influences. Everything, in fact, is thought to exist in the modern individual except his own "pristine consciousness," his hidden self or soul. While looking for a way out of self-absorption, Lawrence preached again the incommunicable, inalienable soul, in which traditional culture once could see its most beautiful self-image. What a mixture of motifs Lawrence has compounded for his doctrine!

The "old religious" faculty in favor of which Lawrence writes, in opposition to mechanist science, is specifically the irrational power of love. With such praise, the pallid reasonable religions favored by the educated classes for two centuries are criticized by implication. Our moral demand systems, Jewish and Christian, were originally developed in direct conflict with a religiosity that Lawrence raised up from a grave it had long shared with certain forms of mysticism, and with scattered heretics in Christian culture. Thus, if Lawrence argues for a revival of religiosity, he argues for the same reason against both the established liberal concentration of the self and any revival of a church-centered culture based on the ascetic type of personality. Lawrence was not a religious intellectual in the sense in which we can apply the term to T. S. Eliot. But it is not unknown for the profoundly religious intellectual to oppose churchliness, as, for example, in the case of Kierkegaard, who opposed the Christianity of his time.

If Lawrence's doctrine carries cultural significance, in what sense then may we rightly speak of the religious dimension in his work? By advocating the "old religious faculty," Lawrence had in mind the freer expression of man's basically erotic character. But in doing so he made the religious capacity a part of that aesthetic attitude which we have called "therapeutic"; his doctrine is a highly literary expression of the remissive motifs that dominate the present phase of the psychohistorical process.

The stage of his cultural development being therapeutic, Lawrence considers the divine as essentially erotic in character; it is a position variously held at least since the time of Plato. But Lawrence is a modern advocate of Eros, and therefore quite unGreek: the divine is realized characteristically in the sexual relation between a man and a woman—and then, in pathos, only fleetingly. Being far better educated than many of his detractors, Lawrence was also aware of alternative conceptions of the divine, both pagan and Christian. But he rejected a culture dominated either by *Agape* or by Reason—by the Christian concept of love or by the Greco-Christian scientific *logos*.

By design, *The Plumed Serpent* is a novel of pagan religiosity, raising the possibility of converting a Western woman to a primitive Indian cult. In imaginative rehabilitation of the Aztec ritual, Lawrence rightly understands sun dancing as an imitation—or a dramatic representation—performed in substantiation of the divine concern with the human being. The lady, Kate, is quite cultured; she knows all about socialism and is beyond commitment in any of its Western institutional appearances. But she accepts her religious duty when it is presented to her sexually, and enters upon the social enjoyment of marriage to the high priest of the cult. Thus, she chooses to participate directly in a passional community instead of merely observing it, as her European upbringing inclined her to do. An embarrassment even to ardent exegetes of Lawrence, *The Plumed Serpent* runs together just these motifs—the sexual, the instinctual unconscious, and the religious—which in the European culture have been strenuously kept apart. For the literary descendants of Lawrence, the European compartmentalization of the sexual and the religious motif has been too successful, won at too great a cost not merely to the sexual but also to the religious quality of Western culture.

Lawrence felt that the Christian possibility had ceased entirely in 1914. His great story *The Man Who Died*, written a decade afterward in contemplation of the definite historic ending of the Christian passion, has a didactic edge. It portrays Jesus himself admitting the error of becoming a Christ. Upon his resurrection, Jesus vaguely understands that he cannot return in honesty to his quest for moral authority. He rediscovers his amatory humanity—the true divinity in him—in a directly sexual way, taught by a blond votary of the Isis cult. There follows the true resurrection of Christ as Jesus. As a man, he has recovered his identity. Lost before in an ideologically encouraged confusion about his mission, Jesus now has no mission; he has achieved, in his encounter with an Oriental erotic religion, his own innocence of consciousness. The arrogance of carrying a moral demand in his very person has entirely evaporated. He understands now that he has misled his poor followers by searching for God the Father in the wrong place. Salvation lies only in the intimate, private life.

In *The Man Who Died*, Lawrence shows himself the most powerful advocate of a remissive religiosity in modern English literature. In *Psychoanalysis*, and at greater length in *Fantasia*, he tried to explain what this remissive religiosity amounted to. In sum, he declared his trust in the irrational, in precisely that human energy distrusted by culture. Moreover, he declared himself for an innocence of mind that will permit the Western man to accept himself again as being in harmony with other parts of the universe. His passion was for the private message, often given esoterically. But the message is clear in his own intimate correspondence with men he considered candidates for his revolutionary moral instruction on how to save themselves, and thus possibly culture. "For heaven's sake," he writes, in all seriousness, to the supremely intellectual Bertrand Russell, "don't think—be a baby, and not a savant any more. Don't *do* anything any more—but for heaven's sake begin to *be*—start at the very beginning and be a perfect baby: in the name of courage."

This appeal to "child consciousness" will puzzle only if it is not taken in the context of Lawrence's insistence on the innocence of the child. Not that Lawrence believed that the child was innocent of sexuality. Rather, this sexuality is precisely the condition permitting the innocence of childhood. For in its unconsidered sexual drives—to and from objects—a child cannot abide by any fixed ideals. From this, Lawrence makes it follow that little children, if understood, may lead men toward the good life. To Lawrence, taking thought is not a virtue. The degree of goodness and the relation of goodness to truth depend upon how well men learn to stop taking thought of themselves. Of the cardinal virtues, Lawrence would preserve only two: fortitude and justice. Restraint and prudence do not seem conducive to the good life to him, as they were to Christian moralists—and, significantly, to Freud. More importantly, theorizing about life conspires with a vice to render all virtues ambiguous. Lawrence prefers the purity of ignorance to the impurities of our civilizing education. Such a desire for the possibility of a free man to express himself spontaneously has not appeared in literature drawn so powerfully since Blake's *Songs of Innocence*.

Freud, on the other hand, felt that culture, however burdensome, could be trusted more than spontaneity. It is understandable therefore that Lawrence should oppose so vehemently the Freudian doctrine. Freud too intended to help mankind break away from its habitual fixation upon ideals; but, from long clinical experience he knew better than present the child as a counter-ideal. There is nothing in man, except his trained intelligence, that is not already in the child. In order to overcome the child in himself, while not denying it, a man can only resort to this added quality: the moral contents of intellect that constitute, in fact, culture. No two doctrines could be more dead set against each other on how to treat the quality of childhood in maturity than the doctrine of Lawrence and that of Freud.

Lawrence never really knew children. He saw them without the aid of either clinical or parental intimacy. Otherwise, he would have noticed their craving for order. However changeable, under manipulation by more adult minds, the passions of a child are so dogged that they remain active in adult memory—or so painful, in frustration, that they have to be repressed. The passions of childhood far outlast their objects and at times develop therefore the quality of an obsession. Badly informed as Lawrence was about children, nevertheless, he could commend with confidence to adults the spontaneous and arbitrary purposiveness of the childlike in man, and do so for his own didactic purposes.

From his idealization of the passions as he supposed they were, fresh in childhood, Lawrence derived, in part, his two main criteria for the living of life: first, the need to unite with another in the alternately straining and easing relationship of love; second, the special masculine need for a "passionate purpose" in life, quite apart from an erotic engagement with its release. The second need is satisfied in tension, as Freud thought too, with the first. There is a strain of misogyny in both Lawrence and Freud: women distract men from those missions in the world upon which they must embark. Femininity is specifically anti-cultural, embodying remissive rather than controlling forces. Given his ambivalent attitude toward high culture, Lawrence's mixed hostility and awe of the feminine becomes more understandable. His hostile manliness constantly serves as a critical balance of his awe of the feminine, permitting him to reject it. Alone, or in the company of like-minded men, a husband must set out from his home to make something new and better in the world. If passionate purposes are to be effective, they must be steady; and if they are steady, then they develop inevitably into "fixed ideals."

Yet just this steadiness of purpose, Lawrence considers, needs breaking. This second and higher satisfaction of the religious need in the working half of mankind, consisting in passionate purpose, dissolves under analysis into mere passion for purpose. Lawrence arrives, in a literary style packed with the ballast of religiosity, at a spurious therapy of commitment to nothing in particular. Culturally, the canon of Lawrence's writing expresses his nihilism as an artist.

Like the faith of those for whom faith means mainly a continuing capacity to believe in the possibility of finding themselves, not in finding something beyond the exercise of seeking, Lawrence's personal religion is all going to church and never getting there. The erotic life in his fiction seems always more strongly argued, compensating for the weakness of the other urge, that toward passionateness of purpose. Yet such a development of purpose is, for Lawrence, the final stage in erotic life.

Ultimately, Lawrence believed, each self in its distinctiveness has one purpose only: to come into the "fullness of its being." Any fixed direction or fast commitment can only distract from this fulfillment. To recognize the fact of otherness, to accept the good life as an erotic crucible that can, for sacred moments, fuse together self and another—these alone can proximate fulfillment. Thus, taking for granted both the distances and proximities of love completes in maturity the innocent eroticism of childhood.

Freud, with his ingenious talent for self-suspicion, no longer believed in such fulfillments. He begins really where Lawrence, for lack of sufficient analytic patience, leaves off—at the compatibility of love and hatred in family relations, at the mystery of the ambivalent relationship that unites man and woman, and from which they patch their domestic arrangements. It is not at all clear whether even the higher animals are not self-divided into both subject and object, burdened with the rudiments of a double consciousness. Lawrence's piety toward the possibility of living in continuity with the universe, which he elaborates in his discussion of the alienation from true selfhood in the latter half of *Fantasia*, specifies his religious hope for a condition of innocence, a return to that naïveté which can persist beyond the oceanic feelings of identity known at times to mystics and perhaps (Lawrence thought) to life in the womb. The Lawrencian God represents precisely what Freud called an "oceanic feeling." In fact, Lawrence explicitly invokes elsewhere the "Oceanic God." Nowhere, if not in man, does the Oceanic God represent that state of feeling in the residual psychological womb which cossets early infancy. In this state, the human being ordinarily experiences unqualified and unreflective love, in particular from the mother (or, at least, from the pre-Freudian mother). Lawrence makes an elaborate plea for this unmanipulative state of consciousness in *Fantasia*, having concluded that he had failed in putting across the same point to the readers of *Psychoanalysis*.

This state was better known to the ages preceding the emancipation of women—an advance in society which, like the political enfranchisement of the masses, Lawrence bitterly regretted for the corruption of innocence it had imposed on its beneficiaries. Limited by their sexuality, both women and the masses have been made unhappy by the political responsibilities conferred upon them. The biological warmth that kept families together was more and more missing from modern democratic culture. The family, more than other institutions, was atomized by the new free individual in search of as many of his selves as he could find. To Lawrence, only a biologically warm family, but not the freedom of self-searching, could preserve "the human being all his life fresh and alive, a true individual." Compared to this individual consciousness of contiguity with all other selves, our polite social consciousness created individuals in relations of manipulative tension with one another. The modern family, tolerant and atomized, represented to Lawrence our lowest point of alienation from other selves and not our harmony with them. The alternative to a family the members of which are casually warm toward one another is the cool democratic family of the emergent culture: a family educated in the liberal art of togetherness, well-tempered love, mutual consideration, and the modern option of treating first marriages as trial runs—a sort of growing-up period for grown-ups, with children as evidence of the intimate nature of the learning experience.

To save themselves from false otherness, in which they are miseducated by an immoral intellectualism, individuals are urged to follow their own particular "Holy Ghost." In burnishing yet another dark literary mirror in which to catch the most remissive elements in Christian culture, Lawrence shows something more than literary artifice. As a post-Christian, he was profoundly troubled by the problem of how men in this time shall find their own God. Nowadays, patently, there is no Savior—no cure-all, so to say. As the novels expressing his own fantasies of leadership indicate, the best answer to our religious need would be for the Oceanic God to throw up a fresh Savior. Lawrence was fascinated by the possibility of bringing religiosity (i.e., the simulacrum of faith) back into politics; the theme is adumbrated in *The Plumed Serpent*, *Aaron's Rod*, and *Kangaroo*. But, except in his literary fantasies, no erotic leader appeared. He abandoned hope of politics, and also of the possibility that the soul could be rehabilitated through the agency of one fatherly man. The search for God would have to be carried inward first, each man coming to terms with the incommunicable love that is his own soul, and retraining his own will.

Lawrence's sense of the divinity of loving appears anything but Christian. Pagan fertility meant more to him than Christian charity. Yet even in his deliberate revolt against it, the Christian inheritance dominates Lawrence. This dominance expresses itself in his fiction in the pathetic groping for charity between his violent lovers. The more violent their erotic feelings the more his lovers grope and stumble after charity. There are scores of passages in Lawrence's writings where he thunders loud enough against our contemporary confusion of "mental lust" with fleshly love to satisfy the strictest Christian postmaster.

The desire Lawrence built into the uncomplicated act of having of an *other* is the more pathetic for his intuition of the impossibility of its satisfaction. Desires that bring genuine union also bring about a marriage. Sexual union, however, puts the partners in a family way. Love, when complete, complicates life further, for it will involve now a group that grows along the line drawn by the original love relation. The ultimate question that tests erotic behavior is whether one can become a good parent. Bad lovers make bad parents. Especially in *Fantasia*, Lawrence concentrates on the consequences of the original love relation for those loved. Without that sense of otherness which balances the capacity for warmth between lovers, in the role of parents they would kill their children with domineering kindness; on the other hand, alienated from each other, they would use their children as substitute lovers, as Lawrence knew mothers often to do. It is not the child but the parent (and, in particular, the modern mother) who invents the incest problem. Only toward the end of his doctrinal volumes does the attack on Freud's idea of the incest taboo, with which Lawrence begins, become clear and more plausible. The reader has to be patient with Lawrence: he was never a systematic writer but something better—a seer.

As a concept, the incest taboo, like any other Freudian hypothesis, represents a scientific projection of the false standards governing erotic relations within the family. Thus, the incest taboo articulates the possessive love with which modern mothers, no longer libidinally related to their husbands, manage to keep their sons even after they become mothers-in-law. The sons, even when they marry, remain bound to the one true love they have known as infants. Freud merely "idealized" as it were this failure of parental willingness to recognize in the child an inviolate *other*, and thus projected the incest taboo into universal existence. The experience of anthropologists and psychologists with pre-modern and non-Christian cultures no more confirms Lawrence's criticism of Freud than it conclusively confirms the Freudian concept. But the weight of evidence inclines heavily to the side of Freud. The ubiquity of an incest taboo, even in cultures without our peculiar ideational condition of mothers fixated upon their sons, indicates that the Freudian concept is no mere projection into science of some occasionally distorted notion of intimacy considered proper from one generation to another. Incest taboos seem particularizations of a universal moral demand.

Nevertheless, Lawrence's practical advice on the conduct of family life seems to be sound; it is also sad, for in the personal life of this pointedly prophetic figure the love relation with his mate, Frieda, remained childless. As a prophet, Lawrence drove himself, as much as he was driven, in search of the exemplary life. To accept himself he had to indulge in the absurd fantasy of rejecting England. "Fullness of being," "fulfillment of self," always seems to carry this implication of hysterical arrogance, inexhaustible in its capacity to answer all questions—even national ones—with expressions of self-concern. Viewed from the perspective of prophecy, the personal life of D. H. Lawrence was a failure. Because of his ambition to be an exemplar, his life shows the more conspicuously its patches of familiar compromise. He was a second husband. His wife had already had two chidren by a man whom she no longer loved—if ever she had done so. This preacher of family as well as of conjugal passion never experienced in his own life that which he advocated. His own family history could only have taught him what it is he had to criticize, not, except by abstract negation, what to praise. Moreover, while preaching sheer physical exuberance, Lawrence was a sick shell of a man. The gospel of health was carried in a thin, hollow vessel. If ever strength of will and intelligence triumphed over weakness of body, this triumph belongs to Lawrence, the panegyrist of the body.

Further, in contradiction of his own stated doctrine, Lawrence could not avoid transforming the love relation between man and woman into a model therapy of commitment, complete in its very limitation. In reading Lawrence on love, it is well to remember that, in his inherited religious sense, the object of love is by the nature of the case incapable of being possessed; the worshiper has no means of satisfying his desire completely. For Freud, incompleteness is in the nature of satisfaction; for Lawrence, incompleteness derives from the object of satisfaction. Lawrence divinizes the sense of otherness. Men and women must naturally want to possess each other completely, just as they must also want to be free of each other. They are unable to fulfill either impulse of this duality of life to their satisfaction. By virtue of this sense of the *other*, remote yet tense with erotic capacity, Lawrence portrays people as most exquisite isolates—ultimately even from themselves: the self, being the God in every man, cannot be fully entered into. Between the moments of advance and withdrawal, there is that painful middle distance within which we practice our civilities toward those for whom we harbor most uncivil emotions. Notice the suffering of husband and wife in the story, "New

Eve and Old Adam," another of the many Lawrence stories metamorphosing the Christian search for God into a secular search for the *other*. In this story, the wife accuses the husband of withdrawing into himself at the same time that she has succeeded in disengaging herself from him and become "in the deepest sense . . . free of him" so that "above, in the open, she [could] live." Such an isolated life of freedom must, Lawrence proposes, corrupt the very individuality of the soul, whose nature it is to seek another. The corruption of freedom is nothing like the innocence of one "private, sacred heart" seeking the beating rhythm of another. Expect more than a complementarity of separate life rhythms and every marriage must seem as "comparative failure"—as the "Old Adam" concludes about his own. If one accepts the "real separation of souls," then marriage becomes all it can be. Eros must be cherished, tenderly pursued, loved for the exercise that it gives in the chase and prized in moments of capture. Lawrence believed in the ultimacy of means and in the illusoriness of ends. This is the ultimate meaning built into all secular therapies of commitment. His moral doctrine is one of the most modern: neither an ethics of responsibility nor an ethics of conscience, but an ethics of action. Figures as far apart as Georges Sorel and John Dewey would have understood perfectly this aspect of the Lawrencian gospel. That others, like Paul Tillich, committed to their own doctrine, adapt the Lawrencian gospel too easily measures the default of thought in some of the highest reaches of contemporary Christian theology.

For Lawrence, there is perfect action in the act of love; in it, we become free of both conscience and responsibility. We merely *are*; we cease to care, consider, reflect. This doctrine of ecstatic erotic action is in no way original to Lawrence. He may have read it in Nietzsche's *Birth of Tragedy*, for which he developed a youthful enthusiasm. For brief moments, wrote Nietzsche, we become "primordial Being itself, and feel its indomitable desire for being, and joy in existence. The struggle, the pain, the destruction of phenomena appear to us something necessary . . . considering the fertility of the universal will." Generation is holy. Passion is holy. Screams of violence are more full of life than the hushed tones of tolerance. Only the isolates, the quieters of life, who act thus in the name of thought and care, offend Lawrence.

"Blood consciousness" is nothing new in the English literary tradition; Shakespeare had it, as already mentioned. What is new in Lawrence is his hymn-singing attitude toward the physicality of life. Lawrence's piety for the body is not vulgar; it is merely gratuitous. The world affirms itself. What is needed is not a religion of affirmation; rather, a vital religion of denial. This does not mean that denial will estrange man further from life, but that it would permit a human being, tempted as he is to constant affirmations, to criticize them, freed now from the treacherous involvement in life. Nevertheless, Lawrence's hymns of affirmation are understandable, particularly in their insistence on the sexual. All such affirmations are not an expression of aesthetic sensibility as they were for the Greeks. Rather, the emphasis on the sexual in modern culture and the obsession with private aspects of life are an implicit criticism of the ugly and deforming thing that our sociability has become. The tradition of literary psychologizing expresses an almost complete absence of faith in the controlling motifs of Western culture.

Lawrence's erotic fiction has the function of critical myth. Narrow-minded partisans of the rationalist tradition find him therefore a morally subversive writer, for they invariably advocate living on the surface of consciousness, as far away from the religious unconscious as they can get. Lawrence's literary psychology is based upon his critical religious sensibility. Ultimately his psychology and religion merge. The "pure Unconscious" contrasts sharply with the impure Unconscious, defined by its repressed contents, as proposed by Freud. In its purity, the Unconscious is identical with (in Lawrence's further explanatory phrase) the "pristine consciousness," which in turn describes the state of "innocence" that man must seek. Here, in the term "innocence," the psychological and religious terms in Lawrence's vocabulary become one.

It is the purpose of Lawrence's fiction as critical myth to permit an experience of the divine to be encountered anew. Outside art, the numinous experience is not ordinarily available to modern men of culture. In this sense, all great art is therapeutic. Myth, and an art which expresses the mythic, permits a second level of experience; the experience of the divine comes to the reader through the imagination of the writer, this time indirectly, and is endowed with the form of his own life and his special concerns. For this reason, the interest in the personal history of the writer is inextricable from an interest in his fiction; the two interests feed on each other.

The Freudian therapeutic process parodies the mythic. As a second experience, it is intended to reduce rather than renew the meaning of the first. Lawrence, too, is therapeutic, but with the intention of renewal rather than reduction. Art, as therapy, takes on a certain theurgic (or supernatural) quality, exactly the reverse of therapy applied scientifically. Thus, in his theurgic capacity as an artist, Lawrence could write that "a book is a holy thing, and must be made so again." For this reason alone, Lawrence's life would be part of his art, for it went obviously into the making of his books. Correspondingly, his art reveals the pathos of his life, for the two are as far apart as an interpretation can be from that which is interpreted.

Fiction has taken over the teaching functions of myth in modern culture; this fact describes its importance. Lawrence's fiction mirrors the activity of myth in numerous instances. *Fantasia* opens with a critical little "just-so" story about the creation of our world as the opposite of the beautiful world that once was. Where there are seas now, there was land; what once was knowledge, is now "ritual, gesture, and myth-story." The entire Lawrencian art has the prophetic intention of recalling us to "half-forgotten" knowledge, buried as emotion in the unconscious.

Lawrence would not have approved the scent of sanctity that now surrounds art. Yet that scent is as inevitable as the scent of churches. The cultured of this era strive to relate themselves to art as to a way of recapturing the experience of the divine in which otherwise they no longer can believe and participate. Through the mediation of a writer, painter, composer, movie director, the work of art is experienced as a thing in itself, bracketed and raised above the ordinary workaday world, yet related to that world as revelation is related to that which is revealed—superior and saving. The work of art becomes that *wholly other*, present and yet inviolate, by means of which the cultivated may escape, for the time of this relation, their self-isolation. Thus, for significant numbers of people in contemporary culture, the aesthetic relation takes on religious import. To some it may become even more important than direct human contacts, or as somehow superior to such contacts because of the relative frequency with which passional communions may occur in confronting the surrogates of life in art.

There is certainly a parallel between the neurotic and the artistic process: in each case, surrogates may become more satisfying than the real thing. Even an art that preaches life, as Lawrence's did, may perversely sacrifice life to art. For when art becomes invested with religious meaning, it may become the vehicle of nothing more than its own continuance. In art, the producer may secure for himself the communion missing from his lived life. Although a mere consumer undergoes a milder therapy, through his relation to the finished work of art, the cult of the art object current in Western culture, quite apart from its dynamics of prestige, illustrates just that vicariousness of the erotic opposed by Lawrence.

Coming out from behind the fictional arts to speak directly for himself in his polemics against Freud, Lawrence argues vigorously for each man steering straight toward his own sort of collision with the power of emotions; this Lawrence considers the very core of religious experience—an experience of self. It is this ruthless driving inward, toward the hidden self as the quarry, that characterizes at once the motif of Lawrence's fiction and Freud's psychotherapy. In very different ways and yet for similar purposes, both encourage as well as express the dominant inward movement of our time, as a first means of carrying men outward, toward a new externality. . . .

In the writings of Lawrence, love is made to sanction as well as heal the separation between subject and object which he considered the original sin of "mental consciousness" through which all men daily recapitulate the first fall, led on to more and more self-destructive knowledge by science. When, through erotic experience, we repair the damage done by abstract thought, we are in fact loving the divine substance in things. Lawrence's intuitions are, essentially, post-Christian. In the Christian myth, loving oneself derives from experiencing the fact that one is loved by God. But, in the Lawrencian version, God having died, nothing remains except self-love. Coming thus at the very end of the personalistic tradition—as one finds it variously expressed in the Song of Solomon, in Augustine, in the doctrine of Luther—Lawrence deliberately played on the Christian mythology. He is caught in his time, a Trinitarian who understood that the first two Persons had gone the way of all myth-figures and that only the third, the Holy Ghost, had some chance of survival.

Lawrence's concern with the Holy Ghost is no cheap resonance of the religious motif; rather, that resonance is essential to the doctrine at the roots of his art. After all, Trinitarian Christianity is responsible for our present inclination to attribute an aura of divinity to the person as such—an inclination derived from the original attribution of personality to God. The Hebrew God was a distinct person: in the Christian myth, that person became more complicated, expressing an awareness of the complexity of love which no longer could be understood merely under the rubric of Law. Thus, in Augustine, the three persons of the Trinity—Father, Son, and Holy Ghost—become analogous to the three parts of love. The Father is the original He who loves; the Son originally the one who is loved, as God-man, and therefore (as Jung rightly says) an archetype of the Self; finally, the Holy Ghost is the power of love in that Self. In another place, Augustine analogizes the Trinity of memory, intelligence, and will. All that remains alive in this myth is the third person, will, upon which is founded both the Freudian science and the Lawrencian art. Freed from theological encumbrance, will—the third person, Holy Ghost, power of love—survives as the object of Freud's analysis and Lawrence's advocacy. But, as Freud knew and Lawrence did not, behind the Holy Ghost is the figure of the Mother, the original third person of the Trinity, now returning to psychological power. In the age-old struggle between Father and Son, Lawrence, through his art, enacted the role of the rebel Son and sided with the figure of the Mother, as Christianity did in its struggle against the patriarchal faith that is Israel. Having abandoned that patriarchal faith, yet feeling the gravity of his loss, Freud became a conservative of culture in the name of science rather than faith, meliorating the tension between Father and Son and reducing the remissive power of the Mother. Like every true revolutionary, Lawrence, in his avowed post-Christianity, himself expresses a powerful unconscious motif in the very tradition against which he reacted. In Lawrence's art, as in the Christian unconscious, the Holy Ghost is specifically the sexual agency, which traces back, as Ernest Jones brilliantly said, to the "fantastic 'woman with the penis,' the primal Mother." It is to this primal Mother that both of Lawrence's books on the unconscious are really devoted. And by reason of this devotion, Lawrence is called sex-mad by those who, unaware, worship gods rather than goddesses. Yet Lawrence himself is not an unqualified worshiper of the mother-goddess, in her disguise as the Holy Ghost, which Freud insisted on further depersonalizing as Libido. There is an ambivalence in Lawrence's art that almost shatters it, for although Lawrence is self-converted to the underlying feminism of the tradition of the Holy Ghost, he is unwilling nevertheless to accept the homosexual consequences of that conversion when it occurs outside the Christian symbolic frame. In his ambivalent advocacy of the returning feminine, Lawrence found in Freud an ideal enemy: for, far from advocating the sexual anti-culture for which Lawrence stands, Freud set out to the devise explicitly masculine (read "rational") means for its control.

Freud possessed a coherent and conservative imagination, the one conservative genius of modern culture, defending in it only what can possibly be defended. Lawrence's was an incoherent and revolutionary imagination—incoherent because heavily on the side of the remissions. In our own immediate time, the incoherence of the remissive imagination, as we find it expressed in art and poetry, is a consequence of the decline of the necessary and permitting condition out of which remissive imagination can develop: the vitality of the received controls. Once the dialectic of controls and remissions had been shattered, the remissive imagination was distorted. Because we have no real churches, we can have no reformations.

What ties Lawrence close to an ancient reforming tradition is his belief that the decisive function in man is will or desire—not intellect. Here, in his polemic against Freud, Lawrence reproduces the great struggle in Western culture between voluntarism and intellectualism. Lawrence, the voluntarist, trusts will; Freud, the intellectualist, trusts reason. To Lawrence, therefore, Freud is the great enemy spokesman, engaged to the analysis but not to the advocacy of the Unconscious from which there might develop, as Lawrence hoped, a culture freed from missionary morality, in either theological or psychoanalytic terms.

FRANK KERMODE

Lawrence and the Apocalyptic Types

Writing novels is more like writing history than we often choose to think. The relationships between events, the selection of incident, even, in sophisticated fictions, the built-in scepticism as to the validity of procedures and assumptions, all these raise questions familiar to philosophers of history as problems relating to historical explanation.

One such problem is explanation by types. Types are obviously important in novels, for without them there would be no 'structure'. How do they work in history? How do we recognise, for instance, a revolution? The events of a selected series cease to look random when we assimilate them to other selected series which have been identified and classified under some such terms as 'revolution'. Similarly for series which can be filed under 'crisis', or under 'transitional epoch'. There is the added complication that personalities involved in the events under consideration may very well have done the typing themselves, as revolutionaries generally do, and this means that historical like fictive events can in some measure be caused to occur in conformity with the types. Furthermore, since everybody's behaviour is indeterminately modified by the conviction that he is living through a crisis, it might be argued that history can, though with unpredictable variations, be prepared for such a conformity, even without the intervention of conscious theory. But the element of indeterminacy is so gross that we can perhaps forget this.

There are, very broadly speaking, two quite distinct and mutually hostile ways of considering 'typical' explanations. One is to assume that, with varying and acceptable degrees of 'displacement', histories and fictions cannot avoid conforming with types, so that the most useful thing that can be done is to demonstrate this conformity. However sophisticated and cautious the exponent of this doctine may be, his thinking is likely, in the last analysis, to be sentimentally ritualistic and circular. He is nowadays much more likely to be a critic of fiction than an historian. Historians and modern theologians nowadays employ typology in a much more empirical way, a way consistent with a more linear notion of history. The historian will agree with the discovery of a motive in some action or series of actions involves classifying it as belonging to a certain type. Unless that is done it will not appear that a motive has been discovered. Of course he will also, as a rule, agree that the material available is not always so classifiable; and so will the novelist. The distinction between these kinds of event is roughly that defined by Bultmann in respect of biblical history as a contrast between what is *historisch* and what is *geschichtlich*. The novelist, as a rule, has rather more interest than the historian in the latter, that is, he more completely ignores the multitude of events that might be supposed to have occurred along with the ones he chooses to treat as specially significant. His position is neatly put by Conrad: "Fiction is history, human history, or it is nothing. But it is also more than that; it starts on firmer ground, being based on the reality of forms." Forms are systematized typological insights; they are, or should be, always under very critical scrutiny, because they can tempt us into unjustified archaism.

The modern theologian is forced to understand the difference between sentimental or archaistic typology and the kind which is appropriate to a belief which has had to emigrate, like the Jews, from myth into history. He professes to use the old scriptural types only as indices of the contemporaneity of the New Testament, and not as elements in a miraculous plot, devised by the Holy Ghost, to keep Old and New Testaments, and the whole of history, in a condition of miraculous concord. Of course there are atavistic theologians as well as atavistic historians, literary critics, and novelists, though it is to me an interesting reflection that modern theology got really deeply into de-mythologizing at about the time when literary critics began to go overboard for mythology.

I will not pursue that, but ask why literary people should be so liable to this atavism. One reasonably simple explanation is that our immense scepticism, our deep concern with the nature of the tools we are using, is only one of the traditions to which we are heirs. Another is a tradition of mythological primitivism which has branches of many kinds:

occultism, Frazerian Cambridge anthropology; and Freud and Jung. In the period which was formative for us there was also a fashionably circular historiography, provided by Spengler; a revival of primitive art; and, of course, a large and seminal literature which was in various ways primitivistic and favourable to archaic typologising. Thus, when novels are closest to history we may still ask whether their fidelity to certain types is wholly consistent with a just representation of human history.

II

I begin with this dogmatic introduction in order to make it clear in what relations I am considering D. H. Lawrence. Among the reasons why he continues to be thought of as a particularly important novelist is this: he believed himself to be living in a time of cosmic crisis, and partly justified this conviction by archaic typologising. History was for him a plot devised by the Holy Ghost, and 'scientific' explanations (which would first examine and then reject this as a fiction) he found hateful. Unlike George Eliot, a predecessor in The Great Tradition, he could not separate the intuition that he lived in the great age of transition from explanations devoid of empirical interest but interesting enough to all primitivists, and indeed historians of ideas. He knew a great deal (anti-intellectualists need to) and was exceptionally aware of the nature and history of his typologies; for example, he was a great student not only of mystery rituals but also of Apocalypse, and commentary on Apocalypse. This essay is about what he knew, and how it is expressed in various books, notably *Women in Love*.

In the 'Study of Thomas Hardy', which belongs in time to much the same period as *The Rainbow* and *Women in Love*, Lawrence observed that a man can only view the universe in the light of a theory, and since the novel is a microcosm, it has to reflect a microtheory, 'some theory of being, some metaphysic'. Of course this metaphysic mustn't obtrude and turn the novel into a tract, nor must the novelist make himself a metaphysic of self-justification, and then 'apply the world to this, instead of applying this to the world', a practice of which he found a striking instance in the ascetic Tolstoy, whom he describes as 'a child of the Law'. The fact is that Lawrence was at the moment when he wrote that passage troubled about the 'metaphysic' of the work he had in hand. That he should use so curious an expression of Tolstoy—'a child of the Law'—gives one a strong hint as to the character of that metaphysic.

Lawrence was obsessed with apocalypse from early youth, and he remembered the chiliastic chapel hymns of his childhood. During the war the apocalyptic coloration of his language is especially striking; sometimes it strongly recalls seventeenth-century puritanism. He considered the world to be undergoing a rapid decline which should issue in a renovation, and expected the English to have some part in this, much as Milton put the burden on God's Englishmen; Lawrence, however, dwelt more on the decadence, and seemed to think the English were rotting with especial rapidity in order to be ready. He spoke of the coming resurrection—'Except a seed die, it bringeth not forth', he advises Bertrand Russell in May, 1915. 'Our death must be accomplished first, then we will rise up.' 'Wait only a little while'; these were the last days, the 'last wave of time', he told Ottoline Morell. There would be a new age and a new ethical law.

The nature of Lawrence's pronouncements on the new age and the new ethic is such that he can very well be described as a 'moral terrorist', Kant's term for historians who think that the evident corruption of the world presages an immediate appearance, in one form or another, of anti-Christ. But he was also what Kant, in the same work (*The Disputation of the Faculties*) calls an 'abderitist', namely one who explains history in terms of culture-cycles. More specifically, and perhaps more recognisably, he was a Joachite.

Where Lawrence, who was to call himself Joachim in *The Plumed Serpent*, got his Joachitism from one can only guess. A possible source is Huysmans' *Là-Bas* ('Two of the Persons of the Trinity have shown themselves. As a matter of logic, the Third must appear'). But Joachitism is a hardy plant, and as Frank E. Manuel says in *Shapes of Philosophical History*, it was particularly abundant in the literature of the French decadence and so could have formed part of that current of occultist thinking to which Lawrence was so sensitive. The doctrine varies a bit, but broadly it postulates three historical epochs, one for each person of the Trinity, with a transitional age between each. The details are argued out of texts in *Revelation*.

It is hardly too much to claim that the vague and powerful assumptions we all make about historical transition have their roots in Joachism; in Lawrence, however, the relation is much more specific. The war-time Hardy study speaks of our having reached an end, or a 'pause of finality' which is not an end. It is the moment of Transition. There has been an epoch of Law, and an epoch of 'Knowledge or Love', and out of the synthesis of the two will develop the new age, which will be the age of the Holy Spirit. As in some early Joachite sects, the sexual implications of this are especially important. Lawrence holds that the principle of Law is strongest in woman, and that of love in men (which is worth remembering when one considers Ursula and Birkin). Out of their true union in 'Consummate Marriage' will grow that ethic whch is the product of Law and Love but is a third distinct thing, like the Holy Ghost. Although there is every sign that we have reached the point of transition, the art which should reflect it has not yet been invented. Obviously the big double novel he was working on was to be the first attempt at this appropriate art.

Now I dare say that some admirers of Lawrence will go a long way towards allowing one to speak of his thought, on sex and other matters, as having a strong apocalyptic colouring, yet draw the line at this very schematic and detailed application of the idea. Yet it is, I think, incontrovertible. When Lawrence spoke of 'signs' he did not mean only that everything was getting very bad, he meant that there *were* apocalpytic images and signs in the sky. The Zeppelin was one: 'there was war in heaven . . . It seemed as if the cosmic order were gone, as if there had come a new order . . . It seems our cosmos has burst, burst at last . . . it is the end, our world has gone . . . But there must be a new heaven and a new earth.' This is from a letter to Lady Ottoline Morell, in September, 1915. A few days later he again calls the Zeppelin 'a new great sign in the heavens'. When he came to write the famous chapter 'Nightmare' in *Kangaroo* he again remembered the Zeppelin, 'high, high, high, tiny, pale, as one might imagine the Holy Ghost'.

In *Kangaroo* the Holy Ghost is patron of a new age which will dispense with democracy and bosses and be dominated by 'vertebrate telepathy' from a leader. As always in apocalyptic historiography, this renovation is preceded by a decadence; the 'new show' cannot happen until there has been some smashing. Lawrence's image of the transitional smasher was the terrible 'non-mental' mob, often symbolized by the troglodyte miner, one of his recurrent figures and an object of hate and love, fear and admiration. Continually reflecting on the apocalyptic types, Lawrence produced his own brand of Joachitism, as distinctive as that of Blake in *The Everlasting Gospel*, but easily identifiable, just as one can readily see the conformity between his more general apocalyptic thinking and the whole tradition. For convenience one can identify three aspects of this, in addition to the specifically Joachite notion of transition and crisis. They are: the Terrors (the appalling events of *dies illa*, the last day); decadence and renovation, twin concepts that explain one's own discontent and one's own hopes for another Kingdom, somewhere; and finally what I call clerkly scepticism, the reluctance of the literate to credit popular apocalyptism in its crude forms, with consequent historiographical sophistications.

In Lawrence there is a very personal ambiguity in these matters; he was a clerkly writer, but the popular apocalypse fascinated him just the same. He had a doctrine of symbolism which helped him to bridge this gap, and sometimes his allusions are so inexplicit that only if you are a naive fundamentalist (in which case you probably won't be reading Lawrence) or are on the lookout (in which case you are reading abnormally) will you pick them up. A good example of this is the passage in *St. Mawr*, which is in general an apocalyptic story, where Mrs. Witt discusses with Lewis 'a very big, soft star' that falls down the sky. Lewis is led on to talk about the superstitions of his countryside, and finally to explain what the star means to him: 'There's movement in the sky. The world is going to change again'. When Mrs. Witt reminds him of the physical explanation of shooting stars, mentioning that there are always many in August, he just insists that 'stones don't come at us out of the sky for nothing'. Whatever Lewis has in mind, Lawrence is certainly thinking of Rev. vi. 13, 'And the stars of heaven fell unto the earth', which happens at the opening of the sixth seal, when 'the great day of his wrath is come'. Lawrence is explicit enough about the general apocalyptic bearing of the horse itself, and perhaps too explicit about the decadence and the possibility of a new show and Lewis' superior understanding of the situation, but in this little episode there is a set of variations on a hidden apocalyptic symbol which is in some ways even more characteristic.

What we have to see, I think, is that, explicit or inexplicit, this, the apocalyptic, is the chief mould of Lawrence's imaginative activity. In the work of the nineteen-twenties it grows increasingly explicit, for example in the Whitman essay, or in the study of Melville, where the sinking of the *Pequod* is called 'the doom of our white day'. There had always been a racial aspect to his apocalyptic thinking, as we shall see; even in his essays on Dahlberg and Huxley's *Point Counter Point* he affirms the exhaustion of the white racial psyche, the disintegration that will lead to a new show. From 1923, mostly in letters to Frederick Carter, he was offering elaborate interpretations of *Revelation*, based on a study of conventional exegesis (which he despised) and on less orthodox treatments, such as those of James Pryse, Madame Blavatsky, and Carter himself. In 1924 he wrote some articles on the subject, and in his last years worked hard on *Apocalypse*, his own commentary.

In *Apocalypse* Lawrence acknowledges that the book of *Revelation*, and other parts of the Bible, with which he was saturated in childhood, remained in his mind and 'affected all the processes of emotion and thought'. But in the meantime he had come to loathe it, and his long essay is an attempt to explain why, consciously and unconsciously, this 'detested' book could play so large a part in his most serious work. It has to be separated from mere vulgar credulity and subjected to a clerkly scepticism that is still not mere rationalism. Years of labour went into Lawrence's theory that the version we read in the Bible, the hateful book, 'Jewy' and 'chapel', meat for underdogs, was a horribly corrupt version of an earlier work which must have related the ritual of an authentic mystery religion. What he tries to do is to remove the 'Judeo-Roman screen' and penetrate to the fundamental rite, as it was represented in the imagery of the original pre-Christian text. This rite would be a guide to 'emotional-passional knowledge'; the editorial sophistications stood for the non-vital Christian universe. The original was quick, though the corrupt version was dead. And of course Lawrence found in Revelation his mystery ritual. There was the Great Mother, whom the Jewish and Christian editors had dissociated into one good and one bad, the Woman Clothed with the Sun and the Scarlet Woman. There was the ritual descent into hell, and the rebirth. And this *katabasis* was the type of the one the world was at present undergoing. As in the mystery rite the contemporary harrowing of hell is to be accomplished by a sexual act. In the epoch of the Holy Ghost we shall revert 'towards our elementals', as Lawrence put it in that curious homage to the Paraclete, *Fantasia of the Unconscious*; to Adam reborn, love will be a new thing; the man-woman will be relationship remade. But first there has to be death and rebirth.

Although his commentators pay very little and then only embarrassed attention to it, *Apocalypse* is ideologically a climax of Lawrence's work. But because he never ceased to feel that it was not enough merely to describe the crisis, the terrors, the death and rebirth, he wrote over the same years a novel, a novel which should be impregnated with this sexual eschatology. That novel was *Lady Chatterley's Lover*. As I tried to show in an essay published four or five years ago, that book enacts the sevenfold descent into hell and the climactic rebirth by sex. I shan't dwell on it now, because I want to discuss better books, and especially one in which the apocalyptic types have a peculiar historical force, namely *Women in Love*.

III

Ritual descent into hell, followed by rebirth—that is the character of Lawrence's transitional period. That reason why the world misunderstands what is happening is that it knows only a corrupt Apocalypse—it sees, with Mellors, that 'there's a bad time coming, boys', but thinks that the smashing-up will be a way of dislodging the proud, and setting the underdogs up instead. Actually the beneficiaries constitute an elect, isolate in a new consciousness, synthesising Law and Love. A mark of this elect will naturally be the new man-woman relationship; for the woman was law and the man love, and just as these two epochal ethics will be transformed in the third, so will the two Persons, Man and Woman, be, under the new dispensation, merged in a new relationship, and yet remain distinct. The obvious image for this sexual situation is the Trinity, of which the Persons are distinct but not divided. And this epoch of the Holy Ghost has no place for underdogs.

As we have seen, this programme, already implicit in the Hardy study, requires not only a new ethics and new philosophies of culture, but also its own art; so it is not surprising that the novels Lawrence wrote during the war have much apocalyptic figuration. *The Rainbow* came to represent the Old Testament (Law) and *Women in Love* the New Testament (Love). The rainbow at the end of the first novel is the symbol of the old Covenant; the apocalyptic climax of the second reflects the structure of the New Testament. *Women in Love* is an end, where *The Rainbow* was a beginning; it represents the destruction of the old, and enacts the pause before the new world. It projects a kind of Utopia; but it is subjected, like the rest of the apocalyptic material, to Lawrence's own brand of scepticism.

The Rainbow is deliberately rendered as a kind of Genesis. The opening passages have a sort of Blakean gravity, like the illustrations to Job—the gravity is patriarchal. Allusions to Genesis punctuate the book. The death of old Brangwen, drunk, after a flood, makes him a sort of distorted antitype of Noah. George Ford's extremely interesting book on Lawrence (*Double Measure*) makes these and other connections with Genesis, including the references to the coming together of the sons of God and the daughters of man, which establish a typical basic for Ursula. *The Rainbow* also contains some faint but characteristic premonitions of the apocalpyse to come: as when Anna sneers at the lamb-and-flag window of the church, calling it 'the biggest joke of the parish'. The lamb and flag constitutes a traditional icon of apocalypse, but Anna is sneering at her husband's interest in such symbolism, as her daughter will later deride Birkin's more sophisticated apocalypse. Women are sceptics, they cling, like Anna, 'to the worship of human knowledge', they hanker after the Law. In fact Brangwen is a sort of decadent typologist, with an underdog chapel apocalypse; we are not surprised when we meet him briefly in *Women in Love* and find him grown insensitive, proletarian, obsolete.

The lamb-and-flag window is one of those glancing allusions, like the falling star in *St. Mawr*, which show how these figures possessed Lawrence. The great chapter of the horses is more explicitly apocalyptic; Lawrence's discussion of the horse in *Apocalypse* establishes a direct connexion with *Revelation*; and in the same section he once again quotes that text from Genesis, earlier used in *The Rainbow*, about the sons of God visiting the daughters of men, adding that according to Enoch these angels had 'the members of horses'. The passage is extremely complicated, as always when Lawrence's imagination is fully extended on this theme. These horses stand for the lost potency of white civilisation; (and specifically of England: there is a gloomy patriotic element in Lawrence's eschatology); they also stand for sexual terrors of the kind he associated with them in *Fantasia of the Unconscious*. Of course sexual terror and racial decadence were closely related subjects, as one sees most vividly in *Women in Love*.

IV

In fact *Women in Love* exhibits all the apocalyptic types in their Lawrentian version: decadence and renovation in a painful transition or crisis, élitism, patriotic fervour, sex and mystery. Its subject, like that of *Lady Chatterley*, is, basically, England, and by extension the decline of 'white' racial culture to be unimaginably redeemed in a sexual mystery. The characteristic pattern occurs with peculiar clarity in a letter of 1926: 'they've pushed a spear through the side of my England', means, superficially, that the country round Nottingham had been ruined and disfigured by 'miners—and pickets—and policemen' during the great strike; but underneath there is the imagery of death and a new love: dancing, disciples, a new 'England to come'. There is a sort of Blakean patriotism, even in *The Rainbow*; but Ursula in *Women in Love*, *is* England, for her, as for Connie, that other sleeping beauty, there is a programme of renovation by sexual shock. We find her, after the water-party, 'at the end of her line of life', her 'next step was into death'. This death, she finds, is preferable to mechanical life. But the death-flow of her mood is interrupted by the arrival of Birkin. At once she hates him. 'He was the enemy, fine as a diamond, and as hard and jewel-like, the quintessence of all that was inimical . . . She saw him as a clear stroke of uttermost contradiction.' The life-flow of love and the death-flow of law here clash. Birkin contradicts death, personal, national and cosmic. He himself often meditates on the necessary death of England: 'of race and national death' at the wedding party near the beginning, of the death of England when he and Ursula buy the old chair, of the necessary disappearance of England in the chapter 'Continental', when Gudrun sneers at him and calls him a patriot. But death is for him a preparation for the new life; so he must contain and overthrow Ursula's scepticism; and because she is England he must work the renovation on her body.

This intermittent equation of Ursula and England gives some indication of the means by which Lawrence matched his apocalyptic types with history. For *Women in Love* is an historical novel. Like *Middlemarch*, to which it owes so much, *Women in Love* is a novel about a modern crisis; and it deals with it, partly, by concentrating on the condition of women question, which, as George Eliot once remarked, had been from the time of Herodotus one of the most important symptoms of the state of a society. Unlike *Middlemarch*, however, Lawrence's novel contains no positive allusion to actual history. 'I should wish the time to remain unfixed', he wrote, 'so that the bitterness of the war may be taken for granted in the characters.' I shall postpone discussion of this radical difference of method, because the immediate need is simply to assert that *Women in Love* is nonetheless an historical novel, a book about a particular historical crisis. When Dr. Leavis observes of Lawrence that 'as a recorder of essential English history he is a great successor of George Eliot', he is thinking primarily of *The Rainbow*; but he adds that '*Women in Love* has . . . astonishing comprehensiveness in the presentment of contemporary England (the England of 1914).' *The Rainbow* has 'historical depth', and studies the past in which the crisis germinated. *Women in Love* concerns itself less with evocations of a lost world than with a moment of history understood in terms of a crisis archetype. The random events of history assume the patterns of eschatological feeling and speculation.

'The book frightens me: it's so end of the world', said Lawrence in 1916. George Ford points out that among the early titles proposed for *Women in Love* were *The Latter Days* and *Dies Irae*. And this eschatological preoccupation touches everything in the book. Consider, for example, the social aspect. Lawrence's apocalypse, as I have said, is élitist, and like the élite of the medieval Joachite sects, for instance The Brethren of the Free Spirit, his chosen ones exclude the profane from their mysteries. Birkin often remarks that people don't matter; or they matter only in so far as they may produce the terrors, the great mindless shove into the last days. The mood is reflected also in Lawrence's own letters and in *Kangaroo*. The mechanical mob has nothing to do with the true sexual mystery-religion of apocalypse; it was in their name that the Jewish and Greek bottom-dogs corrupted the text of the original Revelation. They have a false, lesser mystery, no true *katabasis*, but merely a parody of it. These *profani*, destructive, even chthonic, were associated in Lawrence's mind with colliers, the 'blackened, slightly distorted human beings with red mouths' who work for Gerald. To Gudrun, who has an instinctive sympathy with their debased power—Lawrence writes several passages to make this point including the very fine one where the workmen lust after her in her fancy stockings—to Gudrun they are 'powerful, underworld men' in whose voices she hears 'the voluptuous resonance of darkness'; she desires them, related as they are to the kind of evil found in the waterplants of 'Sketchbook', and the decadence of Halliday's statue. If Ursula is the Magna Dea in her creative aspect, Gudrun is Hecate, a Queen of the Night. But in the renovated world there is to be no place for her, or for her underworld men.

The real descent into hell and rebirth Lawrence can signify only by sex. The purest expression of it is in *The Man Who Died*, but in some ways the love-death undergone by Ursula and Connie is a fuller image because it amalgamates heaven and hell, life-flow and death-flow, in one act. The act is anal. Lawrence is never explicit about it, whether in the novels or in the essays where one might have expected some explanation of the Holy Ghost's electing so curious an epiphany. But he has in mind what he takes to be the basic figure of the mystery behind revelation—this is the point, for Connie and Ursula and for England also, where life and death meet; when the same induced by Law is defied and burnt out. 'How good it was to be really shameful . . . She was free'. This participation in 'dreadful mysteries beyond the phallic cult', enacts death and rebirth at once, is decadent and renovatory at once.

As the literature shows, this is not easy to discuss. One cannot even distinguish discursively, between the sex Gudrun desires from Loerke, which is obscene and decadent, and that which Ursula experiences with Birkin, which is on balance renovatory. The first comes straight out of Nordau, the second is darkly millennialist, again like that of some medieval sects in their Latter Days; yet in practice they presumably amount to almost the same thing. It is an ambivalence which may have characterised earlier apocalyptic postures, as Fraenger argues in his book on Hieronymus Bosch. Decadence and renovation, death and rebirth, in the last days, are hard to tell apart, being caught up in the terrors.

Does a new world—created in the burning out of sexual shame, in the birth from such an icy womb as that of the last chapters of Lawrence's novel—does such a world await the elect when the terrors of the transition are over? Do the elect rightly look forward to the epoch of the Holy Spirit? The myth in the book says yes. It says so throughout—in image after image and in a long series of antitheses: in 'Rabbit' and in 'Water-Party', in the water-weeds and butterflies, in Gerald's death journey to Gudrun's bed and in Birkin rolling naked in the pine-needles; in the flow of death and the flow of life, the imagery of *Fleurs du mal* and the rose of happiness. But the book also obscures the myth. Between the flow of life and that of death there is 'no difference—and all the difference. Dissolution rolls on, just as production does . . . it ends in universal nothing—the end of the world . . . It means a new cycle of creation after . . .' Birkin is glossing his earlier remark that Aphrodite 'is the flowering mystery of the death-process'. He cannot tell Ursula quite how their Aphrodite is dissociated from that process. And here he invites her scepticism.

As Magna Dea committed to continuance, as woman the voice of Law, and as modern clerk, Ursula is repeatedly the voice of that scepticism which always, in history, attends apocalyptic prophecy. When Birkin rants about the disappearance of England, she knows it cannot 'disappear so cleanly and conveniently'. It is part of the historical tension between myth and history (the long record of disappointed apocalypse) or between what Birkin thinks of as life and death. The novel fights back at myth, and where the myth says yes, the novel and Ursula often say no. The novel, as a kind, belongs to humanism, not to mystery religion; or in terms of Worringer's contemporary distinction, it cannot, because of the society that produced it, abandon empathy entirely in favour of abstraction. Thus our white decadence can never take the obscenely abstract form of Halliday's statue. And Lawrence knew this. Whereas *The Rainbow*, which looks back to a pastoral Genesis, can end with the archetypal sign of the covenant, *Women in Love* must have a modern conclusion in which nothing is concluded, a matter of disappointed love, a pattern incomplete. It allows history some ground unconquered by the types.

'Has *everything* that happens universal significance?' It is Birkin's question, and the novelist's question always. For Birkin it arises out of the repeated assertion that Gerald's type is Cain. Gerald's shooting of his brother is to Gudrun 'the purest form of accident'. But Birkin decides that he 'does not believe there was any such thing as accident. It all hung together, in the deepest sense.' Hence the subsequent death of Gerald's sister, his own visit to the depths of the lake, the region of death, and finally his death in the ice, may be seen as pre-determined. At any rate Lawrence wants us to ask questions about the truth of the types in a novel. The New Testament shows them all fulfilled, in the 'fullness of time'. Can there be such a novelistic *pleroma*, in which no event is random? If so, all the apparent randomness of the book must have significance: cats, rabbits, jewels, floods. This kind of realism finds its *figura* in random event. So the mythic type returns powerfully to its ancient struggle with history. But Lawrence never in fact allowed history to lose altogether, even in *The Plumed Serpent*, even in the narrowly schematic *Lady Chatterley's Lover*. He headed dangerously toward a typological predominance, and paid the price; the more he asserted the fulfilment of preordained types, the less he could depend on that randomness which leaves room for quickness and special grace. Mrs. Morel locked out of her house, experiencing fear but burying her face in the lily—that is the kind of thing that is lost. We still have it in *Women in Love*—in a relevance altogether strange, in unique configurations. There are the naked white men round the 'primitive', an image not subordinated to the element of doctrine involved; or the eurhythmics and the cows in 'Water-Party'. One of Lawrence's powers was a capacity for stunning verisimilitude, a thing precious in itself—one thinks of the passage in *The Rainbow* in which Will Brangwen picks up the factory-girl at the music-hall. There are always untyped graces of this sort in Lawrence; they belong to history, and they are what all good novels ought to have. Lawrence never lost the power, but it must have seemed that its relevance to what he was doing progressively diminished.

Women in Love is the last novel in which he kept the balance. Its radical type is apocalypse, used as an explanation of the great contemporary crisis; for 'it was in 1915 the old world ended' and the great transition began. The great feat is to confront what Auerbach calls 'the disintegration of the continuity of random events'—reflected in the technique of Lawrence's novel—with the unchangingness of the types, and to do it without sinking into a verisimilar discreteness on the one hand, or into a rigid, flux-denying *schema* on the other. *Women in Love* studies crisis without unforgivably insulting reality. Its types do some of the work which historians also do with types.

LOUIS L. MARTZ

Portrait of Miriam

The girl was romantic in her soul.

And she was cut off from ordinary life by her religious intensity which made the world for her either a nunnery garden or a paradise, where sin and knowledge were not, or else an ugly, cruel thing.

And in sacrifice she was proud, in renunciation she was strong, for she did not trust herself to support everyday life.

"You don't want to love—your eternal and abnormal craving is to be loved. You aren't positive, you're negative. You absorb, absorb, as if you must fill yourself up with love, because you've got a shortage somewhere."

With very few exceptions, the commentators on Lawrence's *Sons and Lovers* have tended to accept the view of Miriam's character as thus described by the narrator and by Paul Morel. Mark Spilka, for example, in his stimulating book, bases his interpretation of the novel on the assumption that Miriam has "an unhealthy spirituality," is truly "negative," that she really "wheedles the soul out of things," as Paul Morel says, and that "because of the stifling nature of Miriam's love, Paul refuses to marry her"—justifiably, since "Miriam's frigidity is rooted in her own nature." But I believe that the portrait of Miriam is far more complex than either Paul or the narrator will allow, and that a study of her part in the book will cast some light upon the puzzling and peculiar technique of narration that Lawrence adopts when he comes to the

From *Imagined Worlds: Essays on Some English Novels and Novelists in Honour of John Butt.*

central section of his novel, the five tormented chapters (7–11) running from "Lad-and-Girl Love" through "The Test on Miriam."

As everyone has noticed, Part I of the novel (the first third of the book, concluding with the death of William) is written in the manner of Victorian realism: the omniscient narrator, working with firm control, sets forth the facts objectively. The countryside, the mining village, the family conflicts, the daily life of the household—all is given in clear, precise, convincing detail. The use of local dialect, the echoes of biblical style, the short, concise sentences combine to create in us a confidence in the narrator's command of his materials. His fairness to everyone is evident. If the father is predominantly shown as brutal and drunken, in those savage quarrels with the mother, he is also shown in his younger glory as a man who might have flourished with a different wife: "Gertrude Coppard watched the young miner as he danced, a certain subtle exultation like glamour in his movement, and his face the flower of his body, ruddy, with tumbled black hair, and laughing alike whatever partner he bowed above." Even when the wife has turned away from him she can enjoy his music:

> Quite early, before six o'clock, she heard him whistling away to himself downstairs. He had a pleasant way of whistling, lively and musical. He nearly always whistled hymns. He had been a choir-boy with a beautiful voice, and had taken solos in Southwell cathedral. His morning whistling alone betrayed it.
>
> His wife lay listening to him tinkering away in the garden, his whistling ringing out as he sawed and hammered away. It always gave her a sense of warmth and peace to hear him thus as she lay in bed, the children not yet awake, in the bright early morning, happy in his man's fashion.

We watch Morel's relish in getting his breakfast and his joy in walking across the fields to his work in the early morning; we learn of those happy times when Morel is cobbling the family's boots, or mending kettles, or making fuses; we recognize his faithful labour at his gruelling job; and particularly we notice the love for him felt by the youngest child Arthur: "Mrs. Morel was glad this child loved the father." All these things give a sense of balance and proportion to Part I, making it clear that Paul's view is partial, unfair to the father, ignoring his basic humanity.

Paul's blindness towards his father's very existence as a human being is cruelly shown in the scene where Morel emerges from the pit to hear of William's death:

> "And William is dead, and my mother's in London, and what will she be doing?" the boy asked himself, as if it were a conundrum.

> He watched chair after chair come up, and still no father. At last, standing beside a waggon, a man's form! The chair sank on its rests, Morel stepped off. He was slightly lame from an accident.
>
> "Is it thee, Paul? Is 'e worse?"
>
> "You've got to go to London."
>
> The two walked off the pit-bank, where men were watching curiously. As they came out and went along the railway, with the sunny autumn field on one side and a wall of trucks on the other, Morel said in a frightened voice:
>
> " 'E's niver gone, child?"
>
> "Yes."
>
> "When wor't?"
>
> The miner's voice was terrified.
>
> "Last night. We had a telegram from my mother."
>
> Morel walked on a few strides, then leaned up against a truck side, his hand over his eyes. He was not crying. Paul stood looking round, waiting. On the weighing-machine a truck trundled slowly. Paul saw everything, except his father leaning against the truck as if he were tired.

"Paul saw everything, except his father." Only the omniscient narrator reveals the man Morel, battered from his work, frightened for his son's life, sunk in dumb agony at the news, while his intimate dialect plays off pitifully against the formal language of Paul, to stress the total division between the two.

Part I, then, is a triumph of narration in the old Victorian style. It is a long prologue, in which the issues are clearly defined, and in which, above all, the mother's overpowering influence is shown in the death of one son, while she turns toward Paul as her only remaining hope: " 'I should have watched the living, not the dead,' she told herself."

Meanwhile, as William is engaged in his fatal courtship, the figure of Miriam has been quietly introduced, in the natural, harmonious setting of the farm: "Mother and son went into the small railed garden, where was a scent of red gillivers. By the open door were some floury loaves, put out to cool. A hen was just coming to peck them. Then, in the doorway suddenly appeared a girl in a dirty apron. She was about fourteen years old, had a rosy dark face, a bunch of short black curls, very fine and free, and dark eyes; shy, questioning, a little resentful of the strangers, she disappeared." Shortly after this follows the vivid incident in which the brothers jeer at Miriam for being afraid to let the hen peck the corn out of her hand:

> "Now, Miriam," said Maurice, "you come an' 'ave a go."
>
> "No," she cried, shrinking back.

> "Ha! baby. The mardy-kid!" said her brothers.
> "It doesn't hurt a bit," said Paul. "It only just nips rather nicely."
> "No," she still cried, shaking her black curls and shrinking.
> "She dursn't," said Geoffrey. "She niver durst do anything except recite poitry."
> "Dursn't jump off a gate, dursn't tweedle, dursn't go on a slide, dursn't stop a girl hittin' her. She can do nowt but go about thinkin' herself somebody. 'The Lady of the Lake.' Yah!" cried Maurice.

We are bound to align this with the later incident of the swing, both of which might be taken "as revelations of Miriam's diminished vitality, her tendency to shrink back from life, whether she is making love, feeding chickens, trying to cope with Mrs. Morel's dislike of her, or merely looking at flowers." But we should note that immediately after the passage just quoted Paul witnesses another aspect of Miriam:

> As he went round the back, he saw Miriam kneeling in front of the hen-coop, some maize in her hand, biting her lip, and crouching in an intense attitude. The hen was eyeing her wickedly. Very gingerly she put forward her hand. The hen bobbed for her. She drew back quickly with a cry, half of fear, half of chagrin.
> "It won't hurt you," said Paul.
> She flushed crimson and started up.
> "I only wanted to try," she said in a low voice.
> "See, it doesn't hurt," he said, and, putting only two corns in his palm, he let the hen peck, peck, peck at his bare hand. "It only makes you laugh," he said.
> She put her hand forward, and dragged it away, tried again, and started back with a cry. He frowned.
> "Why, I'd let her take corn from my face," said Paul, "only she bumps a bit. She's ever so neat. If she wasn't, look how much ground she'd peck up every day."
> He waited grimly, and watched. At last Miriam let the bird peck from her hand. She gave a little cry—fear, and pain because of fear—rather pathetic. But she had done it, and she did it again.
> "There, you see," said the boy. "It doesn't hurt, does it?"
> She looked at him with dilated dark eyes.
> "No," she laughed, trembling.

The scene shows more than timidity; it shows, also, her extreme sensitivity, along with her shy desire for new experience: she wants to try, she wants to learn; if rightly encouraged she will and can learn, and then she can respond with laughter and trembling excitement. This first view of Miriam, seen through the eyes of the objective narrator, is astir with life: for all her shyness and shrinking she is nevertheless capable of a strong response. The whole initial sketch is suffused with her "beautiful warm colouring" and accompanied by her "musical, quiet voice." She is a girl of rich potential.

II

As Part II opens we become at once aware of a drastic shift in method. The first two pages are given over to an elaborate interpretation of Miriam's character before she again appears, "nearly sixteen, very beautiful, with her warm colouring, her gravity, her eyes dilating suddenly like an ecstasy." No such extended analysis of anyone has appeared in Part I; there the characters have been allowed to act out their parts before us, with only brief guiding touches by the objective narrator. But here we sense a peculiar intensity in the analysis: the narrator seems to be preparing the way for some new and difficult problem, and in so doing he seems to be dropping his manner of impartiality. He is determined to set our minds in a certain direction, and this aim is reflected in the drifting length and involution of the sentences. The style of writing here seems designed to reflect the "mistiness" of the character he is describing, her remoteness from life:

> Her great companion was her mother. They were both brown-eyed, and inclined to be mystical, such women as treasure religion inside them, breathe it in their nostrils, and see the whole of life in a mist thereof. So to Miriam, Christ and God made one great figure, which she loved tremblingly and passionately when a tremendous sunset burned out the western sky, and Ediths, and Lucys, and Rowenas, Brian de Bois Guilberts, Rob Roys, and Guy Mannerings, rustled the sunny leaves in the morning, or sat in her bedroom aloft, alone, when it snowed. That was life to her. For the rest, she drudged in the house, which work she would not have minded had not her clean red floor been mucked up immediately by the trampling farm-boots of her brothers. She madly wanted her little brother of four to let her swathe him and stifle him in her love; she went to church reverently, with bowed head, and quivered in anguish from the vulgarity of the other choir-girls and from the common-sounding voice of the curate; she fought with her brothers, whom she considered brutal louts; and she held not her father in too high esteem because he did not carry any mystical ideals cherished in his heart, but only wanted to have as easy a time as he could, and his meals when he was ready for them.

She is also a girl who is "mad to have learning whereon to pride herself"; and for all these causes she neglects and ignores her physical being: "Her beauty—that of a shy, wild, quiveringly sensitive thing—seemed nothing to her. Even her soul, so strong for rhapsody, was not enough. She must have something to reinforce her pride, because she felt different from other people." At the same time, her misty emotions lead her towards a desire to dominate Paul: "Then he was so ill, and she felt he would be weak. Then she would be stronger than he. Then she could love him. If she could be mistress of him in his weakness, take care of him, if he could depend on her, if she could, as it were, have him in her arms, how she would love him!"

In all this the narrator is anticipating the views of Miriam frequently expressed by Paul himself: that she is too spiritual, too abstract, that she shrinks away from physical reality, and that she has a stifling desire to absorb and possess his soul. The incident of the swing that follows shortly after would seem to bear out some of this: she is afraid to let Paul swing her high, and Lawrence phrases her fear in language that has unmistakable sexual overtones: "She felt the accuracy with which he caught her, exactly at the right moment, and the exactly proportionate strength of his thrust, and she was afraid. Down to her bowels went the hot wave of fear. She was in his hands. Again, firm and inevitable came the thrust at the right moment. She gripped the rope, almost swooning." Yet she has led Paul to the swing, and she is fascinated by his free swinging: "It roused a warmth in her. It were almost as if he were a flame that had lit a warmth in her whilst he swung in the middle air." Who can say that Miriam is unable to learn this too, as she has learned with the hen, and as she is later shown to overcome her fear of crossing fences?

> Occasionally she ran with Paul down the fields. Then her eyes blazed naked in a kind of esctasy that frightened him. But she was physically afraid. If she were getting over a stile, she gripped his hands in a little hard anguish, and began to lose her presence of mind. And he could not persuade her to jump from even a small height. Her eyes dilated, became exposed and palpitating.
>
> "No!" she cried, half laughing in terror—"no!"
>
> "You shall!" he cried once, and, jerking her forward, he brought her falling from the fence. But her wild "Ah!" of pain, as if she were losing consciousness, cut him. She landed on her feet safely, and afterwards had courage in this respect.

Certainly she wants to learn; only a few lines after the swing episode we find this all-important passage:

> But the girl gradually sought him out. If he brought up his sketchbook, it was she who pondered longest over the last picture. Then she would look

up at him. Suddenly, her dark eyes alight like water that shakes with a stream of gold in the dark, she would ask:

"Why do I like this so?"

Always something in his breast shrank from these close, intimate, dazzled looks of hers.

"Why *do* you?" he asked.

"I don't know. It seems so true."

"It's because—it's because there is scarcely any shadow in it; it's more shimmery, as if I'd painted the shimmering protoplasm in the leaves and everywhere, and not the stiffness of the shape. That seems dead to me. Only this shimmeriness is the real living. The shape is a dead crust. The shimmer is inside really."

And she, with her little finger in her mouth, would ponder these sayings. They gave her a feeling of life again, and vivified things which had meant nothing to her. She managed to find some meaning in his struggling, abstract speeches. And they were the medium through which she came distinctly at her beloved objects.

It seems as though she is learning to reach out towards the "shimmeriness" that is the "real living"; with his help she is coming out of her "mist" towards a distinct sight of "her beloved objects." *She* is learning, while *he* shrinks away from her intimate, shimmering eyes ("like water that shakes with a stream of gold in the dark"). She senses the meaning of his "abstract speeches," she gets "so near him," she creates in him "a strange, roused sensation"—and as a result she enrages him for reasons that he cannot grasp. Is it because he is refusing to face the shimmer that is really inside Miriam?

So, when he sees her embracing her youngest brother "almost as if she were in a trance, and swaying also as if she were swooned in an ecstasy of love," he bursts out with his irritation:

"What do you make such a *fuss* for?" cried Paul, all in suffering because of her extreme emotion. "Why can't you be ordinary with him?"

She let the child go, and rose, and said nothing. Her intensity, which would leave no emotion on a normal plane, irritated the youth into a frenzy. And this fearful, naked contact of her on small occasions shocked him. He was used to his mother's reserve. And on such occasions he was thankful in his heart and soul that he had his mother, so sane and wholesome.

One senses, as Miriam does at a later point, an alien influence here, twisting the mind of Paul and the narrator away from Miriam. Two pages later we see a dramatic juxtaposition of two warring actualities:

He used to tell his mother all these things.

"I'm going to teach Miriam algebra," he said.

> "Well," replied Mrs. Morel, "I hope she'll get fat on it."
>
> When he went up to the farm on the Monday evening, it was drawing twilight. Miriam was just sweeping up the kitchen, and was kneeling at the hearth when he entered. Everyone was out but her. She looked round at him, flushed, her dark eyes shining, her fine hair falling about her face.
>
> "Hello!" she said, soft and musical. "I knew it was you."
>
> "How?"
>
> "I knew your step. Nobody treads so quick and firm."
>
> He sat down, sighing.
>
> "Ready to do some algebra?" he asked, drawing a little book from his pocket.

Who is sane and wholesome, we may well ask? And whose thoughts are abstracted from life? We are beginning to learn that we cannot wholly trust the narrator's remarks in this central portion of the book, for his commentary represents mainly an extension of Paul's consciousness; everywhere, in this portion of the book, the voice of the narrator tends to echo and magnify the confusions that are arising within Paul himself. These are the contradictions in which some readers have seen a failure or a faltering in the novel, because "the point of view is never adequately objectified and sustained to tell us which is true." But I feel rather that Lawrence has invented a successful technique by which he can manage the deep autobiographical problems that underlie the book. We are watching the strong graft of a stream of consciousness growing out of the live trunk of that Victorian prologue, and intertwining with the objectively presented action. The point of view adopted is that of Paul; but since confusion, self-deception, and desperate self-justification are essential to that point of view, we can never tell, from that stream of consciousness alone, where the real truth lies. But we can tell it from the action; we can tell it by seeking out the portrait of Miriam that lies beneath the over-painted commentary of the Paul-narrator. This technique of painting and overpainting produces a strange and unique tension in this part of the novel. The image of Miriam appears and then is clouded over; it is as though we were looking at her through a clouded window that is constantly being cleared, and fogged, and cleared again. It is an unprecedented and inimitable technique, discovered for this one necessary occasion. But it works.

How it works, we may see by looking once again at the frequently quoted passage where Miriam leads Paul, despite his reluctance ("They grumble so if I'm late") into the woods at dusk to find the "wild-rose bush she had discovered."

> The tree was tall and straggling. It had thrown its briers over a hawthorn-bush, and its long streamers trailed thick, right down to the grass, splashing the darkness everywhere with great split stars, pure white. In bosses of ivory and in large splashed stars the roses gleamed on the darkness of foliage and stems and grass. Paul and Miriam stood close together, silent, and watched. Point after point the steady roses shone out to them, seeming to kindle something in their souls. The dusk came like smoke around, and still did not put out the roses.
>
> Paul looked into Miriam's eyes. She was pale and expectant with wonder, her lips were parted, and her dark eyes lay open to him. His look seemed to travel down into her. Her soul quivered. It was the communion she wanted. He turned aside, as if pained. He turned to the bush.
>
> "They seem as if they walk like butterflies, and shake themselves," he said.
>
> She looked at her roses. They were white, some incurved and holy, others expanded in an ecstasy. The tree was dark as a shadow. She lifted her hand impulsively to the flowers; she went forward and touched them in worship.
>
> "Let us go," he said.
>
> There was a cool scent of ivory roses—a white, virgin scent. Something made him feel anxious and imprisoned. The two walked in silence.

What is this "something" that makes him "feel anxious and imprisoned"? Is he like the hawthorn-bush, caught in the trailing streamers of the rose-bush? Is it because she has insisted on a moment of soul-communion which represents her tendency towards "a blasphemous possessorship"? The narrator seems to be urging us in this direction. Yet in itself the scene may be taken to represent, amid this wild profusion of natural growth, a moment of natural communion in the human relationship, a potential marriage of senses and the soul. This is, for Miriam, an "ecstasy" in which nature is not abstracted, but realized in all its wild perfection. Paul breaks the mood and runs away towards home. And when he reaches home we may grasp the true manner of his imprisonment:

> Always when he went with Miriam, and it grew rather late, he knew his mother was fretting and getting angry about him—why, he could not understand. As he went into the house, flinging down his cap, his mother looked up at the clock. She had been sitting thinking because a chill to her eyes prevented her reading. She could feel Paul being drawn away by this girl. And she did not care for Miriam. "She is one of those who will want to suck a man's soul out till he has none of his own left," she said to herself; "and he is just such a gaby as to let himself be absorbed. She will never let him become a man; she never will." So, while he was away with Miriam, Mrs. Morel grew more and more worked up.

> She glanced at the clock and said, coldly and rather tired:
> "You have been far enough to-night."
> His soul, warm and exposed from contact with the girl, shrank.

Miriam offers him the freedom of natural growth within a mature relation, though Paul soon adopts the mother's view of Miriam's "possessive" nature. He cannot help himself, but there is no reason why readers of the book should accept the mother's view of Miriam, which is everywhere shown to be motivated by the mother's own possessiveness. The mother has described only herself in the above quotation; she has not described Miriam, who is quite a different being and has quite a different effect on Paul. The fact is that Paul needs both his mother and Miriam for his true development, as he seems to realize quite early in the conflict: "A sketch finished, he always wanted to take it to Miriam. Then he was stimulated into knowledge of the work he had produced unconsciously. In contact with Miriam he gained insight; his vision went deeper. From his mother he drew the life-warmth, the strength to produce; Miriam urged this warmth into intensity like a white light." Or earlier we hear that Miriam's family "kindled him and made him glow to his work, whereas his mother's influence was to make him quietly determined, patient, dogged, unwearied."

But the mother cannot bear to release him. Miriam must be met by her with cold, unfriendly curtness, while the married woman, Clara, may receive a friendly welcome from the mother. Clara offers no threat: "Mrs. Morel measured herself against the younger woman, and found herself easily stronger." "Yes, I liked her", she says in answer to Paul's inquiry. "But you'll tire of her, my son; you know you will." And so she encourages the affair with Clara: the adulterous relation will serve the son's physical needs, while the mother can retain the son's deeper love and loyalty. Mrs. Morel senses what she is doing, but evades the facts:

> Mrs. Morel considered. She would have been glad now for her son to fall in love with some woman who would—she did not know what. But he fretted so, got so furious suddenly, and again was melancholic. She wished he knew some nice woman—She did not know what she wished, but left it vague. At any rate she was not hostile to the idea of Clara.

The mother's devices are pitiful, and at the same time contemptible, as we have already seen from the painful episode in which she overwhelms her son with raw and naked emotion:

> He had taken off his collar and tie, and rose, bare-throated, to go to bed. As he stooped to kiss his mother, she threw her arms round his neck, hid her face on his shoulder, and cried, in a whimpering voice, so unlike her own that he writhed in agony:

> "I can't bear it. I could let another woman—but not her. She'd leave me no room, not a bit of room—"
>
> And immediately he hated Miriam bitterly.
>
> "And I've never—you know, Paul—I've never had a husband—not really—"
>
> He stroked his mother's hair, and his mouth was on her throat.
>
> "And she exults so in taking you from me—she's not like ordinary girls."
>
> "Well, I don't love her, mother," he murmured, bowing his head and hiding his eyes on her shoulder in misery. His mother kissed him a long, fervent kiss.
>
> "My boy!" she said, in a voice trembling with passionate love.

"At your mischief again?" says the father, "venomously," as he interrupts this scene of illicitly possessive passion. Mischief it is, corrosive and destructive to the marriage that Paul needs, the full relationship that Miriam offers, with her intimate love for nature.

It will be evident that I do not agree with the view that Spilka and others have taken of that flower-picking episode with Miriam and Clara, the view that takes the scene as a revelation of a basic flaw in Miriam: "she kills life and has no right to it."

> "Ah!" cried Miriam, and she looked at Paul, her dark eyes dilating. He smiled. Together they enjoyed the field of flowers. Clara, a little way off, was looking at the cowslips disconsolately. Paul and Miriam stayed close together, talking in subdued tones. He kneeled on one knee, quickly gathering the best blossoms, moving from tuft to tuft restlessly, talking softly all the time. Miriam plucked the flowers lovingly, lingering over them. He always seemed to her too quick and almost scientific. Yet his bunches had a natural beauty more than hers. He loved them, but as if they were his and he had a right to them. She had more reverence for them: they held something she had not.

The last clause has a wonderful ambiguity. If we take Paul's point of view, we will say that she is "negative," that she lacks true life. If we ponder the whole action of the book, we will say that what she lacks is the full organic life of the flower, sexually complete within itself. She cannot grow into her full life without the principle that Paul, with his masculine creativity, here displays. The passage shows a man and a woman who are true counterparts, in mind and body. When, a little later, Paul sprinkles the flowers over Clara, he is performing an exclusively sensuous ritual that threatens more than a pagan love-death:

> Her breasts swung slightly in her blouse. The arching curve of her back was beautiful and strong; she wore no stays. Suddenly, without knowing, he was scattering a handful of cowslips over her hair and neck, saying:

"Ashes to ashes, and dust to dust,
If the Lord won't have you the devil must."

The chill flowers fell on her neck. She looked up at him, with almost pitiful, scared grey eyes, wondering what he was doing. Flowers fell on her face, and she shut her eyes.

Suddenly, standing there above her, he felt awkward.

"I thought you wanted a funeral," he said, ill at ease.

It is Paul, under his mother's domination, who kills life, by refusing to move in organic relation with Miriam:

He would not have it that they were lovers. The intimacy between them had been kept so abstract, such a matter of the soul, all thought and weary struggle into consciousness, that he saw it only as a platonic friendship. He stoutly denied there was anything else between them. Miriam was silent, or else she very quietly agreed. He was a fool who did not know what was happening to himself. By tacit agreement they ignored the remarks and insinuations of their acquaintances.

"We aren't lovers, we are friends," he said to her. "*We* know it. Let them talk. What does it matter what they say."

Sometimes, as they were walking together, she slipped her arm timidly into his. But he always resented it, and she knew it. It caused a violent conflict in him. With Miriam he was always on the high plane of abstraction, when his natural fire of love was transmitted into the fine steam of thought. She would have it so.

The last sentence is a fine example of the way in which the commentary of the Paul-narrator can contradict the tenor of the action: "she slipped her arm timidly into his." Clara knows better and tells Paul the truth in that revealing conversation just before "the test on Miriam." Paul has been describing how Miriam "wants the soul out of my body": "I know she wants a sort of soul union."

"But how do you know what she wants?"

"I've been with her for seven years."

"And you haven't found out the very first thing about her."

"What's that?"

"That she doesn't want any of your soul communion. That's your own imagination. She wants you."

He pondered over this. Perhaps he was wrong.

"But she seems—" he began.

"You've never tried," she answered.

This is not to deny that Miriam is shy, intense, spiritual, and, as a result of her upbringing, fearful and evasive of sexual facts. All these qualities belong to her character, for she is young, sensitive, and modest.

My point is that her portrait does not consist simply of a static presentation of these aspects: her portrait is being enriched dynamically and progressively before our eyes, over a long period of years, from her early adolescence, through an awakening and potential fulfilment, to the utter extinction of her inner life and hope.

The truth of Clara's view has been borne out long before, as far back as that scene where Paul accuses Miriam of never laughing real laughter:

> "But"—and she looked up at him with eyes frightened and struggling—"I do laugh at you—I *do*."
>
> "Never! There's always a kind of intensity. When you laugh I could always cry; it seems as if it shows up your suffering. Oh, you make me knit the brows of my very soul and cogitate."
>
> Slowly she shook her head despairingly.
>
> "I'm sure I don't want to," she said.
>
> "I'm so damned spiritual with *you* always!" he cried.
>
> She remained silent, thinking, "Then why don't you be otherwise." But he saw her crouching, brooding figure, and it seemed to tear him in two.

And then, on the next page, as Paul repairs the bicycle tyre, we have an unmistakable glimpse of the vital image of Miriam, her strong physical feeling for him, and her true laughter:

> "Fetch me a drop of water in a bowl," he said to her. "I shall be late, and then I s'll catch it."
>
> He lighted the hurricane lamp, took off his coat, turned up the bicycle, and set speedily to work. Miriam came with the bowl of water and stood close to him, watching. She loved to see his hands doing things. He was slim and vigorous, with a kind of easiness even in his most hasty movements. And busy at his work, he seemed to forget her. She loved him absorbedly. She wanted to run her hands down his sides. She always wanted to embrace him, so long as he did not want her.
>
> "There!" he said, rising suddenly. "Now, could you have done it quicker?"
>
> "No!" she laughed.
>
> He straightened himself. His back was towards her. She put her two hands on his sides, and ran them quickly down.
>
> "You are so *fine*!" she said.
>
> He laughed, hating her voice, but his blood roused to a wave of flame by her hands. She did not seem to realise *him* in all this. He might have been an object. She never realised the male he was.

Those last three sentences, the outgrowth of his torment, and the earlier remark, "so long as he did not want her," provide clear examples of the way in which the overpainted commentary tends to obscure the basic portrait of Miriam. It is the same in the episode at Nethermere: "He could not bear to look at Miriam. She seemed to want him, and he resisted. He resisted all the time. He wanted now to give her passion and tenderness, and he could not. He felt that she wanted the soul out of his body, and not him."

> He went on, in his dead fashion:
>
> "If only you could want *me*, and not want what I can reel off for you!"
>
> "I!" she cried bitterly—"I! Why, when would you let me take you?"

His bursts of anger and "hate", his feeling that Miriam is pulling the soul out of his body, are only his own tormented reactions to the agony he feels in being pulled so strongly away from his mother, as Daniel Weiss has said: "It is that for the first time in his life he is facing a mature relationship between himself and another woman, *not* his mother, and that a different mode of love is being demanded from him. It is Miriam's refusal to allow him to regress to the Nirvana, the paradisal state of the infant, her insistence that he recognize her, that fills him with anguish."

As though to warn us against accepting Paul's responses and interpretations, Lawrence inserts in the middle of the crucial chapter, "Strife in Love," a long, vigorous, attractive, and surprising scene where the father is shown totally in command of the household, on a Friday evening, when the miners make their reckoning in Morel's house. Complaining with warm, vigorous dialect about the cold room, as he emerges from his bath, Morel draws even his wife into laughter and reminiscent admiration:

> Morel looked down ruefully at his sides.
>
> "Me!" he exclaimed. "I'm nowt b'r a skinned rabbit. My bones fair juts out on me."
>
> "I should like to know where," retorted his wife.
>
> "Iv'ry-wheer! I'm nobbut a sack o' faggots."
>
> Mrs. Morel laughed. He had still a wonderfully young body, muscular, without any fat. His skin was smooth and clear. It might have been the body of a man of twenty-eight, except that there were, perhaps, too many blue scars, like tattoo-marks, where the coal-dust remained under the skin, and that his chest was too hairy. But he put his hand on his sides ruefully. It was his fixed belief that, because he did not get fat, he was as thin as a starved rat.
>
> Paul looked at his father's thick, brownish hands all scarred, with broken nails, rubbing the fine smoothness of his sides, and the incongruity struck him. It seemed strange they were the same flesh.
>
> "I suppose," he said to his father, "you had a good figure once."

> "Eh!" exclaimed the miner, glancing round, startled and timid, like a child.
>
> "He had," exclaimed Mrs. Morel, "if he didn't hurtle himself up as if he was trying to get in the smallest space he could."
>
> "Me!" exclaimed Morel—"me a good figure! I wor niver much more n'r a skeleton."
>
> "Man!" cried his wife, "don't be such a pulamiter!"
>
> " 'Strewth!" he said. "Tha's niver knowed me but what I looked as if I wor goin' off in a rapid decline."
>
> She sat and laughed.
>
> "You've had a constitution like iron," she said; "and never a man had a better start, if it was body that counted. You should have seen him as a young man," she cried suddenly to Paul, drawing herself up to imitate her husband's once handsome bearing.
>
> Morel watched her shyly. He saw again the passion she had had for him. It blazed upon her for a moment. He was shy, rather scared, and humble. Yet again he felt his old glow. And then immediately he felt the ruin he had made during these years. He wanted to bustle about, to run away from it.

Paul is the "outsider" here, the one who does not enter into the family warmth, as we have seen a few lines earlier from his cold comment on his father's vigorous exclamations ("Why is a door-knob deader than anything else?"), and as we see a little later from the way in which he turns "impatiently" from his books and pencil, after his father has asked him "humbly" to count up the money. And at the close of the episode he dismisses his father viciously: "It won't be long," he says to his mother. "You can have my money. Let him go to hell." Morel does not deserve this, we feel, after all the warmth and vigour of his action here. Paul is cruel to anyone who threatens his mother's dominion, however briefly.

This Miriam feels instinctively, a few minutes later, when she looks at the stencilled design that Paul has made for his mother:

> "Ah, how beautiful!" she cried.
>
> The spread cloth, with its wonderful reddish roses and dark green stems, all so simple, and somehow so wicked-looking, lay at her feet. She went on her knees before it, her dark curls dropping. He saw her crouched voluptuously before his work, and his heart beat quickly. Suddenly she looked up at him.
>
> "Why does it seem cruel?" she asked.
>
> "What?"
>
> "There seems a feeling of cruelty about it," she said.
>
> "It's jolly good, whether or not," he replied, folding up his work with a lover's hands.

He has also made a "smaller piece" for Miriam; but when he sees her fingering the work "with trembling hands" he can only turn with embarrassment to tend the bread in the oven, and when she looks up at him "with her dark eyes one flame of love" he can only laugh "uncomfortably" and begin to talk "about the design." "All his passion, all his wild blood, went into this intercourse with her, when he talked and conceived his work. She brought forth to him his imaginations. She did not understand, any more than a woman understands when she conceives a child in her womb. But this was life for her and for him." But, as the imagery of conception ironically implies, such talk is not all of life for either of them.

Immediately after this, the physical scuffle and flirtation with Beatrice shows another need, which Miriam recognizes and would like to satisfy: "His thick hair was tumbled over his forehead. Why might she not push it back for him, and remove the marks of Beatrice's comb? Why might she not press his body with her two hands? It looked so firm, and every whit living. And he would let other girls, why not her?" A moment later, as usual, Paul tries to "abstract" their relationship into a French lesson, only to find that her French diary is "mostly a love-letter" to him:

> "Look," he said quietly, "the past participle conjugated with *avoir* agrees with the direct object when it precedes."
>
> She bent forward, trying to see and to understand. Her free, fine curls tickled his face. He started as if they had been red hot, shuddering. He saw her peering forward at the page, her red lips parted piteously, the black hair springing in fine strands across her tawny, ruddy cheek. She was coloured like a pomegranate for richness. His breath came short as he watched her. Suddenly she looked up at him. Her dark eyes were naked with their love, afraid, and yearning. His eyes, too, were dark, and they hurt her. They seemed to master her. She lost all her self-control, was exposed in fear. And he knew, before he could kiss her, he must drive something out of himself. And a touch of hate for her crept back again into his heart. He returned to her exercise.

Miriam does not bear the slightest blame for the failure of this relationship: she is "like a pomegranate for richness," like the bride in the Song of Solomon; she combines a pure beauty of sensuous appeal with all the soul that Paul the artist needs for his further development. And like that bride she is not passive, she tries to draw Paul out of his imprisonment, tries to draw his attention towards the wild beauty of "the yellow, bursten flowers." His response is to level at her the most cruel of all his desperate charges:

> "Aren't they magnificent?" she murmured.
>
> "Magnificent! it's a bit thick—they're pretty!"

> She bowed again to her flowers at his censure of her praise. He watched her crouching, sipping the flowers with fervid kisses.
>
> "Why must you always be fondling things!" he said irritably.
>
> "But I love to touch them," she replied, hurt.
>
> "Can you never like things without clutching them as if you wanted to pull the heart out of them? Why don't you have a bit more restraint, or reserve, or something?"
>
> She looked up at him full of pain, then continued slowly to stroke her lips against a ruffled flower. Their scent, as she smelled it, was so much kinder than he; it almost made her cry.
>
> "You wheedle the soul out of things," he said. "I would never wheedle—at any rate, I'd go straight."
>
> He scarcely knew what he was saying. These things came from him mechanically. She looked at him. His body seemed one weapon, firm and hard against her.
>
> "You're always begging things to love you," he said, "as if you were a beggar for love. Even the flowers, you have to fawn on them—"
>
> Rhythmically, Miriam was swaying and stroking the flower with her mouth, inhaling the scent which ever after made her shudder as it came to her nostrils.
>
> "You don't want to love—your eternal and abnormal craving is to be loved. You aren't positive, you're negative. You absorb, absorb, as if you must fill yourself up with love, because you've got a shortage somewhere."
>
> She was stunned by his cruelty, and did not hear. He had not the faintest notion of what he was saying. It was as if his fretted, tortured soul, run hot by thwarted passion, jetted off these sayings like sparks from electricity.

The shortage is in Paul; and she fondles the flowers so warmly because they offer solace from his ruthless rejection of her natural being. Her closeness to flowers throughout the book shows her as an innocent Persephone who needs only to be carried away by the power that Paul might possess if he were a whole man. But he is not. He is a child, with a child's limited outlook. His mother's influence has reduced all other human beings to unreality. This the narrator makes plain in one of his rare moments of illumination:

> He had come back to his mother. Hers was the strongest tie in his life. When he thought round, Miriam shrank away. There was a vague, unreal feel about her. And nobody else mattered. There was one place in the world that stood solid and did not melt into unreality: the place where his mother was. Everybody else could grow shadowy, almost non-existent to him, but she could not. It was as if the pivot and pole of his life, from which he could not escape, was his mother.

So then for Paul the warm reality of Miriam must fade away into spirituality and soulfulness, and she must suffer the cruel accusation summed up in the falsely composed letter that he writes at the end of the chapter, "Defeat of Miriam"—a letter of stilted, inflated rhetoric, false in every way:

> May I speak of our old, worn love, this last time. It, too, is changing, is it not? Say, has not the body of that love died, and left you its invulnerable soul? You see, I can give you a spirit love, I have given it you this long, long time; but not embodied passion. See, you are a nun. I have given you what I would give a holy nun—as a mystic monk to a mystic nun. Surely you esteem it best. Yet you regret—no, have regretted—the other. In all our relations no body enters. I do not talk to you through the senses—rather through the spirit. That is why we cannot love in the common sense. Ours is not an everyday affection. As yet we are mortal, and to live side by side with one another would be dreadful, for somehow with you I cannot long be trivial, and, you know, to be always beyond this mortal state would be to lose it. If people marry, they must live together as affectionate humans, who may be common-place with each other without feeling awkward—not as two souls. So I feel it.

So she feels it too, and the hopeless rejection of her true character gives a death-blow to her inner vitality. " 'You are a nun—you are a nun.' The words went into her heart again and again. Nothing he ever had said had gone into her so deeply, fixedly, like a mortal wound."

After such a wound, his later effort to carry on sexual relations with her is bound to be a failure. She tries, as she always has tried, but her inner life is ebbing. This is not the marriage that she yearns for, not the union that he needs. Paul hardly knows that she is there, as a person; indeed he does not want to know her as a human being. "He had always, almost wilfully, to put her out of count, and act from the brute strength of his own feelings." The title of the chapter, "The Test of Miriam," is bitterly ironic, for what the chapter presents is the test on Paul's ability to free himself from the imprisonment which he feels, but does not understand. This is clear from Paul's stream of consciousness at the very outset of the chapter: "There was some obstacle; and what was the obstacle? It lay in the physical bondage. He shrank from the physical contact. But why? With her he felt bound up inside himself. He could not go out to her." His only refuge is to turn towards a sort of mindless evasion of his torments, a rejection of his own humanity:

> He courted her now like a lover. Often, when he grew hot, she put his face from her, held it between her hands, and looked in his eyes. He could not meet her gaze. Her dark eyes, full of love, earnest and

> searching, made him turn away. Not for an instant would she let him forget. Back again he had to torure himself into a sense of his responsibility and hers. Never any relaxing, never any leaving himself to the great hunger and impersonality of passion; he must be brought back to a deliberate, reflective creature. As if from a swoon of passion she called him back to the littleness, the personal relationship.

So Paul, near the end of this chapter, is reduced to pitiful, even contemptible, littleness. Miriam, in her violent despair, at last cries out the essential truth: "It has been one long battle between us—you fighting away from me." His response is shock and utter amazement: in his self-absorption he has never even begun to see it from her point of view. And he turns at once towards a painful series of self-justifications, throwing the blame on her: "He was full of a feeling that she had deceived him. She had despised him when he thought she worshipped him. She had let him say wrong things, and had not contradicted him. She had let him fight alone . . . She had not played fair." Yet at the very end of the chapter, the bitter truth of what he has done to her emerges poignantly out of self-deception:

> "She never thought she'd have me, mother, not from the first, and so she's not disappointed."
>
> "I'm afraid," said his mother, "she doesn't give up hopes of you yet."
>
> "No," he said, "perhaps not."
>
> "You'll find it's better to have done," she said.
>
> "*I* don't know," he said desperately.
>
> "Well, leave her alone," replied his mother.
>
> So he left her, and she was alone. Very few people cared for her, and she for very few people. She remained alone with herself, waiting.

COLIN CLARKE

Reductive Energy in "The Rainbow"

In *The Rainbow* as in Lawrence's work at large, the vitalistic virtues—spontaneity, untamed energy, intensity of being, power—are endorsed elaborately. But the endorsement is noticeably more ambiguous on some occasions than on others. The vitality of the young Will Brangwen (he reminds Anna 'of some animal, some mysterious animal that lived in the darkness under the leaves and never came out, but which lived vividly, swift and intense') is one thing; the vitality that Will and Anna eventually release in themselves in their bouts of natural-unnatural sensuality is another. So for that matter is Ursula's fierce salt-burning corrosiveness under the moon, or the corrupt African potency of Skrebensky. In the one instance life is affirmed directly, positively, unambiguously, if also with potential ferocity and violence—but in the other instances reductively, in disintegration or corruption. . . .

In the chapter 'Anna Victrix' we remark the partial emergence of a syndrome of images that was to prove crucial in the articulation of the reductive theme in *Women in Love*; and no passage is more prophetic than the following, with its ambiguous stress on enforced *downward* movement.

> At first she went on blithely enough with him shut down beside her. But then his spell began to take hold of her. The dark, seething potency of him, the power of a creature that lies hidden and exerts its will to the destruction of the free-running creature, as the tiger lying in the darkness of the leaves steadily enforces the fall and death of the light creatures

> that drink by the waterside in the morning, gradually began to take effect on her. Though he lay there in his darkness and did not move, yet she knew he lay waiting for her. She felt his will fastening on her and pulling her down, even whilst he was silent and obscure.
>
> She found that, in all her outgoings and her incomings, he prevented her. Gradually she realized that she was being borne down by him, borne down by the clinging, heavy weight of him, that he was pulling her down as a leopard clings to a wild cow and exhausts her and pulls her down. . . .
>
> Why did he want to drag her down, and kill her spirit? Why did he want to deny her spirit? Why did he deny her spirituality, hold her for a body only? And was he to claim her carcase? . . . 'What do you do to me?' she cried . . . 'There is something horrible in you, something dark and beastly in your will'.

Will's reductive activity is potent, vital, sanctioned by Nature (assimilated, that is, to the splendid destructiveness of leopards and tigers) but also debilitating, *un*-natural, monstrous. The downward tug is a degradation, an obscenity: 'And was he to claim her carcase?' Whether Will is 'actually' as monstrous as he seems to Anna is not of course a critical issue. There is no way of going behind the words themselves to unverbalized facts, and what the words present us with is something like an antinomy—a vision of horror and preversity imposed, immediately, upon a no less cogent vision of potency and life. What we carry away is an impression not so much of complexity of 'character' as of the value-and-cost of living within the darkness.

And the same is true of the way Will's impressively rendered sensuality is directly overlaid by his agonizing sense of vacuity and dependence; he is extremely vulnerable, and at the same time powerful. This point needs to be laboured a little, because of the way the dependence and weakness have been dwelt upon in critical commentaries and the potency correspondingly ignored. Of the potency we are assured again and again:

> There was something thick, dark, dense, powerful about him that irritated her too deeply for her to speak of it.

or:

> And ever and again he appeared as the dread flame of power. Sometimes, when he stood in the doorway, his face lit up, he seemed like an Annunciation to her, her heart beat fast. And she watched him, suspended. He had a dark, burning being that she dreaded and resisted.

Yet Daleski permits himself to remark that Will is 'the weak, if not quite the broken, end of the arch'; and he concludes that the conflict between

Will and Anna 'derives, ultimately, from *his* imperfections'. One wonders then how it is that Anna should come in time to sustain herself with her husband's subterranean strength:

> She learned not to dread and to hate him, but to fill herself with him, to give herself to his black, sensual power, that was hidden all the daytime.

On the other hand we are not allowed to forget that the power Will mediates in the darkness is paid for by an acquaintance with the *terrors* of the darkness—and the obscenities too.

> She wanted to desert him, to leave him a prey to the open, with the unclean dogs of the darkness setting on to devour him. He must beat her, and make her stay with him.

In the paragraph immediately preceding we find this:

> And, at the bottom of her soul, she felt he wanted her to be dark, unnatural. Sometimes, when he seemed like the darkness covering and smothering her, she revolted almost in horror, and struck at him.

Will is terrified of the unclean creatures of the dark; yet in Anna's eyes he is one of those creatures himself, potent, sinister, horrifying. In short, what at one moment is potency becomes at the next, with a sudden shift of perspective, vulnerability. Nor are terror and horror absolute qualities—or static; they create, or convert themselves into their opposites: '*Because* she dreaded him and held him in horror, he became wicked, he wanted to destroy'; 'And he began to shudder . . . He must beat her, and make her stay with him'. In both Will and Anna power is a function of vulnerability and vulnerability of power.

The reading Leavis offers then seems to me to do these scenes less than justice:

> Anna, on the face of it, might seem to be the aggressor. The relevant aspect of her has its clear dramatization in the scene that led to the banning of the book; the scene in which she is surprised by Will dancing the defiant triumph of her pregnancy, naked in her bedroom. She is the Magna Mater, the type-figure adverted to so much in *Women in Love* of a feminine dominance that must defeat the growth of any prosperous long-term relation between a man and a woman.
>
> But we have to recognize that this dominance in Anna has for its complement a dependence in Will. There are passages that convey to us with the most disturbing force the paradoxical insufferableness to Anna of such a dependence, and its self-frustrating disastrousness. This inability to stand alone constitutes a criticism of a positive trait of Will's towards which Anna feels a deep antipathy. In a sense that Lawrence's

> art defines very clearly, he is religious. It is a religiousness that provokes in Anna a destructive rationalism, and the scenes that give us the clash leave us in no doubt that both attitudes are being criticized. The whole treatment of religion in this chapter, called 'Anna Victrix', which deals with it directly in a sustained way, is very subtle in its distinctions and its delicacies.

This, surely, is too rationalistic, and moralistic, to convey a full sense of the paradoxical richness of the text. Will doesn't, or shouldn't, lose marks for his inability to stand alone. What should register with us rather is the manifest weakness-in-strength; this, we have to recognize, is what it is like to be a natural inhabitant of the darkness. In other words, it is not so much that 'attitudes are being criticized' as that we are being made aware of the cost of a certain kind of human experience. The potency and the capacity of degradation—the fear of the night and the splendid dark sensuality—belong to a single individual, and what is being deviously suggested is that the potency can't be had *without* the degradation. The more sophisticated strategy of *Women in Love* is already within sight.

If the endorsement of reductive power in 'Anna Victrix' is largely oblique, by the time we reach the chapter 'The Child' it has become explicit, though not, for that reason, unambiguous. First there is the account of Will's unconsummated seduction of the young girl he meets in Nottingham. A moralistic interpretation of this scene, entailing a simple ethical judgment on Will's perversity and pursuit of sensation for its own sake, would drastically impoverish its significance.

> He did not care about her, except that he wanted to overcome her resistance, to have her in his power, fully and exhaustively to enjoy her.

This and similar passages, taken out of context, could be used to support the view that the whole episode points the distance between a fully human sexuality and the aridness of unassimilated desire.

> Just his own senses were supreme. All the rest was external, insignificant, leaving him alone with this girl whom he wanted to absorb, whose properties he wanted to absorb into his own senses. . . .
>
> But he was patiently working for her relaxation, patiently, his whole being fixed in the smile of latent gratification, his whole body electric with a subtle, powerful, reducing force upon her.

Yet this premeditated sensuality (one notes how often Lawrence resorts to the image of electricity to suggest the *frisson* of white or sensational sex) opens up for Will a new world of Absolute Beauty.

> And his hand that grasped her side felt one curve of her, and it seemed like a new creation to him, a reality, an absolute, an existing tangible beauty of the absolute.

Clearly, the human value of Will's experience is by no means easily determined. Indeed its final value *cannot* be determined; the effect of Lawrence's art is to discourage in the reader any tendency to reach a single and ready-defined judgment. The destruction of the flesh in conscious sensuality is presented very deliberately for contemplation, as though the intention were to invite a dismissive moral judgment; but, just as deliberately, any such judgment is held at bay. The perversity and destructiveness are fully conceded and, artistically, fully realized; but so is the beauty, the 'amazing beauty and pleasure'. As so often in Lawrence's work the effect is one of double exposure: we register the impulse to destruction even while we acknowledge the enhancement of life.

These complexities and tensions are sustained and indeed intensified in the sequence that follows when Will, returning home, incites Anna to a new kind of love-making, 'a sensuality violent and extreme as death'.

> There was no tenderness, no love between them any more, only the maddening, sensuous lust for discovery and the insatiable, exorbitant gratification in the sensual beauties of her body. . . .
> They accepted shame, and were one with it in their most unlicensed pleasures. It was incorporated. It was a bud that blossomed into beauty and heavy, fundamental gratification.

Mark Spilka's comment on these pages, in *The Love Ethic of D. H. Lawrence*, runs as follows:

> They revel in one another, as Tom Brangwen and his wife had revelled before them, and as Rupert and Ursula (Brangwen) Birkin would revel after them, in order to root out all shame, all fear of the body's secrets: . . .
>
> Here Lawrence seems to find a place, in marriage, for cold, lustful desire (as opposed, apparently, to 'hot, living desire'); and its function—a limited one—is discovery and purification: a sensual revel, a phallic 'hunting out' which leaves one free for the deeper, warmer love he generally upholds. But more than this, the experience sets Brangwen free to attend to his public tasks, which he had hitherto endured as so much mechanical activity. Now his purposive self is roused and released, and he begins at 30 to teach woodwork classes at the Cossethay night-school. About ten years later he returns to his own creative work in wood and other materials, and soon afterwards he receives an appointment as Art and Handwork Instructor for the County of Nottingham. Through the purgation process, both he and his wife have been aroused to active,

> purposive life—she, from the long sleep of motherhood; he, from social sterility to a point of social and self-respect.

And in a footnote, after quoting a comparable scene from *Lady Chatterley's Lover* ('Burning out the shames, the deepest, oldest shames, in the most secret places . . .') he adds:

> What the experience does for Constance Chatterley it also does for Will and Anna Brangwen. It is a purgation process, and less the norm of love than a release to full, creative life.

This reading is faithful to the text up to a point, for Brangwen's profound sensual activity does release in him a socially purposive self. And yet what we observe first and foremost is that the new licentiousness has an absolute, or non-instrumental, value. Obviously (for the language is quite explicit) Will's sensuality is disintegrative. A deliberate, piece-meal exploitation of the body takes the place of tenderness and love. Yet the disintegrative sex is now discovered to be a way-in to life, and, above all, a revelation of beauty, 'supreme, immoral, Absolute Beauty'. This is the bold truth we are required to confront; and Spilka's reading tends to dissipate it. It is the final paragraphs of the chapter that that reading is most relevant to, for there we find ourselves in a more reassuring, not to say cosy, world where social purposiveness is triumphant and even lust turns (eventually) a moral mill.

> He wanted to be unanimous with the whole of purposive mankind . . . For the first time he began to take real interest in a public affair. He had at length, from his profound sensual activity, developed a real purposive self.

The *rapprochement* effected between the reductive and the creative in these last paragraphs impresses one as willed and glib, indeed as largely unreal. We are not to be convinced by mere assertion that social purposiveness can develop out of sensuality and a profound moral indifference; this, surely, is something that calls for patient demonstration.

On the other hand the 'mere assertion' was in itself an achievement; Lawrence was breaking new ground, even if he was doing so at a purely discursive level. To gauge the distance, as it were, between the 'argument' of the paragraphs under review and the 'argument' of the paragraphs that conclude the preceding chapter, 'The Cathedral', is one way of enforcing this point.

> He still remained motionless, seething with inchoate rage, when his whole nature seemed to disintegrate. He seemed to live with a strain upon himself, and occasionally came these dark, chaotic rages, the lust

> for destruction. She then fought with him, and their fights were horrible, murderous. And then the passion between them came just as black and awful. . . .
>
> He made himself a woodwork shed, in which to restore things which were destroyed in the church. So he had plenty to do: his wife, his child, the church, the woodwork, and his wage-earning, all occupying him. If only there were not some limit to him, some darkness across his eyes! . . . He was unready for fulfilment. Something undeveloped in him, there was a darkness in him which he *could* not unfold, which would never unfold in him.

This might well seem to be more honest than the conclusion to the chapter that follows; for Will's lust for destruction, of which we have heard so much and which we now recognize as a basic fact about him, is not lost sight of at all, even while we are being assured of his constructiveness and purposiveness. In other words, the creative and the reductive co-exist throughout; the one is not simply *substituted* for the other, as in the later passage, which seems by comparison a good deal too smooth. On the other hand the theme of the later passage is intrinsically more 'difficult'. Whereas in the earlier instance Will's creativeness and destructiveness, if undissociated are also causally unconnected, in the later instance it is actually *from* the destructiveness (in this case disintegrative sensuality) that the creativeness, we are to believe, proceeds, or develops. In cold fact however, the total failure to dramatize this development means that the destructive and the creative seem no more inwardly affiliated than they were in the earlier sequence. Indeed less so; virtually they lost contact.

And it is a loss of contact of just this kind that we frequently remark in the remaining chapters. The story repeatedly concerns itself with disintegration and destructiveness; and we can scarcely fail to assume, as we proceed, that it will be part of this concern to discover and define a significant pattern of relationships between *kinds* of disintegration: *this* disintegrative process will prove to have a bearing on *that*. But in the event no such pattern emerges; 'cross-reference' seems both to be encouraged and not encouraged. There is the fiercely corrosive and violently destructive activity of Ursula in the moonlight; there is the corruption and social disintegration at Wiggiston, and the corresponding despair of Ursula herself—('She had no connexion with other people. Her lot was isolated and deadly. There was nothing for her anywhere, but this black disintegration'); there is the splendid-sinister potency of Skrebensky, corrupt, fecund, destructive ('He kissed her, and she quivered as if she were being destroyed, shattered'); and there is Ursula's vision of advancing corruption at the very end of the novel. But to what extent these kinds of disintegration bear upon each other is not clear. Whereas in *Women in Love* the densely reticulated imagery is constantly persuading us to see identities in difference, to make discriminations and discover analogies, in the latter part of *The Rainbow* we seem to be invited teasingly to embark on this same procedure only in the end to be frustrated.

But these judgments require substantiating and I turn first to the scene, in the chapter 'First Love', in which the adolescent Ursula annihilates her lover under the moon. Once again (as in the case of Will Brangwen, 'the sensual male seeking his pleasure') we find ourselves acknowledging a value in activity patently opposed to the creative and integrative. 'But hard and fierce she had fastened upon him, cold as the moon and burning as a fierce salt . . . seething like some cruel, corrosive salt'. 'Cold . . . and burning': the oxymoron (a common one wherever Lawrence is concerned with the reductive processes) focusses the sense of an inverse vitality running counter to growth and to warm organic blood desire. Nowhere in the novel is human personality reduced more obviously and more drastically to the inhuman and inorganic, and yet nowhere are we more aware of power and energy humanly mediated. The recurrent images—moonlight, steel, corrosive salt, the sea—exclude the organic entirely, and one thinks of the famous letter on Marinetti and the Futurists (5 June, 1914):

> . . . it is the inhuman will, call it physiology, or like Marinetti—physiology of matter, that fascinates me. I don't so much care about what the woman *feels*—in the ordinary usage of the word. That presumes an *ego* to feel with. . . . You mustn't look in my novel for the old stable *ego* of the character.

In a stimulating article on *The Narrative Technique of "The Rainbow"*, Roger Sale has considered the literary means by which Lawrence contrived to 'break down "the old stable ego of character" '. It is not so much Sale's argument itself that concerns me here as the significance of that metaphor of 'breaking down'.

> The simplest declarative sentence is one of the main aids the novelist has in building up a stable ego, an identity. . . .
>
> If we turn to a passage in *The Rainbow*, we can show how Lawrence tries there to break down this natural building-up process . . .

The phrasing could not be more apt—or revealing; for 'breaking down' is a common Laurentian synonym for 'reduction'. So Sale pays his tribute unconsciously to the iconic power of Lawrence's art, and demonstrates indirectly that the major novels are about the reductive process not only in the most obvious or literal sense but in the further sense that they themselves image that process. In the episode under review we remark how the fiercely corrosive activity of the fictive Ursula is matched, and to that extent endorsed, by the corrosive activity—no less vigorous—of the artist himself. And this endorsement goes far towards explaining why our moral sense should fail to be outraged by Ursula's 'enormous wilfulness'. Her attitude to Skrebensky is inhuman, but then so is the novelist's art, in the sense that part of what he is engaged in is the reduction of human personality to an inhuman or material substratum. But this involves no diminishing of artistic intensity; indeed it has the reverse effect, and the novelist creates a notable artificial beauty—a beauty 'immoral and against mankind'.

Probably the best gloss on these pages is a passage . . . from *The Crown* . . .

> Leonardo knew this: he knew the strange endlessness of the flux of corruption. It is Mona Lisa's ironic smile. Even Michael Angelo knew it. It is in his *Leda and the Swan*. For the swan is one of the symbols of divine corruption with its reptile feet buried in the ooze and mud, its voluptuous form yielding and embracing the ooze of water, its beauty white and cold and terrifying, like the dead beauty of the moon, like the water-lily, the sacred lotus, its neck and head like the snake, it is for us a flame of the cold white fire of flux, the phosphorescence of corruption, the salt, cold burning of the sea which corrodes all it touches, coldly reduces every sun-built form to ash, to the original elements. This is the beauty of the swan, the lotus, the snake, this cold white salty fire of infinite reduction. And there was some suggestion of this in the Christ of the early Christians, the Christ who was the Fish.

The paradoxes are a good deal sharper in the novel than in the essay (with the exception of that last equation of Christ and Fish), for the obvious reason that Ursula, a human being, is further removed than snake or swan from 'the original elements', so that in the novel the reductive process is that much more spectacular. For all that, we are not more interested in the morality of Ursula's behaviour, essentially, than we would be in the behaviour of swan or snake. Or, to make the point perhaps less provocatively, we are interested in the morality of her behaviour only to the extent that we are interested in her dehumanization. It is relevant to recall that remarkable passage in E.T.'s Memoir where an account is given of three occasions on which Lawrence became wildly distraught—possessed—under the combined influence of moonlight and sea:

> I was really frightened then—not physically, but deep in my soul. He created an atmosphere not of death which after all is part of mortality, but of an utter negation of life, as though he had become dehumanized.

Analogously, in the scene in *The Rainbow*, one is impressed not so much by Ursula's will to separateness, or her frenetic feminine assertiveness, though these qualities are doubtless evident enough, as by her intimidating inhuman-ness. Yet the further she departs from the warmly living the more evidence she gives of vitality of a different kind—inverse, disintegrative. Inverse is Birkin's word; and indeed his notion of 'inverse process' is loosely relevant to the whole episode.

> When the stream of synthetic creation lapses, we find ourselves part of the inverse process, the blood of destructive creation. Aphrodite is born in the first spasm of universal dissolution—then the snakes and swans and lotus—marsh-flowers—and Gudrun and Gerald—born in the process of destructive creation . . . It is a progressive process—and it ends in universal nothing . . .

The process can end only in a re-assimilation to the anonymous energies of nature; yet it is productive of a deadly and distinctive beauty. And in *The Rainbow*, likewise, beauty is a product of the reductive process, a function of reductive power.

> She stood for some moments out in the overwhelming luminosity of the moon. She seemed a beam of gleaming power. She was afraid of what she was. Looking at him, at his shadowy, unreal, wavering presence a sudden lust seized her, to lay hold of him and tear him and make him into nothing. Her hands and wrists felt immeasurably hard and strong, like blades.

This revelation of life and beauty where we might scarcely be supposed to expect it, in a process that brutally affronts our sympathies—in a progressive departure from the human—is what the episode is centrally about. (It is for the most part a fully realized rhetorical beauty and rhetorical life, though there is, surely, some overwriting.) To identify with Ursula's daytime consciousness, and accept as self-validating the slow horror she experiences as she gradually recovers herself . . . is clearly inappropriate. Primarily, Ursula's horror is there to measure the recession of the magical and mythic. There is no suggestion that the familiar order of reality is the more valid or true; it is simply different.

And indeed the sheer fact of difference is stated as cogently as could well be. It is a question however whether the statement is not in fact too cogent. I have suggested, apropos of the final paragraphs of the chapter 'The Child', that Lawrence's task is to communicate a sense of the distinction between pure creation and destructive creation—or the vital and the perversely vital—without effecting a simple dissociation between them. In the earlier sequences involving Tom and Lydia, and Anna and

Will, the constant modulation from the mythic to the commonplace, and vice versa, has established the existence of a consciousness at once distinct from our familiar daytime consciousness and at the same time prone to assert itself in the context of daytime living. Will's murderously reductive activity in the chapter 'Anna Victrix' is a quality of his everyday behaviour and also the utterance of a self that can seem at moments extravagantly alien. But from the stackyard scene on there is a tendency for the magical and the everyday—the subterranean self and the social self—to move apart. And the abrupt dissociation of personae at the end of the scene, when Ursula repudiates her 'corrosive self' with horror (while the night is suddenly 'struck back into its old, accustomed, mild reality') is, in this connection, only too suggestive of what is to come. A truth is enforced, but at the expense of a counter-truth; Ursula's ruthless energy is made to seem *merely* alien.

It is Skrebensky's character however that tends most conspicuously to bifurcate, and in a way that bears even more suggestively on my argument. If it is a mistake to interpret Ursula's lurid behaviour under the moon with a moralistic bias, it is a parallel mistake to ignore the corrupt vitality of her lover and to write him off as a hollow man *simpliciter*. Leavis has perhaps led the way here; at any rate he has concerned himself exclusively with Skrebensky's shortcomings, laying stress upon his 'good-citizen acceptance of the social function as the ultimate meaning of life' and pointing to the connection between this acceptance and his 'inadequacy as a lover'. Others, designedly or not, have followed suit. S. L. Goldberg lumps Skrebensky with Winifred Inger and Tom Brangwen, 'the irrevocably lost'. Daleski, quoting the argument between Ursula and Skrebensky about being a soldier, comments:

> This passage establishes not only that Skrebensky is 'not exactly' a soldier, but that he is not exactly anything. If, unlike Will, he does not deny the outside world, he accepts his place in it with a mechanical and unadventurous complacency. . . .
> Skrebensky is even less defined as a man than either Tom or Will; lacking the rooted stability of the one and the passionate aspiration of the other, he has no real identity.

But what of the Skrebensky who, like Ursula herself, can be a vehicle of intense vitality, positive-reductive, potent, corrupt?

> He talked to her all the while in low tones about Africa, conveying something strange and sensual to her: the negro, with his loose, soft passion that could envelop one like a bath. Gradually he transferred to her the hot, fecund darkness that possessed his own blood. He was strangely secret. The whole world must be abolished. . . .

> He seemed like the living darkness upon her, she was in the embrace of the strong darkness. He held her enclosed, soft, unutterably soft, and with the unrelaxing softness of fate, the relentless softness of fecundity. . . .
>
> It was bliss, it was the nucleolating of the fecund darkness. Once the vessel had vibrated till it was shattered, the light of consciousness gone, then the darkness reigned, and the unutterable satisfaction.

Here again is that effect of double exposure to which I have already alluded: on the one hand an impression of cultural and organic regression, on the other hand the sensual transfiguration, 'the unutterable satisfaction'. It is the familiar paradox:

> Corruption will at last break down for us the deadened forms, and release us into the infinity.

The image of the turgid African night is parallel to those other images of potency-in-disintegration, the flaring moon and the salt-burning sea. Skrebensky's sensuality is at once reductive, regressive, a breaking down ('One breathes it, like a smell of blood', 'The whole world must be abolished') and a release into infinity. The sensual ecstasy has its roots in corruption. The lovers inhabit an 'umblemished darkness'; yet the matrix (as it were) of this darkness is that other, sinister darkness of Africa. This latter is the darkness that sustains them, ultimately—as the swan has its reptile feet buried in the ooze and mud. We are in the world of *Women in Love*. The teeming night is recognizably Birkin's 'dark river of dissolution': 'massive and *fluid* with terror', 'his loose, soft passion that could envelop one like a *bath*', 'they walked the darkness beside the massive *river*', 'the soft *flow* of his kiss . . . the warm fecund flow of his kiss', 'one fecund nucleus of the *fluid* darkness'. This is very obviously in the spirit of the later novel. It anticipates Birkin's '*fountain* of mystic corruption'.

Yet the Ursula-Skrebensky story, it is commonly agreed, is not, by a long way, as coherent or compelling as for the most part the story of *Women in Love* is. And one reason at least is plain. The final movement of *The Rainbow* is organized around a single human relationship. Inevitably this deprives Lawrence of the scope he needed for elaborating those paradoxical themes which, all the evidence goes to show, were now so deeply engaging his imagination. It is no accident that the single pair of lovers became two pairs of lovers in the sequel; they had to. Skrebensky is called on to discharge the functions of both Birkin *and* Gerald, to 'figure', in Jamesian phrase, the possibilities both for life *and* death in reductive sexuality. Not surprisingly he proves unequal to the task. At a non-narrative level the paradox about living disintegration can be developed and protracted as far as ingenuity will allow; but at the narrative level the limits to this process are stricter. *The Rainbow* is a novel, with a story. Skrebensky cannot, in the story, be given over finally to disintegration and also be redeemed. And, in the event, under these novelistic pressures his character falls apart into *two* characters.

On the one hand there is Skrebensky the darkly potent lover, inhabitant of the fecund universal night.

> Everything he did was a voluptuous pleasure to him—either to ride on horseback, or to walk, or to lie in the sun, or to drink in a public-house. He had no use for people, nor for words. He had an amused pleasure in everything, a great sense of voluptuous richness in himself . . .

There is little doubt that we are to accept this vitality as real. Moreover it entails a certain correlative distinction at a more personal and conscious level.

> She took him home, and he stayed a week-end at Beldover with her family. She loved having him in the house. Strange how he seemed to come into the atmosphere of her family, with his laughing, insidious grace. They all loved him, he was kin to them. His raillery, his warm, voluptuous mocking presence was meat and joy to the Brangwen household. For this house was always quivering with darkness, they put off their puppet from when they came home, to lie and drowse in the sun.

The emphasis here is still on the dark under-life; yet laughing insidious grace, raillery, warmth and voluptuous mockery also suggest less esoteric qualities—more 'human' and social—and a corresponding fulness or completeness of being. At any rate we are left in no doubt of the richness and abundance of life which the relationship with Skrebensky, for all its limitations, does release. The lovers are held together *only* in the sensual subconsciousness, yet that only includes so much.

> Then he turned and kissed her, and she waited for him. The pain to her was the pain she wanted, the agony was the agony she wanted. She was caught up, entangled in the powerful vibration of the night. The man, what was he?—a dark, powerful vibration that encompassed her. She passed away as on a dark wind, far, far away, into the pristine darkness of paradise, into the original immortality. She entered the dark fields of immortality.

In the face of this and similar passages it is scarcely adequate to say of Skrebensky that though he satisfies Ursula 'time after time in their physical relations he fails her at the last in the "beyondness of sex" . . . —where Birkin in *Women in Love* will not fail with Ursula later'. Something like this, it is true, is Ursula's own reading of the situation:

> The salt, bitter passion of the sea, its indifference to the earth, its swinging definite motion, its strength, its attack, and its salt burning, seemed to provoke her to a pitch of madness, tantalizing her with vast suggestions of fulfilment. And then, for personification, would come Skrebensky, Skrebensky, whom she knew, whom she was fond of, who was attractive, but whose soul could not contain her in its waves of strength, nor his breast compel her in burning, salty passion:

But we remember not only how she and Skrebensky had 'stood together, dark, fluid, *infinitely* potent, giving the living lie to the dead whole which contained them' or had passed away 'into the pristine darkness of paradise', or how 'perfectly and supremely free' they were, 'proud beyond all question, and *surpassing mortal conditions*', but also the sinister African potency, the destructiveness and indifference to humanity which Skrebensky had darkly communicated and which, I have argued, are analogous to the 'salt, bitter passion' which, we now learn, he is utterly deficient in.

But then of course there is the other Skrebensky.

> His life lay in the established order of things. He had his five senses too. They were to be gratified. . . .
>
> The good of the greatest number was all that mattered. That which was the greatest good for them all, collectively, was the greatest good for the individual.

This is the Skrebensky the commentators have fixed upon—a vacuity; a mere social integer, essentially without identity and living in pure externality through the senses.

It is true that the contrast between the two Skrebenskys is not always as steep as the passages quoted might suggest. There are moments when the vacuity and the power live together convincingly, are accepted as belonging to a single person.

> He seemed so balanced and sure, he made such a confident presence. He was a great rider, so there was about him some of a horseman's sureness, and habitual definiteness of decision, also some of the horseman's animal darkness. Yet his soul was only the more wavering, vague . . . She could only feel the dark, heavy fixity of his animal desire. . . . all must be kept so dark, the consciousness must admit nothing . . . He was always side-tracking always side-tracking his own soul. She could see him so well out there, in India—one of the governing class, superimposed upon an old civilisation, lord and master of a clumsier civilisation than his own.

Here Skrebensky's limitations are a believable aspect of his strength; the animal darkness, the fixity of animal desire, the disinclination to bring things to consciousness, the side-tracking of his own soul—this all hangs together. If his soul is wavering and vague, if he virtually has no soul, this is not because he lives purely in the senses, but because he has the inarticulateness of an animal—both its dark power and its heavy fixity.

And if Skrebensky's sensual being impresses us as far shallower on some occasions than on others, something similar is true of Ursula. She however is always exempted from adverse judgment.

> Yet she loved him, the body of him, whatever his decisions might be . . . She caught his brilliant, burnished glamour. Her heart and her soul were shut away fast down below, hidden. She was free of them. She was to have her satisfaction.

We may compare this with the earlier comment on Skrebensky: 'He had his five senses too. They were to be gratified'. But whereas in the one instance dissociated sensuality releases a glow and splendour of life ('She became proud and erect, like a flower, putting itself forth in its proper strength') in the other it is a token of death ('Skrebensky, somehow, had created a deadness around her, a sterility, as if the world were ashes . . . Why did he never really want a woman, not with the whole of him: never love, never worship, only just physically want her?') When Skrebensky finally fails Ursula at the end, they are engaged in a pursuit of just that kind of satisfaction which she herself had set up as a goal ('Her heart and soul were shut away . . . She was to have her satisfaction'); yet responsibility for this failure seems to be laid exclusively at Skrebensky's door.

> She liked it, the electric fire of the silk under his hands upon her limbs . . . Yet she did not feel beautiful. All the time, she felt she was not beautiful to him, only exciting. She let him take her, and he seemed mad, mad with excited passion. But she, as she lay afterwards on the cold, soft sand, looking up at the blotted, faintly luminous sky, felt that she was as cold now as she had been before.

The transfiguration in the flesh which Ursula had unquestionably enjoyed with Skrebensky is here repudiated, and the intoxication of the senses which they shared is conceived of as having ended in itself; it involved, apparently, 'no connexion with the unknown'. But the reader's recollections, as I have suggested, are different from Ursula's, and are not so rapidly erased.

One can conceive easily enough of an ending to the novel which would seem to resolve these warring tensions: Ursula, looking back in gratitude to the very real satisfaction and fulfilment Skrebensky had brought, might yet acknowledge that in the end the sensual ecstasy could not in itself sustain her. Yet, clearly, tensions as powerful as these are not to be resolved so neatly and rationally. For Lawrence is under an evident compulsion to make *incompatible* statements about voluptuousness or dissociated sensuality, and is struggling to find a novelistic pattern sufficiently flexible to allow him to do so. The pattern to which he is committed is transparently *not* sufficiently flexible; so we find him asserting of Skrebensky that his sensuality ends in sensuality and yet also that it leads into the unknown.

There is an essay of this period, *The Lemon Gardens* (it appeared in the *English Review* in September 1913) in which this doubleness of attitude to self-conscious sensuality is articulated with especial clarity.

> This is the soul of the Italian since the Renaissance. In the sunshine he basks asleep, gathering up a vintage into his veins which in the night-time he will distil into ecstatic sensual delight, the intense, white-cold ecstasy of darkness and moonlight, the raucous, cat-like, destructive enjoyment, the senses conscious and crying out in their consciousness in the pangs of the enjoyment, which has consumed the southern nation, perhaps all the Latin races, since the Renaissance. . . .
>
> This is one way of transfiguration into the eternal flame, the transfiguration through ecstasy in the flesh. . . . And this is why the Italian is attractive, supple, and beautiful, because he worships the Godhead in the flesh. We envy him, we feel pale and insignificant beside him. Yet at the same time we feel superior to him, as if he were a child and we adult.
>
> Wherein are we superior? Only because we went beyond the phallus in the search of the Godhead, the creative origin. And we found the physical forces and the secrets of science. . . .
>
> But we have exhausted ourselves in the process. We have found great treasures, and we are now impotent to use them. So we have said: 'What good are these treasures, they are vulgar nothings.' We have said: 'Let us go back from this adventuring, let us enjoy our own flesh, like the Italian.' But our habit of life, our very constitution, prevents our being quite like the Italian. The phallus will never serve us as a Godhead, because we do not believe in it: no Northern race does. Therefore, either we set ourselves to serve our children, calling them 'the future', or else we turn perverse and destructive, give ourselves joy in the destruction of the flesh.

'Perverse and destructive': the tone is distinctly unsympathetic. 'This is one way of transfiguration into the eternal flame': the tone is far from unsympathetic. Yet the topic is essentially the same on each occasion. True, the Italian's worship of the Godhead in the flesh is genuine, whereas the northerner's is derivative and mechanical. Yet the theme in each instance is the self-consciousness of the flesh, destructive enjoyment, the pursuit of maximum sensation, the senses conscious and crying out in their consciousness. And these in effect are the ambiguities of the Ursula-Skrebensky story. We may compare:

> She vibrated like a jet of electric, firm fluid in response. Yet she did not feel beautiful. All the time, she felt she was not beautiful to him, only exciting.

And

> But the fire is cold, as in the eyes of a cat, it is a green fire. It is fluid, electric.

In the essay the cold fire has a splendour absent from the episode in the novel.

> This is the supremacy of the flesh, which devours all, and becomes transfigured into a magnificent brindled flame, a burning bush indeed.

But as I have suggested, a dismissive note—corresponding to the 'not beautiful . . . only exciting' of the novel—is there in the essay too, in the unsympathetic attitude to the northerner's merely mechanical sensation-hunting.

And so it is that the character of Skrebensky fails in the last analysis to cohere. He is made a butt, like the northerner, because he seeks the destruction of the flesh, or pure gratification through the senses; yet just the capacity to live through the flesh, reductively, like the Italian, is his strength. It is only with *Women in Love* that Lawrence finds for this teasing paradox an appropriate dramatic correlative. . . .

In the handling of this theme of corruption in *The Rainbow* one is indeed haunted by a sense of half-realized significance. There is the treatment of Ursula's uncle Tom for instance. Before the meeting at Wiggiston he had already made a decisive impact upon her imagination, when she saw him at the farm after the drowning of his father.

> She could see him, in all his elegant demeanour, bestial, almost corrupt. And she was frightened. She never forgot to look for the bestial, frightening side of him, after this.
>
> He said 'Good-bye' to his mother and went away at once. Ursula almost shrank from his kiss, now. She wanted it nevertheless, and the little revulsion as well.

And we remember this when he appears next, at the wedding (the passage is too long to quote in full).

> A kind of flame of physical desire was gradually beating up in the Marsh. . . . Tom Brangwen, with all his secret power, seemed to fan the flame that was rising. . . .

> The music began, and the bonds began to slip. Tom Brangwen was dancing with the bride, quick and fluid and as if in another element, inaccessible as the creatures that move in the water. . . . One couple after another was washed and absorbed into the deep underwater of the dance.
>
> 'Come', said Ursula to Skrebensky, laying her hand on his arm. . . .
>
> It was his will and her will locked in a trance of motion, two wills locked in one motion, yet never fusing, never yielding one to the other. It was a glaucous, intertwining, delicious flux and contest in flux.

The dichotomies of the moralist are hopelessly irrelevant here. The underworld over which the half-sinister Tom Brangwen presides is a place of dangerous licence, of enchantment, of heightened life, a place for the privileged to enter. Yet if here, in his equivocal way, Tom releases life, and later, at Wiggiston, is an unequivocal agent of death, nothing is made of this duality; it generates no significance. There is no ironic juxtaposition of his two roles, as there would be in *Women in Love*; we are not manoeuvred into adopting, simultaneously or nearly so, conflicting attitudes to corruption or decay.

The final paragraphs of the novel, which are commonly acknowledged to be unconvincing, bear upon my argument with especial force. There is a demonstrable confusion of imagery in these paragraphs, amounting in fact to a sort of trickery—but of a kind that shows Lawrence feeling his way towards the richer effects of *Women in Love*.

> She knew that the sordid people who crept hardscaled and separate on the face of the world's corruption were living still. . . . She saw in the rainbow the earth's new architecture, the old, brittle corruption of houses and factories swept away, the world built up in a living fabric of Truth, fitting to the over-arching heaven.

The hardness that Ursula discovers around her is both the hardness of death and a hardness that conceals new life. We are asked to believe that the one kind of hardness can become or virtually *is* the other, and on grounds that appear to be little more than verbal. 'The terrible corruption spreading over the face of the land' is *hard, dry, brittle*; and equally hard, dry and brittle is the 'horny covering of disintegration', 'the husk of an old fruition' in which Ursula can observe 'the swelling and the heaving contour of the new germination'. Lawrence insists on the completeness and seeming finality of the corruption—it is 'triumphant and unopposed'—and yet it is in the very extremity of the corruption that consolation is discovered. If organisms have everywhere disintegrated almost to dust, so much the better. The more dust-like, the more easily 'swept away'! Some such spurious logic would seem to be implied, surely, in the collocation of 'swept away', 'brittle corruption' and 'disintegration', and even if this were not so, one's other objection would remain: the hardness of corruption ('corruption so pure that it is hard and brittle') cannot be translated by mere verbal sleight-of-hand into the hardness of the husk that encloses new life.

In any case, we are left with the impression that corruption is merely *antithetical* to this new life—an impression that quite fails to correspond with the fact that the novel has been moving towards the discovery that corruption can also energize and renew. The sequence in which this movement is most emphatic is that concerned with Skrebensky's sinister African sensuality, where, as we have seen, the language affirms both the menace of corruption and its life-giving potency. (The concept of corruption is not invoked explicitly in the passage, but it is clearly within call; the African night is at once hot and fluid, and there is a powerful suggestion of over-abundant growth.) In the novel as a whole however, the movement in question, the tendency towards a simultaneous affirmation of corruption and vitality, is at least as much promise as realization.

> Awful and threatening it was, dangerous to a degree, even whilst he gave himself to it. It was pure darkness, also. All the shameful things of the body revealed themselves to him now with a sort of sinister, tropical beauty. All the shameful natural and unnatural acts of sensual voluptuousness which he and the woman partook of together, created together, they had their heavy beauty and their delight. Shame, what was it? It was part of extreme delight. It was that part of delight of which man is usually afraid. Why afraid? The secret, shameful things are most terribly beautiful.

There is not much horror in these tropics, obviously. 'Sort of' necessarily deprives 'sinister' of some of its force, and the analogy in any case is only a glancing one (by contrast one thinks of the African sequence, later, and of that very real Negro 'with his loose, soft passion'). In short, while the beauty and the energizing power of corruption (or something like corruption) are made sufficiently real, the alternative possibilities of ugliness and nausea tend to be distanced. And though this is a strategy that might appear to be locally justified, in the larger perspective it begins to look suspect. For it is in keeping with the too-easy translation of the reductive impulses into the constructive which I have already commented on apropos of the conclusion of this episode, and to that extent contributes significantly to the relative disorganization of the novel in its latter phases.

And in this respect even the African sequence suffers, excellent as it is in itself; it too is more or less dissociated. For instance, no attempt is made to relate Skrebensky's African corruption to the no less lurid corruption at Wiggiston; and yet at one level, with his belief in the priority of social values and the unimportance of the individual, Skrebensky is heading straight for that 'disintegrated lifelessness of soul' which Uncle Tom (the Wiggiston colliery-owner) and Winifred Inger, Ursula's teacher, so patently embody.

> She saw gross, ugly movements in her mistress, she saw a clayey, inert, unquickened flesh, that reminded her of the great prehistoric lizards. One day her Uncle Tom came in out of the broiling sunshine heated from walking. Then the perspiration stood out upon his head and brow, his hand was wet and hot and suffocating in its clasp. He too had something marshy about him—the succulent moistness and turgidity, and the same brackish, nauseating effect of a marsh, where life and decaying are one.

'Prehistoric', 'marshy', 'turgidity': it is very like the African jungle. Yet there is no particular reason why we should recall this passage, when Skrebensky's splendid-corruptive African potency is later established.

Nor does the disintegration at Wiggiston bear as suggestively as it might upon Ursula's disintegrative or destructive attitude to that disintegration. Nor for that matter is her destructive social attitude sharply enough related to the destructive violence she directs against Skrebensky. . . .

The destructiveness Ursula unleashes on Skrebensky has a far more ambiguous value than the pure 'apocalyptic' destructiveness implicit in her attitude to society. So it cannot just be said that the one *is* the other. However, a valid point remains: there is certainly an identity in the difference. Yet not enough is done to help us to an awareness either of the difference or of the identity: Lawrence's grasp on the relationship is not a fully inward one.

These are the kinds of dissociation then that characterize the latter part of the novel. For all that, Lawrence is travelling perceptibly in these pages towards the tauter organization of *Women in Love*, a work in which the notion that 'life and decaying are one' is a shaping presence throughout.

DAVID CAVITCH

"Aaron's Rod"; "The Plumed Serpent"

In *Aaron's Rod* and *Kangaroo* Lawrence is represented both as an authorial voice, confiding and expostulating with his "dear reader," and as a character who is a small, chirpy, irascible, half-comical man. As Rawdon Lilly or as Lovatt Somers, the Lawrence persona pursues through travel and writing the same investigations of life that engaged Lawrence in England, Italy, and Australia while he wrote the novels. He is a restless figure who is impelled by whim or the slightest occasion to abandon one living-place after another. Yet he believes in the imminent possibility of a stable personal and societal life, and he would like to assume a leading role in a movement or party to initiate the new order. With his cronies he tirelessly discusses love, marriage, and social reconstruction based on manly love and leadership. At *Kaffeklatschen* in Florence or political meetings in Sydney, the fascinating but stagey dialogues give the reader an impression of overhearing the author's recent conversations with his acquaintances. Like Lawrence, the persona recognizes that his social impulse is frustrated by his skepticism and his terrible insight to other people's motives for action. Regarding his own motives, each persona is continually subject to criticism and ridicule from his indomitable wife, as Lawrence was often challenged by Frieda in their notorious conflicts. The reader is urged to recognize the similarities between the fictional and the real couple by the unmistakable, deliberate caricature in the descriptions of man and wife. In all, the thinly veiled

---

disguise thrown revealingly about himself keeps us mindful that the fiction we are reading is chiefly the fictionalized immediate experience of the author, as Lawrence wishes it to be known.

In *Aaron's Rod* the Lawrence persona is a secondary though not a minor character. He is a socially obscure but charismatic figure to whom Aaron Sisson is drawn after he leaves his wife and children in the Midlands because domestic life came to an end for him—as naturally and inexplicably as birth or death, he says. The first two chapters which show Aaron brooding in Beldover before taking flight are among the best passages Lawrence wrote in the realistic manner of *Sons and Lovers*. But soon the author intrudes to break the spell of pure fiction and to insist upon the actuality of his personal hand in the contrivance of novel writing. He joshes the reader and frets about the difficulty of getting his diverse characters assembled and his story under way. After the opening chapters, Aaron's experience through the novel—some of which would seem unlikely, at best—is made fictitious by the author's continual confidences to the reader. When Aaron in Italy finally considers the deep causes of his estrangement from his wife, the psychological immediacy of this important passage is repeatedly undercut by the authorial voice:

> Thoughts something in this manner ran through Aaron's subconscious mind as he sat still in the strange house. He could not have fired it all off at any listener, as these pages are fired off at any chance reader. Nevertheless there it was, risen to half consciousness in him.
>
> Don't grumble at me then, gentle reader, and swear at me that this damned fellow wasn't half clever enough to think all these smart things, and realise all these fine-drawn-out-subtleties. You are quite right, he wasn't, yet it all resolved itself in him as I say, and it is for you to prove that it didn't.
>
> (XIII)

Yet, the author's asides and cajolery are often amusing, like clever conversation. When Aaron is led to his guest-room up the grand staircase of a palatial villa into a further, modest stairway beyond a little door, Lawrence observes the irony: "Man can so rarely keep it up all the way, the grandeur." His voice maintains the generally light tone of the novel. It is a book that one must read with detachment and a willingness to be diverted from the fiction to the anterior, "real" world in which the author works and offers his own personality for attention. We are not allowed to accept Aaron's story with willing suspension of our disbelief; and for this reason it is all the easier to recognize in Rawdon Lilly the figure of Lawrence himself.

Lilly speaks authoritatively about how people should live. He argues with a knighted British philanthropist that man should rid himself of individual economic purpose and live with trust in Providence. Among a group of jaded and effeminate men, he agrees with their analysis of marriage and their condemnation of modern woman for being sexually possessive. In a political discussion that includes a Jewish socialist and a crusty Scottish reactionary, Lilly argues like a fascist, and then adopts a palatable vagueness about the integrity of individuals:

> "I agree in the rough with Argyle. You've got to have a sort of slavery again. People are not *men:* they are insects and instruments, and their destiny is slavery. They are too many for me, and so what I think is ineffectual. But ultimately they will be brought to agree—after sufficient extermination—and then they will elect for themselves a proper and healthy and energetic slavery."
>
> "I should like to know what you mean by slavery [Levison asks]. Because to me it is impossible that slavery should be healthy and energetic. You seem to have some other idea in your mind, and you merely use the word slavery out of exasperation—"
>
> "I mean it none the less. I mean a real committal of the life-issue of inferior beings to the responsibility of a superior being."
>
> "It'll take a bit of knowing, who are the inferior and which is the superior," said Levison sarcastically.
>
> "Not a bit. It is written between a man's brows, which he is."
>
> "I'm afraid we shall all read differently."
>
> "So long as we're liars."
>
> "And putting that question aside: I presume that you mean that this committal of the life-issue of inferior beings to someone higher shall be made voluntarily—a sort of voluntary self-gift of the inferiors—"
>
> "Yes—more or less—and a voluntary acceptance. For it's no pretty gift, after all.—But once made it must be held fast by genuine power. Oh yes—no playing and fooling about with it. Permanent and very efficacious power."
>
> "You mean military power?"
>
> "I do, of course."
>
> Here Levison smiled a long, slow, subtle smile of ridicule. It all seemed to him the preposterous pretentiousness of a megalomaniac—one whom, after a while, humanity would probably have the satisfaction of putting into prison, or into a lunatic asylum. And Levison felt strong, overwhelmingly strong, in the huge social power with which he, insignificant as he was, was armed against such criminal-imbecile pretensions as those above set forth. Prison or the lunatic asylum. The face of the fellow gloated in these two inevitable engines of his disapproval.
>
> "It will take you some time before you'll get your doctrines accepted," he said.

> "Accepted! I'd be sorry. I don't want a lot of swine snouting and sniffling at me with their acceptance.—Bah, Levison—one can easily make a fool of you. Do you take this as my gospel?"
>
> "I take it you are speaking seriously."
>
> Here Lilly broke into that peculiar, gay, whimsical smile.
>
> "But I should say the blank opposite with just as much fervour," he declared.
>
> "Do you mean to say you don't *mean* what you've been saying?" said Levison, now really looking angry.
>
> "Why, I'll tell you the real truth," said Lilly. "I think every man is a sacred and holy individual, *never* to be violated. I think there is only one thing I hate to the verge of madness, and that is *bullying*. To see any living creature *bullied*, in *any* way, almost makes a murderer of me. That is true. Do you believe it—?"
>
> "Yes," said Levison unwillingly. "That may be true as well. You have no doubt, like most of us, got a complex nature which—"
>
> (XX)

At that moment of possible resolution to the debate, an anarchist's bomb explodes in the café where they are sitting and the scene of bloodshed and indiscriminate destruction is the emblematic conclusion to the conflict of ideologies. Lawrence dreaded the resurgence of war; yet, as a man preternaturally sensitive to the violence in the life of his era, he acknowledged in himself the attitudes that were soon articulated by the fascists, and for a time he accepted the recourse to totalitarianism that swept over Europe. Even his ironic treatment of Levison prophetically belittles the confidences in rationality that blinded his era's liberals.

For Lawrence the political reorganization of life would be valuable only as a procedure for liberating the sensual man from the bonds of an overly rationalistic culture. Aaron Sisson's malaise is not the result of social or economic conditions; his emotional illness indicates a sensual failure within his private world of narrowly domestic experience. He feels that his soul has been broken into and violated by the possessiveness and dependency of his wife, whose idea of marriage is "that the highest her man could ever know or ever reach, was to be perfectly enveloped in her all-beneficent love." (XIII) After Aaron leaves her, he comes to understand that he is rejecting the principle of the marriage relationship in which he was expected to repudiate his "intrinsic and central aloneness." This kind of threat against his integrity disrupts his marriage and more of such love saps his power to live, for when Aaron is later seduced by a young woman, he falls ill and becomes mordantly dejected. Only Lilly—who believes in his own superior grace to govern life in lesser beings—can revive Aaron's will to recover health. Lilly apparently transfers his vitality into Aaron's body by entrancedly rubbing him with oil until he shows signs of "regaining himself." With his life-rousing, "mindless" rubbing of Aaron's "lower body," Lilly claims Aaron's allegiance to his power. By submitting to the authority of a greater male soul, Aaron could extricate himself from woman's fixed conception of love, and he would come into full possession of his own nature. Aaron, however, finds it difficult to comprehend and trust an allegiance with masculine power.

In Lilly's parting words to Aaron, Lawrence delivers his analysis of unrest among individuals in postwar Europe and he prescribes a political solution that most of Europe adopted—but which Lawrence soon rejected after testing his social philosophy in the imaginative world of his writings and finding its ideas ultimately repellent. The kind of social organization that he prescribed for the liberation of man's varied sensuality could not be achieved by mere political means, however extreme, and Lawrence gradually dismissed his belief in totalitarian order. In the final passage of *Aaron's Rod*, however, the despair and devaluation of life that underlie the novel's ironic levity emerge clearly in the form of doctrines that were to dominate a sick world:

> "I told you there were two urges—two great life-urges, didn't I? There may be more. But it comes on me so strongly, now, that there are two: love, and power. And we've been trying to work ourselves, at least as individuals, from the love-urge exclusively, hating the power-urge, and repressing it. And now I find we've got to accept the very thing we've hated.
>
> "We've exhausted our love-urge, for the moment. And yet we try to force it to continue working. So we get inevitably anarchy and murder. It's no good. We've got to accept the power motive, accept it in deep responsibility, do you understand me? It is a great life motive. It was that great dark power-urge which kept Egypt so intensely living for so many centuries. It is a vast dark source of life and strength in us now, waiting either to issue into true action, or to burst into cataclysm. Power—the power-urge. The will-to-power—but not in Nietzsche's sense. Not intellectual power. Not mental power. Not conscious will-power. Not even wisdom. But dark, living fructifying power. . . .
>
> ". . . That's where Nietzsche was wrong. His was the conscious and benevolent will, in fact, the love-will. But the deep power-urge is not conscious of its aims: and it is certainly not consciously benevolent or love-directed. . . .
>
> ". . . The mode of our being is such that we can only live and have our being whilst we are implicit in one of the great dynamic modes. We *must* either love, or rule. And once the love-mode changes, as change it must, for we are worn out and becoming evil in its persistence, then the other mode will take place in us. And there will be profound,

> profound obedience in place of this love-crying, obedience to the incalculable power-urge. And men must submit to the great soul in a man, for their guidance: and women must submit to the postive power-soul in man, for their being."
>
> "You'll never get it," said Aaron.
>
> "You will, when all men want it. All men say, they want a leader. Then let them in their souls *submit* to some greater soul than theirs. At present, when they say they want a leader, they mean they want an instrument, like Lloyd George. A mere instrument for their use. But it's more than that. It's the reverse. It's the deep, fathomless submission to the heroic soul in a greater man. You, Aaron, you too have the need to submit. You, too, have the need livingly to yield to a more heroic soul, to give yourself. You know you have. And you know it isn't love. It is life-submission. And you know it. But you kick against the pricks. And perhaps you'd rather die than yield. And so, die you must. It is your affair."
>
> There was a long pause. Then Aaron looked up into Lilly's face. It was dark and remote-seeming. It was like a Byzantine eikon at the moment.
>
> "And whom shall I submit to?" he said.
>
> "Your soul will tell you," replied the other.
>
> (XXI)

By comparing Lilly to a Byzantine eikon Lawrence means to suggest a holy power evident in his intent face, and the novel concludes with this image of Lawrence proposing that men must die or submit their souls to persons like himself. The egomania of the final pages overcomes the author's irony that is the viewpoint through most of the book. The apotheosis of Lilly is an embarrassment to the reader, and perhaps it was also to Lawrence at some level of consciousness; for while finishing *Aaron's Rod* he was taking another glance at himself in *Sea and Sardinia*, and in that book he sees a limited, half-comical, wholly mortal man—whose attractiveness is only in his sutble awareness of life, including his self-awareness.

II

The psychologically decisive effort of writing *The Plumed Serpent* made Lawrence regard the book, for a short time, as "my most important novel, so far"—the one lying "nearer my heart than any other work of mine." To many readers for whom it is a ponderous and pretentious book, Lawrence's special fondness for this novel seems weirdly misplaced. The fiction is a fantasy of the sort that Lawrence could make profoundly beautiful in a short tale, but in this long novel the laboriously sustained and minutely detailed implausibilities grow offensive. His overestimation of the work, however, accurately reflects his feeling that the particular creative process from which it issued was a most important experience for him.

Like the women of the three preceding tales, Kate Leslie, the heroine, delivers herself to violent forces connected with the land—in this instance, to "the horror and climax of death-rattles, which is Mexico." Years before, she divorced her first husband to marry a renowned Irish revolutionary leader. Now she feels that everything in her past was finished for her when Leslie was killed in his fight "to *change* the world, to make it freer, more alive." She has come to Mexico to escape from any further intimate connection with people or worldly activity. Wondering why she has chosen "this high plateau of death," she soon becomes oddly fascinated by the purposiveness of two revolutionaries, whom she blindly never associates with her dead husband. Kate joins with Don Ramon and Don Cipriano who revive the Aztec cult of Quetzalcoatl to supplant Christianity in Mexico. This nationalist folk-movement renews a "virginal" self in her; she dances with peasants, sings hymns of Quetzalcoatl which Ramon composes, and allows herself to be married to Cipriano, who requires that she remain passive during sexual intercourse. She agrees to become a goddess of earth and death in a new pantheon that includes Cipriano and Ramon, and she learns to accept even human sacrifice proudly without a shudder of revulsion.

The narrative is made up of many startling incidents of sacrifices, assaults, skirmishes, insurrections, betrayals, physical violations, and atrocious murders; but they are mostly emptied of any real frightfulness by the excess of violence. All the potential horror of the action is spent extravagantly in a swirl of foreground activity, leaving no sense of deep undercurrents of destructive motivations. The violence, as superficial as a comic-strip's, is overshadowed by the thematic patterning of the tumultuous narrative. The intention of the cult is to make motives into rituals, to dramatize essential human nature to the last varied detail. Ramon's hymns and sermons, which overweigh the novel with monotonous digressions from the story and characters, emphasize the reconciliation of all opposites in the principle of the living Quetzalcoatl, "the Lord of the Two Ways." As the chief god of the new worship, Quetzalcoatl symbolizes the union of male and female qualities singly represented by Cipriano, who is the living fire-god Huitzilopochtli, and Kate, the eternal Woman Malintzi. Substantiating the doctrine of the trinity, all nature offers symbolic examples of similar reconciliation of conflicting qualities in balanced cooperation. The sacred images in the new religion are rain falling on the earth, pre-dawn and twilight appearing between the night and day, Morning Star and Evening Star, fire in the darkness, the circle of the Lake of Sayula in the dry expanse of Mexico, and the union of coition.

The main action of the fiction is the effort to elevate degraded human existence to a level where humanity is godlike. The new religion makes gods out of the principle characters and its designed effect on all believers is to rouse a conviction of their essential divinity. Lawrence uses realistic details of Mexican culture to represent the psychic degradation in which contemporary man lives, and the novel begins with two realistic chapters that establish his morbid repugnance for the world around him. The opening bullfight episode stresses the oppression of soul in a loutish mobocracy, and the climactic image for Lawrence's view of Mexican life is the maddened bull goring the anus of a picador's disabled horse while its bowels spill out. From such horror of brutal degeneracy, the novel eventually turns to describe a new religion of human redemption and transcendence.

Don Ramon, the savior-designate, is not disturbed by the circumstances of impoverished and exploited life within his society, and he is not impelled to change Mexico on the surface. He refuses an opportunity to become next in line for the national presidency, and his idea of social reform is to gather peasants together in farm-and-crafts communes where they make Quetzalcoatl costumes and learn the new hymns. His purpose is solely to revive the Aztec cult for the redemption of the Indian soul in Mexico. The one activity in life that he wants to change is sexual relations. He believes that the present practice of "letting oneself go" in sex involves a man ravishing a woman, or a woman ravishing a man: "There is such a thing as sin, and that's the centre of it. Men and women keep on ravishing one another. . . . Letting oneself go, is either ravishing or being ravished." (XVIII) From this center, sin spreads into all human relations, for they consist chiefly of people ravishing others and offering themselves for ravishment. His view of civilization is not far from the novel's emblematic opening picture of the horse and bull.

The religion he institutes centers in a ritual of sex and a sacrament of marriage that demand woman's "submission absolute, like the earth under the sky." Only her "supreme passivity" preserves gentleness in man and woman alike. Presumably, as individuals reject the disintegrative frenzy of sexual release, they organize the coherence of their inner natures. In a strange reversal of his earlier prescriptive views about sex, Lawrence implies that people can become serene and godlike as they learn to forgo orgasm and transcend the frictional passion of their ordinary intercourse.

The clay feet of the gods are never so embarrassing, however, as in the events on "Huitzilopochtli's Night," when Kate accepts her new role as Eternal Woman. The ceremony of Cipriano's apotheosis as the vengeful fire-god is the point late in the novel where the literal story line must be absorbed by the Aztec myth. Quetzalcoatl can be revivified in the fiction only as his legend comes to structure the characters' ensuing experience, but the myth never convincingly justifies the events that occur. The Catholic peasants who have attacked Ramon's hacienda and tried to kill him must be executed—not by law, but by the will of the gods. Cipriano in body paint and feathers stabs or strangles the victims, according to the courage they displayed in the attack. The bodies are then laid before the altar and Ramon as Quetzalcoatl accepts the offerings. The whole of this elaborate and critically important ritual does not succeed in sweeping Kate's imagination to a new level of symbolic perception—and certainly not the reader's either. Kate's immediate response is to find the ceremony brutal and loathsome, and the reader never forgets that it is preposterous. Kate recognizes that in spite of all the costumes and liturgies Ramon and Cipriano "seemed nothing but men." Her reaction indicates the failure of the symbolic elements of the novel to assert their meaning for us: "As is so often the case with any spell, it did not bind her completely. She was spell-bound, but not utterly acquiescent. In one corner of her soul was revulsion and a touch of shame." (XXIV)

The difficult effort of persuading herself that the cult is meaningful is left to Kate's own specious reasoning. After witnessing the sacrifice, Kate sits brooding at home and she thinks to herself that, after all, individualism is an illusion. She should abandon herself in submission to Cipriano and fulfill her generic Womanhood. At that moment Cipriano enters her house and coaxes her to come to the church where they have intercourse before the altar where the sacrificed bodies had lain. Kate, continuing to cogitate uninterruptedly during intercourse, finally accepts the role that she denied in the preceding pages:

> And she pressed him to her breast, convulsively. His innermost flame was always virginal, it was always the first time. And it made her again always a virgin girl. She could feel their two flames flowing together.
>
> How else, she said to herself, is one to begin again, save by refinding one's virginity? And when one finds one's virginity, one realises one is among the gods. He is of the gods, and so am I. Why should I judge him!
>
> So, when she thought of him and his soldiers, tales of swift cruelty she had heard of him: when she remembered his stabbing the three helpless peons, she thought: Why should I judge him? He is of the gods. And when he comes to me he lays his pure, quick flame to mine, and

> every time I am a young girl again, and every time he takes the flower of my virginity, and I his. It leaves me insouciant like a young girl. What do I care if he kills people? His flame is young and clean. He is Huitzilopochtli, and I am Malintzi. What do I care, what Cipriano Viedma does or doesn't do? Or even what Kate Leslie does or doesn't do!
>
> (XXIV)

The context of the passage and the demands of the myth make Kate's sexual intercourse the very moment of her apotheosis. But her surprising transformation into Malintzi is accomplished only by her own casuistry. Her incredible mental detachment from her sexual experience at that instant is so bizarre that Lawrence's obvious fudging leaves us unconvinced of her new role.

Just before he completed *The Plumed Serpent*—and one would like to think it shows a twinge of artistic misgivings—Lawrence dashed off four travel essays about his daily life in Oaxaca that reveal him feeling sheepish as an author, perhaps already embarrassed by what he was driven to write in his Mexican novel. Later published as the first four chapters of *Mornings in Mexico*, the Oaxaca sketches each dramatize a single day during the week before Christmas. The opening comedy of "Corasmin and the Parrots" presents Lawrence full of laughter, finding man's pretensions, including his own, amazingly ridiculous. Men, like dogs and parrots, find it impossibly difficult to drop the gestures of self-importance which only parody their obvious limits and uniqueness. In the three other essays of the series Lawrence's witty, tolerant report of Mexican life continues to give mankind the lie in the teeth: all egotistical stances are self-evidently absurd when the ignorance, the frailty, the self-pity of an actual man are concretely shown. There was that grace of irony in Lawrence that could anticipate his repudiation of the overblown fantasy he was writing even while his emotional self had to pursue it to the end.

The whole symbolic effort of the novel is unsuccessful in respect to its religious and sexual formulations; Lawrence was simply incapable of deifying terror and slavery in sex. But the primary assertion in the conclusion of the novel depends on neither of these hypostatizations. Kate's personal attachment to Ramon and Cipriano together, and their mutual dependence on her, affirms the familial relations of child and parents that the mythology implies. She appears in the last chapters not as Malintzi but as a middle-aged woman fearful of loneliness, appreciative of calm, occasional sex, and connected to Mexico by love for both her husband and Ramon—who is represented in the Quetzalcoatl myth as a young god born from the principle of their marriage. In the conclusion of the narrative, Kate is reinstated with a husband whom this time she does not abandon for another. In Ramon she is given a mature son similar to her former boy-husband Leslie; and Ramon, unlike the earlier revolutionary, does not supplant an older man as her lover and end up dead in his usurpation. Kate in her final role promises motherly love to Ramon and perfect obedience to Cipriano. One successful effect of the deflation of exaggerated violence throughout the novel is that Kate is relieved of the dangerously attractive powers and betraying compulsions that accompany the sexual nature of Helena, Gertrude Morel, Ursula and Gudrun Brangwen, Lou Carrington, the nameless Woman, and the Princess. But *The Plumed Serpent* shows that, given Lawrence's views of the savagery of phallicism and the rapaciousness of independent women, his only recourse was to devalue sexual activity entirely, in favor of quiescence. The one myth in *The Plumed Serpent* that is fully supported by the author's feelings is the characters' descent from sexual exaltations to an aging, familial order of life.

SANDRA M. GILBERT

The Longest Journey: Lawrence's Ship of Death

In the famous and sonorous series of verses entitled "The Ship of Death" the journey motif is most fully and convincingly elaborated. Here for the first time Lawrence becomes absolutely explicit about his own death and the death that every man is dying during every moment of his life. The first section, with its ellipses and its air of Rilkean *einsehen*, is certainly the most portentous.

> Now it is autumn and the falling fruit
> and the long journey towards oblivion.
>
> The apples falling like great drops of dew
> to bruise themselves an exit from themselves.
>
> And it is time to go, to bid farewell
> to one's own self, and find an exit
> from the fallen self.

The death of the apples sets the tone and states the theme of the whole work. When the apple falls, the seed, the germinal new self, destroys the ripe fruit like a death-bullet. And the old apples, no more than "great drops of dew," lapse back into the ground. So the pure new self, the soul of each man, must "find an exit/from the fallen self."

Yet despite the serene commitment to natural process that the apple metaphor implies, Lawrence concedes in part two that the death-journey is painful, even for the most faithful man. The autumn frost is

From *Acts of Attention: The Poems of D. H. Lawrence.* Copyright © 1972 by Cornell University. Cornell University Press.

"grim," and apples fall "thick, almost thunderous, on the hardened earth," recalling the terror of "the thunderers, the sunderers," and "death is on the air like a smell of ashes!" Ashes, like dew, dissolve or disintegrate to nothingness, but unlike dew, which we associate with morning-freshness, with beginnings, they are the endings of life, all that is left to the self when the life-flame has burned itself out.

> And in the bruised body, the frightened soul
> finds itself shrinking, wincing from the cold
> that blows upon it through the orifices

It is not easy to "bid farewell."

In part three Lawrence explores one of the alternatives that may occur to the frightened soul: suicide. The suicide controls fate by choosing the time of his own death. Lawrence describes such action with an allusion from *Hamlet* ("And can a man his own quietus make /with a bare bodkin?"), a reference which, though he later built it into an important pun, is a little too knowingly clever to be entirely successful. Still, Hamlet's speech is philosophically appropriate, for, like Hamlet, Lawrence sees death as "an undiscovered country" into which the shivering soul must travel. And, like Hamlet, in facing death he rejects the alternative of suicide—"for how could murder, even self-murder/ever a quietus make?" Murder, perhaps especially self-murder, is an act of will which, like the scientism of Anaxagoras, hurls one into the isolating "abyss of immortality." "O let us talk of quiet that we know," Lawrence pleads in section four, "the deep and lovely quiet /of a strong heart at peace!" The only quietus available to man is the true quietus of "Pax" or of "Silence," rather than the artificial quietus of suicide. Again, one must yield oneself—quietly, peacefully, silently—to the inevitable process of one's life, the process of dying.

In parts four through eight Lawrence describes the death-journey itself more specifically than ever before. His ship metaphor is a traditional one, drawn from Egyptian and Etruscan sources, and probably from Shelley and Tennyson as well. But through a delicate and precise elaboration of details he makes it quite his own. The soul, he tells us, in preparation for its longest journey, must build

> A little ship, with oars and food
> and little dishes, and all accoutrements
> fitting and ready.

And what might seem like sentimental allegory in his subsequent description of "the fragile soul /in the fragile ship of courage, the ark of faith" is tempered by the homely specificity of the boat's "store of food and little cooking pans /and change of clothes." Yet these details function allegorically too, for the spirit, as we have seen throughout *Last Poems*, requires nourishment on its journey, the sustenance of prayer and belief, and when it puts off the body, the clothing of the old life (as Yeats and Carlyle also saw), it must have another garment, another self, for the new life.

Even so, when the soul sails out onto the sea of oblivion, everything disappears.

> There is no port, there is nowhere to go
> only the deepening blackness darkening still
> blacker upon the soundless, ungurgling flood
> darkness at one with darkness, up and down
> and sideways utterly dark, so there is no direction any more,
> and the little ship is there; yet she is gone.
> She is not seen, for there is nothing to see her by.
> She is gone! gone! and yet
> somewhere she is there.
> Nowhere!

"The deepening blackness darkening still," a subtle paradox (for how can black be blacker than black?), is reminiscent of the "darker and darker stairs, where blue is darkened on blueness" down which the poet imagined himself descending into Pluto's kingdom. Yet though the little ship for a moment disappears into this profound and impossible darkness, though it is "gone!" somewhere that is nowhere, it never vanishes into the *grey* nothingness of mechanistic evil—"the grey mist of movement which moves not." Such evil, said Lawrence in "Evil is Homeless," "shows neither light nor dark,/and has no home, no home anywhere." The little ship of the journeying soul experiences, emphatically, first dark, then darker darkness, then light again. Though in the moment of oblivion there is an illusion of ending, of stopping ("It is the end, it is oblivion") the journey never really stops.

In parts nine and ten Lawrence describes what was for him by now an article of faith, the mystical rebirth of the soul.

> And . . . out of eternity, a thread
> separates itself on the blackness,
> a horizontal thread
> that fumes a little with pallor upon the dark.

Literally, it is the line of dawn on a far horizon; figuratively, it is the thread of life which, because life is an endless journey "onwards, we know not whither," can never really snap. "A flush of rose"—the faintest rekindling of the "scarlet flame" of life—"and the whole thing starts again."

> The flood subsides, and the body like a worn sea-shell
> emerges strange and lovely.
> And the little ship wings home, faltering and lapsing
> on the pink flood,
> and the frail soul steps out, into her house again
> filling the heart with peace.

A number of critics have puzzled over the exact intention of these lines. Was Lawrence proposing a kind of oriental or Pythagorean metempsychosis, or was he suggesting something like the Christian concept of resurrection? But while he was no doubt influenced by both these theologies (and, too, by the kind of theosophical thinking that he incorporated into *The Plumed Serpent*), he had always vehemently rejected the dogmatic structure of any creed. He never particularized his beliefs beyond a faith in the majesty of a *Kosmodynamic* God whose processes he saw working themselves out everywhere, in apples and peaches and pomegranates and, by analogy, in men. He felt that in the economy of nature nothing is ever wasted or cast aside, but believed that to attempt an intellectual definition of what can only be known intuitively, through symbol and metaphor, would be an arrogant effort to comprehend "the incomprehensible."

Lawrence's own ship of death, then, was finally an "ark of faith," an ark unencumbered with the particulars of Christian or Buddhist or pre-Socratic dogma, but impelled toward oblivion by a "fragile courage" to let being take its own course. And specifically the ship of faith that he built for himself in these last months of his life was made up of the *Last Poems* themselves, poems which, in imaginatively drawing nearer and nearer to the mystery of death, and in exploring the experience of oblivion that is to come, prepare the poet to endure the experience itself—what he knows will be its ashen bitterness as well as what he believes will be its "cruel dawn of coming back to life." What is finally most impressive about "The Ship of Death" is not the wit with which Lawrence elaborates a traditional metaphor, not the skill of the incantatory free verse (whose meter comes closer to traditional iambic pentameter than that of most of his later poetry) but the sense of personal religious urgency it communicates.

> Have you built your ship of death, O have you?
> O build your ship of death, for you will need it . . .
> death is on the air like a smell of ashes!
> Ah! can't you smell it?

Oh build your ship of death, your little ark
and furnish it with food, with little cakes, and wine
for the dark flight down oblivion. . . .

We are dying, we are dying, we are all of us dying,
and nothing will stay the death-flood rising within us,
and soon it will rise on the world, on the outside world. . . .

It is not really the imagery of the voyage nor the traditional symbol of sacramental cakes and wine that affects us in such passages as these, but the prophetic exhortation the dying poet addresses to the reader and to all men, the oldest reminder that can be given to any man: "To everything there is a season, a time to sow and a time to reap." "Dust thou art and unto dust thou shalt return."

To say, however, that Lawrence is preparing himself (and us) to endure death, is not to say that death appeared to him a wholly painful or cruel experience. He concluded that the process of halving and healing could be frightening, the journey into oblivion sad, but he felt, too, that oblivion brings health at last. "Sing the song of death, O sing it!" he exclaims in "Song of Death," one of a series of short pieces that are essentially explanatory addenda to "The Ship of Death" itself,

for without the song of death, the song of life
becomes pointless and silly.

And this is just a colloquial Lawrentian formulation of what Stevens says in "Sunday Morning" or Whitman in "Whispers of Heavenly Death" and other poems. Sleep, which men have always named "Death's second self," promises this healing oblivion, Lawrence writes in "Sleep" and "Sleep and Waking."

Did you sleep well?
Ah yes, the sleep of God!
The world is created afresh.

Therefore he reasons, like Donne addresssing death, that if

From rest and sleepe, which but thy pictures bee,
Much pleasure, then from thee, much more must flow.

Furthermore, because death is a sleep it is a *forgetting*, and again, while forgetting is difficult, it is healing and necessary. "Very still and sunny here," Lawrence wrote to Laurence Pollinger in September 1929, the "slow, sad" month in which "Bavarian Gentians" is set. "*Olvidar—vergessen—oublier—dimenticare*—forget—So difficult to forget." Yet one must, ultimately, lose one's memories, for in losing them one sloughs off the old self, makes room for the new.

To be able to forget is to be able to yield
to God who dwells in deep oblivion.
Only in sheer oblivion are we with God.
For when we know in full, we have left off knowing.

he explains in "Forget." Only when we have lost our memories—indeed, lost our minds—do we pass into the state of final knowledge that is beyond nerve-brain knowledge, the state into which the poet mystically enters in "Bavarian Gentians" and "The Ship of Death."

The beautiful and simple poem "Shadows" is Lawrence's last and most moving attempt to explore the oblivion, the forgetfulness, the not-knowing that is death's (and God's) final gift. Here at last he speaks in his own person and speaks directly of his own illness, as if his persistent attention to cosmos and *Kosmodynamos* throughout *Last Poems* has given him the courage—the ark of faith—with which to confront not only the destiny of all men but his own fate in particular.

And if tonight my soul may find her peace
in sleep, and sink in good oblivion,
and in the morning wake like a new-opened flower
then I have been dipped again in God, and new-created.
And if, as weeks go round, in the dark of the moon
my spirit darkens and goes out, and soft, strange gloom
pervades my movements and my thoughts and words
then I shall know that I am walking still
with God, we are close together now the moon's in shadow.

The gravely religious tone here is absolutely authentic, though it lacks the rather ostentatious dogmatic structure of, for instance, Eliot's

End of the endless
Journey to no end
Conclusion of all that
Is inconclusible
Speech without word and
Word of no speech
Grace to the Mother
For the Garden
Where all love ends.

Indeed, as a religious poet Lawrence is strangely reminiscent not only of such obvious forebears as the Romantics Keats, Whitman, Rilke and Stevens, but of the seventeenth-century Anglican George Herbert. Like Herbert, he speaks in his best religious verses ("Shadows," for example, and "The Ship of Death" and "Phoenix") with a quiet assurance, a faith that does not need to rely on the doctrinaire and even morbid melodrama that sometimes seems to characterize the writings of Eliot and even those of Donne. The serenity and directness of "Shadows" parallels, for instance, the calm conclusion of Herbert's "Even-Song."

> I muse which shows more love,
> The day or night; that is the gale, this th' harbour;
> That is the walk, and this the arbour;
> Or that the garden, this the grove.
>
> My God, thou art all love:
> Not one poore minute 'scapes thy breast,
> But brings a favour from above;
> And in this love, more than in bed, I rest.

And the faith that is expressed in lines like these from "Shadows"—

> And if, in the changing phases of man's life
> I fall in sickness and in misery
> my wrists seem broken and my heart seems dead
> and strength is gone, and my life
> is only the leavings of a life . . .
>
> then I must know that still
> I am in the hands [of] the unknown God,
> he is breaking me down to his own oblivion
> to send me forth on a new morning, a new man,

is not so different, after all, from Herbert's.

Oddly enough, it is not so different from Eliot's either, despite the latter's conviction that Lawrence wrote about strange gods. In "Ash Wednesday," for instance, Eliot had not only prayed "to God to have mercy upon us," but also prayed

> that I may forget
> These matters that with myself I too much discuss
> Too much explain . . .

and had asked God to

> Teach us to care and not to care.
> Teach us to sit still.

This is essentially what Lawrence has been asking too, in poems like "The Ship of Death," "Pax," and "Shadows." Yet, perhaps even more surprisingly, it seems to me that in the end Lawrence's words carry more conviction than Eliot's, though Eliot's poems are often considerably smoother. Like Wright Morris, I believe that "in this world—the one in which we must live—the strange gods of D. H. Lawrence appear to be less strange than those of Mr. Eliot."

I do not introduce the author of "Ash Wednesday" and the *Four Quartets* so as to attack his religious poetry, but in order to make a specific point about Lawrence's work in *Last Poems*. The best of these poems succeed, as Eliot's do not, precisely because throughout the collection Lawrence has worked to make his religion *plausible* to us. His long and careful exploration of the nature of God; his examination of the relationship between body and soul, blood and nerve; his attention to the mysterious experience of death—all these endeavors bear fruit in our willingness to accept the calm and simple faith of "Shadows." Eliot, working, as R. P. Blackmur approvingly points out, in a structure of Christian orthodoxy he assumes we will accept, never explains who his God is, or why he believes in Him. Yet, "in this world in which we must live," such an explanation is just what a religious poet must offer, and just what Lawrence's *Last Poems*, taken all together, constitute. Indeed, even where Lawrence uses fairly conventional religious metaphors, as in "The Ship of Death," "Phoenix," or "Lord's Prayer," he does so with an explanatory specificity, a concreteness—and hence a plausibility—that makes the dogmatic orthodoxy of lines from "Ash Wednesday" like "Sovegna vos," or "Lord I am not worthy" seem shallow and even pretentious, because it has no fundamental reality for most of us.

But then "one of the great virtues of Lawrence," as Father Tiverton notes, "was his sense of the ISness rather than the OUGHTness of religion," —that is, his attention to reality. As a religious poet, Lawrence rarely lost sight of the ontology he defines in "Lord's Prayer," the relationship between God—

> For thine is the kingdom,
> the power and the glory.
>
> Hallowed be thy name, then,
> thou who art nameless,

and himself—

> I, a naked man, calling,
> calling to thee for my mana,
> my kingdom, my power, and my glory.

And surely our sense of the plausibility of poems like "The Man of Tyre," "Whales Weep Not!," "Bavarian Gentians," "The Ship of Death" and "Shadows"—poems in which attention becomes meditation, meditation becomes prayer, prayer renewal—justifies his life-long aesthetic faith that "an act of pure attention, if you are capable of it, will bring its own answer."

BARBARA HARDY

Women in D.H. Lawrence's Works

It is easy to see Lawrence as the enemy. He is hard on women. He creates saints and monsters as he sheds and fails to shed his Oedipal sicknesses, admitting, denying, and re-admitting his mother's stranglehold, asking her to free him by dying, then succumbing to the seductiveness of that last sacrifice. He criticises and harangues women for coming too close, for being too personal, for wanting to be loved, for having too much mind, for having too much cunt. He disapproves what he himself invents, in Miriam's intensities, in Pussum's mindlessness, in Hermione's will, in Helena's dreaming, in Gudrun's life-denying and aggressive libertinism. He approves what he himself invents, in Ursula's life-affirming sexual freedoms, in Kate's exalted relinquishing of her orgasm, in Connie Chatterley's gratitude for hers, in the immolation of the Woman Who Rode Away. He yearns after touch and tenderness in male friendships but finds Lesbianism repulsive. He allows Ursula and Harriet to criticise his *Salvator Mundi* touch, but always gives himself the last word. . . .

Jessie Chambers and Helen Corke agreed that it was hard for him to accept mind in women, and there is plenty of crude anti-female and anti-feminist anger, spite, fear, and pity in his poems. He can be silly, as in 'These Clever Women':

> Now stop carping at me! Do you want me to hate you?
> Am I a kaleidoscope
> For you to shake and shake, and it won't come right?

Am I doomed in a long coition of words to mate you?
    Unsatisfied! Is there no hope
Between your thighs, far, far from your peering sight?

He can be more consciously amusing on the same subject, in 'Purple Anemones' where the idea of the anemones as 'husband-splendid, serpent heads' getting after Persephone and Ceres, 'those two enfranchised women', shows him exuberantly, cheaply and not uncharacteristically teetering on the verge of wit. There are some places where he even seems to appreciate feminism for its energy and passion, as in a series of verses in *Pansies* which shift from the rueful hope that a properly re-directed male energy might cure the 'modern Circe-dom', to a grudging recognition that women are the Lord's favourite vessels of wrath, usefully and alarmingly collecting the foreskins for Him. Occasionally he hits the right tone, amused, wary, mocking but not unappreciative:

What has happened in the world?
the women are like little volcanoes
all more or less in eruption.
It is very unnerving, moving in a world of smouldering volcanoes.
It is rather agitating, sleeping with a little Vesuvius.
And exhausting, penetrating the lava-crater of a tiny Ixtaccihuatl
and never knowing when you'll provoke an earthquake.

In [a] letter to Savage, Lawrence has this to say: 'I don't agree with you about our separation from women. The only thing that is very separate—our bodies—is the via media for union again, if we would have it so.' His phrases for such union in *Women in Love* are familiar: it is a 'freedom together' and 'two single equal stars balanced in conjunction'. When Birkin despairs of explaining his images to Ursula, he decides that talking is no good, 'it must happen beyond the sound of words. . . . This was a paradisal bird that could never be netted, it must fly by itself to the heart.' His poetry is closer to this soundlessness than his novels, being more sustainedly sensuous as it traces the particulars of feeling without debate and analysis. Although it is not only in the poetry that Lawrence denies the separation of men and women, it is easier to begin with it. His early poems, *Look! We Have Come Through!*, and the late collection, *More Pansies*, are not just to be negatively praised for admitting that men and women are alike, but valued for their knowledge of sexual feeling.

Some of the poems in *More Pansies* shift from man to woman within poems or within groups of poems. One pair of poems, 'The Gods! The Gods!' and 'Name the Gods!' balances the image of a god in a women's body and a man's, the woman showing 'the glimmer of the presence of the gods . . . like lilies' as she washes, the mower revealing the god not in his own body but in the 'falling flatness' of the wheat, 'the pale-gold flesh of Priapus dropping asleep'. This turning from man to woman or woman to man is a marked two-beat rhythm. Many of these poems show an insistent self-consciousness about the well known deficiency in our language, its lack of an equivalent of the German *Mensch*, which lacks the ambiguity and condescension of *Man* and the flatness of *person*. Particularly in the late poems, Lawrence will use 'person' as he will use 'creatures' or 'individuals' or 'people'. He often uses 'Man' all-embracingly, but its possible condescensions are obliterated, if we read the poems as we should, as they flow and grow into each other, by the rhythm which turns from the man to the woman, separating in order to join in common experience: 'man or woman', 'man and woman', 'most men, most women', 'no man knows, no woman knows', 'a fellow-man or fellow-woman', 'men and women', 'when most men die, today/when most women die', 'living women and men', 'it is no woman, it is no man'.

In 'The Cross' he remakes that image which was ironically and aggressively phallic in 'Last Words to Miriam', proclaiming the frailty of the sexual distinction, and merging it in that 'man' which must be more urgently distinguished from the robot:

> Behold your Cross, Christians!
> With the upright division into sex
> men on this side, women on that side
> without any division into inferiority and superiority
> only differences,
> divided in the mystic, tangible and intangible difference.
>
> And then, truth much more bitter to accept,
> the horizontal division of mankind
> into that which is below the level, and that which is above. . . .
>
> That which is truly man, and that which is robot,
> the ego-bound.

The lustrous noon in 'Andraitx-Pomegranate Flowers' reveals 'a man, a woman there'. The pulsing content of 'The Heart of Man' is shut off from both sexes, 'no man knows, no woman knows'. The naked 'I' of 'Moral Clothing' approaches a 'fellow-man or a fellow-woman' who must be naked too. When Lawrence attacked and decided to give up what he called 'image-making love' it was because he had spent his life fixing and then unfixing sexual images. But certain natural and social truths forced him to see men and women as persons and not as men and women. The second letter to Savage declares that 'Sex is the fountain head, where life bubbles up into the person from the unknown. . . .' The word 'person' is a vital one.

Never trust the artist, trust the tale. And since tales create certain fixities of ego and action that poety can avoid, never trust the tale, trust the poem. Amongst the persuasive and not quite persuasive indictments of Eliseo Vivas's *D. H. Lawrence: the failure and triumph of art* (Northwestern University Press, Evanston, 1960), is the suggestion that Lawrence's concern was with eros, and the loss of self through sex, as distinct from agape, and its loss of self in generous outgoing. Vivas is confident that Lawrence admits the reflexiveness of eros, and quotes an example from Ursula and Skrebensky's lovemaking in *The Rainbow*, which leaves each lover with the sense of maximal vitality, from which he concludes that self-knowledge is all Lawrence thought we gained from eros. There is some danger in relying on the far from beneficent relation of these lovers, who went a fair way in mutual destruction, seeming to suggest the limits and threats of pure self-possession through sex, a point which I'd have thought he was making again through Gudrun and Gerald in *Women in Love*. But it is difficult to argue briefly about the novels, and all I can do here is to suggest that Vivas could not have come to this conclusion so easily had he also been working with the poems. It is knowledge that bubbles through the unknown, in sex, and the poetry of *Look! We Have Come Through!* seems to invoke a more companionable eros than that of Ursula and Skrebensky, a loving which is a mode of other-knowledge as well as self-knowledge, while admittedly being rather less heroic than agape.

Look! We Have Come Through! has a title which announces the theme of a sexual and a moral triumph. Its 'We' is the 'We' of lovers sufficiently freed by love from anxiety, fear, and bewilderment, to make a passionate analysis of passionate love. (Lawrence shied away from the word 'love', but it seems simplest to stick to it.) One convention of love-poetry and love which he questions in these poems is the lover's praise of the beloved's beauty, and this radical questioning is made as part of his argument about liberation, for man and woman. Birkin's declared lack of interest in Ursula's good looks in *Women in Love* is of course part of the general re-definition of love argued there, but the protest against aesthetic appreciation in sex is most sensitively and lucidly found in the poems. 'She Said As Well To Me' begins with the woman's praise of the man's body, and sets against it the man's protest against her appreciation. He objects not just because aesthetic celebration is shallow (as of course it often is) but because her compliments hold sinister suggestions of instrumentality, thanks for services excellently rendered to her ego. She argues, in a way which manages to be both superficial and overpoweringly rapturous, that lovers should be free to gaze, admire, and show each other their naked beauty, but as she tries to talk him out of what she calls the typical male timidity, she does rather dwell on function. It is certainly not surprising that the man begins 'to wonder', and decides that what she says doesn't make him free but 'trammelled and hurt'. His defence is made through images of animal freedom very like those in *Birds, Beasts and Flowers*, the poems which try to do for animals what he wants her to do for him, to respect the individuality of others, and to hesitate before its strength and privacy. But such respect depends on some knowledge of the other, and is not reflexive. In all this, the *noli me tangere* felt but given up in *The Man Who Died* is not by any means shown as a matter of male feeling only. The woman in the poem generalises, matronisingly—'Men are the shyest creatures, they never will come out of their covers'—but the things that answer and defy her are both male and female:

> Now I say to her: 'No tool, no instrument, no God!
> Don't touch and appreciate me.
> It is an infamy.
> You would think twice before you touched a weasel on a fence
> as it lifts its straight white throat.
> Your hand would not be so flig and easy.
> Nor the adder we saw asleep with her head on her shoulder,
> curled up in the sunshine like a princess;
> when she lifted her head in delicate, startled wonder
> you did not stretch forward to caress her
> though she looked rarely beautiful
> and a miracle as she glided delicately away, with such dignity.
> And the young bull in the field, with his wrinkled, sad face,
> you are afraid if he rises to his feet. . . .'

It is easy to argue that Lawrence's rejection of intimate praise and fondness comes from his Oedipal wound and produces his dangerous fascination with violence. It is easy to see the retreat from Miriam's intensities, as Jessie Chambers herself saw it, only as a fiction made in order to strengthen his mother's image. I think it is also necessary to see that such rejection of praise and appreciation beats a wise retreat from that instrumentality familiar to lovers and to artists. It was not only a response which Lawrence had to the intrusiveness of loving women, but a temptation he may have felt for himself as an artist. It was certainly one which he sometimes did and sometimes didn't resist.

The rejections and the appreciations in *The White Peacock* and *Sons and Lovers* are clearly made in the interests of defining the man; they help to show and analyse George Saxton's degeneration and Paul Morel's coming of age. Helen Corke, always unstridently alert to Lawrence's use of women, says as much in her brief essay on *The White Peacock*: 'These women are fully drawn, but Lawrence is not interested in them as individuals. He sees them only in relation to their men. "Take," he would seem to say to his reader, "a male creature! We shall now study its reactions to these various forms of feminine stimuli." ' Her essay ends with the image of Erda, whose single concern is with the race, who cuts away the psyche 'so that the reproductive physical self cannot develop individually, and the woman, in motherhood, is absorbed into the lives of her children . . . sister to the servant of the One Talent'. Helen Corke seemed to Lawrence to be the defiantly dreaming and thinking woman who could resist him, and in what she calls the 'deferred conversation' in *Lawrence's Apocalypse*, she accuses him of too simply and crudely separating masculine and feminine extremities of what she saw as a spectrum of sexuality. There are occasions in both letters and fiction, when Lawrence seems to reduce the individual woman to an outline, a type, or a complex convenience, but it is essential to recognise that such reductions are not confined to his portraits of women.

There is the denigration of his father in *Sons and Lovers*, of Bertrand Russell and Middleton Murry in *Women in Love*, not to mention the reductions of Sir Clifford Chatterley. Moreover, even where Lawrence's women present tendentious types or images, their needs and passions often turn out to derive from his own intimate experience and fantasies. Although in 'The Woman Who Rode Away' Lawrence chose a woman as an appropriate victim of *ennui*, wildness and masochistic sacrifice, there is no doubt that the feelings and values of his immolated heroine lay within his own experience. In his finest volume, 'The Ship of Death', the poems most fluidly and shiftingly create their repetitions, modulations, and permutations on the themes of death and rebirth, and we see that the crude lines of the brutal little fable have an intimate connection with Lawrence's imaginative experience of dying, dying away from deadly society, from human attachments, from a sick body. Where he seems most chauvinistic he is probably most personal. Anyone who can see 'The Woman Who Rode Away' simply as a man's sadistic immolation of woman cannot have looked properly at 'The Ship of Death', or, for that matter, compared Lawrence with de Sade.

Lawrence, like other artists, lapses into crudity when he is refusing to work with sufficient imaginative energy and thought. The allegorical modes and moments in his fiction are often reductions of human complexity which place male and female in opposition to each other instead of showing them as human beings engaged in similar struggles with class, sex, education, work, art, and mortality. But Lawrence's allegory is sometimes subtler than it appears, and we should always be very wary of accepting his characters' instant interpretations. In the 'Mino' chapter in *Women in Love*, for instance, Birkin takes Ursula through his revised syllabus of love by using the demonstration-model of male and female cats. As the female cat waits submissively, cuffed and longing, Ursula tells the cat that he is 'a bully like all males', an observation which seems especially abstract and unfair if we remember her beaked passion and hostility at the end of *The Rainbow*. (The abstraction and unfairness is of course not hers but her author's.) The Ursula of *Women in Love* has more Frieda and less Lawrence in her than the Ursula of *The Rainbow*, and so needs the lecture:

> 'No,' said Birkin, 'he is justified. He is not a bully. He is only insisting to the poor stray that she shall acknowledge him as a sort of fate, her own fate: because you can see she is fluffy and promiscuous as the wind. I am with him entirely. He wants superfine stability.
>
> "Yes, I know!' cried Ursula. 'He wants his own way—I know what your fine words work down to—bossiness, I call it, bossiness.'
>
> The young cat again glanced at Birkin in disdain of the noisy woman.
>
> "I quite agree with you, Miciotto,' said Birkin to the cat. 'Keep your male dignity, and your higher understanding.'

And he goes on provoking Ursula's fury about 'this assumption of male superiority'. It is worth observing, however, that Birkin, despite his ironical looks and laughs, is actually not talking about male superiority but about stability, strays, and wildness. It is equally true that Ursula's impetuous attack is created by superiority, whether it had its origin in Frieda Lawrence's jeers, as seems likely, or not. (The cat, incidentally, looks at Birkin with a look of 'pure superiority'.) Birkin insists that what the cats represent is not Gerald's bullying of the mare, the 'Wille zur Macht', but 'The desire to bring this female cat into a pure stable equilibrium, a transcendent and abiding *rapport* with the single male' because without him 'she is a mere stray, a fluffy sporadic bit of chaos'. It is essential to see the she-cat as a stray, though I wouldn't suggest that Lawrence presents the debate very ingratiatingly, especially for women readers. It suggests the need for permanence, not the need to be knocked into shape by the male.

The conjunction of stars and the fluffy bit of chaos recur in *Look! We Have Come Through!*, not surprisingly, since the early stages of Lawrence's struggles and successes with Frieda are told both in *Women in Love* and in these early unrhymed poems. The fluidity of poetry, and of this free verse in particular, has its advantage over the fixities of the prose fiction. Its dialectic is more shifting, its impersonations less hard, its moods less tethered to history and personality. In addition, irony and comedy are happily absent, for Lawrence is not at his best in either. *Women in Love* is of course a novel which refuses to be linear. It resembles poetry in its reliance on lyrical and symbolic statement, but it still has the novel's characteristic continuity. When Birkin gives up a mood or a thought in exhaustion, irony or bewilderment, it is still registered in continuous and casual patterns, whereas the poems dealing with similar ideas and feelings jump without link or explanation from one mood to another. One result of this discontinuity seems to be a greater freedom from male and female stereotypes. In the fiction, even imagery may be attached to character and therefore to gender. In the poetry, the emphasis can be placed on states of mind and passion.

Sometimes, of course, the poetry simply fills out the novel's outline. When Lawrence retreats from the woman's gratified praise of his body's fineness and function, we see precisely what he meant by that subservience to the ego of which he accuses Ursula in *Women in Love*. The poetry is fuller of feeling and is thus more lucid than the novel, with its commitments to history, debate, and character. The risen Christ's *noli me tangere* and Birkin's stoning of the reflections of Aphrodite are explained in the poems, which ruminate lengthily on the retreat into solitude, on the sense of independence and separateness, and on the conjunction of the separate persons. This poetry is about persons rather than about men and women, or man and woman. It is true to those feelings which are common to both (or all) the sexes, and proves what the novels asserted and dropped. It is the poetry, not the fiction, which really destroys the old ego of sexual difference. What the novel does is to show the attempt to break, and its difficulty.

'Song Of A Man Who Is Loved' may at a glance look like the ineffaceable mother's image, but it develops a particularity, physical and emotional, which makes it larger and newer. The lover is secured by permanence and conjunction from the surrounding space, hardness, and chaos. Here is a guarantee of rest and peace:

> So I hope I shall spend eternity
> With my face down buried between her breasts;
> With my still heart full of security,
> And my still hands full of her breasts.

The abstract concepts of security and permanence take on the definite forms of solid bone and its soft covering, both needed, bone for a lasting support, flesh for something softer than the world outside. That world's hardness and evasiveness are both present, too, in sensation and sound:

Having known the world so long, I have never confessed
How it impresses me, how hard and compressed
Rocks seem, and earth, and air uneasy, and waters still ebbing west.

But the hard things are human, as well as natural, including 'Assertions! Assertions! stones, women and men!' Lawrence's unpleasant qualities, his hating and his superiority, allow him to sound aggressive about human beings as well as assertions and stones, but his more endearing need for stability links him with Ursula and the stray cat. He is not simply a provider of peace, he knows chaos too, and it is a chaos sensuously realized as it never was in the debates and arguments of the novel:

And the chaos that bounces and rattles like shrapnel, at least
Has for me a door into peace, warm dawn in the east
Where her bosom softens towards me, and the turmoil has ceased.

When conjunction has happened, the gains can be demonstrated by man or woman. The knowledge cannot be simply reflexive. The man uses for himself the image of chaos and in 'One Woman To All Women' lets her use his star symbol, the 'other beauty, the way of the stars', which is also now, as Coleridge might say, attached to the reality it represents, being brought into the sensuous area of sexual rhythm, motion, and propulsion:

If you knew how I swerve in peace, in the equipoise
With the man, if you knew how my flesh enjoys
The swinging bliss no shattering ever destroys.

Admittedly, the last splendid line which brings the cosmos into the lover's bed, is diminished by the refrain and title of the poem, 'You other women'. The ultimate boast and gratification can seem (immediately) rather pettily feminine and (ultimately) pettily masculine, though the poem is concerned to dismiss conventional beauty, and its rejections of cosmetic and narcissistic devices conveniently express the ego-binding of aesthetic vanities, and perhaps excuse the unattractive competitiveness.

In one of the best poems in the volume, 'New Heaven and Earth' there is a refusal to differentiate, a nervous-seeming but ultimately confident glancing from what seems a man's experience to what is felt also as a woman's. The song becomes that of a human being who is loved. Lawrence's usual way is to impersonate the woman or to speak as the man, but here he shifts from the one to the other, as he does again, momentarily, in 'Both Sides of the Medal' where he insists and shows that she has a passion for him as he has for her. 'New Heaven and Earth' is a poem which most clearly deals with the proof of sexual knowledge, with the knowledge of self, of otherness, of newness, of strangeness. It creates an exotic sexual landscape which achieves something less frequently found in Lawrence than in Donne, the sweet and violent jolt through a conceit into fresh experience, the shock given to mind through senses, here creating and re-creating the twinned delights of finding the self in finding the other human creature:

> I am thrown upon the shore.
> I am covering myself with the sand.
> I am filling my mouth with the earth.
> I am burrowing my body into the soil.
> The unknown, the new world!

This landing of the desperate castaway is followed by the sudden shock of translation. The man and his reader are grounded, in a new impact:

> It was the flank of my wife
> I touched with my hand, I clutched with my hand
> rising, new-awakened from the tomb!
> It was the flank of my wife
> whom I married years ago
> at whose side I have lain for over a thousand nights
> and all that previous while, she was I, she was I;
> I touched her, it was I who touched and I who was touched.

Lawrence does better here than in *Women in Love* with the sense of eternal *rapport*. His image of the past is in several senses more solidly persuasive than the novel's statements about the future, in a new version of the traditions of amorous pre-knowledge and eureka-feeling. The woman's flank is the strand of the new world:

> White sand and fruits unknown and perfumes that never
> can blow across the dark seas to our usual world!
> And land that beats with a pulse!
> And valleys that draw close in love!
> And strange ways where I fall into oblivion of uttermost living!—
> Also she who is the other has strange-mounded breasts and strange
> sheer slopes, and white levels.

The erotic and exotic geography works brilliantly: whiteness, curves, scents, and foreignness belonging plainly to the human body and the new world, beating pulse and closing valleys transferring an amorous life to the land, and making it more extraordinary and intense. The rapturous poem—perhaps the most Whitman-like of Lawrence's poems—delights in conjunction, separateness, and joy, with vividness which shows what the novel's debate is about.

It shows this more intricately than I have suggested, because it begins with a sense of self-nausea, itself related to the various hatefulnesses of war, the tomb, and imprisonment in self. We move to that sense of rapturous landing from an unpleasantly striking image of a man making love to himself, and of a loathsome hermaphroditic fruitfulness, 'begetting and conceiving in my own body'. The slopes are breasts, the valleys close in, the images belong to female physiology, but Lawrence can also force a sharing of the image which makes even clearer the common experience of sex, for both man and woman, as he does in 'Wedlock' which uses more obvious domestic distinctions, to make the same point about common experience. It starts with the sense of the man protecting the woman, wrapping her round, but almost immediately refuses to preserve the vital and phallic images for himself:

> Do you feel me wrap you
> Up with myself and my warmth, like a flame round the wick?
>
> And how I am not at all, except a flame that mounts off you.
> Where I touch you, I flame into being;—but is it me, or you?

The imagery of flame ceases to be phallic, passes from the obviously male candle and wick to something larger and less differentiated, 'a bonfire of oneness, my flame I flung leaping round you / You the core of the flame, crept into me'. The image is shared, like the passion. The poem stretches to take in both lovers, itself an act of love. . . .

Lawrence's sense of human liberation is realized when he forgets the 'he and she', in a way undreamed of by Donne. This is most fully achieved in the poems, but even in the constraints of the prose fiction there emerges some sense that women and men share the same struggle. The woman in *The Woman Who Rode Away* is, as a woman, the best equipped human being for submission and sacrifice, society having after all freely encouraged female masochism. The women at the beginning of *The Rainbow* not surprisingly resemble their sisters (and contemporaries) in the novels of George Eliot, who also look ahead into history and out into the public world. The Brangwen women look because they have windows to look through, children to plan for, the doctors and parsons to talk to, while the men of the agricultural community work with the animals in the fields behind. Ursula, like Dorothea Brooke, Isabel Archer, Little Dorrit, and Tess, is an appropriately female image of Victorian aspiration. Lawrence couldn't sympathise with the suffragettes, but he could sympathise with Ursula's attempt at liberation, permitting her to do such modern things as reject her college education for its irrelevance, choose and use the wrong lover and leave him, become pregnant and have a symbolic and convenient miscarriage. Some of which things the Victorian heroines were not free to try. But Ursula, like Dorothea and Dorrit, rebels and protests against social limits which are oppressive to the woman but also oppressive to the man. Just as George Eliot moved from Maggie to Tom, from Dorothea to Lydgate, to show not only the woman's limitations but the man's, to achieve not only a feminist plea but also a human one, just as Hardy moved from Jude to Sue, so Lawrence moves from Ursula to Birkin. I would not want to exaggerate the success of his analysis. George Eliot, a woman who had to put on the indignity of a male name, for reasons both sexual and literary, and Thomas Hardy, least chauvinist of all nineteenth-century male English writers except Meredith, were capable of achieving and maintaining a balance between the plight of man and woman. But when Lawrence moved on that hinge between *The Rainbow* and *Women in Love*, his heroine became more orthodox, less introspective, forgot some of her past, changed to become more conventionally in need of an education from the man.

At the beginning of *Women in Love* Ursula and Gudrun are not making a narrowly female plea when they question marriage and the family. In the episode of the chair, both Ursula and Birkin are together, man and woman, in rejecting the furniture and fittings of family life, despite their will to permanence. Their atypical freedom has of course been observed by several critics, including Leavis and Vivas, as coming straight from Lawrence's own situation. Only in *Lady Chatterley*, did he fully admit that the problem of sexual freedom and fulfilment was bound up with property, family, households, and children. Only Connie is actually allowed the urge to conceive, perhaps as a belated reflection of Frieda's maternity. She is to have a child as well as acts and utterance, though off stage. Lawrence 'neglects' the family, perhaps because his marriage was sterile, perhaps because his attachment to his mother had been almost sterilising, perhaps because it is the man, rather than the woman, who occupies the centre of the novel. The result is that he often pays man and woman the compliment of valuing them as particular persons, not as parents and ancestors.

Lawrence set the human couple together at the end of *Lady Chatterley's Lover* in an abstract social world, almost as far removed from the average daily life as the Mexico of *The Plumed Serpent* or the Australia of *Kangaroo*. But throughout the novels there are moments when the human being can be set in her environment, to represent not only a woman's life, but something larger. In *Sons and Lovers*, where the women are subordinate to the picture of the man's development and growing-up, there is the remarkable social detail of the scene in Clara's house when Paul Morel finds her and her mother at their lace-making:

> That was a little, darkish room too, but it was smothered in white lace. The mother had seated herself again by the cupboard, and was drawing thread from a vast web of lace. A clump of fluff and ravelled cotton was at her right hand, a heap of three-quarter-inch lace lay on her left, whilst in front of her was the mountain of lace web, piling the hearthrug. Threads of curly cotton, pulled out from between the lengths of lace, strewed over the fender and the fireplace. Paul dared not go forward, for fear of treading on piles of white stuff.
>
> On the table was a jenny for carding the lace. There was a pack of brown cardboard squares, a pack of cards of lace, a little box of pins, and on the sofa lay a heap of drawn lace.
>
> The room was all lace, and it was so dark and warm that the white, snowy stuff seemed the more distinct.
>
> 'If you're coming in you won't have to mind the work,' said Mrs. Radford. 'I know we're about blocked up. But sit you down.' . . .
>
> Clara began to work. Her jenny spun with a subdued buzz; the white lace hopped from between her fingers on to the card. It was filled; she snipped off the length, and pinned the end down to the banded lace. Then she put a new card in her jenny. Paul watched her. She sat square and magnificent. Her throat and arms were bare. The blood still mantled below her ears; she bent her head in shame of her humility. Her face was set on her work. . . .
>
> Clara broke in, and he told her his message. She spoke humbly to him. He had surprised her in her drudgery. To have her humble made him feel as if he were lifting his head in expectation.
>
> 'Do you like jennying?' he asked.
>
> 'What can a woman do!' she replied bitterly.
>
> 'Is it sweated?'
>
> 'More or less. Isn't *all* woman's work? That's another trick the men have played, since we force ourselves into the labour market.'
>
> 'Now then, you shut up about the men,' said her mother. 'If the women wasn't fools, the men wouldn't be bad uns, that's what I say. No man was ever that bad wi' me but what he got it back again. Not but what they're a lousy lot, there's no denying it.'
>
> 'But they're all right really, aren't they?' he asked.
>
> 'Well, they're a bit different from women,' she answered.

Clara is a suffragette, and Lawrence (and Paul) eventually pack her off again to crude old Baxter Dawes, thus settling that bit of Paul's *Bildung*. But to say that, even though it is quite true, ignores the powerful life of those scenes where full weight is given to sensuous and emotional truth, where the tale can be trusted. We see precisely why she was a feminist, perhaps also, a little, why she could go back to her bad marriage, liberated as she is into the imprisoning world of work. The white lace smothers and blocks the room. Humiliations of labour blend with humiliations of sex. It is the men who sweat the women, it is an employer and a lover who watches: 'her throat and arms were bare. . . . She bent her head in shame of her humility. . . . To have her humble made him feel as if he were lifting his head in expectation'. Here are traces of that peculiar Victorian perversion, the gentleman's excitement at the woman's hard drudgery, discussed most candidly in *Munby*, most romantically in Clough's *The Botkie*. But it is a moment which doesn't belong only to a problem of women, but links with the whole world of work.

Paul Morel felt the humiliation of the factory too, though Lawrence toned down some of the more brutal aspects of his own experience. The miners are smothered and blocked also. Lawrence had a clear understanding of the tedium and brutality of industrial work, for men and women, and when we think of his own domestic zest for washing up saucepans or laying tables, with care and creativity, we should remember that it was a free and chosen work that he delighted in. He is quick to seize what joy there is, even in the mines, and does so in Morel's marvellous stories, which have their part to play in casting that fatal and transient glamour over Gertrude Morel. He also realized, or at least showed, that woman had to get into the world of work, that the domestic drudgery of Miriam's mother had no zest, was all grind and service, and that Miriam was desperate to learn, to move up and move on. In her story too, for all its distortions, we see the most explicable moments of humility as she struggles to enter the desired and difficult world of learning. Her desires are Mrs Morel's for her sons, Paul's for himself. In the world of work some escape into the rare creative chance, others are imprisoned by the routines of the inhuman machine Lawrence was to indict, fight, and escape. The pressures of that world form the most striking part of Lawrence's argument against industry and science, and as he shows them in action, as he remembers and imagines, he sees the continuity of human feeling. It flows through love and labour, links men and women, calls on their energy and sometimes defeats it.

Lawrence never faced the question of the identity of man and woman's political predicament, except perhaps intuitively, but he recorded their common struggle to survive in the industrial world. Even a novel which uses women as instruments in the male artist's *Bildung* has moments which show the women, like men, as human beings, individuals, persons.

F. R. LEAVIS

"The Rainbow"

The Rainbow and *Women in Love* are intimately related, but surprisingly unlike—though they are both obviously by D. H. Lawrence. Lawrence writes to Edward Garnett in a letter dated 30 December 1913: 'In a few days' time I shall send you the first half of *The Sisters*—which I should rather call *The Wedding Ring*— . . . It is very different from *Sons and Lovers*: written in another language almost.' *The Sisters*, one is told, is what became *Women in Love*, though I am bound to question whether in this instance it became anything but *The Rainbow*. Probably, when Lawrence threw out the other suggested title for it, it hadn't wholly emerged as itself from the one projected novel on which Lawrence had embarked, and of which he wrote to A. D. McLeod in April 1913: 'I am doing a novel which I have never grasped. Damn its eyes, there I am at page 145, and I've no notion what it's about. I hate it. F. says it is good. But it's like a novel in a foreign language I don't know very well—I can only just make out what it is about.'

This is not affectation, but an emphatic way of describing the emergence, as he experienced it, of original thought out of the ungrasped apprehended—the intuitively, the vaguely but insistently apprehended: first the stir of apprehension, and then the prolonged repetitious wrestle to persuade it into words. We have the two novels that separated out in the organic working of that first creative impulsion: *The Rainbow* and *Women in Love*. And of the later book he might have said: 'It is *very* different from *The Rainbow*: written in another language almost.' We can only marvel at the rapidity with which his genius developed. Both books are incredibly original. He said justly (where at least the achieved was in question) to

Edward Marsh in a letter dated 6 November 1915: 'You jeered rather at *The Rainbow*, but notwithstanding it is a big book. I tell you, who know.' Of *Women in Love* we can guess pretty shrewdly that he didn't doubt it to be capable of standing by itself and to be the greater achievement. And if he wrote in a letter, '*The Rainbow* and *Women in Love* are really an organic artistic whole,' that expresses his sense of their having emerged from the same creative intuition, and of his need to have written *The Rainbow* in order to tackle successfully his diagnostic and prophetic study of what was in 1914 contemporary England—and modern civilization.

The Rainbow clearly led up to *Women in Love*; we see well enough why Lawrence, in several letters, refers to the latter as a 'sequel' to *The Rainbow*. He looked back from his own time, and seeking to understand that, and whither England was tending or driving, asked what essential growth, what development, lay behind the present—which, as he lived in it, was becoming something else. He could hardly have written *The Rainbow* without at the same time shaping in the process a sequel—not merely an 'idea' of it, unless an idea can be concrete, and the forming idea be the creative writer's thought in its characteristically concrete formation. 'Art-speech is the only speech'—the only speech that can render living thought; and Lawrence's problem was how to achieve precision and cogency in that.

Though his present in *Women in Love* is, of its nature, dynamic, and, as such, straining urgently, and very responsive to impulsions of change, it is nevertheless a present—England now. The distinctive offer of *The Rainbow* is to render development concretely—the complex change from generation to generation and the interweaving of the generations. *His* present, which is nothing in the nature of a newspaper present, has to be created, and only a great genius could create it so that one had to agree: this *is* the present. And who questions (the 'who' is to be taken as interrogatory, so that—from my point of view—a questioner would probably expose himself to a placing comment) that *Women in Love* gives the present of a half-century ago? The England, the 'English life' evoked is of course selective; but so is any 'objectivity' that thought offers to bring in front of us. The question, where Lawrence is concerned, regards the criteria implicit in the reality he presents us with, and, in such a matter, they are peculiarly evasive when dealt with discursively; they elude analytic-descriptive generalities. It is in an immediate way that one is convinced; one's conviction is confirmed by thought, the life of which the process of confirmation at the same time nourishes. Of course there have been developments in half-a-century, but they go essentially to confirm Lawrence's insight; so that he remains the incomparable promoter of perception and judgment where *our* present is in question.

For all the marked difference in style between the two books, the implicit criteria, and something characteristic of the method of *Women in Love*, are what have been worked out in the writing of *The Rainbow*. The criteria are those of the great writer who said: 'At the maximum of our imagination we are religious.' As I remarked on one of the occasions on which I have quoted this utterance before, 'imagination' and 'religious' are important words in the context of Lawrence's thought, but as they stand in the isolated sentence they are far from unambiguous. Of course, reading them there in what we know to be a Laurentian maxim, we take the Laurentian charge they transmit. As good a way of intimating—that is, of achieving a due explicitness about—the nature of that charge as any, it seems to me, is to consider the case of Skrebensky, who is, in the last third of *The Rainbow*, the man in Ursula Brangwen's developing emotional life. Already in the chapter (XI) called 'First Love' we have this, which leaves us in no doubt as to his life-deficiency:

> He went about his duties, giving himself up to them. At the bottom of his heart his self, the soul that aspired and had true hope of self-effectuation lay as dead, still-born, a dead weight in his womb. Who was he, to hold important his personal connection? What did a man matter personally? He was just a brick in the whole great social fabric, the nation, the modern humanity. His personal movements were small, and entirely subsidiary. The whole form must be ensured, not ruptured for any personal reason whatsoever, since no personal reason could justify such a breaking. What did personal intimacy matter? One had to fill one's place in the whole, the great scheme of man's elaborate civilization, that was all. The whole mattered—but the unit, the person, had no importance, except as he represented the Whole. So Skrebensky left the girl out and went his way, serving what he had to serve, and enduring what he had to endure, without remark. To his own intrinsic life, he was dead. . . . He had his five senses too. They were to be gratified.

It is made plain to us that he is not a mere vulgar cynic. He takes duty seriously, and duty for him is to 'the established order of things'. In fact, he serves to enforce the meaning of 'responsibility' in the profound Laurentian sense of the word—to enforce it by bringing out its immeasurable difference from anything suggested by 'duty'. It is made plain for us too that Skrebensky is not without some kind of awareness of the unmanning contradiction involved for him in his inner life. The effect on Ursula gives us a Laurentian theme that again plays a major part in *Women in Love*, this time as involved in the relations between Gudrun and Gerald

Crich. It is a prolonged ordeal for both sisters—in *The Rainbow* the ordeal is Ursula's:

> So there came over Skrebensky a sort of nullity which more and more terrified Ursula. She felt there was something hopeless she had to submit to.

The adjective 'hopeless' is not a word that it is Lawrence's way anywhere to throw in slackly, as suggesting a vague intensity in the state vaguely deplored, and most certainly not in *The Rainbow*. In the brief quoted passage it refers us to the title of the book. We all know that the rainbow is a symbol, and we associate it with promise and hope. But there is more in it than that, otherwise Lawrence wouldn't have made it the title of the novel that has for its sequel *Women in Love*. For in the title there is no irony, and in the sequel no changed Laurentian attitude. What I call 'attitude' here I qualify as Laurentian because it is basic to Lawrence's thought. True, what he makes of the symbol was potential in it; but the actual value, the complex significance, that Lawrence's novel creates for it and invests it with is distinctively and pregnantly Laurentian.

The attitude and tone can't be called optimistic, and how misleading it would be to lay the stress on hope and promise the following passage serves to intimate. I pick it from an essay in *Phoenix I* because it brings in the Ark with the rainbow:

> Catastrophe alone never helped man. The only thing that ever avails is the living adventurous spark in the souls of men. If there is no living adventurous spark, then death and disaster are as meaningless as tomorrow's newspaper.
>
> Take the fall of Rome. During the Dark Ages of the fifth, sixth, seventh centuries A.D., the catastrophes that befell the Roman Empire didn't alter the Romans a bit. They went on just the same, rather as we go on to-day, having a good time when they could get it, and not caring. Meanwhile Huns, Goths, Vandals, Visigoths, and all the rest wiped them out.
>
> With what result? The flood of barbarism rose and covered Europe from end to end.
>
> But bless your life, there was Noah in his Ark with the animals. There was young Christianity. There were the lonely fortified monasteries, like little arks floating and keeping the adventure afloat. There is no break in the great adventure in consciousness. Throughout the howling deluge, some few brave souls are steering the ark under the rainbow.
>
> The monks and bishops of the Early Church carried the soul and spirit of man unbroken, unabated, undiminished over the howling flood of the Dark Ages. Then this spirit of undying courage was fused into the

> barbarians, in Gaul, in Italy, and the new Europe began. But the germ had never been allowed to die.
>
> Once all men in the world lost their courage and their newness, the world would come to an end.

Not, then, just hope or the reassurance implicit in a promise that can be relied on because it is from God. The peace that Lawrence counsels us to seek and secure isn't that. Rather it is the peace of basic responsibility fully accepted—'responsibility' as the young ship's-captain of 'The Secret Sharer' so naturally assumed it as his. Responsibility in that profound sense goes with the imagination that makes possible a liberation from the imprisoning ego; it calls for the developed intelligence that (depending as it does on developed intuition) can make—if the courage is there—the individual being the disinterested servant of life. But Conrad's distinctive attitude and tone are such that, challenged to describe them as we have them in the work of his kindled imagination, one would hardly find oneself prompted to bring in, for any positive major use, the word 'religious'. Rather, it is Ramón of *The Plumed Serpent* who, in that early intimate exchange with Kate, describes in Laurentian terms what 'responsibility' implies as it actually prevails in Lawrence's art.

But we didn't create ourselves; and the sole access to the promptings to be gathered from the unknown—from which life and creativity enter us—is by the well-head, which is deep below our valid thought. Submission to the promptings is the escape from the ego and its will; but such submission is, of its nature, a very active matter, demanding self-knowledge, intensive cultivation of the most delicate intuitiveness, and the courage to arrive at conclusions the precision and finality of which are not guaranteed: the responsibility for them is ours, and where it is not taken up there is no genuine responsibility. 'But Noah, of course, is always in an unpopular minority'—it doesn't occur to Skrebensky to belong to that; that is, he leaves responsibility to the Whole, or to the community, or to the greatest good of the greatest number.

Ursula, who is no more than a girl learning about love and life, and committed (she is intelligent) to discovering what her own 'life-responsibility' dictates, is first, for all Skrebensky's young-love irresistibleness, made uneasy by her sense of his inner nullity as a man, and then, as she matures, brought to a decided placing judgment against him. The very end of the book gives us one of the two or three main quotable passages in it in which the rainbow symbol figures. The passage is essentially explicitness relating immediately to the significance of the symbol, and forms part of her reflections as she lies in bed recovering from an illness brought on by uncertainty, apprehension and emotional conflict.

> In everything she saw she grasped and groped to find the creation of the living God, instead of the old, hard barren form of bygone living. Sometimes great terror possessed her. Sometimes she lost touch, she lost her feeling, she could only know the old horror of the husk which bound in her and all mankind. They were all in prison, they were all going mad.
>
> . . . And then, in the blowing clouds, she saw a band of faint iridescence colouring in faint colours a portion of the hill. And forgetting, startled, she looked for the hovering colour and saw a rainbow forming itself. In one place it gleamed fiercely, and, her heart anguished with hope, she sought the shadow of iris where the bow should be. Steadily the colour gathered, mysteriously, from nowhere, it took presence upon itself, there was a faint, vast rainbow. The arc bended and strengthened itself till it arched indomitable, making great architecture of light and colour and the space of heaven, its pedestals luminous in the corruption of new houses on the low hill, its arch the top of heaven.
>
> And the rainbow stood on the earth. She knew that the sordid people who crept hard-scaled and separate on the face of the world's corruption were living still, that the rainbow was arched in their blood . . .

This is the form taken by Ursula's reaction against Skrebensky. To estimate its signficance fairly we need to remind ourselves that Ursula is a major character in the sequel, *Women in Love*, too, and finally marries Birkin. Birkin, of course, is very different from Skrebensky; but then so is Ursula from Lawrence. It was Lawrence who created the complex charge of significance, the subtle value that fitted the symbol to the title of his novel: Ursula's rainbow isn't Lawrence's.

I think (it is not an unrelated matter) of the difference between Ursula's fortune in love and Gudrun's. Birkin isn't a novelist or a poet; but he is nevertheless much more like Lawrence than Ramón of *The Plumed Serpent* is—*The Plumed Serpent*, 'the most important thing I have done so far'. The two fictional characters, Ramón and Birkin, are extremely unlike one another—extremely but not utterly; for they have this in common: they have both revolted against the enclosed ego and attained to human responsibility. Lawrence stresses the feminine in the title—and more than the title—of *Women in Love*; that is necessary to his insistence that the ideas of equality and inequality are irrelevant—and worse, the relevant stress falling on *difference*, and the difference being essential to life (and not merely, in humanity, to the biological continuance of the species).

Ursula is an intelligent girl of strong character and proper pride. Her reaction against Skrebensky has a Laurentian significance; it leads up to the battle that is an important constituent in the chapter called 'Moony' and the later chapter called 'Excurse'. Birkin is very unlike Skrebensky; though without Skrebensky's charm, he is far from being a spiritual nullity. He is the man who, though he would like to save Gerald from his mechanistic fate, and have him for his friend, diagnoses Gerald's disease and sees him as modern civilization speeding towards the death-break—the cessation of life (which is creativity) in a 'frozen world'. In fact, he shares Lawrence's diagnostic insight. He shares, too, Lawrence's view of the difference between woman and man. The immediately necessary point is made, I think, when I quote again from 'Moony' this:

> 'I always think I am going to be loved—and then I am let down. You *don't* love me, you know. You don't want to serve me. You only want yourself.'
>
> A shiver of rage went over his veins at this repeated: 'You don't want to serve me.' All the paradisal disappeared from him. 'No,' he said, irritated, 'I don't want to serve you, because there is nothing there to serve. What you want me to serve is nothing, mere nothing. It isn't even you, it is your mere female quality. And I wouldn't give a straw for your female ego —it's a rag doll.'

Birkin speaks in exasperation, for in fact he truly and profoundly loves her. He is exasperated at the hopelessness of trying to talk her into conviction. 'It must happen beyond the sound of words.' It is a question of what love is and what marriage should be; and actually she is brought to recognize the force of his point and tacitly admit conversion—brought to it merely by the genuineness and power of what he is.

She is luckier than her sister Gudrun. Gudrun is attracted by Gerald Crich's male beauty and the masterfulness of his organizing talent and will; and then repelled by the emptiness of his intrinsic being—just as Ursula had been by Skrebensky's conventional nullity—as a centre of life. It is for the man to foster in himself openness, necessarily creative, to the unknown—to strive towards free, unbiased and uncommitted receptivity at the well-head; his living spiritual authority is a matter of that. The woman driven to conclude that he is null reacts as Ursula and Gudrun do. Gudrun wants prestige and power, but, in the proximity of the chilling fact of death, discovers the vacuum in Gerald where she looked for the creative living centre—discovers too that she can't forgive the lack in a man she might, possibly, have otherwise thought of as hers. Her reaction is to fall back on the bullying superiority of Loerke, the artist-cynic.

I have been exemplifying how impossible it is, in an attempted expository treatment of Lawrence's thought, to achieve an expository ordering. This is not to offer an adverse criticism, but to bear involuntary testimony to the wholeness, the organic unity, inseparable in Lawrence's thought from his distinctive emphasis on life. My last point regarded both the difference and the relations between woman and man. I was about to go back to the problem of doing justice to the pregnancy, in the title of the book, of the symbolic rainbow, when I remembered that Ursula's mother, Anna, had, in introspective self-questioning, Ursula being then a new-born baby, herself dwelt expansively on the symbol. When I looked up the place in Chapter VI, 'Anna Victrix,' I was reminded further that Will Brangwen, her husband, was involved too—in a way that gave significance to their quarrel (for it amounted to that) about Lincoln Cathedral.

This is the passage from 'Anna Victrix'; it gives us an essential element in the total Laurentian charge—the charge that explains why the novel was called *The Rainbow*:

> Anna loved the child very much, oh, very much. Yet still she was not quite fulfilled. She had a slight expectant feeling, as of a door half opened. Here she was, safe and still in Cossethay. But she felt as if she were not in Cossethay at all. She was straining her eyes to something beyond. And from her Pisgah mount, which she had attained, what could she see? A faint, gleaming horizon, a long way off, and a rainbow like an archway, a shadow-door with faintly coloured coping above it. Must she be moving thither?
>
> Something she had not, something she did not grasp, could not arrive at. There was something beyond her. But why must she start on the journey? She stood so safely on the Pisgah mountain.
>
> Dawn and sunset were the feet of the rainbow that spanned the day, and she saw the hope, the promise. Why should she travel any further?

Her husband's 'sense of something more' (for he had such a sense, though there is no rainbow for him) is different; the rainbow is hers. We say this to ourselves because it is pretty obvious that we are meant to: it is not for nothing that the page or so evoking him ends immediately before the just-quoted passage begins. The juxtaposition is significant.

This is Will Brangwen:

> And what more? What more would be necessary? The great mass of activity in which mankind was engaged meant nothing to him. By nature he had no part in it. What did he live for, then? For Anna only, and for the sake of living? What did he want on this earth? Anna only, and his children, and his life with his children and her? Was there no more?
>
> He was attended by a sense of something more, something further, which gave him absolute being. It was as if now he existed in Eternity, let Time be what it might. What was there outside?

'Nothing': that is the answer assumed. This is plain from the way in which Will, in the next chapter ('The Cathedral'), the substance of which precedes chronologically what happens in the chapter just quoted from, reacts when Anna asserts, and sticks to it, that she doesn't accept the significance he imputes to Lincoln Cathedral. She too is filled with awe at the marvel of the interior; and so also is Lawrence himself, as is shown in the sustained power of the prose in which he evokes the marvel: words will do this only when the charged and possessed imagination of the great artist informs them. But in the wonderfully controlled ecstatic prose there is something that, when it asserts itself, makes the ecstasy specifically Will Brangwen's, as it does explicitly here—triggering off rebellion in Anna:

> And there was no time nor life nor death, but only this, this timeless consummation, where the thrust from earth met the thrust from earth and the arch was locked on the keystone of ecstasy. This was all, this was everything. Till he came to himself in the world below. Then again he gathered himself together, in transit, every jet of him strained and leaped, leaped clear into the darkness above, to the fecundity and the unique mystery, to the touch, the clasp, the consummation, the climax of eternity, the apex of the arch.

But—of Anna—there follows this:

> She too was overcome, but silenced rather than tuned to the place. She loved it as a world not quite her own, she resented his transports and ecstasies. His passion in the cathedral at first awed her, then made her angry.

She remembered that the open sky was no blue vault, and told herself protestingly that it was shut out. And she taunted Will with the faces carved where possible by the irreverent masons:

> These sly little faces peeped out of the grand tide of the cathedral like something that knew better. They knew quite well, these little imps that retorted on man's own illusion, that the cathedral was not absolute. They winked and leered, giving suggestion of the many things that had been left out of the great concept of the church.

This, of course, is Lawrence himself—our awareness of that is overriding, without our being disabled from accepting it as Anna. 'God burned no more in that bush': that, extracted from the prose of the context, with which it doesn't quarrel, is close to speech—which might be either's.

The tensions that complicate the married life of Will and Anna (it was a 'love-marriage') are dealt with by a novelist of first-hand perception and rare powers of subtle thought. The difference that sparks between them on the visit to Lincoln Cathedral is one of them; but my immediate concern with it is the help it gives towards 'defining' the charge of 'value', the significance, that Lawrence creates for the rainbow of his chosen title. Anna, in her creative sense, her apprehension, of the rainbow in the chapter, 'Anna Victrix', makes it something more complex than simply hope and promise: 'She was straining her eyes to something beyond . . . Something she had not, something she could not grasp, could not arrive at.' And it is through Anna that Lawrence registers his self-dissociation from Will's way of being religious. Whatever the way in which the adjective applies to Lawrence's sense and service of the unknown, these amount to something fundamentally other than Will's cult of the cathedral and what the cathedral represents.

It seems to me that Lawrence's basic attitude is religious in the most vital, the most living, way: it is the way compelled by a properly indocile perception of what our civilization is doing to life. It contrasts not only with Will Brangwen's; it contrasts equally with T. S. Eliot's—as these sentences announce ambiguously (they were written long before the first of the *Four Quartets*):

> We derive from the unknown, and we result into the unknown. But for us the beginning is not the end; for us the two are not one.

Lawrence believes in the reality of time, for he believes in the reality of development and essential change—the appearance in the universe of what didn't exist before. For him the relation between the creator and created life is utterly unlike what it is for Eliot—but then for Lawrence the unknowable supreme principle and potency and life itself are utterly unlike Eliot's God and Eliot's mankind.

The brief implicitly anti-Eliotic utterance I have quoted comes from an essay in *Phoenix I* entitled 'Life', in which Lawrence is explicit about man's unique status as he envisages it.

> Midway between the beginning and the end is man, midway between that which creates and that which is created, midway in another world, partaking of both, yet transcending.
>
> All the while man is referred back. He cannot create himself. At no moment can man create himself. He can but submit to the creator, to the primal unknown out of which issues the all. At every moment we issue like a balanced flame from the primal unknown. We are not self-contained or self-accomplished. At every moment we issue from the unknown.

To be a great creative writer, born in England, at Eastwood, of a miner's family, at that moment in history, was for a Lawrence to find himself committed to a prophetic role. He was impelled inevitably, by his astonishing gifts, into a questioning examination of the deepest underlying conditions of civilized life. Was the continuance of civilization in the spirit of its modern accelerating development possible? Wasn't overt human disaster certainly ahead, and not far distant, and essential human disaster already upon us? Thus his preoccupation with human responsibility and the relation of man to the unknown was everywhere urgent and insistent; it was in and of the creative drive behind his thought and art. This *was*, to invoke his own injunction, to cultivate 'consciousness'.

It is all in keeping that Lawrence in various places gives us some explicitness about the nature of responsibility and (it follows) of the self-discipline it calls for. In the essay, 'Life', for instance, we have this suggestive paragraph:

> I turn my face, which is blind and yet which knows, like a blind man turning to the sun, I turn my face to the unknown, which is the beginning, and like a blind man who lifts his face to the sun I know the sweetness of the influx from the source of creation into me. Blind, forever blind, yet knowing, I receive the gift, I know myself the ingress of the creative unknown. Like a seed, which unknowing receives the sun and is made whole, I open onto the great warmth of primal creativity and begin to be fulfilled.

Responsibility involves scrupulous delicacy of apprehension at the well-head, and therefore the cultivation of natural aptitude and delicate scruple.

> We shall never know what is the beginning. We shall never know how it comes to pass that we have form and being. But we may always know how through the doorways of the spirit and the body enters the vivid unknown, which is made known in us. Who comes, who is it that we hear outside in the night? Who knocks, who knocks again? Who is it that unlatches the painful door?
>
> Then behold, there is something new in our midst. We blink our eyes, we cannot see. We lift the lamp of previous understanding, we illuminate the stranger with the light of our established knowledge. Then at last we accept the newcomer, he is enrolled among us.

The image, 'seed', in 'like a seed' helps in the business of evocative definition. The seed responds livingly to sun and moisture because, we say, it is potential life itself—and we rest too easily, in blank assumption, on the assumed value of the word 'potential'. Let us say, rather, that the life in the seed is asleep; it can certainly die. But when it wakes, and develops in the warmth of the sun, it develops to an old pattern; we don't expect a mutation. What we are concerned with now is newness. The seed analogy holds in so far as it suggests that the man in whom his attained and realized 'manhood' is active *is* life, pre-eminently life, on our side of the well-head, and so is especially quick—let us bear in mind Lawrence's archaic use of the word—to apprehend the new life-promptings from the unknown, whence life enters us. But the stranger is new, and the newness and 'our established knowledge' have to accomodate themselves to each other. There is no absolute certainty and no finality; for, even if there is no growth, no change, in the unknown, the most scrupulous constatation may contain error.

Justified near-certitude regarding the new involves, as life does, creativity. The creativity in me isn't mine—it doesn't belong to me; yet I am responsible for what it does. Is, then, what it takes a master of 'art-speech' to constate 'objective'? Well, it means to be; how far it is (or isn't) is left to me to judge; it is my responsibility—which may take, as where Lawrence was concerned, a very long time to discharge to one's satisfaction. 'Verifiable' has a different meaning in regard to judgments about life from what it has for the scientist.

Major creative writers are rare: I put it in this way, because the newly apprehended at the well-head, to affect a culture, must be realized in producible thought. And even so, producible and (one would think) overwhelming, it may make little difference; what difference has Lawrence made? In writing it, I meant this question as rhetorical, but feel now that it had better be, just a little, an inquiry too. Lawrence succeeded in making a living for himself and Frieda with his pen: his art in the short stories and the tales was compelling, but it appears to me very possible that his novels were read for the misunderstood characteristics that earned him a name for immorality. In any case his thought (and that is his art) was in general—I include myself in the generalization—uncomprehended, it was basically too new and important.

And yet it is perhaps too early to say that he made no difference. Perhaps the confidence of such a judgment reveals a certain crudity of assumption about the way in which a dynamism like Lawrence's could work. There has undoubtedly been a change for the worse in cultural conditions since he died, a change that might seem to make any hope that he could tell as an influence on the prevailing culture merely ridiculous. The forming of such an intellectual community as he irradiated at Eastwood, was life-centre to, and drew life from, is in today's conditions inconceivable. He was launched as an author with astonishing ease, and found little in the way of making the kinds of contact he needed: he couldn't doubt that there was still an influential educated public in England. Yet the prospects of civilization, as he saw them, were not cheerful, but distinctly chilling: the paragraph I printed as epigraph to my last book, *The Living Principle*, represented his profound conviction:

> I knew then, and I know now, it is no use trying to do anything—I speak only for myself—publicly. It is no use trying merely to modify present forms. The whole great form of our era will have to go.

The first sentence, it is true, regarded the war which made Horatio Bottomley a power in England; but 'I knew then' is followed by 'and I know now'; so it doesn't regard merely that. Lawrence was convinced that England—and he was right—hadn't begun to recover, and wouldn't. How could it? The war accelerated, the drive of modern civilization that Birkin, in *Women in Love*, sees as irresistible. Birkin, however, doesn't the less fight with all his being against the irresistible drive. Nor does Lawrence. In spite of his saying, 'It is no use trying to do anything . . . in public', what more could anyone do, and do in a public way, than carry on war against the disease with that marvellous output of books and essays and tales? The life in him was something like unshaken invincible faith; it affirmed itself, and was the proof of the affirmation; he couldn't have believed at a deep level that such implicitly affirming creativity was doomed to make no difference.

Wasn't it this difficult faith, this paradoxical quasi-hope, that Lawrence's rainbow symbolized for him as the upshot of his novel? The Laurentian rainbow meant faith-in-life overhung by frightening menace—menace yoked, for the 'conscious', with a paradoxical contradiction. The novel offers to bring before us the immediate past of the England of *Women in Love*. The generation it starts with is Tom Brangwen's, who is the old rural England. But already the embanked canal, carried along the valley, has shut off the farm from the industrialized world it now supplies. Brangwen needs no rainbow; his problem is to find the woman with whom to make a life together. Simply, sanely and touchingly (which means convincingly), he solves his problem: he and the Polish lady, with such different backgrounds, have little in common except that they attract one another, and, for all the difference between them, are both such that they can trust the intuitive conviction that the other will be the right life-long mate. In this respect, though she is a lady and knows the outside world—both very important facts, they answer to this part of the account of the characteristic Brangwen husband and wife: 'They were two very separate beings, vitally connected, knowing nothing of each other, yet living in their separate ways from one root.'

We have here what serves as a foil (not a wholly felicitous word, yet the other, 'norm', that suggests itself seems a good deal more unsuitable) against which the tensions and miseries attendant on the growing complexity of the conditions of life in the two succeeding generations are set off. The marriage between Will and Anna, the wholly Polish girl, is a young-love match that Tom Brangwen knows it would be useless to forbid, and I have already dealt with the friction that soon manifests itself between husband and wife. As for her rainbow vision, which meant not merely hope or promise, but 'straining her eyes to something beyond', we know: 'She did not turn to her husband, for him to lead her.' Also: 'And soon again she was with child. Which made her satisfied, and took away her discontent.' And further: 'With satisfaction, she relinquished the adventure to the unknown. She was bearing her children.'—'She was a door and a threshold, she herself.' A relevant, and very important point, about the difference between woman and man is made here.

Ursula, her daughter, cares so much about 'responsibility', which she knows intuitively and by experience in the family (there's her 'grandfather', Tom Brangwen) is the business of the man, that she can't forgive Skrebensky his complete and shameless lack of it. Ursula, then, has character and distinction. They ensure her a wide experience in the world of her time; experience—the diversities of it are largely painful—which is evoked for us by a master who has already proved himself to be one of the greatest of novelists. The end is defeat, or what looks like final disaster.

The chapter in which Ursula has to contemplate this, and her own 'nullity'—it is the concluding chapter of the book—has for title. 'The Rainbow'. It begins: 'Ursula went home to Beldover', and ends with the symbolic rainbow. 'She could scarcely speak or notice' when she came home, and 'the weeks crawled by'. On a listless walk by herself, she suffers the pathological nightmare of the horses, staggers home, and collapses into bed. It is convalescing in her bedroom that, at the window, she has her rainbow vision. The final paragraph of the book closes: 'She saw in the rainbow the earth's new architecture, the old, brittle corruption of houses and factories swept away, the world built up in a living fabric of Truth, fitting to the overarching heavens.'

This is indeed quasi-hope—undaunted faith—overhung by dark menace. For we certainly have to take it as, in a way, endorsed by Lawrence himself: there can be no irony. The paradox I point to with my 'quasi-hope' and 'faith' is there in the opening chapter. Lawrence doesn't for one moment let us suppose that, in sum, he would have wished to preserve, if he could, the old Brangwen civilization ('We've been here above *two* hundred years', he tells the Polish lady when courting). The marriage of Tom Brangwen to Lydia Lensky furthered the development that led to the Eastwood in which Lawrence was born. In the old rural civilization the lively intellectual milieu in which Lawrence formed and nourished his genius wouldn't have been possible. Yet Eastwood was a characteristic product of that developing civilization regarding which he was so sure that, of its very nature, it was heading to the most final of disasters. The paradox was the life in him which perceived, and fought against the irreversible drive, the lethal upshot of which seemed certain, and at the same time cherished the certitude that life would refuse ever to suffer final defeat. The Laurentian rainbow of the title was the assurance.

The novel ends on Ursula's rainbow vision; but there is no rainbow in the sequel. There could hardly be; the communication of *Women in Love* is, in its Laurentian cogency, too complete.

> Was this then all that remained? Was there left nothing but to break off from the happy creative being, was the time up—Is our day of creative life finished?

I have quoted these questions before; they form part of Birkin's brooding, in the chapter where he throws stones to disperse the reflected moon in the millpond, over the inevitable disaster towards which our civilization is taking us. When, at the end of *Women in Love*, he comes back with Ursula from Verona to see to Gerald's frozen corpse, it is as if the answer to those questions were given: 'Yes.' Birkin's earlier apprehensions—by which he 'was frightened'—were justified.

No rainbow, then. Yet Ursula was with him, and there is every sign that the problem of marriage was, for them, solved— solved permanently. This is the point at which to emphasize the title that Lawrence chose for his novel. It reminds one for how much, where Lawrence was concerned, the relations between woman and man counted in any question regarding the livingness of a culture, the health of a civilization. Where the habit, economy and institutional ethos of a civilization should tend to make proper relations—relations involving recognition of the total difference between them and of the nature of their essential need of each other—impossible, there could be, Lawrence clearly believed, little livingness and no hope.

It would be a delicate and exacting business holding forth on the relative significance of Gerald's ominous death on the one hand and of the felicitous mating between Ursula and Birkin on the other—the significances, that is, weighed against one another in their bearing on the effect of the total novel. But what there was of paradox in the book was inescapable in the nature of the enterprise it represented. You could hardly expose the nature of the unsuccess of the one pair without creating a successful pair as a kind of norm—at any rate, if you were Lawrence. He wouldn't have committed himself to the inquest into civilization in England if he hadn't been the gifted being who said, 'Nothing is important but life.' Thus *Women in Love* is paradoxically an affirmation; to serve life is the implicit and inseparable intention, the very spirit, of the creativity that produced it. It couldn't accomodate an equivalent of the rainbow passage with which Ursula concludes *The Rainbow*; but that Lawrence wrote *The Rainbow* and insisted that *Women in Love* was the sequel has a clear significance.

GARRETT STEWART

Lawrence, "Being," and the Allotropic Style

Surely no other author in English of Lawrence's acknowledged stature and influence, and of so distinctive a prose voice, has had such scant attention paid, in the way of considered and sophisticated estimation, to the words he used to gain his leverage on the literary imagination. The earliest critics, taken by surprise, could seldom refrain from remarks against the rhetoric, and before long it went almost without saying, however partisan the omission, that Lawrence's language, great as he might be at character and event, was at best a noble effort on the side of overexertion. In its rash verbal gambles and extravagances, the jargonish Lawrencian rhetoric seldom seemed gainfully employed, and might well be arraigned, if not for mere sloganizing and artistic bankruptcy, at least for some criminal neglect of the law of diminishing returns. Though manifestly furious with old novelistic solutions to the problem of speaking truth, the offensive new style becomes rapidly insolvent, and fails to pay its way in meaning. Briefs for the defense are difficult to file when the charges and detractions are not articulated with any degree of attention to the habits they summarily berate. Contemporary reviews lamented in passing Lawrence's "perfervid futuristic style" with its "morbidly perverted ingenuity," the "crazy iterations and benumbing violence" of its "curiously vicious rhythm," the "flinging about of heavy words" in a "turgid, exasperated" rhetoric, a "yelling" style rather than a telling one. This earliest dismay over the affronts and infelicities of Lawrence's expression has found its way, even if merely to be tamed and overcome, into much recent commentary, where the specter of the rhapsodic sermonizer, all rant and chant, is still vestigially with us, his rhetoric, for all its power at times, too often a shotgun marriage of cant and incantation. Quality in Lawrence's style is still a subject mostly for those who don't care for him, and who discuss it as an absence, with his defenders leaving the prose, unaided, to speak for itself when it honorably can. Yet certainly the best reply to the charges against Lawrence's style is not that it is sometimes wonderful, but that it is, and can be demonstrated to be, characteristically good, complex, and uniquely resonant.

The most recent attempt to do so at all systematically is Colin Clarke's study of the language of paradox (arguably a special, exacerbated case of ambiguity) in the novels, especially *Women in Love*, and the effort has been rebuked, though with the best intentions of his own for the study of style in Lawrence, by Mark Spilka himself, who objects to Clarke's looking "*at* language rather than *through* it." Consider how unthinkable this objection would be for recognized "stylists" and verbal manipulators from Sterne through Dickens to Joyce or Woolf, and one realizes what a special case Lawrence is thought to be by Spilka. He commends to our attention for its healthy, corrective approach, and for its noteworthy contribution to the "meagre work on Lawrence's style," an essay by Alan Friedman that he hopes will serve "as an antidote to Lawrencian style myopically misconceived as verbal paradox." Yet Friedman's spirited, incisive essay is interesting here primarily for what it, too, leaves out of consideration. Isolating, as he thinks Lawrence did, "the nearly insuperable problem" as "verbalization" itself, yet recognizing that the "unsayable is stylistically embarrassing," Friedman sees Lawrence taking a crucially different tack from "Joyce's brilliant solution to the problem—*distorting* conventional verbalization in order to render preconscious and unconscious material." Rather, Lawrence, "in order to take us elsewhere, into his own particular and very different region of the unconscious . . . distorts not words and not grammar, but the conventional signals for emotions." That is, one must suppose, the distortions operate almost sub-stylistically, therefore eluding any definitive linguistic analysis. On the contrary, there is a natural latitude within both definition and syntax, a plasticity of usage and ligature that promotes, whether deliberately or not for a given writer, what we call ambiguity, and that Lawrence defiantly frees up, maximizes, and exploits. It is this decidedly un-Joycean but equally verbal experiment which Friedman seems closer to when he later characterizes Lawrence's style as "writing which runs roughshod over idiomatic English." Where else could this bullying possibly be registered but in the "distortion" of "words" (meanings if not spellings), and "grammar"? I propose to look neither exclusively *at* nor exclusively *through* these components of Lawrence's unsettled idiom, and hope to avoid the far more common error of looking merely *around* them. Instead, I intend to look *with* style at the underlying reality it is meant to reveal, in the way I believe language was for Lawrence himself a way of seeing, the investigative license of his poetic means, the "way through" the opacities of deceit and self-delusion. . . .

It is hard to imagine why a statement like the following at the close of Lawrence's foreward to *Women in Love*, candidly prefixed to the very novel in which the question of stylistic motive is so widely vexing and hotly debated, should have given such infrequent pause to the critics: "In point of style, fault is often found with the continual, slightly modified repetition. The only answer is that it is natural to the author; and that every natural crisis in emotion or passion or understanding comes from this pulsing, frictional to-and-fro which works up to culmination." The implication is, one would think, bluntly obvious. The rhetoric of incremental self-generation takes its metaphor from the generative act itself in this image of a "frictional" style, a useful way of labelling the sexual element in Lawrence's prose. Blackmur was looking for some of the right things in one of the wrong places, for a poetry of finish in a poetry of self-effectuation. As with Lawrence's verse, the language of his novels is also not a shaped but a process prose, working itself up and out as it goes. In his landmark study from the early fifties, an essay otherwise notable for a strong and accurate fix on the Lawrencian sensibility, Mark Schorer wildly misses the point of Lawrence's prefatory note: "The attempt," he regrets to say, "to duplicate, in syntactical movement itself, the dialectical flow of the theme is perhaps a mistaken aesthetic ambition." If what Lawrence meant by frictional culmination was dialectics, then Hegel was the greatest pornographer of the nineteenth century. The truth is, of course, less oblique, and offers a rather straightforward way out of the dilemma in which Stoehr thinks Lawrence has trapped himself. Sex can be kept "out of the head" even when explored by prose discourse if it is embodied rather than overseen, intimately registered rather than analyzed. Sex does not have to turn cerebral simply by being said, for by what Schorer calls "syntactic movement" prose can attune itself to the vital rhythms it is meant more to approximate than to examine. That is, the dilemma of the verbal consciousness versus the anti-mentalizing sexual conscience, of aesthetic potential versus the staunchly guarded ethic of the instinctual life, is more thoroughly stylistic in its bearings than Stoehr demonstrates, though his textual evidence quite properly centers on *Lady*

Chatterley's Lover. It is in that last novel where we find the most strenuous and prolonged efforts at that driven, insistent style which Lawrence's negative critics have felt, watching it develop through *The Rainbow* and *Women in Love*, illustrates the most injurious strain (both senses) in his exploratory technique. To give it a working label, we may call it for now the orgastic style, a prose that paces itself to the rhythm and tempo of sexual climax while simultaneously investigating the psychic contours of such "dyings," answering once and for all, I think, the questions its own extremity of effect raises most acutely about the place of verbalization in sex and in love.

Repetition, apposition, parataxis, the ambivalences of syntactic elision, the patterns of echo and assonance, the functional shifts of diction within and between phrases, the thrust, swerve, and conversion of imagery—the whole lunging, unstable dynamic of Lawrence's style, never more furiously displayed than in the passage below from *Lady Chatterley's Lover*—substitutes for a mentalized portrait, certainly for any observations rationally derived or dialectically arrived at, a visceral rhythm that is the furthest development in English of the Romantic rhapsody. And it does this, here as elsewhere, in scenes that are themselves an account of the death of mentalized response. To disinfect sex from any taint of morbid intellectuality—or of pornography, as Lawrence defines it—to keep it clean and felt and intoxicated even while casting it up into words, he had to let it speak for itself, rhythmic and half inarticulate, a pulse and not an exposition. To the formidable liabilities of this procedure the style of *Lady Chatterley* surrenders itself wholesale, like Connie to Mellors in this scene:

> She yielded with a quiver that was like death. . . .
>
> She quivered again at the potent inexorable entry inside her, so strange and terrible. It might come with the thrust of a sword in her softly-opened body, and that would be death. She clung in a sudden anguish of terror. But it came with a strange slow thrust of peace, the dark thrust of peace and a ponderous primordial tenderness, such as made the world in the beginning. And her terror subsided in her breast, her breast dared to be gone in peace, she held nothing. She dared let go everything, all herself, and be gone in the flood.

The ambiguity in "all herself" of "all by herself" and "her entire self" seems to propel, in company with the basic frictional momentum, the relentless unfolding of the next paragraph:

> And it seemed she was like the sea, nothing but dark waves rising and heaving, heaving with a great swell, so that slowly her whole darkness was in motion, and she was ocean rolling its dark, dumb mass. Oh, and

> far down inside her the deeps parted and rolled asunder, in long, far-travelling billows, and ever, at the quick of her, the depths parted and rolled asunder, from the center of soft plunging, as the plunger went deeper and deeper, touching lower, and she was deeper and deeper and deeper disclosed, and heavier the billows of her rolled away to some shore, uncovering her, and closer and closer plunged the palpable unknown, and further and further rolled the waves of herself away from herself, leaving her, till suddenly, in a soft, shuddering convulsion, the quick of all her plasm was touched, she knew herself touched, the consummation was upon her, and she was gone. She was gone, she was not, and she was born: a woman.

This may heave and plunge once too often, but like the phonic thickening of "deeps" into "depths" there is a progression and strategic deepening to be noted. Just before the turning point at "still suddenly," inversion shuttles to the end of the pivotal clause, slightly varied from its earlier appearance, the crucial pronouns of what we might call, borrowing from the physical death of Tom Brangwen in *The Rainbow*, "the stripped moment of transit from life into death." For as "further and further rolled the waves of herself away from herself, leaving her," she is finally divested, "her" stripped of "self," a "leaving" that in the second sense of this participle also leaves the essential "her" behind, freed of the self-reflective awareness which has until now blocked her sexual release. "Isn't Connie Chatterley just as self-regarding in this scene," Stoehr asks, as any of the self-conscious, posturing lovers in the kind of pornography Lawrence detested? But the answer is not sought in the changes rung on the self-reflexive grammar in the actual sentences Lawrence gives us, especially as it is salvaged for a more genuine, tactile intuition of self that is not overly mentalized, when "she knew herself touched, the consummation was upon her, and she was gone."

With this most feverishly detailed and unalleviated sexual death scene in all of Lawrence's major fiction in front of us, we are in a position as never before to recognize the greatest of Lawrence's contributions to the literature of sexuality, and to its literary language. In his famous essay "Night Words," speaking about the necessary impoverishment of pornography as a genre, George Steiner notes that the "list of writers who have had the genius to enlarge our active compass of sexual awareness . . . is very small," and though he does not mention Lawrence, he does allude to the tradition of which the novelist's sexual vocabulary is the final flowering: "The close, delicately plotted concordance between orgasm and death in Baroque and Metaphysical poetry and art clearly enriched our legacy of excitement, as had the earlier focus on virginity." Building on the earliest achievements of Richardson, Emily Brontë, and Flaubert in the novel, and of Keats and Shelley especially among the Romantic poets, Lawrence becomes the greatest modern representative on this increasingly small list of authors. By extending and cross-indexing the "concordance" in every direction, Lawrence matured the Metaphysical trope into a metaphysic, and, pushing the link between libido and oblivion to its logical extreme, reinterpreted life as an erotic continuity with sensual annihilation and brought into prominence as no writer before him the idea of a sexual afterlife—the new heaven and earth of the redefined self, the "to be" that arises, phoenix-like, from the ashes of the extinguished ego. But Lawrence has not only given us a number of subsequent entries in such an index and lexicon of sexuality, he has also bestowed on English prose a largely original grammar of orgasm, in which the posture and pace of his style, its stance and frictional mode of advance, are at once an exercise in, and an expression of through language, the sexual imagination. In the last sentence of that paragraph from *Lady Chatterley*, as in the one just before it, apparent serial grammar has the ambiguous feel of simultaneity at the moment of transit: "She was gone, she was not, and she was born: a woman." Looking back from this point over the entire passage, we realize that Lawrence's pulsing, frictional style, as described in the foreword to *Women in Love*, is readied for the mimetic approximation not only of a sexual climax, or negatively of that "terrible frictional violence of death" between Gerald and Gudrun in *Women in Love*, but also the oscillating rhythms of catharsis and parturition, emotional purge and rebirth.

I have begun by discussing the orgastic rhythms of Lawrence's prose because, as Stoehr shows, they offer the most graphic test case for the self-critique of verbalization. But they are to Lawrence's entire rhetoric as sex is to life: no more than an important part. And probably an even greater challenge is offered to expressive language in the simulation not of the sexual death but of the ensuing peace that is passed away to, and that in its turn passes understanding, and words. On the way to this voiceless transcendence of the redefined "being," it is necessary to see that language does not doubt its own legitimacy for emotional registration so much as insist on its unremitting self-analysis and revalidation. "To know, to give utterance" is never to rest complacent, but to "break a way through" the barriers of inexpressiveness itself. The most mistaken attacks on Lawrence's style are those that assume the rhetoric as subservient to, sometimes even abject before, the philosophy. Better to see the gradual building toward a philosophy of rhetoric, turning the style back on itself to produce an argument in and for a revisionist language of fiction.

Lawrence has to be the most polemical of the great novelists, and hence the most deeply rhetorical, more deeply than has yet been thought. Style looks beneath its own surface for the governing principles of anchorage and transformation. Lawrence writes a prose of tested, not flouted limits, most speculative where it is thought to be most cocksure and blustering, a style contesting its own rules. This self-mediated debate, with implications far beyond the linguistic purview of a writer's craft, is ranged and waged from the level of habitual diction to the characteristic scaffolding of whole sentences, from puns and paradoxical phrases, for example—that by putting both ends against an unachieved middle cast doubts upon or ultimately fulfill the possibilities of synthesis—to the large-scale stationing of repetitions, incremental or not, that tax, and, by so doing, test the principles of recurrence and mutability. Lawrence's use of pronouns and reflexives at times suggests a quarrel with the whole idea of antecedence, continuity, and identity in a subjective flux, his deployment of singular and plural verbs a caution against crippling limitations on our ideas of unity and oneness. The disposition of voice, mood, and case—as in passive or transitive predicates, or in the balancing of nominative against accusative forms—serves to assess and at times demur from the received arrangement of subject, object, and agent in sexual relationships, the evident vectors of cause and effect. In similar fashion his serial syntax argues with the tyranny of rigid transitions and his revolutionary use of appositives becomes a debate over the lower and upper limits of the apposite, almost a redefinition of synonymy and metaphor, identity and transformation. Sprung so often from the concrete, the fleshed and blooded, the near tactility of Lawrence's best abstract diction is finally an indictment of evacuated categorical language, a brilliant willing of weight and texture upon ideality. And of special interest for this essay, the pressure Lawrence brings to bear on the verb "to be" and the declension, so to speak, of its gerund form, "being," goes beyond anything in our fictional literature in anatomizing the vocabulary and grammar of existence.

In Lawrence's renegade rhetoric, the most ponderous and idiosyncratic "deliberation" turns out to be just that: a self-adjudication. Not to make the writing sound falsely measured and cerebral, we must nevertheless hear it as an inquiry of passion as well as a cry. The metaphors of arraignment and judgment with which I began discussing the charges against Lawrence's rhetoric are rightly internalized for his prose, which becomes in more than one way trying. But the tables get quickly turned, and to hear Lawrence's style properly emerges as the hearing of a case against anything less flexible, his best effects constantly enlisted as exhibits for the new prosecution. We must begin weighing evidence for the expressive supremacy of Lawrence's non-orgastic rhetoric long before *Lady Chatterley's Lover*, and the book Lawrence thought of as his first sustained breakthrough in experimental techniques, *The Rainbow*, is a good place to start gathering testimony for Lawrence's deft, fertile ambiguities. In the first generation of the narrative, the Polish widow Lydia Lensky represents to Tom Brangwen that influx of foreign glamor that makes habitable again his annulled native ground after the death of his mother. She is the personification of the new and strange, and the pun on her national origin (Lawrence defecting to Joyce's camp?) made by the servant Tilly catches the antipodal magnetism to which Tom is eager to submit: "Mrs. Bentley says as she's fra the Pole—else she *is* a Pole, or summat." She is all three to Tom, a pole of experience to be felt and known, an epitome of otherness, indeed a "summit" to be reached.

I mention the Joycean—or call it Dickensian—touch only as a point of departure for the more thoroughly original and peculiarly Lawrencian effects to come, the syntactic latitudes and subdued punning, for instance, in the passionate betrothal scene of Tom and Lydia, as the increments of serial grammar overlap in a sequence of metamorphic stages impossible to mark off precisely: "And he bent down and kissed her on the lips. And the dawn blazed in them, their new life came to pass, it was beyond all conceiving good, it was so good, that it was almost like a passing-away, a trespass." Tom, whose worst trauma in grammar school arose from his inability to write "in the real composition style," now has his sexual fulfilment sung by Lawrence in a style schooled in the resolute dismantling of grammatical convention and compositional "commonplaces." The style's sliding transformation taxies past us in a paratactic sequence deliberately interknit and elided: not *a, b, c,* but *ab, bc, cd.* Does the modest, pivotal understatement "it was so good" attach backwards or forwards? "It was so good that it was beyond all conceiving" or "It was so good as to be like a passing-away?" Both, of course, especially when we recognize the calculated demolition of idiom taking place along with the syntactic detachments. The experience is "beyond all conceiving" because it is the post-conceptive birth throes of a new life, a life which "came to pass" both as an occurrence and a "passing-away." This ingenious fiddling with idiom reaches a climax in the appositional "trespass." In connection with Lawrence's first novel, *The Trespasser*—with neither explanation nor example, though it is one of the few mentions of Lawrence's word play anywhere in print—Frank Kermode alludes to the noun "trespass" as "a favorite French pun of Lawrence's." The French *trépas* is "death," and what Lawrence has come upon, and made to seem a profound linguistic coincidence, is a single set of letters, approximately, that covers the central ambiguity in his sexual encounters, the transport that is a passing away, the exstasis that becomes a crossing to the unknown. One of the most complex of his fictional experiences is thus halved into articulation and fused again by the bilingual duplicity. Death in Lawrence, when it is other than extinction, is both a world apart and a transgression thereupon, the terminus and the transit, a bound as at once a limit and a leap beyond.

The genius and formal originality of *The Rainbow* resides in its tendency to render these leaps evolutionary. What results is the psychological internalization of the chronicle novel format, so that its three-tiered plot line, like so much of the syntax that locally articulates it, is elided, overlapped, the travails and achievements of one generation made to seem in spiritual apposition to its precursor—with (to adopt perhaps the only commonplace about Lawrence's style to the generational grammar of *The Rainbow* as a whole) new stages of the family biography becoming "incremental repetitions" of their predecessors. The narrative shape of the novel unfolds a composite and progressive psyche that is finally given the name "Ursula," after being designated "Tom" and "Anna" in their turn, but which is always some refraction of the central Brangwen spirit. I trust that a bit more evidence will make clear the rich correspondence between the overall logic of narrative transmutation in this novel and the self-augmenting transformations of Lawrence's rhetoric as they are carried beyond the experiments of *Sons and Lovers*.

To this end there is a vital document. Edward Garnett received the best known letter Lawrence ever wrote, quoted as often and as inevitably as a half dozen of Keats's most renowned letters in any discussion of their author's characteristic artistry. "You mustn't look in my novel," Lawrence both warned and boasted to Garnett, "for the old stable ego—of the character." The hesitation at the dash, if it is more than emphasis, hints at a distinction between the stable ego of character, which you won't find, and some other kind of stable ego which you will, rather than at something beyond or beneath the ego altogether, as this statement is often taken to mean. For the moment Lawrence seems explicit enough: "There is another *ego*, according to whose action the individual is unrecognisable, and passes through, as it were, allotropic states which it needs a deeper sense than any we've been used to exercise, to discover are states of the same single radically unchanged element." Here we seem to have a useful working metaphor for the segmented generations of *The Rainbow*, in which Tom, Anna, and Ursula are not separate egos but allotropes of the Brangwen element, as diamond and coal (to use Lawrence's analogies in this letter) are to the primary carbon. Yet a preceding passage in this letter has tended to mislead readers and confuse the issue. "I don't so much care about what the woman *feels*—in the ordinary usage of the word," says Lawrence, speaking generally about any woman in fiction, any character. "That presumes an *ego* to feel with. I only care about what the woman *is*—what she IS—inhumanly, physiologically, materially . . . what she *is* as a phenomenon (or as representing some greater, inhuman will) instead of what she feels according to the human conception." So the question is unavoidably twofold, if not contradictory. We must look beneath the ego in characterization for the vital phenomenon, and we must look beyond character for the phenomenon of the continuous ego. To give the theory local habitation and a set of names, we note that the truth about the first Tom Brangwen, for instance, as about his daughter and his granddaughter, must be probed for beneath personality and character; but what is found will not distinguish one human entity from the other so much as lead us back to the unifying phenomenon: the family ego, "as representing some greater, inhuman will." The biological dictum that ontogeny recapitulates phylogeny turns biographical in *The Rainbow* and holds for the special case of the Brangwens, where successive characters in the species undergo the metamorphic ordeals of their predecessors in order to trespass for themselves, through a kind of death and rebirth, upon the next evolutionary stage. The underlying continuity is thus both allotropic and hierarchical.

But where does this lead us with respect to style? The letter to Garnett, perused often and minutely, has never been read to suggest anything very specific about the language which, in one verbal experiment after another, aids in precipitating, as it were, Lawrence's new art of characterization. That metaphor from chemistry, on the large scale as well as the small, is just the one we want, for Lawrence's high-risk experimental idiom is precipitate and headlong in the hope that something will eventually settle out, isolate itself into unheard of clarity. Lawrence's revolutionary emphasis on allotropes of the self in fictional narrative thus mandates a change in the very nature of novelistic prose. In the pun on "trespass" we have an example of Lawrence's new elemental diction, whose isolable, separate meanings operate on this allotropic principle. But "trespass" is not simply a pun; it is also, when it suggests death, a metaphor of motion. In this regard it is no accident that another term for figure of speech, "trope," and the chemical term "allotrope" derive from the same Greek root for "turning," whether "aside" or "into," which is indeed the process tropes and allotropes can be seen to result from: figurative diversion and transformation, metaphoric revision in the one and radical metamorphosis in the other. "Trespass" is an especially good allotropic sample because one of its operable meanings names the transitional mobility it at the same time exemplifies, an entrance into or a transgression upon its own alternate definition. The scientific model also works for dubieties of syntax, where two seemingly different parsings of a grammatical arrangement can be resolved as allotropes of a twofold unity hitherto unobserved. So that syntactic ambiguities not only distribute allotropic diction but demonstrate the principle in their own mutable working out. Frequently set in motion by the presence of an unstable syntactic bond, a paratactic loosening of structure for instance, words are alchemized into their own ambiguous allotropes, phrases and clauses into their grammatical alter-egos. This is the eccentric chemistry of lexicon and syntax in Lawrence's style, and suggests a private linguistics in which ambivalence finds its model in chemical valence paradox in nuclear polarization, and where the alternate possibilities of a pun or the repulsing poles of an oxymoron are discovered to be merely aspects "of the same single radically unchanged element," the unitary and harmonizing substance Lawrence is restlessly seeking beneath the play and fluctuation of his surface matter and which can only be made accessible to us if we develop a "deeper sense than any we've been used to exercising."

If this is a new verbal science, it is also a new poetry. Lawrence is the only major English novelist of this century, the first since Hardy, who is also a major poet, and yet next to nothing has been said about the fertile, shifting ground held in common by the poems and the novels as their eminent verbal domain. A single excursion into the ambiguous topography of one of Lawrence's better-known poems should begin to make clear some crucial similarities in his prose and verse styles. The poem is one of many about sexual death and regeneration, with the persona "carried by the current in death over to the new world"; it is called "New Heaven and Earth," and in her book *New Heaven, New Earth* it is singled out by Joyce Carol Oates as a poem whose language is "continually straining its boundaries in an effort to make the strangeness of his experience coherent." Linguistically figured, these are the ultimate boundaries of life and death as they converge in a transformed new space that is simultaneously, on the far and near side of the mortal divide at the instant when the border vanishes, a new heaven and a renewed earth. The opening two stanzas compose one of the finest and most characteristic death "passages" in his verse, turning (as it happens) on that allotropic pun "trespass":

> And so I cross into another world
> shyly and in homage linger for an invitation
> from this unknown that I would trespass on.

I am very glad, and all alone in the world,
all alone, and very glad, in a new world
where I am disembarked at last.

Lawrence is fond of the opening *in medias res* (to what is "And" conjoined?) and here he also opens *in medias legis*, halfway between two denotations of his second word, "so" (between "therefore" and "thus," or "consequently" and "in this manner")—the action described being not only the decisive choice or announced first move of the transforming experience but also the thing itself in process, a duality which the subsequent diction and grammar bear out. The play on "trespass" suggests again both an exit and a deathly accession, a transgression upon not "that unknown" but "this," not over there somewhere but right here, a surprising variant of what Lawrence identifies in a poem called "Silence" as "the great hush of going from this into that." In "New Heaven and Earth" the entire process of arrival is latent in the single demonstrative "this." It is a grammar of encroach and trespass. The chiastic syntax that pivots the next stanza—very glad, all alone, all alone, very glad—is a fitting instance of Lawrence's serial grammar passing over into apposition, fitted precisely to the evoked parallel and gradual identification between the two worlds at the moment of passage, with the mortal distinction between "the world" and "a new world" relinquished by the transfiguration. Even the willful formality of the passive "am disembarked"—instead of the transitive "disembark"—answers both to the grace of agency by which the easy transit is made and to the simultaneity of past and present tenses ("I am arrived," rather than "I have arrived") in this selfless, unassertive transport.

Such an argument for complexities of phrase in Lawrence's poetic language, too often read as an exercise in metrical vagrancy and uninstructed effusion, should attract itself by association to the prose of his novels, which attempts in its own curious motions to elicit certain underlying principles of transformation and identity. Only when Lawrence has provisionally convinced us that the two or more faces of an ambiguity may be stages of a definition in transit, allotropes of a single evolving unity, has he fully equipped his style to invoke and investigate his thematic preoccupations. "The ordinary novel would trace the history of the diamond," Lawrence wrote in that letter to Garnett, "—but I say, 'Diamond, what! This is carbon.' And my diamond might be coal or soot, and my theme is carbon." Life, what! This is being, and his version of life might be death or annihilation, yet his theme is the deeper principle of being. His grammar might seem paratactic or appositional, but his theme is transformation. His noun might suggest either "passage" or the French for "death," but his theme, "trespass," is what they have in common. This is the way Lawrence's imagination has begun, with *The Rainbow*, to explore the secret springs and surface currents of characterization, and I am submitting that it was only natural for a similar sense of language to find itself evolving at the same time in the noticeably more mannered style of this fourth novel. For manner in the best of Lawrence is never sheer mannerism but an expressive means, in the case of *The Rainbow*, and especially of *Women in Love*, a breaking away from the traditional forms of *Sons and Lovers*—and a way through, to the poetry of refurnished "utterance."

The betrothal scene in *The Rainbow* with which I began this part of the discussion was preceded by another version of death and resurgence in the first passionate embrace between Tom and Lydia, during which the hero was struck almost unconscious. "He returned gradually, but newly created, as after a gestation, a new birth, in the womb of darkness. Aerial and light everything was, new as a morning, fresh and newly-begun." The actual moment of metamorphosis and rebirth is signaled by that pivotal grammar which transforms the probable "Everything was aerial and light" into its curiously inverted form. The unidiomatic inflection of the resulting clause lands an odd accent on the verb of being, partially displacing it from its equative status into a verb of simple predication, simple existence, as if to say that only by being so transmuted into the aerial and the bright can reality be honestly said to have come into being at all. Existence itself has been subjected to a limiting but beautiful redefinition by the ability of a single verb, and the syntax it governs, to hover between alternatives. It is indeed the Hamletized verb "to be" and its various deployments—especially the ambiguities loosed by its appearance as "being"—which I wish to concentrate on for the rest of this essay, a task which will seem, I trust, only as narrow as a modest passageway: an entrance, marked off and cleared away, into the enormity of Lawrence's stylistic innovation and the swarm of questions it raises about the role and perimeters of "utterance." This will be, I recognize, not so much a reading of Lawrence as a prolegomenon to one, not a circumscribed essay on his fiction but rather a prelude to any number of them—an article whose primary rewards will therefore be still only in sight, not yet visited upon its pages, when they have come to a close. I might have produced a roster of puns and syntactic uncertainties by way of confirming that Lawrence's style works in the way I believe it does—and works its strange, unexampled magic. Instead I have tried not to prove this, but to put just a few of these stylistic ventures to the proof by giving some hint of their full aesthetic power and authority. The main burden of what remains will fall on two crucial but little-discussed passages in *The Rainbow* and *Women in*

Love, Ursula at the microscope in Chapter XV of the former, Birkin and Ursula on the night before their wedding in Chapter XXVII of the latter, scenes whose climaxes arrive, respectively, with the phrases "a consummation, a being infinite" and "a consummation of my being and of her being in a new one." Criticism, however sensitive, is necessarily less concise than poetry, even a novelist's poetry, and it is no fault of stylistics, only a testament to the evocative and concentrating powers of Lawrence's style, that it takes so many more words for analysis to bring the full reach of art to light. My hope is that when thus highlighted, the genius of Lawrence's often perverse style will stand revealed for what it is, an effort on behalf of that bright book of life, as Lawrence called the novel, to make it all the more lustrous and illuminating.

In the last important fiction Lawrence completed before his death, the use of an ambiguous "to be" variant is still part of his stylistic stock-in-trade, and is accompanied by a more obvious play with diction. When Isis first touches Christ's wounds in *The Man Who Died*, they are healed to ecstasy: " 'They are suns!' he said. 'They shine from your touch. They are my atonement with you'." The noun "atonement," especially in connection with Christ's mortified flesh, is an ironic reinterpretation of the Christian "Passion," the suffering for and remission of sins. The sexual passion of the man who died is a unification by touch, here the touch of Isis, on the next page of the entire living and inanimate universe, not a reparation for so much as an atoning *with*, the deeper repair of the soul's sexless isolation: "This is the great atonement, the being in touch. The gray sea and the rain, the wet narcissus and the woman I wait for, the invisible Isis and the unseen sun are all in touch, and at one." The redefined grace of "atonement" is by this point a manifest pun on "attunement" as well, both allotropic nouns resonating, just as they do within the single spelling, within the larger harmony of passionate and universal concord. There is also an ambiguous glimmer in the appostive phrase "the being in touch." The immediate idiomatic sense of the words does not, if we are used to Lawrence by now, overrule the possibility of an alternate reading, so that the phrase as written is felt to have emerged from a blended resolution of two allotropic base sentences: "He is in touch" and "He exists only in touch." This is the atonement—the restitution that becomes a restoration—by which the man who died realizes that in touch and only in touch is predicated his true being.

The distinction between kinds of "being" has lasted through to Lawrence's last long story from an experiment with it in his first great novel, *Sons and Lovers*. That inching over of "to be" from copula to intransitive we saw in *The Rainbow*'s inversion, "Aerial and light everything was," had taken a small but moving part two years before in the subterranean verbal drama enacted at the end of *Sons and Lovers*, a schizophrenic dialogue between Paul Morel and the voice of his own despair over the death of his mother:

> Then, quite mechanically and more distinctly, the conversation began again inside him.
>
> "She's dead. What was it all for—her struggle?"
> That was his despair wanting to go after her.
> "You're alive."
> "She's not."
> "She is—in you."
> Suddenly he felt tired with the burden of it.
> "You've got to keep alive for her sake," said his will in him.

As if the psychological fissuring of the scene runs so deep as to divide not only voice but verbal structure as well, there is a movement toward ambiguity in this exchange from patterns of clear attribution ("She's dead," "You're alive") through an elliptical format, with "alive" understood, that takes a deceptively parallel track into pure predication as the verb of being breaks out from its contracted form ("She's not," "She is"). There is no contradiction, just a double perspective; the language of negation is not equivalent to the language of nothing, and this is a linguistic fact which Lawrence raises to metaphysical status. Granted that his mother is not alive, she can still be, exist, in him. This is the blessing and the burden of immortality through love. Death kills, yes, but it does not necessarily cancel, and after life there is still being by being loved. The metalinguistic distance between "she is not alive" and "she is not" can be as great as eternity.

LEO BERSANI

Lawrentian Stillness

Matter moves; the spirit is still. The opposition between agitation and stillness in D. H. Lawrence has almost the diagrammatic neatness of the Cartesian dualism between matter and mind. In *Women in Love*, the nonhuman is identified with the mechanical, and the mechanical is associated with "infinitely repeated motion." Like Descartes, Gerald Crich dreams of the conquest of matter by mind. But for Descartes, the conquest is made possible by intellectual procedures which systematize the mind's unique capacity for knowledge (and therefore illustrate the intrinsic opposition between mind and matter). Gerald, the Industrial Magnate, begins with a kind of militant Cartesian sense of mankind as "mystically contradistinguished against inanimate Matter," but his conquest of matter (specifically, his struggle "with the earth and the coal it enclosed") depends on his *imitating* certain qualities of matter. Man subjugates nature through his will, but will in Lawrence is the inhuman principle of the mind, and in constructing machines which embody his will, Gerald makes himself like matter in order to subdue it:

> There were two opposites, his will and the resistant Matter of the earth. And between these he could establish the very expression of his will, the incarnation of his power, a great and perfect machine, a system, an activity of pure order, pure mechanical repetition, repetition ad infinitum, hence eternal and infinite. He found his eternal and his infinite in the pure machine-principle of perfect co-ordination into one pure, complex, infinitely repeated motion, like the spinning of a wheel; but a productive spinning, as the revolving of the universe may be called a productive spinning, a productive repetition through eternity, to infinity.

From *The Yale Review* 1, vol. 65 (October 1975).

"Infinitely repeated motion" is the fundamental property—at once terrifying and desirable—of the nonhuman universe. It is terrifying because any repeated motion—from a particular compulsive ritual to the "productive spinning" of the universe itself—can, by its very nature, never be penetrated by consciousness. Pure, undifferentiated repetition is always (even when it lasts only a short time) intrinsically infinite, eternal, and nonhuman. We can imagine the *end* (the temporal finitude) of a series only when we can perceive differences among the units of the series. The perception of differences acts for us as a guarantee of both renewal and death: to be aware of difference, in mental and physical phenomena, is to know that life exists, that is, that things appear and disappear, that there are birth and death. Even the difference between two logical propositions, or two rocks, or two rays of light can operate as an epistemologically useful metaphor for the organic processes which make of life continual change.

Now nothing is more timeless than mechanical time; a clock endlessly repeats, at precisely identical intervals, the sound by which it marks what we call the passage of time but which we *hear* as the repetition of changeless intervals. In *Women in Love*, it is appropriate that Gudrun—a creature, like Gerald, of mechanical will—should express her terror of repetition in terms of the monotonous movements of a clock. Life with Gerald would be "the terrible bondage of this tick-tack of time, this twitching of the hands of the clock, this eternal repetition of hours and days"; and even in Gerald's love she finds "the same ticking, the same twitching across the dial, a horrible mechanical twitching forward over the face of the hours." All life, for Gudrun, resolves itself into a tick-tack from which there is no escape. For pure repetition can't even be thought about; it can only be borne. The clock in Gudrun's parlor has "a ruddy, round, slant-eyed, joyous-painted face" inserted in its dial; with the ticks of the clock, the face wags back and forth "with the most ridiculous ogle," giving to Gudrun (overcome by a "maddened disgust") "an obstrusive 'glad-eye' " at each movement. The image marvelously expresses a sense of helplessness in the face of mechanical repetition. A relentless, nonhuman movement is hallucinated into a kind of conniving and obscene mockery of the entrapped mind. Gudrun's horror is her intuition that one's primary experience of life may be merely one of indefinite repetition; it is the horror of a metaphysical rather than an anecdotal boredom.

But there is also something desirable in "infinitely repeated motion." It is Loerke, the industrial artist, who preaches most explicitly in the novel what almost amounts to a religion of continuous motion. The granite frieze he is doing for a granite factory in Cologne is "a representation of a fair, with peasants and artisans in an orgy of enjoyment," in "a frenzy of chaotic motion." Man at the fair, he tells Ursula and Gudrun, " 'is fulfilling the counterpart of labour—the machine works him instead of he the machine. He enjoys the mechanical motion in his own body.' " And when Gudrun asks him if there is " 'nothing but work—mechanical work,' " he answers: " 'No, it is nothing but this, serving a machine, or enjoying the motion of a machine—motion, that is all. You have never worked for hunger, or you would know what god governs us.' " The appeal of repeated motion is identical with its horror: it lies in the illusion of being an immortal machine, or inorganic matter, rather than a mortal human being. The maddening tick-tack of the clock can suddenly become a principle of liberation. The beauty of a machine is that its nature is perfectly fulfilled by its movements; it exists only within its own operations. What Lawrence calls the will is that human faculty by which we manage to function without interruption, to continue "moving" as if we had severed all connections with our own disruptive desires and anxieties as well as those of other people. "To work for hunger" is indeed an excellent apprenticeship in the skill of mechanical being, for in extreme material need the preservation of life itself depends on our ability to go on repeating the deathlike motions of a continuously efficient machine. One can stop a machine, but one can't distract it; it has no connections beyond its own system of organized motions. And for human beings, will is what allows us to continue as if nothing were happening to us apart from the process of continuing.

The perfection of Loerke's nature is precisely this inability to be distracted from his work (his operations, or functioning). And he can be "a pure, unconnected will, stoical and momentaneous" because "in the last issue he cared about nothing, he was troubled about nothing, he made not the slightest attempt to be at one with anything." Gudrun's shift of loyalty from Gerald to Loerke is a choice *against* relations, in favor of unconnected singleness. She will now live perhaps entirely in the world of the tick-tack. And, as Lawrence brilliantly suggests, in a world of infinite, eternal motion, the only *possibility* is death. We can see the logic of this truth in both Gerald and Gudrun. Gerald exalts the will and the machine in order to flee from the organic death which terrifies him. And in a sense, as I've suggested, "infinitely repeated motion" is indeed a form of immortality; the repetition of the same is not a process of organic matter. But it's also true that without differences and without connections (and connections bring differences into the history of our movements), nothing can happen, no matter how long we "repeat ourselves." Or rather, since the body does change even if the mind has committed itself to what Lawrence calls indestructible Matter, death is all that can happen. Gerald's life is, most profoundly, a chase after death, and Lawrence says of Gudrun at the end of the novel that "the lovely, iridescent, indefinite charm" which she finds in the notion of pure possibility ("Anything might come to pass on the morrow") is equivalent to the charm of "pure illusion. All possibility—because death was inevitable, and *nothing* was possible but death."

The rejection of life gives the illusion of immortality and of infinite possibility. But the triumph of will is essentially the triumph of the impulse to die. Death is the only interesting event—the only event to look forward to—in a life of perfectly regulated repetitions designed to save the self from unexpected changes and connections. "Infinitely repeated motion" is thus curiously linked to the end of all movement. Repetition, as Freud suggests in *Beyond the Pleasure Principle*, is the activity which brings together the pleasure principle and the death impulse. If pleasure results from the reduction of tension due to stimuli, the ultimate pleasure is the elimination of all stimuli, and the wish to die is a fantasy of ecstatic inertia. In order to conserve itself, the organism chooses to repeat rather than to change; repetition is the movement which is meant to save us from all movement. Repetition, in a deeply paradoxical way, is the *activity of inertia*. Doomed to live, we can express our urge to "return" to the peace of inanimate matter only by maintaining the tension of constantly performing identical movements.

Motion serves death; and Birkin, Lawrence's spokesman in *Women in Love*, tries to teach and live the difficult lesson of a life-preserving stillness. The critique of repeated motion extends to all kinds of activity. It is perhaps most interesting—and most surprising—when it is made with respect to sexual activity. Ursula's need for agitation in love brings a discordant note into her relation with Birkin, even at moments when they seem most harmoniously at one with each other. "She wished he were passionate," Lawrence writes of Ursula in the chapter called "Excurse," "because in passion she was at home. But this [the "new heaven" of Birkin's eyes "beautiful and soft and immune from stress or excitement"] was so still and frail, as space is more frightening than force." Within sex, there is good sex and bad sex, and—in striking conformity to the argument we've been following—the best Lawrentian sex seems to involve the least movement. The villain in sex is friction. Before making love with Mellors, Lady Chatterley would get her satisfaction in sex by working herself up and down on Mick's penis after he had had his orgasm. Not only was this sex frictional, but the friction, so to speak, went on twice as long as "necessary" because Connie would begin her sex when Mick had finished his. With Mellors, Connie gets beyond the sharp pleasures of rubbing and rubbed skin; he initiates her into a kind of rippling, liquefying orgasm, into an "unspeakable motion that was not really motion, but pure deepening whirlpools of sensation swirling deeper and deeper through all her tissue and consciousness, till she was one perfect concentric fluid of feeling." In the same way, Cipriano educates Kate, in *The Plumed Serpent*, out of her need for "the white ecstasy of frictional satisfaction, the throes of Aphrodite of the foam." He brings her "to the new, soft, heavy, hot flow, when she was like a fountain gushing noiseless and with urgent softness from the volcanic deeps."

There is frictional sex, and there is frictional thought. In *The Plumed Serpent*, Lawrence describes the pleasure of the former as "one final spasm of white ecstasy which was like sheer knowing." With Loerke, Gudrun enjoys a kind of frictional knowledge, "the last subtle activities of analysis and breaking down." Gerald is for Gudrun "the most crucial instance of the existing world," and when she all but murdered him, she is finished with life and with the world, and there is only what Lawrence calls "the inner, individual darkness, sensation within the ego, the obscene religious mystery of ultimate reduction, the mystic frictional activities of diabolic reducing down, disintegrating the vital organic body of life." Reductive analysis is the mental equivalent of frictional sex. In the same way that the ecstasy of frictional sex results from the repetition of distinct thrusting motions, "the subtle thrills" of reductive knowledge come from a kind of rubbing of experience until it breaks down into a series of distinct units. Reduction is the intellectual screwing of life through repetition and relentlessly regular thrust of analytical understanding.

The "love" beyond love to which Birkin brings a reluctant Ursula is, in its most perfect expression, a "star-equilibrium which alone is freedom," a juxtaposition in which they connect but don't fuse. The connection described toward the end of "Excurse" is physical but nonsexual; it is mystical but within the body ("pure mystical nodality of physical being"); and it is a connection between minds without thought, one coming from "that other basic mind, the deepest physical mind." I emphasize, as Lawrence does, these apparent paradoxes partly to stress the difficulty of making logical sense of the passage in question. The second half of "Excurse" is the section in *Women in Love* where Lawrence is obviously taking the greatest novelistic risks. He must put into the "agitations" of speech, into the "movements" of thought, a state about which there may be nothing to say except that it is inaccessible to whatever might be said or thought. Nonetheless, Lawrence makes the attempt to put something of this state into words, although he has to rely on such apparently self-canceling expressions as "physical mind" and "mystical nodality of physical being" to suggest the literally unspeakable nature of his "star-equilibrium." (He also relies on a certain heightening of tone which can easily be found ridiculous, and which indeed most critics have eagerly pounced on. As we enter something that is "neither love nor passion," we also move from the narrative voice of a realistic, often satirical modern novel to the incantatory tone of biblical affirmations: "It was the daughters of men coming back to the sons of God, the strange inhuman sons of God who are in the beginning," and: "She had found one of the sons of God from the Beginning, and he had found one of the first most luminous daughters of men." The jolting shifts in "Excurse" between "sons of God" [or "an Egyptian Pharaoh"] and Birkin's car or his bickering with Ursula give a good idea of the difficulties, for realistic fiction, in this mingling of mystical intuition with prosaic details of modern life.)

The paradoxical expressions I mentioned a moment ago are perhaps only superficially self-canceling. They keep meaning poised between two contradictory words or expressions, they immobilize thought in an equilibrium of opposites. "Mind" is not meant to cancel out "physical" in "physical mind." Unlike Mallarméan negation, Lawrentian paradox (and paradox in general) maintains all its incompatible terms. A first term is never erased; but the thought that might use that term as a point of departure is paralyzed by the juxtaposition of another term which gives us an unthinkable phrase. In a sense, there is nothing to "understand"; we are merely asked to maintain a connection between two words. The narrative continues, but it thus manages to suggest its own arrest. An enforced stillness on the stylistic level runs parallel to the characters' spiritual stillness. Now there is, apparently, some movement in this state. At the back of Birkin's thighs, Ursula feels "the strange mystery of his life-motion," and "a rich new circuit, a new current of passional electric energy" floods them both with a new and rich peace. "There were strange fountains in his body," and "deeper, further in mystery than the phallic source [the source of friction], came the floods of ineffable darkness and ineffable riches." But Lawrence suggests that even this movement is compatible with, is perhaps even equivalent to, stillness: "the strange and magical current of force in [Birkin's] back and loins, and down his legs" is "so perfect that it stayed him immobile." Fundamentally, there would seem to be no compromise possible between friction and stillness. *Women in Love* moves between the opposite poles of "infinitely repeated motion" and Pharaoh-like stillness. And while there are gradations from one extreme to the other, the polarity between the two is anything but a "star-equilibrium"; it is polarity of pure antagonism.

To what extent does the Lawrentian contrast between agitation and stillness accommodate novelistic characters? In a well-known letter to Edward Garnett (15 June 1914), Lawrence spoke of his indifference to the psychology of traditional fiction: "You mustn't look in my novel for the old stable *ego* of the character. There is another ego, according to whose action the individual is unrecognizable, and passes through, as it were, allotropic states which it needs a deeper sense than any other we've been used to exercise, to discover are states of the same single radically unchanged element." And in one of the essays of *The Reality of Peace* (published in the summer of 1917, shortly after Lawrence finished his rewriting of *Women in Love*), Lawrence seems to be explicitly defining what the content of that other ego might be: "For there are ultimately only two desires, the desire of life and the desire of death. Beyond these is pure being, where I am absolved from desire and made perfect." The fact which most interests Lawrence about human beings is the extent to which they are being carried along by either currents of life energy or currents of death energy. Now the impulse to live and the impulse to die are not exactly attributes of personality; rather, they are attempts to enlarge on or to obliterate the very field in which the anecdotes of personality are possible. Personality must therefore be read as a system of signs or of choices which can be deciphered back to a primary choice of life or of death. And the deciphering takes almost no time at all in Lawrence. Interpretation is immediate, and tends to bypass the mediating and distorting vehicle of language. There are flashes of recognition instead of an interpretive process. Lawrentian desire has to be extricated from language, for life and death energies *in* language are already tamed or derived energies. Or, to put it another way, they are desires already on display, both showing and hiding themselves in an essentially social theatre. In the kind of simplifying vision which Lawrence's characters have of one another, individuality in the usual sense is disregarded and only the organism's inclination to destroy or to survive and grow is registered. Perhaps Lawrence asks us really to accept only one assumption about human beings: that it is possible to know at once (although it may not be formulated at once) if people's impulse to live is stronger than their impulse to die, or vice versa.

These intuitions account for the sudden shifts of language in *Women in Love*—shifts which may puzzle or irritate us—from the prosaic to the extravagant. When the connection is made between two life currents or two death currents, minds "go," people "lapse out" and "swoon," they have "transports" and "keen paroxysms," and the "veil" of "ultimate consciousness" is "torn." Nothing is more disorienting in *Women in Love* than the use of such expressions as descriptive narrative accompaniments to the most banal action or the most controlled, unremarkable dialogue. Hermione enters the church for Laura Crich's wedding, sees that Birkin isn't there, and apparently without the slightest change in her behavior, "A terrible storm came over her, as if she were drowning. . . . It was beyond death, so utterly null, desert." The first time Gudrun sees Gerald, she is immediately "magnetised" by the appearance of a man "so new, unbroached, pure as an arctic thing." She has "a keen paroxysm, a transport . . . all her veins were in a paroxysm of violent sensation," and she feels herself already enveloped, alone with him, in " 'some pale gold, arctic light.' " Now these sudden crises of "swooning" or "lapsing out" can make a Lawrentian narrative seem both quite mad and quite monotonous. The variety of social encounters and the richness of psychological textures are constantly being dismissed by unrelentingly repetitious references to those currents of life and death energies which underlie both social history and the nuances of individual psychology. What is involved here is nonetheless a radical redefinition of character and desire in fiction. Proust—who might be used as an instructive point of comparison—is much more hesitant than Lawrence in his subversion of what Lawrence calls in *The Plumed Serpent* the "assembled self." Literature for the Proustian narrator is in part a resolution of crises in which he feels emptied of all being. The literary work provides him with reassuring evidence of "an individual, identical and permanent self." It is a document of ontological security; literature can give to Marcel the stable and fixed image of an identity he finds neither in introspection (to turn inward is to find only "an empty apparatus") nor in the anguishing otherness of the external world. Writing fixes the writer's self in an external self-portrait which never escapes from the writer's control. . . .

For Lawrence, language is, at worst, a kind of abstract frictional activity which allows individuals and civilizations both to obfuscate and secretly to satisfy their impulse toward death. Surely, as we shall see in a moment, language can at least make us aware of how easily it can be enlisted in the service of death, and thereby help to stimulate the opposite impulse to reach a life-producing, silent stillness.

One of Lawrence's central problems is to find a way to identify individuals within a mode of characterization which discards the usual signs of individuality. In part, he relies on the individualizing psychology of realistic fiction. His characters have distinct physical, psychological, and social identities. Each one has a recognizable and separate style of being; conventional personalities make for a general clarity of characterization. In a sense, the realistic character-portrait provides Lawrence with a safety valve in his risky experimentation with character as a mass of life and death energies. Furthermore, conventional characterization is especially useful since Lawrence, in his redefinition of character, doesn't discard individuality; it is, in fact, an ideal which personality prevents us from attaining. Personality is the trap in which the individual gets lost. It is the sign of the self's inability to remain alone, an alluring invitation to self-destroying fusions. But, Birkin insists, " 'there is a real impersonal me, that is beyond love, beyond any emotional relationship. . . . The root is beyond love, a naked kind of isolation, an isolated me, that does *not* meet and mingle, and never can.' " Beyond personality, " 'there is no speech and no terms of agreement . . . no standard for action . . . because one is outside the pale of all that is accepted, and nothing known applies.' " Lawrence must therefore describe or at least suggest an individuality to which the individualizing attributes of personality are irrelevant. And he must also find a way to differentiate among characters about whom the only essential thing to be said is that they wish to die or that they wish to live.

The latter enterprise is all the more difficult in that life energies and death energies are often manifested in almost identical interests and almost identical speech. There is realistic diversification of character in *Women in Love*, but there are also striking continuities among the characters. And the thematic recurrences in the novel will create considerable confusion for us if we insist on keeping doctrinal distinctions absolutely clear. The characters in Lawrence's novel seem to have been conceived as almost imperceptible variations on a few major themes. And a scale of occasionally blurred gradations among the various versions of a theme is nonetheless meant to illustrate a sharp and fundamental opposition between the will to live and the will to die. It is particularly striking that almost all the other characters repeat Birkin's ideas in one way or another. They don't merely illustrate what he says about people; they often say what he says, and even seem to live as he lives. And yet they are clearly meant to be negative embodiments of his ideas and his life.

What, for example, are we to think of the opposition between sensual spontaneity and cerebral knowledge in the novel? Hermione's attack on modern self-consciousness (the young, she says, are " 'burdened to death with self-consciousness' ") is a fairly good recitation of a favorite Lawrentian idea, but Rupert angrily answers that young people don't " 'have too much mind, but too little.' " But he also argues for the " 'dark sensual body of life.' " Hermione wants passion and the instincts only through her head: " 'You have only your will and your conceit of consciousness,' " Birkin brutally tells her, " 'and your lust for power, to *know.*' " On the other hand, when he tries, later in the novel, to resolve the contradictions he recognizes in his always talking about "sensual fulfilment," he concludes that "he did not want a further sensual experience." He imagines what happened in Africa thousands of years ago as a "lapse from pure integral being, from creation and liberty," a fall into "mindless progressive knowledge through the senses, knowledge arrested and ending in the senses." What he wants with Ursula is "another way, . . . the paradisal entry into pure, single being, . . . a lovely state of free proud singleness" apparently different from those frightening "sensual subtle realities" of Africa which are "far beyond the scope of phallic investigation." But the fulfillment described in "Excurse" comes, as we have seen, from "the deepest physical mind." Ursula releases "a new current of passional electric energy" in Birkin's body, and she thereby discovers a bodily "source deeper than the phallic source"—but, I suppose, different from the "awful" meta-phallic "sensual subtle realities" of African art. For the Africans, to go beyond the phallic is to reach "knowledge such as the beetles have, which live purely within the world of corruption and cold dissolution." For Birkin and Ursula, to go beyond the phallic is to come upon "floods of ineffable darkness and ineffable richness"; it is "to be awake and potent in that other basic mind, the deepest physical mind."

I don't think there is much to be gained from trying to figure out exactly what differences Lawrence means to establish between a bad sensuality of the mind (Hermione), a meta-phallic corrupt sensuality (Africa), and a good meta-phallic sensuality of what he calls "the deepest physical mind." We can make sense of the distinctions only by being very abstract about them, and Lawrence himself—rather admirably—is at times willing to admit that he is floundering among his own concepts. It is more interesting to look at some of the effects in the novel of these blurred distinctions among characters and ideas. They make, curiously, for a tendency toward fusion: separate beings, separate cultures, and separate ideas in the novel are constantly being rubbed against one another in unharmonious friction. There are numerous examples of this not quite identical, frictional repetition. In Birkin, "singleness" is a positive term. But the word is also used to describe Loerke: Gudrun finds in him "an uncanny singleness, a quality of being by himself, not in contact with anybody else, that marked out an artist to her." There is, then, a wholly unconnected singleness, and there is also, as Birkin tells Ursula, the singleness that makes possible " 'an equilibrium, a pure balance of two single beings:—as the stars balance each other.' " It would surely be unjust to apply to Birkin Lawrence's remark that Loerke "made not the slightest attempt to be at one with anything." Nevertheless, there is a certain indifference in Birkin too, and Gerald suffers from his "consciousness of the young, animal-like spontaneity of detachment" in the other man: "He knew Birkin could do without him—could forget, and not suffer." Lawrence plays dangerously with these similarities; we are always being asked to make crucial but extremely subtle distinctions. We must keep Birkin's singleness separate from Loerke's and Gudrun's autonomy; we mustn't confuse Gerald's idolatry of organization and Rupert's pursuit of harmony. Winifred Crich is a strange hybrid of Loerke and Birkin: some of the terms used to describe her "nihilistic" nature will be taken up again to characterize Loerke ("she never formed vital connections . . ."), and others remind us of Gerald's judgment of Birkin (her will "was so strangely and easily free," she is like "a soulless bird . . . without attachment or responsibility beyond the moment").

Finally, what does it mean to be an artist? Gudrun's art is a function of her need to murder other people spiritually by reaching some final knowledge about them. (And of course her need to know reminds us of Hermione's obsessive lust for knowledge.) Gudrun likes to place people "in their true light, give them their own surroundings, settle them for ever." Thus she disposes of the guests at Laura Crich's wedding in Chapter One: "She knew them, they were finished, sealed and stamped and finished with, for her." She "loves" Gerald until she feels that she knows him completely. "She wanted to touch him and touch him and touch him, till she had him all in her hands, till she had strained him into her knowledge." And this is exactly the attitude which Gudrun brings to her painting. As she sketches water-plants, she "sees" them rising from the mud; and her seeing is a kind of knowledge untranslatable into words: ". . . she could feel their turgid fleshy structure in a sensuous vision, she *knew* how they rose out of the mud, she *knew* how they thrust out from themselves, how they stood stiff and succulent against the air." Now final knowledge about anything is deathlike. " 'You can only have knowledge strictly,' " Birkin announces in "Breadalby," " 'of things concluded, in the past. It's like bottling the liberty of last summer in the bottled gooseberries.' " But, first of all, there are similarities between Gudrun's obsessive need to know through touch and that "unspeakable communication in touch" which Birkin and Ursula enjoy. For the latter is also a kind of knowledge, although it is knowledge of something "never to be seen with the eye, or known with the mind, only known as a palpable revelation of living otherness." Furthermore, Birkin's notion of art includes the idea of complete knowledge. It's true that, like Ursula, he would reject Loerke's (and Gudrun's) absolute separation of art from life, but when he explains to Gerald why the carved African figure of a woman in labor is "art," he says: "It conveys a complete truth. . . . It contains the whole truth of that state, whatever you feel about it." Finally, we are by no means meant to feel that Gudrun's art is bad or uninteresting (Birkin praises it), and, more significantly, Birkin explains why he is copying a Chinese drawing of geese in almost exactly the same terms used to describe Gudrun's sensuous knowledge of the water-plants. He " 'gets more of China, copying this picture, than reading all the books.' " He satisfies a kind of ontological curiosity about other people's most intimate perception of reality: " 'I know what centres they live from—what they perceive and feel—the hot, stinging centrality of a goose in the flux of cold water and mud—the curious bitter stinging heat of a goose's blood, entering their own blood like an inoculation of corruptive fire—fire of the cold-burning mud—the lotus mystery.' "

From the point of view of traditional fiction, these transparent analogies subvert a desirable diversity of character and plot. Like Proust, Lawrence nonchalantly exposes what the realistic novelist seems anxious to disguise: the derivation of his work from a single creative imagination. The characters of *Women in Love*, like those of *A la Recherche du temps perdu*, repeat, with variations, a single psychology. And the clarity of the repetitions in both works tends to destroy the realistic myth of distance between the novelist and his work. There is no difference of being between the author and the world he describes; fiction is always a form of autobiography, and the writer's relation to his work is fundamentally one of paternity. But in Lawrence the psychological and thematic repetitions which I've just briefly outlined undermine an explicit credo of singleness. The distinctions among characters are blurred by similarities of attitude and of temperament; and the mystical notion of singleness risks being compromised by a tendency toward fusion, or psychological community, on the level of realistic personality. On the one hand, such fusions are clearly not what Lawrence intends. In the foreword to *Women in Love*, Lawrence takes note of the fact that "in point of style, fault is often found with the continual, slightly modified repetition." His first answer to this criticism is that such repetitions are "natural" to him, and then he adds: ". . . every natural crisis in emotion or passion or understanding comes from this pulsing, frictional to-and-fro which works up to culmination." It is as if he found an analogous type of frictional characterization necessary in order to work toward that spiritual culmination in distinct singleness which Ursula and Birkin come close to attaining at the end of "Excurse." We have, then, a curious case of frictional movement in the service of life-creating stillness. Frictional repetition is not merely a negative quality in Lawrence's world. *Women in Love* is a succession of scenes in which *nearly* identical points of view antagonistically confront, or rub up against, one another. All the characters repeat, with more or less subtle variations, a few principal themes. But the very blurring of points of view which results from these repetitions is meant to serve the most finely differentiating activity. In part, the Lawrentian technique of characterization expresses the tentative and experimental nature of Lawrence's fiction. Each novel tries out several possibly destructive or life-creating selves. Novelistic character is a means of testing the life and death potentialities of certain styles of being; and the fate of a specific character, as it slowly takes shape in the course of a novel, reveals the value of his or her style, its complicity with life or with death.

But the goal of frictional characterization is nonetheless stillness of being, a state beyond movement and even character. And there would be nothing to say about that state: a case of true singleness could have no point of reference, it could not even be compared to another example of " 'an isolated me, that does *not* meet and mingle, and never can.' " We can perhaps now appreciate the full significance of Lawrence's implied comparison of stylistic repetition to the pulsing to-and-fro of frictional sex. Friction in sex "works up to culmination," which means to the end of friction and of sex. The only tolerable aspect of frictional sex for Lawrence seems to be that it leads to a kind of collapse, to an at least temporary, nonsexual stillness which he finds more desirable than the agitations of sexual passion. In the same way, what makes frictional characterization acceptable may be that it points the way to a "culmination" in, say, the inexpressible Pharaoh-like stillness of Birkin in "Excurse." And if that stillness were definitive, neither sex, nor character, nor the novel would any longer be necessary. Nearly identical versions of being would finally give way to a single version of being. The gaps separating characters would be closed, and the already limited range of characterization would be reduced to the single "point" of the ideal spiritual state. As the orgasm relieves the body of tiring movement, so perfect stillness would relieve the novelist of the fatiguing obligation to move constantly back and forth among identical but antagonistic versions of the energies which produce life and death.

In exactly what way does the love between Birkin and Ursula serve life? There is a curious resemblance between Birkin's and Gerald's ideas of "perfect union" with a woman. Gerald pursues Gudrun in order to escape from the exhausting struggle of his conscious will against "the hollow void of death in his soul." When he first makes love to her, "the miraculous soft effluence of her breast suffused over him, over his seared, damaged brain, like a healing lymph, like a soft, soothing flow of life itself, perfect as if he were bathed in the womb again." But this "soothing flow of life" is of course also a deathlike peace. With Gudrun, Gerald escapes not from the void of death, but rather from his resistance to his profound desire to die. Toward the end of the novel, Gudrun resentfully thinks that "the secret of his passion, his for ever unquenched desire for her [was] that he needed her to put him to sleep, to give him repose." In a sense, she allows him to satisfy his impulse to be murdered—an impulse which largely accounts for his sexual appeal. He has an exciting passivity; just below the surface of his active will, there is a willingness to be penetrated or violated to which even Birkin is by no means insensitive. Sex with Gudrun is a preliminary version of Gerald's final sleep in the snow; love is a seductive version of death.

How different from this is the peace which Birkin seeks? Perhaps beyond what we might call the secondary ambiguities of sex in Lawrence (lack of genital vitality, disgust of female sexuality, anal eroticism), there is the more fundamental ambiguity of love as a longing to die disguised as a formula for life. We have seen the connections between "infinitely repeated motion" and death; but there may be even more profound connections between a nondesiring stillness and death. Birkin sees the connection: he tells Ursula that he wants "love that is like sleep," and that love should be like sleep "so that it is like death," but he makes this admission respectable, so to speak, by falling back on the ancient notion that the old self must die in order for a new self to be born. But even his attempts to describe the new self bring us back to suggestions of death. In "Moony," Lawrence is careful to point out that Birkin's peace with Ursula is not sleep, but what he describes is, so to speak, a conscious sleep: "To be content in bliss, without desire or insistence anywhere, this was heaven: to be together in happy stillness." The ultimate Lawrentian goal is the death of desire.

To desire is to experience a lack or an absence; and the sign of desire is movement (actual physical movement or the mental movements of thought and fantasy). We move in order to remove the lack, to make something absent present. Such movement is also the sign of individual life. It indicates my sense of my particular existence, that is, my sense of myself as not being all reality. I begin to live psychically as an individual when I recognize, in desire, the existence of realities distinct from myself. My desires provide a kind of negative of my individuality: they implicitly define me by explicitly defining what I lack. Thus individual life is inseparable from desire and movement. This is of course by no means the same thing as saying that individuality itself is desirable; there may be no reason to prefer individuality to an experience of peaceful, nondesiring fusion with the universe. But then we should realize that we are aspiring, precisely, to our death as individuals. Lawrence, however, wants to propose the peace of being without desire as the condition for true singleness or individuality. Furthermore, such peace is meant to be creative of life. Now it's true that the movements of desire, if they express or indeed create the reality of an individual life, also erode life. We *spend* life in our agitated pursuit of more life. To live is to accept a process of dying, and we can escape (or think we are escaping) the dying which we initiate by living only if we eliminate desire from life. And one way to do this is, as I suggested at the beginning of this essay, to engage in a type of movement which has no history. This "solution" is the illusory immortality of "infinitely repeated motion," of which, as we have seen, Lawrence provides a brilliant critique. Exact repetition implicitly denies the desiring individual (and therefore individual life); it would make the self eternal by removing its activity from all contingencies (history doesn't affect repetition). I called such repetition the activity of inertia. And what I'm now suggesting is a secret complicity in Lawrence between "infinitely repeated motion" and the idea of still singleness. The peace of Lawrentian love is the literal inertia which "infinitely repeated motion" paradoxically achieves through purposeless agitation.

There is nothing to do in Lawrentian love but sustain it. And the novel, as an artistic form, mercilessly exposes the difficulties of such a task. Lawrence has chosen to place his characters, for better or for worse, in the framework of a generally realistic fiction, and it is a virtue—at once dull and impressive—of realistic fiction to pursue the consequences of mystical ecstasy in everyday relations. The end of *Women in Love* suggests a certain staleness in the lovers' union, and the danger of their beginning to look merely old and tired. Lawrence's perfect lovers would be engaged in the hopeless task of repeating an intensity without movement, a state without content. To a certain extent, Birkin (without of course admitting or even knowing it) has merely found a *doctrine* to justify Gerald's impulse to rest in the definitive sleep of death. It is a doctrine which claims individualizing and life-creating energies for a deathlike stillness. Birkin, like Gerald, must find a way out of the exhausting erosions of desire. Love is an escape from a desiring life which does in fact both vitalize and kill us: it is the panacea which unites both the death-seekers and the supposed life-seekers of Lawrence's fiction in the peace of nonverbal, nonmoving, nondesiring spiritual death.

Finally, however, the peace of "Excurse" is by no means followed only by boredom; the lovers also return to conflict. About a third of

Women in Love takes place after "Excurse," and the latter chapters are certainly not free of frictional antagonism between Birkin and Ursula. They were happy, Lawrence says of them before they leave Austria for Italy, "but they were never *quite* together, at the same moment. One was always a little left out." Indeed, the novel ends on a note of conflict between the two—about whether or not Birkin's ideal of "eternal union with a man" is possible. We might consider Birkin's wish abstractly, apart from what it may "mean" psychologically. It can easily enough be interpreted in terms of the principal sexual ambiguities of *Women in Love*: it is, as Ursula says, a "theory," and it may disguise Birkin's dissatisfaction with heterosexuality and the homosexual impulses to which the suppressed prologue to the novel explicitly, and guiltily, confessed. But we can also think of Birkin's desire simply *as* a desire—that is, as a sign of Birkin's inability to be satisfied with nondesiring stillness. His exhortations to "happy stillness" may make us forget how restless he is throughout the novel—certainly more restless than Ursula, whom he accuses of wanting the agitations of passion rather than the quietness of the union he offers her. I don't mean that Birkin's striving is "better" than what he says he is striving toward, but one can't help but admire the casualness with which Lawrence allows Birkin's aims to be questioned by others and tested by time. As Frank Kermode has written: "One of the achievements of the novel is to criticize the metaphysic, both by attacking Birkin and by obscuring doctrine with narrative symbolisms capable in their nature of more general and more doubtful interpretation." There is nothing final about the peace of "Excurse." If the language of that chapter makes it clear that the episode is something crucial which the novel has been struggling to reach, it's also true that the novel's apparent goal is not its climax but merely a narrative unit somewhere in the middle of the work, and that the novel itself works beyond its most exalted achievement.

ELIZABETH BRODY TENENBAUM

The Problematic Self

In Lawrence's writings through *Women in Love* we find repeated suggestions that women, desiring to possess the men they love, constitute a threat to masculine independence. In the works that immediately follow this novel Lawrence strives to reduce the significance of the sexual bond, thereby minimizing woman's power over her mate. In *Fantasia of the Unconscious* he explicitly relegates woman to a secondary role in her partner's life. One of his arguments rests on man's need to surpass woman through his solitary achievements: "Primarily and supremely man is *always* the pioneer of life, adventuring onward into the unknown, *alone with his own temerarious, dauntless soul.* Woman for him exists only in the twilight, by the camp fire, when day has departed" (second italics mine). However, Lawrence completely reverses the basis of his argument only a paragraph later, this time proposing communal rather than individual achievement as man's primary goal: "We have to break away, back to the great unison of manhood in some passionate *purpose*. Now this is not like sex. Sex is always individual . . . We have got to get back to the great purpose of manhood, a passionate unison in actively making a world. This is a real commingling of many. And in such a commingling we forfeit the individual." The juxtaposition of these two contradictory passages suggests that Lawrence's deepest concern at this time is neither individuality nor communion, but rather any purely masculine goal that can free the male from dependence upon a woman.

In the two novels that follow *Women in Love*, as in *Fantasia of the Unconscious*, Lawrence shifts his focus away from heterosexual love, ex-

---

ploring possibilities for eliminating or counterbalancing the bond between a man and a woman. But these works reflect even more clearly than *Women in Love* the paradoxical Romantic desire to raise the individual self to the status of an absolute and also to transcend the isolated ego by merging with a larger whole.

One of the most striking features of both *Aaron's Rod* and *Kangaroo* is the repeated assertion of two antithetical ideas: the absolute singleness and self-responsibility of every individual and the desirability of a social communion based on the submission of the weak to the strong. Rawdon Lilly, the character in *Aaron's Rod* who most closely resembles his creator, openly acknowledges the incompatibility of these two propositions. In a scene that has become infamous for its fascistic overtones, Lilly argues vehemently for "a real committal of the life-issue of inferior beings to the responsibility of a superior being." A moment later, however, he declares, "But I should say the blank opposite with just as much fervour . . . I think every man is a sacred and holy individual, *never* to be violated. I think there is only one thing I hate to the verge of madness, and that is *bullying*." Lilly is by no means simply playing devil's advocate in espousing these mutually exclusive positions, for the earnest dialogue with which the novel concludes reaffirms his commitment to both. In trying to convince Aaron to repudiate his "love urge," Lilly insists on the necessity of taking full responsibility for oneself:

> You can't lose yourself, so stop trying. The responsibility is on your own shoulders all the time, and no God which man has ever struck can take it off. You *are* yourself and so *be* yourself. Stick to it and abide by it. Passion or no passion, ecstasy or no ecstasy, urge or no urge, there's no goal outside you, where you can consummate like an eagle flying into the sun, or a moth into a candle . . . You've got an innermost, integral unique self, and since it's the only thing you have got or ever will have, don't go trying to lose it.

But four pages later he reverses his argument completely, insisting that Aaron's only hope for survival is to submit himself to the power of a greater man: "You, Aaron, you too have the need to submit. You, too, have the need livingly to yield to a more heroic soul, to give yourself. You know you have. And you know it isn't love. It is life-submission. And you know it. But you kick against the pricks. And perhaps you'd rather die than yield. And so, die you must."

Kangaroo reflects the same irreconcilable conflict between individualistic and hierarchical values. Richard Lovat Somers, the Lawrence-like protagonist of this novel, asserts with obsessive frequency the all-importance of the isolate, absolute self. But his ideal of complete self-sufficiency coexists with a belief in a human need for an authoritarian order: "One cannot live a life of entire loneliness, like a monkey on a stick . . . There's got to be meeting: even communion. Well, then, let us have the other communion . . . Sacrifice to the strong, not to the weak. In awe, not in dribbling love. The communion in power."

In *Aaron's Rod* Lawrence suggests that men may have to repudiate women entirely in order to achieve genuine self-fulfillment. The protagonist of *Kangaroo*, however, believes marriage can be a satisfctory arrangement provided the wife agrees to be subordinate to her husband: "She was to submit to the mystic man and male in him, with reverence, and even a little awe . . . You can't have two masters of one ship: neither can you have a ship without a master." But as long as Somers, like Birkin at the end of *Women in Love*, is deprived of any purely male communion, he remains far too dependent upon his wife to succeed in becoming her master: "He was the most forlorn and isolated creature in the world, without even a dog to his command. He was so isolated he was hardly a man at all, among men. He had absolutely nothing but her." Somers's involvement in Australian politics appears to be motivated largely by a need for a purely male activity from which his wife can be excluded:

> For two or three years now, since the war, he had talked like this about doing some work with men alone, sharing some activity with men . . . It would be out of [Harriet's] sphere, outside the personal sphere of their two lives, and he would keep it there. She emphatically opposed this principle of her externality. She agreed with the necessity for impersonal activity, but oh, she insisted on being identified with the activity, impersonal or not. And he insisted that it could not and should not be: that the pure male activity should be womanless, beyond woman."

Ultimately repudiating both the socialistic laborites who advocate rule by the masses and the fascistic "Diggers" who espouse social unity through love, Somers tellingly groups "love," "the masses," "the weak," and "woman" together among the forces whose ascendancy must be ended by a countervailing power: "When the flow is sympathetic, or love, then the weak, the woman, the masses, assume the positivity. But the balance even is only kept by stern *authority* [*sic*], the unflinching obstinacy of the return-force, of power." Somers has sought a pure male activity that would place him beyond woman only to find the male world of politics under the sway of essentially "feminine" forces. Nowhere in the contemporary world can he find the power-based communion that alone seems to offer freedom from the threat of domination through love.

The Plumed Serpent is a very different book from the other two "leadership novels" with which it is frequently grouped. The protagonists of both *Aaron's Rod* and *Kangaroo* are essentially powerless men, and their commitment to both individual singleness and masculine communion seems closely related to their fear of female domination. But the male protagonists of *The Plumed Serpent* have a power within them that assures them of ascendancy over women. When contemplating a world where female subservience is the norm, Lawrence seems to lose his concern for individual singleness. In direct contradiction to a view expounded in *Women in Love*, Lawrence, speaking through Kate, attacks the very concept of individual wholeness: "There was no such animal [as an individual]. Except in the mechanical world. In the world of machines, the individual machine is effectual. The individual, like the perfect being, does not and cannot exist, in the vivid world. We are all fragments. And at the best, halves."

In *Kangaroo* Somers predicts that his wife will submit to him only when he himself submits to the power of his unconscious: "Before Harriet would ever accept him, Richard Lovat, as a Lord and Master, he, this selfsame Richard who was so strong on kingship, must open the doors of his soul and let in a dark Lord and Master for himself, the dark god he had sensed outside the door. Let him once truly submit to the dark majesty, break open his doors to this fearful god who is master, and enters us from below, the lower doors; let himself once admit a Master, the unspeakable god: and the rest would happen." But Somers apparently remains incapable of such submission, and his difficulties with Harriet rest unresolved at the end of the book. In *The Plumed Serpent* the metaphorical dark god identified in this passage finds embodiment in the literal gods of a primitive religion. By submitting themselves to the majesty of these deities, Ramón and Cipriano attain a potency that makes them triumphant leaders of a masculine world and revered masters of women.

The sense of a cohesive community that is so central to *The Plumed Serpent* is absent from Lawrence's last two works of fiction, which, like his earlier novels, seem to hold out hope only for those who reject society entirely. In *Apocalypse*, however, Lawrence provides a final affirmation of a communal ideal that can find fulfillment only in a world very different from our own. Repudiating his earlier glorification of the detached nonconformist, he now perceives a universal desire for personal independence as the fundamental illness of our age: "We *cannot bear connection.* That is our malady. We *must* break away, and be isolate. We call that being free, being individual. Beyond a certain point, which we have reached, it is suicide." At the end of a peripatetic, highly individualistic life that prevented him from being truly a part of any family, community, or nation, Lawrence concludes that human happiness requires a sense of organic connection with a world beyond the self: "My individualism is really an illusion. I am a part of the great whole, and I can never escape. But I *can* deny my connections, break them, and become a fragment. Then I am wretched. What we want is to destroy our false, inorganic connections, especially those related to money, and re-establish the living organic connections, with the cosmos, the sun and earth, with mankind and nation and family." Throughout much of his life Lawrence, like Rousseau, combined an exceptionally intense preoccupation with his own individuality and a deep-rooted longing to transcend the isolated ego. Having enraged their countrymen and alienated their friends, both men spent their final days in virtual isolation celebrating an all-encompassing oneness.

H. M. DALESKI

Aphrodite of the Foam and "The Ladybird" Tales

> . . . But the mode of our being is such that we can only live and have our being whilst we are implicit in one of the great dynamic modes. We *must* either love, or rule. And once the love-mode changes, as change it must, for we are worn out and becoming evil in its persistence, then the other mode will take place in us. And there will be profound, profound obedience in place of this love-crying, obedience to the incalculable power-urge. And men must submit to the greater soul in a man, for their guidance: and women must submit to the positive power-soul in man, for their being.

This pronouncement of Rawdon Lilly in *Aaron's Rod* (1922) may serve as a gloss on the central issue of the three tales published in 1923 in the volume called *The Ladybird.* Despite their difference of milieu and mode, all three tales are primarily concerned with the same theme, with the necessity for the abandonment of romantic love as a basis for relationship between the sexes and with its replacement by the woman's submission to the 'power-soul in man'. *The Ladybird* tales, indeed, are best read in the light of the novels of this period, particularly *The Plumed Serpent* (1926); for in this novel the conception of the new relationship that is first adumbrated in *Aaron's Rod* is fully developed, and Lawrence is explicit about the nature of the submission demanded of the women in the sex act, whereas he is reserved on this matter in the tales.

The sexual submission of the women in *The Plumed Serpent* is total, involving, as it does, her voluntary forgoing of orgasm. It is an extreme position, to which Lawrence had been led in reaction against the kind of assault on a man that is figured in Ursula Brangwen's ferocious 'annihilation' of Skrebensky in *The Rainbow*—an assault that the novelist had come to envisage as a concomitant of romantic love. It is a position, moreover, that he abandoned, for in *Lady Chatterley's Lover* (1928) relationship between a man and a woman is based not on power and submission but on a reciprocal tenderness, and Connie Chatterley achieves a less questionable form of sexual fulfilment with Mellors. *The Ladybird* tales, in other words, should be regarded as exploratory ventures in a large undertaking that was to lead, eventually, to *Lady Chatterley's Lover*. But Lawrence's assertion in these tales of a male dominance unwittingly suggests that the concomitants of the doctrine of power are as unfortunate as those of romantic love. *The Ladybird* is a most impressive volume, a testimony to Lawrence's remarkable power and range in the long story; but it seems to me that both 'The Ladybird' and 'The Fox' are seriously marred.

II

Lady Daphne in *The Ladybird* is introduced as having 'her whole will' fixed in 'her adoption of her mother's creed', fixed, that is, in a belief in loving humanity and in a 'determination that life should be gentle and good and benevolent'. But it is at once intimated that her adherence to such a creed is a perverse denial of her essential self, for she has 'a strong, reckless nature'—she is 'Artemis or Atalanta rather than Daphne'—and her eyes tell of 'a wild energy damned up inside her'. Such a fixing of the will in frustration of natural being is inevitably inimical to life, and Daphne moves, as it were, in death: her two brothers have been killed in the war, her baby has been born dead, and her appearance fills 'the heart with ashes'. She is, indeed, Proserpine—though in a sense different from that in which her husband, Major Basil Apsley, uses the name when he refers to her 'wonderful Proserpine fingers' and says that 'the spring comes' if she lifts her hands. Daphne, though given to life, is wedded to death, embodying in herself the deathliness of the creed of Love.

This deathliness is further projected in the marriage of Daphne and Basil. When he comes back from the war, he is 'like death; like risen death', and 'a new icy note' in his voice goes 'through her veins like death'. We are meant to register, I think, that the death Basil carries in himself is not only the mark of his experiences in the war. A 'white-faced, spiritually intense' man, Basil maintains that, having been through the ordeal of the war, he has arrived at 'a higher state of consciousness, and therefore of life. And so, of course, at a higher plane of love'. It is the constant burden of Lawrence that, where life is viewed in terms of the achievement of a stage of heightened mental consciousness, it is life as well as 'blood-consciousness' that is denied; and it follows that the love which is a correlative of such a state of consciousness is as sterile as the life with which it is equated. This, at all events, is what Basil's love for Daphne is shown to be. After his love-making she has 'to bear herself in torment', she feels 'weak and fretful', she '[aches] with nerves', and cannot eat; he in turn becomes 'ashy and somewhat acrid'. In Basil, we are to understand, the consciousness of loving has usurped the body of love, leaving him ineffectually prostrate before Daphne:

> He suddenly knelt at her feet, and kissed the toe of her slipper, and kissed the instep, and kissed the ankle in the thin, black stocking.
>
> 'I knew,' he said in a muffled voice. 'I knew you would make good. I knew if I had to kneel, it was before you. I knew you were divine, you were the one—Cybele—Isis. I knew I was your slave. I knew. It has all been just a long initiation. I had to learn how to worship you.'
>
> He kissed her feet again and again, without the slightest self-consciousness, or the slightest misgiving. Then he went back to the sofa, and sat there looking at her, saying:
>
> 'It isn't love, it is worship. Love between me and you will be a sacrament, Daphne. That's what I had to learn. You are beyond me. A mystery to me. My God, how great it all is. How marvellous!'

The act of kneeling and the kissing of feet are charged with significance in Lawrence's work of this period. In this instance, we may feel, they are even somewhat over-charged, but their purport is unmistakable. Abnegating his independent manhood, Basil becomes a slavish idolater; and his worship of Daphne turns her into a goddess, turns her, indeed, into Cybele, whose name Birkin invokes when (in the scene at the millpond in *Women in Love*) he attempts to smash the reflection of the moon, thus demonstrating his opposition to the possessive *magna mater* figure that is destructive of a man's virility. When Basil says that his feeling for Daphne 'isn't love' but 'worship', what he means is that he has attained 'a higher plane of love'. It is too ethereal a plane to support life, however, and not unexpectedly his worship of her postulates the kind of sacrifice of self that conceals a desire for death: 'I am no more than a sacrifice to you,' he tells her, 'an offering. I *wish* I could die in giving myself to you, give you all my blood on your altar, for ever.'

Basil is distracted from his worship of Daphne when, returning to the sofa, he slides his hand down between the back and the seat and finds a thimble. The thimble belongs to Daphne, a present given her as a girl by a Bohemian count, Johann Dionys Psanek, with whom, wounded and a prisoner of war in England, she has renewed acquaintance. This interruption of Basil's adoration of his wife is premonitory of the Count's irruption into their relationship. The Count, whose own marriage has failed, regards himself (like the Indians in 'The Woman Who Rode Away') as 'a subject of the sun' rather than of a woman; and a 'dark flame of life' seems to glow through his clothes 'from his body'. 'I belong to the fire-worshippers,' he tells Daphne; and what he slowly, even unwillingly, proceeds to do is to fire her into life, to release the wild energy that is dammed up in her. At the same time, contact with her also helps to heal him—'Let me wrap your hair round my hands, like a bandage,' he says—for he does not at first wish to live.

Daphne's sewing of some shirts for both the Count and her husband is made to reveal the different demands that the two men make of a woman. Basil is enraptured at the thought of having a shirt she has sewn next to his skin: 'I shall feel you all round me, all over me,' he says to her. What he wants in his relationship with her, we see, is to be encompassed, as in a womb. The Count, on the other hand, having told Daphne that the hospital-shirt he is wearing is too long and too big, insists that she herself, and not her maid, should sew a shirt for him: 'Only you,' he maintains, 'might give me what I want, something that buttons round my throat and on my wrists.' What he wants of a shirt is that it be a good fit—just as what he wants of a woman is that she be a 'mate'. 'Everything finds its mate,' he is fond of remarking; and he makes it clear to Daphne that what interests him is not the gentle mating of doves but the fiercer mating of wild creatures. The tale, that is to say, seems to be moving to a Dionysian mating of Artemis and Dionys, for Daphne becomes aware of a 'secret thrilling communion' with the Count, of a dark flow between them; and, though she resists him with her mind and will, she is nevertheless drawn by his account of a 'true love' that is 'a throbbing together in darkness, like the wild-cat in the night, when the green screen [with which her eyes are closed] opens and her eyes are on the darkness'. She comes to recognize too that, in contradistinction to the 'superconscious' finish of Basil and herself, the Count, like her father, has some of 'the unconscious blood-warmth of the lower classes'; and she is prepared to grant that his 'dark flame of life . . . might warm the cold white fire of her own blood'. We are led to expect, in other words, that the union of these two will be the contrary of the deathly 'white love' of Daphne and her husband; in fact the new relationship proves to be merely the obverse of the old.

The new form that Daphne's life appears about to take is symbolized by the thimble the Count has given her, which she puts on when she sews his shirt. The thimble has 'a gold snake at the bottom, and a Mary-beetle of green stone at the top, to push the needle with'. The Mary-beetle or ladybird, placed opposite the snake at the top of the thimble, may be thought of as instinct with flight; and the thimble, I suggest, figures the kind of union that is represented by Quetzalcoatl in *The Plumed Serpent*, a union of bird and serpent, of spirit and flesh. Certainly, as Daphne moves closer and closer to a vital relationship with the Count, it appears to be the hope of a release into unified being that is held out to her. It is the ladybird alone, however, that is the Count's crest, and as such, as 'a descendant of the Egyptian scarabaeus', it is emblematic of a rather different urge on his part. Lord Beveridge declares that the ball-rolling scarab is 'a symbol of the creative principle', but the Count suggests (though he smiles 'as if it were a joke') that, on the contrary, it symbolizes 'the principle of decomposition'. He is not joking, however, for, confronted with a world that 'has gone raving', he has chosen 'the madness of the ladybird' and found his God in 'the blessed god of destruction'. His God is a 'god of anger, who throws down the steeples and the factory chimneys', and he proposes to serve him by helping to beat down 'the world of man'. The Count, it emerges, is bent on disrupting the established order, an order founded on democracy and love, and substituting for it an order based on 'the sacredness of power'. Basil maintains that 'there is really only one supreme contact, the contact of love', but the Count insists that he 'must use another word than love', and suggests several: 'Obedience, submission, faith, belief, responsibility, power'. The Count talks here like Lilly in *Aaron's Rod*, and it is in the novels, particularly in *The Plumed Serpent*, that the political implications of this doctrine of power are pursued to a logical conclusion. In 'The Ladybird' the superiority of the doctrine of power over that of love is asserted domestically, as it were, in the Count's conquest of Basil's wife.

The Count's power as a man is evidenced by the 'spell' he casts on Daphne when, prior to his departure from England, Basil invites him to spend a fortnight at Thoresway, the 'beautiful Elizabethan mansion' of Lord Beveridge. At night, when he is alone in his room, the Count croons to himself 'the old songs of his childhood'. Daphne, who is 'a bad sleeper', and whose nights are 'a torture to her', hears the singing, which, 'like a witchcraft', makes her forget everything. Thereafter it becomes 'almost an obsession to her to listen for him'. She is sure he is calling her, 'out of herself, out of her world', and in the day she is 'bewitched'. One night she cannot resist going into his room, and they sit for some time apart, in the dark:

> Then suddenly, without knowing, he went across in the dark, feeling for the end of the couch. And he sat beside her on the couch. But he did not touch her. Neither did she move. The darkness flowed about them thick like blood, and time seemed dissolved in it. They sat with the small, invisible distance between them, motionless, speechless, thoughtless.
>
> Then suddenly he felt her finger-tips touch his arm, and a flame went over him that left him no more a man. He was something seated in flame, in flame unconscious, seated erect, like an Egyptian King-god in the statues. Her finger-tips slid down him, and she herself slid down in a strange silent rush, and he felt her face against his closed feet and ankles, her hands pressing his ankles. He felt her brow and hair against his ankles, her face against his feet, and there she clung in the dark, as if in space below him. He still sat erect and motionless. Then he bent forward and put his hand on her hair.
>
> 'Do you come to me?' he murmured. 'Do you come to me?'

Great stress is laid here on the lack of consciousness of the lovers: they sit 'speechless, thoughtless', and the Count, having moved to Daphne 'without knowing', sits 'in flame unconscious'. In contradistinction to the superconsciousness of Basil and Daphne, they are immersed in a flow that is thick and dark, 'like blood'; and where Basil is prostrate before her, the Count sits 'erect, like an Egyptian King-god in the statues', sits, that is (like Birkin in *Women in Love*) in 'immemorial potency'. The Count's sense of his own potency certainly communicates itself to Daphne, for it brings her sliding down to his feet. But the relationship which Daphne now embraces is not, after all, so different from that which obtains between her husband and herself. There is a significant reversal of roles, it is true, but the relationship is still founded on the worship of one partner by the other, even though it is now 'the sacredness of power' that elicits the devotion. What is disturbing here is that Lawrence, intent on asserting the Count's power and on emphasizing the difference between his attitude to Daphne and that of Basil, seems to be unaware that Daphne, clinging to the Count's feet and with 'her brow and hair against his ankles', is (for all the heightened prose of the description) in no less objectionable a position than Basil at her feet.

It is a position, we cannot help feeling, that figures more than a woman's necessary sexual submission to a man. The 'small' man has brought the 'tall' woman—their difference of stature is repeatedly stressed—to her knees; and her clinging to his feet is the overt sign of a kind of submission to him that has far-reaching implications for their sexual relations. This is how Daphne is described on the following morning:

> She felt she could sleep, sleep, sleep—for ever. Her face, too, was very still, with a delicate look of virginity that she had never had before. She had always been Aphrodite, the self-conscious one. And her eyes, the green-blue, had been like slow, living jewels, resistant. Now they had unfolded from the hard flower-bud, and had the wonder, and the stillness of a quiet night.

The reiterated allusions to Daphne's stillness at first sight seem to betoken no more than her achievement of the peace of fulfilment after the strain of her sexual relations with Basil, but taken in conjunction with the references to her 'delicate look of virginity' and to her always having been 'Aphrodite'—we remember that Basil, 'in poetry', has called her 'Aphrodite of the foam'—the emphasis on her stillness has a concealed significance. A passage in *The Plumed Serpent* makes clear, I think, what is only hinted at in the story:

> [Kate] realized, with wonder, the death in her of Aphrodite of the foam: the seething, frictional, ecstatic Aphrodite. By a swift dark instinct, Cipriano drew away from this in her. When, in their love, it came back on her, the seething electric female ecstasy, which knows such spasms of delirium, he recoiled from her. It was what she used to call her 'satisfaction'. She had loved Joachim for this, that again, and again, and again he could give her this orgiastic 'satisfaction', in spasms that made her cry aloud.

With Basil, we are told, Daphne has known 'the fierce power of the woman in excelsis', the power of 'incandescent, transcendent, moon-fierce womanhood', but her inability to 'stay intensified' in her 'female mystery' has left her 'fretful and ill and never to be soothed'. What the Count has done, it seems presumably by refusing her 'satisfaction', is to bring her not a release of, but from, her own wild energies. Hence the 'quiet, intact quality of virginity in her' and her 'strange new quiescence' which Basil finds so puzzling; and hence her own sense of having 'suddenly collapsed away from her old self into this darkness, this peace, this quiescence that was like a full dark river flowing eternally in her soul'.

Daphne's achievement of a new self should be distinguished, therefore, from that of Connie Chatterley, of whom she is evidently a prefigurement, for it it said that at Thoresway 'there was a gamekeeper she could have loved—an impudent, ruddy-faced, laughing, ingratiating fellow; she could have loved him, if she had not been isolated beyond the breach of his birth, her culture, her consciousness'. Connie, responding to the tenderness of Mellors, also dies to the Aphrodite in her, but she is reborn as a woman who finds a different kind of 'satisfaction', a consummation that I think we are to understand is denied Daphne, as it is denied Kate in *The Plumed Serpent*:

> Oh, and far down inside [Connie] . . . , at the quick of her, the depths parted and rolled asunder, from the centre of soft plunging . . . , and closer and closer plunged the palpable unknown, and further and further rolled the waves of herself away from herself, leaving her, till suddenly, in a soft, shuddering convulsion, the quick of all her plasm was touched, she knew herself touched, the consummation was upon her, and she was gone. She was gone, she was not, and she was born: a woman.

Daphne's accession into new being, moreover, does not resolve the problem of her relations with the two men. She has to be satisifed, though her relationship with Basil has been demolished, with being 'the wife of the ladybird', for the Count, a prisoner of war, has no alternative but to depart. It is significant, however, that he anyway feels he has 'no future in this life' and that he cannot offer her 'life in the world' because he has 'no power in the day, and no place'. The Count, that is to say, having pledged his power to his god of anger and destruction, appears to have his being in death; and what he finally offers Daphne is a life in the underworld. 'In the night, in the dark, and in death, you are mine,' he tells her; and when he parts from her, he says: 'I shall be king in Hades when I am dead. And you will be at my side.' Proserpine, we see, is Proserpine yet, and the spring seems far behind.

III

'The Fox', until the killing of Banford, has a fine and powerful inevitability of development that makes it, up to that point, one of the most translucent of Lawrence's tales. The established relationship, in this further instance of 'the wicked triangle', is of two girls ('usually known by their surnames'), who have set up home and a farm together. March acts 'the man about the place', but despite their feeling for each other, she and Banford are 'apt to become a little irritable' and seem 'to live too much off themselves'. It is evidently a sterile relationship, March, indeed, being generally 'absent in herself', as if she were not really held by Banford; and this sterility is mirrored in the unproductiveness of the farm, particularly in the 'obstinate refusal' of their hens to lay eggs. Matters are made worse by the depredations of a fox, which carries off hens 'under [their] very noses'.

One evening March, out with her gun, is standing with her consciousness 'held back' when she suddenly sees the fox 'looking up at her'. His eyes meet her eyes, and 'he [knows] her'. She is 'spellbound', does not shoot, and the fox makes off. Thereafter she wanders about 'in strange mindlessness', but she is 'possessed' by the fox and feels that he has 'invisibly [mastered] her spirit'. What is enacted here with admirable economy is parallel to what takes place in repeated meetings between Daphne and the Count. Into the vacancy of March's being there suddenly irrupts, with the force of an epiphany, a manifestation of wild life. Immediately prior to the encounter March has been unaware of the vibrant life around her, of the 'limbs of the pine-tree' shining in the air and the stalks of grass 'all agleam', for she '[sees] it all, and [does] not see it'. Now, at a level deeper than consciousness, she comes under the spell of newly apprehended energies and is possessed by them. What is perhaps specially significant is that she submits to the mastery of the fox—this and the strong sexual overtones of the description preparing the way for her response to the young soldier who suddenly arrives at the farm.

From the moment he appears Henry '[is] the fox' to March. She tries 'to keep her will uppermost' as she watches him, but soon ceases 'to reserve herself' from his presence. Instead she gives herself up 'to a warm, relaxed peace', and, 'accepting the spell' that is on her, she allows herself to 'lapse into the odour of the fox', remaining 'still and soft in her corner like a passive creature in its cave'. In the light of Daphne's experience in 'The Ladybird', March's still, relaxed passivity under the spell is worthy of notice. That it is to a sexual potency in Henry that she is responding is indicated by the dream she has on the night of his arrival. Hearing a strange singing—a call (like the Count's crooning) to a new mode of life—she goes outside and suddenly realizes that it is the fox who is singing. She approaches the fox, but when she puts out her hand to touch him, he suddenly bites her wrist. At the same time, in bounding away, his brush (which seems to be fire) '[sears] and [burns] her mouth with a great pain'. If March in her dream experiences the fire of passion that she desires (for when Henry later kisses her it is 'with a quick brushing kiss' that seems 'to burn through her every fibre'), she is also warned, as it were, not to play with fire, for the fox is no doll, as his bite testifies.

What playing with fire means, in the first instance, is resisting Henry's determination to master her. He is 'a huntsman in spirit', and deciding that he wants to marry her (initially with the shrewd idea of gaining the farm for himself but soon with a genuine and disinterested passion), he sets out to hunt his quarry, knowing 'he [is] master of her'. He also hunts the fox and kills it. It is a remarkable stroke. The killing of the marauder functions, first, as a ritual supplanting of the fox by which March is possessed. At the same time Henry is paradoxically aligned with the fox he kills, and his hunting of it is made the occasion of an extension of his significance:

> As he stood under the oaks of the wood-edge he heard the dogs from the neighbouring cottage up the hill yelling suddenly and startlingly, and the wakened dogs from the farms around barking answer. And suddenly, it seemed to him England was little and tight, he felt the landscape was constricted even in the dark, and that there were too many dogs in the night, making a noise like a fence of sound, like the network of English hedges netting the view. He felt the fox didn't have a chance. For it must be the fox that had started all this hullabaloo.
>
> . . . He knew the fox would be coming. It seemed to him it would be the last of the foxes in this loudly barking thick-voiced England, tight with innumerable little houses.

Henry, we see, should not be regarded merely as a rather nondescript young man who has been fired into the pursuit of a woman. He suddenly emerges here as the representative of a wild, passionate spirit for which there seems to be no room in a tight England. It is a spirit, we are to understand, that has been assailed in England during the war, for the passage should be related to Lord Beveridge's bitter thoughts in 'The Ladybird' of 'the so-called patriots who [have] been howling their mongrel indecency in the public face' and of an 'England fallen under the paws of smelly mongrels'. Henry, like James Joyce's Stephen Dedalus, is determined to fly by the nets that threaten to drag him down; and he wants a freer, more expansive life than seems possible in a land fenced in by the conventional pieties of such as Banford. It is a measure of Lawrence's despair of England at this time that Henry and March are made to leave for Canada at the end of the tale.

But before they can finally come together, Banford's hold on March has to be broken. The way in which Banford is disposed of arouses our gravest doubts; and it is at this point that the crystal-clear depths of the story become suddenly muddied with obsessive matter. Banford is disposed of when Henry, refusing to accept March's withdrawal from her promise to marry him, comes back to the farm to claim her and chops down a tree which falls on and kills his rival. It is true that this climactic event is carefully prepared for. Prior to it March dreams that Banford is dead and that the coffin in which she has to put her is 'the rough wood-box in which the bits of chopped wood' are kept. Not wanting to lay her 'dead darling' in an unlined box, March wraps her up in a fox-skin, which is all she can find. The dream points cleary enough to March's desire for

Banford's death, and, in its association of the dead woman with the fox that Henry has killed, seems to express a wish that he will be the one to bring about her death. It is March's unconscious complicity in Banford's death that in part explains her immediate capitulation to Henry the moment the deed is consummated. It is true, too, that the killing is technically an accident, and that Henry warns Banford to move (though in a manner that ensures her refusal) before he strikes the blows that fell the tree. 'In his heart', however, he has 'decided her death'—and the fact remains that he murders her.

It is furthermore true that the symbolism of the story insidiously suggests that Henry kills Banford as naturally, almost as innocently, as a fox kills chickens, and out of a similar need to live, March being essential to his life. It may also be granted that the killing frees March for life. That does not mean to say, however, that we should celebrate the murder as 'an inspired and creative deed', as Julian Moynahan has suggested. Henry, after all, is not a fox, and calling murder by another name does not make it smell any sweeter. We can only conclude, I think, that when Lawrence, who has such a reverence for life, can be taken to justify murder, it is because the murder is incidental to a compulsive justification of something else.

What strikes us about the murder of Banford is that it is strictly unnecessary. The moment Henry returns to the farm and faces March, her upper lip lifts from her teeth in a 'helpless, fascinated rabbit-look', and as soon as she sees 'his glowing, red face', it is 'all over with her'; she is as 'helpless' as if she were 'bound'. She is as powerless, that is, as a rabbit before a fox; and her helplessness surely implies that Henry has only to insist on her leaving the farm with him for her to yield, irrespective of the opposition they might be expected to encounter from Banford. That Henry is nevertheless made to kill Banford is a means, I suggest, not of freeing March but of ensuring her submission to him as a woman. In *The Plumed Serpent*, when Cipriano executes the men who have tried to kill Don Ramón, he repeatedly intones 'The Lords of Life are Masters of Death'; it seems to be the covert intention behind Henry's murder of Banford that his mastery of death establishes him as a lord of life. For March not only has to be freed from Banford; she has to be released into a new mode of being.

She has to be won, first, to a new conception of relationship between a man and a woman. When she writes to Henry and goes back on her promise to marry him, she says that she has 'been over it all again' in her 'mind', and that she does not see 'on what grounds' she can marry him since he is 'an absolute stranger' to her, they do not 'seem to have a thing in common', and she does not 'really love' him. What she has to be made to respond to, though not with her mind, is the existence of an affinity between them that goes deeper than conventional ideas of love and compatability; what she has to be made to accept, in a word, is the compulsion of a life-force—and of a lord of life. It is this acknowledgement that is wrung from her when Banford is killed, it being an indication of the lengths to which Lawrence is driven in asserting the doctrine of power that murder should be made the means of ensuring the acknowledgement. March faces Henry, gazing at him 'with the last look of resistance', and then 'in a last agonized failure' she begins to cry. 'He [has] won,' we are told; and looking at him with 'a senseless look of helplessness and submission', she realizes that she will 'never leave him again'.

Henry's demonstration of his mastery in the killing of Banford is intended to effect a further submission on March's part once they are married:

> If he spoke to her, she would turn to him with a faint new smile, the strange, quivering little smile of a woman who has died in the old way of love, and can't quite rise to the new way. She still felt she ought to *do* something, to strain herself in some direction. . . . And she could not quite accept the submergence which his new love put upon her. If she was in love, she ought to *exert* herself, in some way, loving. She felt the weary need of our day to *exert* herself in love. But she knew that in fact she must no more exert herself in love. He would not have the love which exerted itself towards him. It made his brow go black. No, he wouldn't let her exert her love towards him. No, she had to be passive, to acquiesce, and to be submerged under the surface of love. . . .

Lawrence is not as explicit here as he is in *The Plumed Serpent*, but in view of the previously quoted comments in that novel on Aphrodite of the foam, I think there can be little doubt what a woman's exertion in love should be taken to mean. March, having 'died in the old way of love', is required (like Daphne) to be reborn into a new passive acquiescence and foamless submergence in the sex act. It is a saving grace that March is left not quite accepting her submergence.

IV

F. R. Leavis has discussed 'The Captain's Doll' at length in his chapter on the tale in *D. H. Lawrence: Novelist*, leaving little to be added to his account. I should merely like to draw attention to the presence in the tale of what might be called the Aphrodite motif. It is perhaps only our recognition of the importance of this motive in 'The Ladybird' and 'The Fox' that makes us aware of it in the third tale in the volume, for in 'The Captain's Doll' it is presented symbolically.

Captain Hepburn, like Count Dionys and Henry, possesses the kind of mastery that casts a spell over a woman. He speaks to Countess Hannele with a 'strange, mindless, soft, suggestive tone' that leaves her 'powerless to disobey'; and when he makes love to her, she is 'heavy and spellbound.' Hannele, in a word, cannot 'help being in love' with him. Nevertheless, Hannele, who makes dolls and cushions and 'suchlike objects of feminine art', has made a doll of the Captain, a 'mannikin' that is 'a perfect portrait' of him as a Scottish officer; and the making of the doll clearly indicates that his mastery over her is far from absolute. At the same time the doll projects an image of the Captain that is not altogether unfair, for we discover that his wife has made a living doll of him: 'Why, on our wedding night,' Mrs. Hepburn tells Hannele, 'he kneeled down in front of me and promised with God's help, to make my life happy. . . . It has been his one aim in life, to make my life happy.' The mannikin, that is, suggests the diminishment of self, of true being, that is implicit in such a limitation of a man's purposive activity. Hepburn is thus both a masterful man and a doll, and it is this complexity that makes the conflict between old and new modes of love a more subtle affair in this story than it is in 'The Ladybird', of which we may be reminded by the recurrence of a man on his knees before a woman. In 'The Captain's Doll' the conflict is first internalized, as it were, for Hepburn himself comes to repudiate 'the business of adoration'. When his wife dies, he realizes that he no longer wants to love in that way; and he insists to Hannele that '*any* woman . . . could start any minute and make a doll' of the man she loves: 'And the doll would be her hero: and her hero would be no more than her doll.' Hannele, however, is inwardly determined that 'he must go down on his knees if he [wants] her love.' The ostensible drama that is played out between them consists in his attempt to make her abandon this position.

But since a man's being no more than a woman's doll also implies that she may use him as a toy in the sex act—implies, indeed, the kind of relationship that Bertha Coutts is said to have forced on Mellors in *Lady Chatterley's Lover*—the drama here not unexpectedly turns out to have a further dimension. We are adverted to this dimension at the beginning of the long, superb description of the excursion which Hannele and Hepburn make to the glacier. Sitting silently in the car that is taking them to the mountains, they watch the glacier river. The river is 'roaring and raging, a glacier river of pale, seething ice-water'; it is a 'foaming river', a 'stony, furious, lion-like river, tawny-coloured'. When the car can go no further, they begin to climb the mountain; and then there follows this passage:

> This valley was just a mountain cleft, cleft sheer in the hard, living rock, with black trees like hair flourishing in this secret, naked place of the earth. At the bottom of the open wedge forever roared the rampant, insatiable water. The sky from above was like a sharp wedge forcing its way into the earth's cleavage, and that eternal ferocious water was like the steel edge of the wedge, the terrible tip biting into the rocks' intensity. Who could have thought that the soft sky of light, and the soft foam of water could thrust and penetrate into the dark, strong earth?

What we have here, it seems clear, is another rendering of 'the intercourse between heaven and earth' that is described at the beginning of *The Rainbow*; and what the 'rampant, insatiable' water, the 'ferocious' water, symbolizes, I suggest, is 'the seething, frictional, ecstatic' Aphrodite of the foam. Such a reading helps us to understand the reactions of Hepburn and Hannele to the scene. He 'hates' and 'loathes' it, finding it 'almost obscene'; she is 'thrilled and excited' by it 'to another sort of savageness'. They proceed on their way to the glacier, and Hepburn suddenly decides he wants to climb on to it: it is 'his one desire—to stand upon it'. The ascent of the glacier is for Hepburn an 'ordeal or mystic battle' and, as he prepares for it, 'the curious vibration of his excitement' makes the scene 'strange, rather horrible to her'; she shudders, but the glacier still seems to her 'to hold the key to all glamour and ecstasy'. He has earlier declared that the mountains 'are less' than he, and been filled with 'a curious, dark, masterful force'. What he demonstrates, I take it, as he climbs 'the naked ice-slope', the ice that looks 'so pure, like flesh', in his determination to pit himself against the source of the seething water and so really to get on top of it.

On the way down Hepburn makes it clear to Hannele that he will not marry her 'on a basis of love'. What he demands of her in marriage, he tells her, is 'honour and obedience: and the proper physical feelings'. The word 'proper', we may feel, is highly ambiguous, but he leaves it at that. Lawrence leaves it at that too, and 'The Captain's Doll' is consequently not marred, as the other two tales are, by an attempt to enforce a total surrender on the woman. After a fierce argument Hannele finally makes her submission, movingly and convincingly, when she tells Hepburn she wants to burn the picture of the doll that he carries with him. The ascent of the glacier has shown beyond question that he is no doll.

JOYCE CAROL OATES

Lawrence's 'Götterdämmerung': The Apocalyptic Vision of "Women in Love"

Women in Love is an inadequate title. The novel concerns itself with far more than simply *women* in love; far more than simply women *in love*. Two violent love affairs are the plot's focus, but the drama of the novel has clearly to do with every sort of emotion, and with every sort of spiritual inanition. Gerald and Birkin and Ursula and Gudrun are immense figures, monstrous creations out of legend, out of mythology; they are unable to alter their fates, like tragic heroes and heroines of old. The mark of Cain has been on Gerald since early childhood, when he accidentally killed his brother; and Gudrun is named for a heroine out of Germanic legend who slew her first husband. The pace of the novel is often frenetic. Time is running out, history is coming to an end, the Apocalypse is at hand. *Dies Irae* and *The Latter Days* (as well as *The Sisters* and *The Wedding Ring*) were titles Lawrence considered for the novel, and though both are too explicit, too shrill, they are more suggestive of the chiliastic mood of the work (which even surprised Lawrence when he read it through after completion in November of 1916: it struck him as "end-of-the-world" and as "purely destructive, not like *The Rainbow*, destructive-consummating").

Women in Love is a strangely ceremonial, even ritualistic work. In very simple terms it celebrates love and marriage as the only possible salvation for twentieth-century man and dramatizes the fate of those who resist the abandonment of the ego demanded by love: a sacrificial rite, an ancient necessity. Yet those who "come through"—Birkin and Ursula—are hardly harmonious; the novel ends with their arguing about Birkin's thwarted desire for an "eternal union with a man," and one is given to feel that the shadow of the dead man will fall across their marriage. And though the structure of the novel is ceremonial, its texture is rich, lush, fanciful, and, since each chapter is organized around a dominant image, rather self-consciously symbolic or imagistic; action is subordinate to theme. The perversity of the novel is such that its great subject of mankind's tragically split nature is demonstrated in the art-work itself, which is sometimes a fairly conventional novel with a forward-moving plot, sometimes a gorgeous, even outrageous prose poem on the order of the work Aloysius Bertrand and Charles Baudelaire were doing in the previous century. Birkin is sometimes a prophetic figure, and sometimes merely garrulous and silly; Ursula is sometimes a mesmerizing archetypal female, at other times shrill and possessive and dismayingly obtuse. In one of Lawrence's most powerful love scenes Gerald Crich comes by night to Gudrun's bedroom after his father's death and is profoundly revitalized by her physical love, but Gudrun cannot help looking upon him with a devastating cynicism, noting his ridiculous trousers and braces and boots, and she is filled with nausea of him despite her fascination. Gudrun herself takes on in Gerald's obsessive imagination certain of the more destructive qualities of the Magna Mater or the devouring female, and she attains an almost mythic power over him; but when we last see her she has become shallow and cheaply ironic, merely a vulgar young woman. It is a measure of Lawrence's genius that every part of his immensely ambitious novel works (with the possible exception of the strained chapter "In The Pompadour") and that the proliferating images coalesce into fairly stable leitmotifs: water, moon, darkness, light, the organic and the sterile.

Our own era is one in which prophetic eschatological art has as great a significance as it did in 1916; Lawrence's despairing conviction that civilization was in the latter days is one shared by a number of our most serious writers, even if there is little belief in the Apocalypse in its classical sense. The notion of antichrist is an archaic one, a sentiment that posits unqualified belief in Christ; and the ushering in of a violent new era, a millennium, necessitates faith in the transcendental properties of the world, or the universe, which contrast sharply with scientific speculations about the fate we are likely to share. Even in his most despairing moments Lawrence remained curiously "religious." It is a tragedy that

Western civilization may be doomed, that a man like Gerald Crich must be destroyed, and yet—does it really matter? Lawrence through Birkin debates the paradox endlessly. He cannot come to any conclusion. Gerald is beloved, yet Gerald is deathly. Gerald is a brilliant young man, yet he is a murderer, he is suicidal, he is rotten at the core. It is a possibility that Birkin's passionate love for him is as foully motivated as Gudrun's and would do no good for either of them. *Can* human beings alter their fates? Though his pessimism would seem to undercut and even negate his art, Lawrence is explicit in this novel about his feelings for mankind; the vituperation expressed is perhaps unequaled in serious literature. Surely it is at the very heart of the work, in Birkin's strident ranting voice:

> I detest what I am, outwardly. I loathe myself as a human being. Humanity is a huge aggregate lie, and a huge lie is less than a small truth. Humanity is less, far less than the individual, because the individual may sometimes be capable of truth, and humanity is a tree of lies. . . .
>
> . . . I abhor humanity, I wish it was swept away. It could go, and there would be no *absolute* loss, if every human being perished to-morrow.

But Ursula also perceives in her lover a contradictory desire to "save" this doomed world, and characteristically judges this desire a weakness, and insidious form of prostitution. Birkin's perverse attachment to the world he hates is not admirable in Ursula's eyes, for Ursula is no ordinary woman but a fiercely intolerant creature who detests all forms of insincerity. She is Birkin's conscience, in a sense; his foil, his gadfly; a taunting form of himself. Yet later, immediately after Birkin declares that he loves her, she is rather disturbed by the starkly nihilistic vision he sets before her; and indeed it strikes us as more tragic than that of Shakespeare:

> We always consider the silver river of life, rolling on and quickening all the world to a brightness, on and on to heaven, flowing into a bright eternal sea, a heaven of angels thronging. But the other is our real reality . . . that dark river of dissolution. You see it rolls in us just as the other rolls—the black river of corruption. And our flowers are of this—our sea-born Aphrodite, all our white phosphorescent flowers of sensuous perfection, all our reality, nowadays.

Aphrodite herself is symptomatic of the death-process, born in what Lawrence calls the "first spasm of universal dissolution." The process cannot be halted. It is beyond the individual, beyond choice. It ends in a universal nothing, a new cycle in which humanity will play no role. The prospect is a chilling one and yet—*does* it really matter? Humanity in the aggregate is contemptible, and many people (like Diana Crich) are better off dead since their living has somehow gone wrong. No, Birkin thinks, it can't *really* matter. His mood shifts, he is no longer frustrated and despairing, he is stoical, almost mystical, like one who has given up all hope. For he has said earlier to Gerald, after their talk of the death of God and the possible necessity of the salvation through love, that reality lies outside the human sphere:

> Well, if mankind is destroyed, if our race is destroyed like Sodom, and there is this beautiful evening with the luminous land and trees, I am satisfied. That which informs it all is there, and can never be lost. After all, what is mankind but just one expression of the incomprehensible. And if mankind passes away, it will only mean that this particular expression is completed and done. . . . Humanity doesn't embody the utterance of the incomprehensible any more. Humanity is a dead letter. There will be a new embodiment, in a new way. Let humanity disappear as quick as possible.

Lawrence's shifts in mood and conviction are passionate, even unsettling. One feels that he writes to discover what he thinks, what is thinking in him, on an unconscious level. Love is an ecstatic experience. Or is it, perhaps, a delusion? Erotic love is a way of salvation—or is it a distraction, a burden? Is it something to be gone through in order that one's deepest self may be stirred to life? Or is it a very simple, utterly natural emotion . . . ? (In *Sons and Lovers* Paul Morel is impatient with Miriam's near-hysterical exaggeration of ordinary emotions; he resents her intensity, her penchant for mythologizing, and finds solace in Clara's far less complex attitude toward sexual love.) Lawrence does not really know, regardless of his dogmatic remarks about "mind-consciousness" and "blood-consciousness." He cannot *know*; he must continually strive to know, and accept continual frustration. . . .

In Lawrence's work one is struck repeatedly by the total absence of concern for community. In the novels after *Sons and Lovers* his most fully developed and self-contained characters express an indifference toward their neighbors that is almost aristocratic. Both Anna and Will Brangwen of *The Rainbow* are oblivious to the world outside their household: the nation does not exist to them; there is no war in South Africa; they are in a "private retreat" that has no nationality. Even as a child Ursula is proudly contemptuous of her classmates, knowing herself set apart from them and, as a Brangwen, superior. She is fated to reject her unimaginative lover Skrebensky who has subordinated his individuality to the nation and who would gladly give up his life to it. ("I belong to the nation," he says solemnly, "and must do my duty by the nation.") Some years later she and Gudrun express a loathing for their parents' home that is astonishing, and even the less passionate Alvina Houghton of *The Lost Girl* surrenders to outbursts of mad, hilarious jeering, so frustrated is she by the limitations of her father's household and of the mining town of Woodhouse in general. (She is a "lost" girl only in terms of England. Though her life in a primitive mountain village in Italy is not a very comfortable one, it is nevertheless superior to her former, virginal life back in provincial England.)

Lawrence might have dramatized the tragedy of his people's rootlessness, especially as it compels them to attempt desperate and often quixotic relationships as a surrogate for social and political involvement (as in *The Plumed Serpent* and *Kangaroo*); but of course he could not give life to convictions he did not feel. The human instinct for something larger than an intense, intimate bond, the instinct for community, is entirely absent in Lawrence, and this absence helps to account for the wildness of his characters' emotions. (Their passionate narrowness is especially evident when contrasted with the tolerance of a character like Leopold Bloom of *Ulysses*. Leopold thinks wistfully of his wife, but he thinks also of innumerable other people, men and women both, the living and the dead; he is a man of the city who is stirred by the myriad trivial excitements of Dublin—an adventurer writ small, but not contemptible in Joyce's eyes. His obsessions are comically perverse, his stratagems pathetic. Acceptance by Simon Dedalus and his friends would mean a great deal to poor Bloom, but of course this acceptance will be withheld; he yearns for community but is denied it.)

For the sake of argument Gudrun challenges Ursula's conviction that one can achieve a new space to be in, apart from the old: "But don't you think you'll *want* the old connection with the world—father and the rest of us, and all that it means, England and the world of thought—don't you think you'll *need* that, really to make a world?" But Ursula speaks for Lawrence in denying all inevitable social and familial connections. "One has a sort of other self, that belongs to a new planet, not to this," she says. The disagreement marks the sisters' break with each other; after this heated discussion they are no longer friends. Gudrun mocks the lovers with her false enthusiasm and deeply insults Ursula. "Go and find your new world, dear. After all, the happiest voyage is the quest of Rupert's Blessed Isles."

Lawrence's utopian plans for Rananim aside, it seems obvious that he could not have been truly interested in establishing a community of any permanence, for such a community would have necessitated a connection between one generation and the next. It would have demanded that faith in a reality beyond the individual and the individual's impulses which is absent in Lawrence—not undeveloped so much as simply absent, undiscovered. For this reason alone he seems to us distinctly un-English in any traditional sense. Fielding and Thackeray and Trollope and Dickens and Eliot and Hardy and Bennett belong to another world, another consciousness entirely. (Lawrence's kinship with Pater and Wilde, his predilection for the intensity of the moment, may have stimulated him to a vigorous glorification of Nietzschean instinct and will to power as a means of resisting aestheticism: for there is a languid cynicism about Birkin not unlike that of Wilde's prematurely weary heroes.)

Halfway around the world, in Australia, Richard Somers discovers that he misses England, for it isn't freedom but mere *vacancy* he finds in this new, disturbingly beautiful world: the absence of civilization, of culture, of inner meaning; the absence of spirit. But so long as Lawrence is in England he evokes the idea of his nation only to do battle with it, to refute it, to be nauseated by it. The upper classes are sterile and worthless, the working classes are stunted aborigines who stare after the Brangwen sisters in the street. Halliday and his London friends are self-consciously decadent—"the most pettifogging calculating Bohemia that ever reckoned its pennies." Only in the mythical structure of a fabulist work like *The Escaped Cock* can Lawrence imagine a harmonious relationship between male and female, yet even here in this Mediterranean setting the individual cannot tolerate other people, nor they him: "the little life of jealousy and property" resumes its sway and forces the man who died to flee. There is, however, no possibility of a tragic awareness in these terms; it is not tragic that the individual is compelled to break with his nation and his community because any unit larger than the individual is tainted and suspect, caught in the downward process of corruption. The community almost by definition is degraded. About this everyone is in agreement—Clifford Chatterley as well as Mellors, Hermione as well as Ursula and Gudrun. Community in the old sense is based on property and possessions and must be rejected, and all human relationships not founded upon an immediate emotional rapport must be broken. "The old ideals are dead as nails—nothing there," Birkin says early in *Women in Love*. "It seems to me there remains only this perfect union with a woman—sort of ultimate marriage—and there isn't anything else." Gerald, however, finds it difficult to agree. Making one's life up out of a woman, one woman only, seems to him impossible, just as the forging of an intense love-connection with another man—which in Lawrence's cosmology would have saved his life—is impossible.

"I only feel what I feel," Gerald says.

The core of our human tragedy has very little to do with society, then, and everything to do with the individual: with the curious self-destructive condition of the human spirit. Having rejected the theological dogma of original sin, Lawrence develops a rather similar psychological dogma to account for the diabolic split within the individual between the dictates of "mind-consciousness" and the impulses of "blood-consciousness." In his essay on Nathaniel Hawthorne in *Studies in Classic American Literature*, he interprets *The Scarlet Letter* as an allegory, a typically American allegory, of the consequences of the violent antagonism between the two ways of being. His explicitness is helpful in terms of *Women in Love*, where a rich verbal texture masks a tragically simple paradox. The cross itself is the symbol of mankind's self-division, as it is the symbol, the final haunting image, in Gerald Crich's life. (Fleeing into the snow, exhausted and broken after his ignoble attempt to strangle Gudrun, Gerald comes upon a half-buried crucifix at the top of a pole. He fears that someone is going to murder him. In terror he realizes "This was the moment when the death was uplifted, and there was no escape. Lord Jesus, was it then bound to be—Lord Jesus! He could feel the blow descending, he knew he was murdered.")

Christ's agony on the cross symbolizes our human agony at having acquired, or having been poisoned by, the "sin" of knowledge and self-consciousness. In the Hawthorne essay Lawrence says:

> Nowadays men do hate the idea of dualism. It's no good, dual we are. The cross. If we accept the symbol, then, virtually we accept the fact. We are divided against ourselves.
>
> For instance, the blood *hates* being KNOWN by the mind. It feels itself destroyed when it is KNOWN. Hence the profound instinct of privacy.
>
> And on the other hand, the mind and the spiritual consciousness of man simply *hates* the dark potency of blood-acts: hates the genuine dark sensual orgasms, which do, for the time being, actually obliterate the mind and the spiritual consciousness, plunge them in a suffocating flood of darkness.
>
> You can't get away from this.
>
> Blood-consciousness overwhelms, obliterates, and annuls mind-consciousness.
>
> Mind-consciousness extinguishes blood-consciousness, and consumes the blood.
>
> We are all of us conscious in both ways. And the two ways are antagonistic in us.
>
> They will always remain so.
>
> That is our cross.

It is obvious that Lawrence identifies with the instinct toward formal allegory and subterfuge in American literature. He understands

Hawthorne, Melville, and Poe from the inside; it is himself he speaks of when he says of Poe that he adventured into the vaults and cellars and horrible underground passages of the human soul, desperate to experience the "prismatic ecstasy" of heightened consciousness and of love. And Poe knew himself to be doomed, necessarily—as Lawrence so frequently thought himself (and his race). Indeed, Poe is far closer to Lawrence than Hawthorne or Melville:

> He died wanting more love, and love killed him. A ghastly disease, love. Poe telling us of his disease: trying even to make his disease fair and attractive. Even succeeding. Which is the inevitable falseness, duplicity of art, American art in particular.

The inevitable duplicity of art: an eccentric statement from the man who says, elsewhere (in an essay on Walt Whitman), and the essential function of art is moral. "Not aesthetic, not decorative, not pastime and recreation. But moral." Yet it is possible to see that the artist too suffers from a tragic self-division, that he is forced to dramatize the radically new shifting over of consciousness primarily in covert, even occult and deathly terms: wanting to write a novel of consummate health and triumph whose controlling symbol is the rainbow, writing in fact a despairing, floridly tragic and rather mad work that resembles poetry and music (Wagnerian music) far more than it resembles the clearly "moral" bright book of life that is the novel, Lawrence finds himself surprised and disturbed by the apocalyptic nature of this greatest effort, as if he had imagined he had written something quite different. The rhythm of Lawrence's writing is that of the American works he analyzes so irreverently and so brilliantly, a "disintegrating and sloughing of the old consciousness" and "the forming of a new consciousness underneath." Such apocalyptic books must be written because old things need to die, because the "old white psyche has to be gradually broken down before anything else can come to pass" (in the essay on Poe). Such art must be violent, it must be outlandish and diabolic at its core because it is revolutionary in the truest sense of the word. It is subversive, even traitorous; but though it seeks to overturn empires, its primary concerns are prophetic, even religious. As Lawrence says in the poem "Nemesis" (from *Pansies*), "If we do not rapidly open all the doors of consciousness /and freshen the putrid little space in which we are cribbed /the sky-blue walls of our unventilated heaven /will be bright red with blood." In any case the true artist does not determine the direction of his art; he surrenders his ego so that his deeper self may be heard. There is no freedom except in compliance with the spirit within, what Lawrence calls the Holy Ghost.

The suppressed Prologue to *Women in Love* sets forth the terms of Birkin's torment with dramatic economy. "Mind-consciousness" and "blood-consciousness" are not mere abstractions, pseudo-philosophical notions, but bitterly existential ways of perceiving and of being. When Birkin and Gerald Crich first meet they experience a subtle bond between each other, a "sudden connection" that is intensified during a mountain-climbing trip in the Tyrol. In the isolation of the rocks and snow they and their companion attain a rare sort of intimacy that is to be denied and consciously rejected when they descend again into their unusual lives. (The parallel with Gerald's death in the snow is obvious; by suppressing the Prologue and beginning with the chapter we have, "Sisters," in which Ursula and Gudrun discuss marriage and the home and the mining town and venture out to watch the wedding, Lawrence sacrificed a great deal. "Sisters" is an entirely satisfactory opening, brilliant in its own lavish way; but the Prologue with its shrill, tender, almost crazed language is far more moving.)

Preliminary to the action of *Women in Love*, and unaccountable in terms of *The Rainbow*, which centers so exclusively upon Ursula, is the passionate and undeclared relationship between Birkin and Gerald, and the tortured split between Birkin's spiritual and "sisterly" love for Hermione and his "passion of desire" for Gerald. Birkin is sickened by his obsession with Gerald; he is repulsed by his overwrought, exclusively mental relationship with Hermione (which is, incidentally, very close to the relationship of sheer nerves Lawrence discusses in his essay on Poe: the obscene love that is the "intensest nervous vibration of unison" without any erotic consummation). That Birkin's dilemma is emblematic of society's confusion in general is made clear, and convincing, by his immersion in educational theory. What is education except the gradual and deliberate building up of consciousness, unit by unit? Each unit of consciousness is the "living unit of that great social, religious, philosophic idea towards which mankind, like an organism seeking its final form, in laboriously growing," but the tragic paradox is that there *is* no great unifying idea at the present time; there is simply aimless, futile activity. For we are in the autumn of civilization, and decay, as such, cannot be acknowledged. As Birkin suffers in his awareness of his own deceitful, frustrated life, he tries to forget himself in work; but he cannot escape a sense of the futility to all attempts at "social constructiveness." The tone of the Prologue is dark indeed, and one hears Lawrence's undisguised despair in every line:

> How to get away from this process of reduction, how escape this phosphorescent passage into the tomb, which was universal though unacknowledged, this was the unconscious problem which tortured Birkin day

> and night. He came to Hermione, and found with her the pure, translucent regions of death itself, of ecstasy. In the world the autumn itself was setting in. What should a man add himself on to?—to science, to social reform, to aestheticism, to sensationalism? The whole world's constructive activity was a fiction, a lie, to hide the great process of decomposition, which had set in. What then to adhere to?

He attempts a physical relationship with Hermione which is a cruel failure, humiliating to them both. He goes in desperation to prostitutes. Like Paul Morel he suffers a familiar split between the "spiritual" woman and the "physical" woman, but his deeper anxiety lies in his unacknowledged passion for Gerald Crich. Surely homoerotic yearning has never been so vividly and so sympathetically presented as it is in Lawrence's Prologue, where Birkin's intelligent complexity, his half-serious desire to rid himself of his soul in order to escape his predicament, and his fear of madness and dissolution as a consequence of his lovelessness give him a tragic depth comparable to Hamlet's. He *wants* to love women, just as he wants to believe in the world's constructive activity; but how can a man create his own feelings? Birkin knows that he cannot: he can only suppress them by an act of sheer will. In danger of going mad or of dying—of possibly killing himself—Birkin continues his deathly relationship with Hermione, keeping his homoerotic feelings to himself and even, in a sense, secret from himself. With keen insight Lawrence analyzes Birkin's own analysis of the situation. "He knew what he felt, but he always kept the knowledge at bay. His a priori were: 'I *should* not feel like this,' and 'It is the ultimate mark of my own deficiency, that I feel like this.' Therefore though he admitted everything, he never really faced the question. He never accepted the desire, and received it as part of himself. He always tried to keep it expelled from him." Not only does Birkin attempt to dissociate himself from an impulse that *is* himself, he attempts to deny the femaleness in his own nature by objectifying (and degrading) it in his treatment of Hermione and of the "slightly bestial" prostitutes. It maddens him that he should feel sexual attraction for the male physique while for the female he is capable of feeling only a kind of fondness, a sacred love, as if for a sister. "The women he seemed to be kin to, he looked for the soul in them." By the age of thirty he is sickly and dissolute, attached to Hermione in a loveless, sadistic relationship, terrified of breaking with her for fear of falling into the abyss. Yet the break is imminent, inevitable—so the action of *Women in Love* begins.

A tragedy, then, of an informal nature, experimental in its gropings toward a resolution of the central crisis: how to integrate the male and female principles, how to integrate the organic and the "civilized," the relentlessly progressive condition of the modern world. It is not enough to be a child of nature, to cling to one's ignorance as if it were a form of blessedness; one cannot deny the reality of the external world, its gradual transformation from the Old England into the New, into an enthusiastic acceptance of the individual as an instrument in the great machine of society. When Hermione goes into her rhapsody about spontaneity and the instincts, echoing Birkin in saying that the mind is death, he contradicts her brutally by claiming that the problem is not that people have too much mind, but too little. As for Hermione herself, she is merely making words because knowledge means everything to her: "Even your animalism, you want it in your head. You don't want to *be* an animal, you want to observe your own animal functions, to get a mental thrill out of them. . . . What is it but the worst and last form of intellectualism, this love of yours for passion and the animal instincts?" But it is really himself he is attacking: Hermione is a ghastly form of himself he would like to destroy, a parody of a woman, a sister of his soul.

Women in Love must have originally been imagined as Birkin's tragedy rather than Gerald's, for though Gerald feels an attraction for Birkin, he is not so obsessed with it as Birkin is; in the Prologue he is characterized as rather less intelligent, less shrewd, than he turns out to be in subsequent chapters. Ursula's role in saving Birkin from dissolution is, then, far greater than she can know. Not only must she arouse and satisfy his spiritual yearnings, she must answer to his physical desire as well: she must, in a sense, take on the active, masculine role in their relationship. (Significantly, it is Ursula who presses them into an erotic relationship after the death of Diana Crich and her young man. It is she who embraces Birkin tightly, wanting to show him that she is no shallow prude, and though he whimpers to himself, "Not this, not this," he nevertheless succumbs to desire for her and they become lovers. Had Ursula not sensed the need to force Birkin into a physical relationship, it is possible their love would have become as spiritualized, and consequently as poisoned, as Birkin's and Hermione's.) Ursula's role in saving Birkin from destruction is comparable to Sonia's fairly magical redemption of Raskolnikov in *Crime and Punishment*, just as Gerald's suicide is comparable to Svidrigaylov's when both men are denied salvation through women by whom they are obsessed. Though the feminine principle is not sufficient to guarantee eternal happiness, it is nevertheless the way through which salvation is attained: sex is an initiation in Lawrence, a necessary and even ritualistic *event* in the process of psychic wholeness. Where in more traditional tragedy—Shakespeare's *King Lear* comes immediately to mind—it is the feminine, irrational, "dark and vicious" elements that must be resisted, since they disturb the status quo, the patriarchal cosmos, in Lawrence it is precisely the darkness, the passion, the mind-obliterating, terrible, and even vicious experience of erotic love that is necessary for salvation. The individual is split and wars futilely against himself, civilization is split and must fall into chaos if male and female principles are opposed. Lawrence's is the sounder psychology, but it does not follow that his world view is more optimistic, for to recognize a truth does not inevitably bring with it the moral strength to realize that truth in one's life.

Birkin's desire for an eternal union with another man is thwarted in *Women in Love*, and his failure leads indirectly to Gerald's death. At least this is Birkin's conviction. "He should have loved me," he says to Ursula and she, frightened, replies without sympathy, "What difference would it have made!" It is only in a symbolic dimension that the men are lovers; consciously, in the daylight world, they are never anything more than friends. In the chapter "Gladiatorial" the men wrestle together in order to stir Gerald from his boredom, and they seem to "drive their white flesh deeper and deeper against each other, as if they would break into a oneness." The effort is such that both men lose consciousness and Birkin falls over Gerald, involuntarily. When their minds are gone their opposition to each other is gone and they can become united—but only temporarily, only until Birkin regains his consciousness and moves away. At the novel's conclusion Birkin is "happily" married, yet incomplete. He will be a reasonably content and normal man, a husband to the passionate Ursula, yet unfulfilled; and one cannot quite believe that his frustrated love for Gerald will not surface in another form. His failure is not merely his own but civilization's as well: male and female are inexorably opposed, the integration of the two halves of the human soul is an impossibility in our time.

Hence the cruel frost-knowledge of *Women in Love*, the death by perfect cold Lawrence has delineated. Long before Gerald's actual death in the mountains Birkin speculates on him as a strange white wonderful demon from the north, fated like his civilization to pass away into universal dissolution, the day of "creative life" being finished. In *Apocalypse* Lawrence speaks of the long slow death of the human being in our time, the victory of repressive and mechanical forces over the organic, the pagan. The mystery religions of antiquity have been destroyed by the systematic, dissecting principle; the artist is driven as a consequence to think in deliberately mythical, archaic, chiliastic terms. How to express the inexpressible? Those poems in *Pansies* that address themselves to the problem—poems like "Wellsian Futures," "Dead People," "Ego-Bound,"

"Climb Down, O Lordly Mind," "Peace and War"—are rhetorical and strident and rather flat; it is in images that Lawrence *thinks* most clearly. He is too brilliant an artist not to breathe life even into those characters who are in opposition to his own principles. In a statement that resembles Yeats's (that the occult spirits of *A Vision* came to bring him images for his poetry) Lawrence indicates a surprising indifference to the very concept of the Apocalypse itself: "We do not care, vitally, about theories of the Apocalypse. . . . What we care about is the release of the imagination. . . . What does the Apocalypse matter, unless in so far as it gives us imaginative release into another vital world?"

This jaunty attitude is qualified by the images that are called forth by the imagination, however: the wolfishness of Gerald and his mother; the ghoulishness of the Beldover miners; the African totems (one has a face that is void and terrible in its mindlessness; the other has a long, elegant body with a tiny head, a face crushed small like a beetle's); Hermione striking her lover with a paperweight of lapis lazuli and fairly swooning with ecstasy; Gerald digging his spurs into his mare's sides, into wounds that are already bleeding; the drowned Diana Crich with her arms still wrapped tightly about the neck of her young man; the demonic energy of Winifred's rabbit, and Gudrun's slashed, bleeding arm which seems to tear across Gerald's brain; the uncanny, terrifying soullessness of Innsbruck; the stunted figure of the artist Loerke; the final vision of Gerald as the frozen carcass of a dead male. These are fearful images, and what has Lawrence to set against them but the embrace of a man and a woman, a visionary transfiguration of the individual by love?—and even the experience of love, of passion and unity, is seen as ephemeral.

Birkin sees Gerald and Gudrun as flowers of dissolution, locked in the death-process; he cannot help but see Gerald as Cain, who killed his brother. Though in one way *Women in Love* is a naturalistic work populated with realistic characters and set in altogether probable environments, in another way it is inflexible and even rather austerely classical: Gerald is Cain from the very first and his fate is settled. Birkin considers his friend's accidental killing of his brother and wonders if it is proper to think in terms of *accident* at all. Has everything that happens a universal significance? Ultimately he does not believe that there is anything accidental in life: "it all hung together, in the deepest sense." (And it follows that no one is murdered accidentally: ". . . a man who is murderable is a man who in a profound if hidden lust desires to be murdered.") Gerald plainly chooses his murderer in Gudrun, and it is in the curious, misshapen form of Loerke that certain of Gerald's inclinations are given their ultimate realization. Gerald's glorification of the machine and of himself as a god of the machine is parodied by Loerke's inhuman willfulness: Gudrun sees him as the rock-bottom of all life. Unfeeling, stoic, he cares about nothing except his work, he makes not the slightest attempt to be at one with anything, he exists a "pure, unconnected will" in a stunted body. His very being excites Gerald to disgusted fury because he is finally all that Gerald has imagined for himself—the subordination of all spontaneity, the triumph of "harmony" in industrial organization.

Of the bizarre nightmare images stirred in Lawrence's imagination by the idea of the Apocalypse, Loerke is perhaps the most powerful. He is at once very human, and quite inhuman. He is reasonable, even rather charming, and at the same time deathly—a "mud-child," a creature of the underworld. His name suggests that of Loki, the Norse god of discord and mischief, the very principle of dissolution. A repulsive and fascinating character, he is described by Lawrence as a gnome, a bat, a rabbit, a troll, a chatterer, a magpie, a maker of disturbing jokes, with the blank look of inorganic misery behind his buffoonery. That he is an artist, and a homosexual as well, cannot be an accident. He is in Lawrence's imagination the diabolic alter ego who rises up to mock all that Lawrence takes to be sacred. Hence his uncanny power, his parodistic talent: he accepts the hypothesis that industry has replaced religion and he accepts his role as artist in terms of industry, without sentimental qualms. Art should interpret industry; the artist fulfills himself in acquiescence to the machine. Is there nothing apart from work, mechanical work?—Gudrun asks. And he says without hesitation, "Nothing but work!"

Loerke disgusts Birkin and Gerald precisely because he embodies certain of their own traits. He is marvelously self-sufficient; he wishes to ingratiate himself with no one; he is an artist who completely understands and controls his art; he excites the admiration of the beautiful Gudrun, and even Ursula, is interested in him for a while. Most painful, perhaps, is his homosexuality. He is not divided against himself, not at all tortured by remorse or conscience. In the Prologue to the novel Birkin half-wishes he might rid himself of his soul, and Loerke is presented as a creature without a soul, one of the "little people" who finds his mate in a human being. It is interesting to note that the rat-like qualities in Loerke are those that have attracted Birkin in other men: Birkin has felt an extraordinary desire to come close to and to know and "as it were to eat" a certain type of Cornish man with dark, fine, stiff hair and dark eyes like holes in his head or like the eyes of a rat (see the Prologue); and he has felt the queer, subterranean, repulsive beauty of a young man with an indomitable manner "like a quick, vital rat" (see the chapter "A Chair"). The Nietzschean quality of Loerke's haughtiness and his loathing of other people, particularly women, remind us of the aristocratic contempt expressed by the middle-aged foreigner whom Tom Brangwen admires so much in the first chapter of *The Rainbow*: the man has a queer monkeyish face that is in its way amost beautiful, he is sardonic, dry-skinned, coldly intelligent, mockingly courteous to the women in his company (one of whom has made love with Tom previously), a creature who strangely rouses Tom's blood and who, in the form of Anna Lensky, will be his mate. There is no doubt but that Lawrence, a very different physical type, and temperamentally quite opposed to the cold, life-denying principle these men embody, was nevertheless powerfully attracted by them. There is an irresistible *life* to Loerke that makes us feel the strength of his nihilistic charm.

Surely not accidental is the fact that Loerke is an artist. He expresses a view of art that all artists share, to some extent, despite their protestations to the contrary. It is Flaubert speaking in Loerke, declaring art supreme and the artist's life of little consequence; when Loerke claims that his statuette of a girl on a horse is no more than an artistic composition, a certain form without relation to anything outside itself, he is echoing Flaubert's contention that there is no such thing as a subject, there is only style. ("What seems beautiful to me, what I should like to write," Flaubert said, in a remark now famous, "is a book about nothing, a book dependent on nothing external. . . .") Loerke angers Ursula by declaring that his art pictures nothing, "absolutely nothing," there is no connection between his art and the everyday world, they are two different and distinct planes of existence, and she must not confuse them. In his disdainful proclamation of an art that refers only to itself, he speaks for the aesthetes of the nineteenth century against whom Lawrence had to define himself as a creator of vital, moral, life-enhancing art. Though Lawrence shared certain of their beliefs—that bourgeois civilization was bankrupt, that the mass of human beings was hopelessly ignorant and contemptible—he did not want to align himself with their extreme rejection of "ordinary" life and of nature itself. (Too unbridled a revulsion against the world would lead one to the sinister self-indulgent fantasies of certain of the decadent poets and artists—the bizarre creations of Oscar Wilde and Huysmans and Baudelaire, and of Gustave Moreau and Odilon Redon and Jan Toorop among others.) Loerke's almost supernatural presence drives Ursula and Birkin away, and brings to the surface the destructive elements in the love of Gudrun and Gerald. He is an artist of decay: his effect upon Gudrun is like that of a subtle poison.

"Life doesn't *really* matter," Gudrun says. "It is one's art which is central."

Symbolically, then, Gerald witnesses the destruction of his love, or of a part of his own soul, by those beliefs that had been a kind of religion to him in his operating of the mines. Lawrence himself plays with certain of his worst fears by giving them over to Loerke and Gudrun, who toy with them, inventing for their amusement a mocking dream of the destruction of the world: humanity invents a perfect explosive that blows up the world, perhaps; or the climate shifts and the world goes cold and snow falls everywhere and "only white creatures, polar-bears, white foxes, and men like awful white snow-birds, persisted in ice cruelty." It is Lawrence's nightmare, the Apocalypse without resurrection, without meaning; a vision as bleak and as tragically unsentimental as Shakespeare's.

Only in parable, in myth, can tragedy be transcended. In that beautiful novella *The Escaped Cock*, written while Lawrence was dying, the Christian and the pagan mate, the male and the female come together in a perfect union, and the process of dissolution is halted. . . . Poetic, Biblical in its rhythms, *The Escaped Cock* is an extraordinary work in that it dramatizes Lawrence's own sense of resurrection from near death (he had come close to dying several times) and that it repudiates his passion for changing the world. . . . Simply to live in a body, to live as a mortal human being—this is enough, and this is everything. Only a man who had come close to dying himself and who had despaired of his efforts to transform the human world could have written a passage like this, in awed celebration of the wonders of the existential world:

> The man who had died looked nakedly onto life, and saw a vast resoluteness everywhere flinging itself up in stormy or subtle wave-crests, foam-tips emerging out of the blue invisible, a black-and-orange cock, or the green flame tongues out of the extremes of the fig-tree. They came forth, these things and creatures of spring, glowing with desire and with assertion. . . . The man who had died looked on the great swing into existence of things that had not died, but he saw no longer their tremulous desire to exist and to be. He heard instead their ringing, defiant challenge to all other things existing. . . . And always, the man who had died saw not the bird alone, but the short, sharp wave of life of which the bird was the crest. He watched the queer, beaky motion of the creature. . . .
>
> And the destiny of life seemed more fierce and compulsive to him even than the destiny of death.

The man who had died asks himself this final question: *From what, and to what, could this infinite whirl be saved?*

The mystic certitude of *The Escaped Cock*, like the serenity of "The Ship of Death" and "Bavarian Gentians," belongs to a consciousness that has transcended the dualism of tragedy. The split has not been healed, it has simply been transcended; nearing death, Lawrence turns instinctively to the allegorical mode, the most primitive and the most sophisticated of all visionary expressions. *Women in Love* is, by contrast, irresolute and contradictory; it offers only the finite, tentative "resurrection" of marriage between two very incomplete people. Like Connie Chatterley and her lover Mellors, the surviving couple of *Women in Love* must fashion their lives in a distinctly unmythic, unidyllic landscape, their fates to be bound up closely with that of their civilization. How are we to escape history? —defy the death-process of our culture? With difficulty. In sorrow. So long as we live, even strengthened as we are by the "mystic conjunction," the "ultimate unison" between men and women, our lives are tempered by the ungovernable contingencies of the world that is no metaphor, but our only home.

GEORGE LEVINE

"*Lady Chatterley's Lover*"

The consciousness of the separation between language and life suggests why *Lady Chatterley's Lover* had to become such a naughty book to the culture Lawrence was trying to reach (despite his own contempt for the effort to shock or *épater le bourgeois*). It stands in parodic relation to the tradition of moral-aesthetic realism, while itself (good parody that it is) belonging to that tradition. It stands almost equally against the developing tradition that was transforming the hero into the artist. It is, at any rate, a novel that refuses to "give up," as one that struggles unevenly by reappropriation of old myths to destroy the conventions of language and society that stood between writer and reality. It is an immensely personal book, caught inevitably in the contradictions of language and art, in which Lawrence nevertheless comes close to succeeding in his quest to stand impersonally free of the frightened will both of his culture and of himself.

Necessarily, then, the novel is importantly about novel writing. Clifford Chatterley and Mrs. Bolton are Victorian realists. Both of them write gossip, as the narrator calls it, and the letter of Mrs. Bolton to Connie in Venice is really a virtuoso parody of the texture of much realist fiction. Clifford's stories are also gossipy, if more intellectual and analytic (as in a later phase of realism): "The observation was extraordinary and peculiar. But there was no touch, no actual contact. It was as if the whole thing took place in a vacuum. And since the field of life is largely an artificially lighted stage today, the stories were curiously true to modern life, to the modern psychology, that is." Like the lovable Philip Wakem

From *The Realistic Imagination: English Fiction from Frankenstein to Lady Chatterley*.

before him, Clifford is a cripple. His capacity to see with such minuteness and to register details so precisely derives from the incapacity to be engaged. He does, indeed, become the perfect representative of the modern writer as we have watched him being imagined by earlier writers.

But more important for my purpose here, Clifford brings together two images—one of the crippled and disenchanted artist seeing clearly by virtue of staying out of "touch," and the other of the merely created being. What we first learn about Clifford is that he was shipped back to England from the war "more or less in bits." Like Frankenstein's monster he is "more or less" put together again. For Lawrence he is no longer human, but merely pieced together mechanical fragments. Life is literally organic, and if Lawrence seems rather brutal and unfeeling about Clifford it is because he takes Clifford as a construction of modern civilization itself: an effect of the war, and a figure reduced physically to what the culture has chosen for itself in the person of those absurdly named intellectuals, Tommy Dukes (the best of them), Charlie May, Arnold B. Hammond, and Winterslow. He is mere mental consciousness. Tommy Dukes, who knows he is himself merely a "Mental-lifer," nevertheless knows as well the consequence of being one. What he says about the relation between ideas and life explains both Clifford's monstrousness and the critical importance of not being satisfied with the observer's stance in which one merely knows without touching: "Hate's a growing thing like anything else. It's the inevitable outcome of forcing ideas on to life, of forcing one's deepest instincts; our deepest instincts we force according to certain ideas. We drive ourselves with a formula, like a machine. The logical mind pretends to rule the roost, and the roost turns into pure hate."

Clifford's world is the world of the machine. In *Lady Chatterley's Lover* we have the final reversal of realism because in it the monster is not the irrational life-energy hidden in the woods beyond society, but society itself. The possibility of redemption lies in those woods, where society feared the monster lurked. All the time, Lawrence implies, it was itself the monster. Clifford is the Benjamin Franklin, that is, the Frankenstein of *Lady Chatterley's Lover*, and the satyr gamekeeper, of course, is the one figure that might restore life, who combines sexual vitality with tenderness and compassion and the capacity to articulate it. Thus, the world encompassed by the conventions of realism is merely an animated corpse; the world belonging to the irrational and mythic energies of nature, Tennyson's "ape and tiger," is the only truly human reality.

It is odd how, in pushing this reversal, Lawrence also signals certain continuities with the best Victorian fiction. In Victorian realism, one also finds a gossipy community too ready to apply general moral maxims and cruelly insensitive to the particular case. Maggie's position in *The Mill on the Floss*, another novel struggling to get beyond the crystallized conventions of a moribund society, is closely analogous to Mellors's and Connie's. Mellors, trapped by a brutal wife, is not very distant from Stephen Blackpool in *Hard Times*, trapped by his wife. Of course, in Lawrence the social regulations have no binding moral force as they have in Dickens, only the stupid force of convention. What Lawrence is determined on is the absolute severance (only partly completed in Hardy) between the social rule and the moral right. Indeed, the idea of "moral right" is irrelevant, and the language of moral convention is mocked and parodied. It is demonstrated to be dead.

For this reason, the whole narrative strategy of the novel seems an almost deliberate slap at our conventions of reading. The narrator is reckless with clichés, and for much of the first half of the book trivializes what should be dramatically powerful with hackneyed phrases that a Victorian novelist would have been embarrassed to use. The first sentence announces that this is a tragic age, but the last sentence of the first paragraph is reduced to "We've got to live, no matter how many skies have fallen." Clifford is "more or less in bits." Connie must "live and learn." Describing Connie's loneliness, the narrator says, "There's lots of good fish in the sea." Listening to the intellectuals, she must sit "quiet as a mouse." Describing the pretty color of the rock burned in the mines, the narrator sneers, "It's an ill-wind that brings nobody good." Such language disappears with Mellors, except when he himself uses it in bitter defensiveness. But the tone is aggressively cheapening as if to announce that all we conventionally value in narrative is merely trivial.

Such language is appropriate, we must feel, to the kind of novel the narrator describes in a very Victorian "intrusion" in chapter 9: "But the novel, like gossip, can . . . excite spurious sympathies and recoils, mechanical and deadening to the psyche. The novel can glorify the most corrupt feelings so long as they are *conventionally* 'pure.' Then the novel, like gossip, becomes at last vicious, and, like gossip, all the more vicious because it is always ostensibly on the side of the angels. Mrs. Bolton's gossip was always on the side of the angels." What one needs is a new language, for the language of realism has become only the language of gossip. "All the great words, it seemed to Connie, were cancelled for her generation: love, joy, happiness, home, mother, father, husband, all these great dynamic words were half dead now, and dying from day to day." So it is that Connie "hated words" because they came "between her and life," and so it is that as Connie begins to break out of the grip of Clifford's mental consciousness the text, in chapter 8, suddenly begins to overflow with literary allusions, strangled among clichés. To "touch" Mellors, Connie must purge herself of "words," and together, Lawrence and Mellors struggle to a new vocabulary, a vocabulary that might at least intimate the wonder of the impersonal organic life from which civilization fled as from a monster. It is for this reason that Lawrence touchingly dwells on "fuck" and "cunt," conscious of how they will disturb his audience, and anxious that they register, through that disturbance, the vitality that lies buried under conventional words and conventional social ordering.

In his rejection of the conventions of realism, Lawrence belongs nevertheless to that great struggle of the realists both to use and to reject literature and language, for the sake of a reality beyond language. He is trapped like those before him in language, though the terms have changed and though he rightly determines that what the Victorians used to register the complexity and streamingless of experience was not hardened and unreal. It was a literary and historical fact that the reality of the Victorian novelists had gone bad. The First World War had blown Clifford and realism to "bits," and in the effort to keep Connie herself from "going to pieces," Lawrence seeks a new vision and a new art.

The Victorian realists had put their faith in the "fact," and the fact had failed them. But the fact of Victorian realism remained beyond the particular surfaces and conventions of order, or disorder, we may find from novel to novel. We can hear in Lawrence's own comments, in *Lady Chatterley's Lover*, on the spirit of genuine fiction, echoes of the ideals and the achievements of the Victorians themselves. In the intensity of his moral engagement, in his radical attempt to reinfuse vitality and meaning into a world from which meaning had been withdrawn, in his quest to find a form that would honor the streamingness of experience without Thackerayan diffusion of plots, in his effort to find a new language to make a vital conjunction between art and experience, Lawrence was perhaps the last of the great Victorians. This is not so clearly distinguishable from George Eliot, after all:

> After all, one may hear the most private affairs of other people, but only in a spirit . . . of fine, discriminative sympathy. For even satire is a form of sympathy. It is the way our sympathy flows and recoils that really determines our lives. And here lies the vast importance of the novel, properly handled. It can inform and lead into new places the flow of our sympathetic consciousness, and it can lead our sympathy away in recoil from things gone dead. Therefore, the novel, properly handled, can reveal the most secret places of life: for it is in the *passional* secret places of life, above all, that the tide of sensitive awareness needs to ebb and flow, cleansing and freshening.

"If art does not enlarge men's sympathies," says George Eliot, "it does nothing morally." "Art is the nearest thing to life."

Lawrence rejects the realists to embrace the monster they feared. In so doing, he transforms, in the very spirit of realism, the language of fiction, the art of the novel. He leaves Connie and Mellors, however, still seeking that consummation implicit in the image of the Grecian urn I invoked at the start. Lawrence knows that he doesn't know, and lives with that knowledge. His language strains toward those "secret places" as Connie and Mellors lean undespairing toward each other.

ROSS C. MURFIN

Lawrence and Shelley

For Lawrence, the destructive eminence of Shelley is generally the tendency of Shelley's poetry to focus on that which is beyond what is attainable in the present moment. This tendency of Shelley's to see always in terms of the far-off is not limited, in Lawrence's opinion, to a destructive and self-annihilating dream of love. Rather, as the later poet tells us time and again through his own writings, the predeccessor always seems to dream of escaping the tangles of present stuff—whatever that stuff may be. Furthermore, these tendencies, which were dreams for Shelley but have become instinct to us all, are, in Lawrence's opinion, worth developing into something truer to the original, primitive reality that Lawrence believes in *because* of the pains he feels when he hearkens too much to what he will call in "Snake," his most famous poem, "the voices" of his "human education."

One of the poems that Lawrence is fondest of recalling in his own poetic search for exiled, tactile, present reality (or rather for the reality that he as a poet is exiled from) is Shelley's "Ode to the West Wind." Working with—and giving us a new feel for—Shelley's terms, Lawrence suggests that his own poetry must nevertheless accomplish a new kind of inspiration and accomplish it, in part, by bending the Romantic poet's force in new directions.

"Not I, not I, but the wind that blows through me!" Lawrence begins his "Song of a Man Who Has Come Through," the exceptionally fine and hopeful lyric he wrote in 1914 after his marriage to Frieda:

A fine wind is blowing the new direction of Time.
If only I let it bear me, carry me, if only it carry me!
If only I am sensitive, subtle, oh, delicate, a winged gift!
If only, most lovely of all, I yield myself and am borrowed
By the fine, fine wind that takes its course through the chaos of
the world
Like a fine, an exquisite chisel, a wedge-blade inserted;
If only I am keen and hard like the sheer tip of a wedge
Driven by invisible blows,
The rock will split, we shall come at the wonder, we shall
find the Hesperides.

Because the "new direction of Time" is borne by a wind that "takes its course through the chaos of the world," the man who wishes not to be an anachronism must let himself be borne by that same wind. The wind that has been "blowing the [old] direction," by implication, must have carried man away from the world's chaos. Its breath may well have been that of the all-too-human voices of civilization, the inspring voices whose dreamy messages have become our very instincts.

The poet generally directs our attention to the subject of the old, exiling sources of inspiration through allusions to a particular poetic inspiration. Shelley becomes almost a metonym for the absent subject, the less-than-fine old winds that have not carried men and women into and "through the chaos of the world / Like a fine, an exquisite chisel." Lawrence's poem, as it charts an antithetical direction, gives itself definition by calling Shelley up as thesis. This, in turn, is accomplished by working inside the predecessor's terms. Shelley had spoken of the wind's "unseen presence" as "breath." Lawrence pictures his fine wind as an unseen hammer instead: that way, his wind can seem at once harder and more effectual. Shelley's figure resides within and just beyond the surface of Lawrence's, which pictures the fine new wind's "invisible blows." Shelley had spoken of his West Wind as the "dirge"

Of the dying year, to which this closing night
Will be the dome of a vast sepulchre,
Vaunted with all thy congregated might

Of vapors, from whose solid atmosphere
Black rain, And fire, and hail will burst: oh hear!
(lines 23–28)

So Lawrence clearly at once identifies and contrasts his wind with Shelley's by making it the clarion call of a new era. It is even, perhaps, the wind that Shelley foresaw but could not yet call upon or write about:

Thine azure sister of the Spring shall blow

Her clarion o'er the dreaming earth, and fill
(Driving sweet buds like flocks to feed in air)
With living hues and odours plain and hill.
(lines 9–12)

It would seem that Lawrence verifies the antithetical nature of his own poetic subject and statement by identifying it with the life-giving counterwind that Shelley only sensed by flashes of prescience. And yet, once again, the compelling power of Shelley's figures is almost eerie; the invisible force by which Lawrence is "like the sheer tip of a wedge / Driven" may seem rather different from the "azure sister" Shelley foresaw as his own wind's counterpart, and yet the earlier poet too had seen the fine new wind "Driving" its earthly subjects.

The most obvious—and important—way in which Lawrence calls Shelley up both as the old wind and as a metonym *for* those winds is by describing his new poetic role in ways that recall Shelley's. He prays for the freedom to be borne:

If only I let it bear me, carry me, if only it carry me!
If only I am sensitive, subtle, oh, delicate, a winged gift!
If only, most lovely of all, I yield myself and am borrowed
By the fine, fine wind that takes its course through the chaos
of the world.

Shelley's wish had not sounded so different, after all:

If I were a dead leaf thou mightest bear;
If I were a swift cloud to fly with thee;
A wave to pant beneath thy power, and share

The impulse of thy strength, only less free
Than thou, O uncontrollable!
(lines 43–47)

"Oh, lift me as a wave, a leaf, a cloud!" Shelley continues. "I fall upon the thorns of life! I bleed!"

A heavy weight of hours has chained and bowed
One too like thee: tameless and swift, and proud.
(lines 53–56)

Lawrence's eloquent plea to be borne in the direction of thorn and rock and chaos, to be carried along in time and flux rather than to be "chained and bowed" by "A heavy weight of hours" on one hand or to escape them on the other—this wish is given power and meaning by its familiarity with

Shelley. Implicit in Lawrence's lines is the realization that the quest for a new inspiration must locate the old one or at least some representative of it and raise powerful questions about its honesty and advisability. This involves recollection, which is by necessity a resubmission to the old influence or inspiration. Lawrence seems to sense that the apprehension of the new wind and the bending of the old one are twin halves of one event: neither activity can take place without the other. The essential self's apprehension of a still unknown way depends upon an almost inexplicable feeling of dissatisfaction with the only one it has ever known, whether it be the high old way of Romantic love, the casual roadside way of Hardy's dark-eyed "gentleman," or the Shelleyan way of putting the inspired self at the center of poems.

In the first line of his "Song," Lawrence associates the new direction with the habit of singing nothing of the self. He does not even say, "I sing not of myself but of the wind that blows through myself." Rather, his first sentence—"Not I . . . but the wind that blows through me"—seeks to be impersonal to the point that it is not even a sentence. The verb "sing" or "speak," though expected, is conspicuously absent, and any guesses about the part of speech played by the personal pronoun are bound to remain hazardous. Because Lawrence alludes to an old inspiration, begs to move in a new direction, and implies that the yet untravelled way will be the way of "not I, but the wind," we, by a loose process of deduction, arrive at the understanding that Shelley and those he stands for were poets only of the I. They were singers who sang with and about their own breath, who invoked natural forces or objects (such as the wind) and even claimed to be singing of the world, but who were in fact making our world out of their dream-bearing breath. If we return to Shelley's poem after immersing ourselves in Lawrence's, can we find the contradiction of which the later man's poem is a flash of comprehension? (As in his love poems, Lawrence does not fully "come through" in his "Song of a Man Who Has Come Through," except to the extent that by recognizing an epistemological contradiction one moves in a new direction, for if the central self lived fully in the old epistemology, no contradictions would be seen, or rather, they would be thought and called consistencies.)

There is indeed a certain sense in which the "Ode to the West Wind" gives evidence of a desperate confusion. One of the first things that may strike a modern reader of the poem is the way in which the poet's extremely urgent address to the wind turns on itself. That is to say, the increasing vigor of Shelley's cries and, finally, his *demands* to be lightly borne as a leaf or "wingéd seed" make him all the more a separate force, a vexed and vexing power apart, the opposite of what Lawrence knows a naturally inspired man must be when he wishes to be "sensitive, subtle, oh, delicate, a winged gift!" It might be argued that all poetic prayers for all kinds of inspiration are inevitably really commands ("Sing Heavenly Muse"), and therefore whenever a poet tells a muse he needs some motivation, he is really trying to motivate a muse, move divinity or nature, pay himself the ultimate compliment by becoming a muse's muse, and prove the veracity of the compliment by proceeding to write an inspired poem. This is especially true of Shelley and, even more, of his address and petition to the West Wind. As early as the first line there is a studied breathiness in Shelley's invocation, a breathiness which requires the reader who reads aloud to look like Aeolus himself as he or she puffs and puffs through the line ("O wild West wind, thou breath . . ."). By the last line of this first stanza there is a loud, breathy, exclamatory repetition ("hear, oh hear!") that makes us simultaneously picture the poet as wind and as one who tells the wind what to do.

To the modern reader who looks hard at Shelley's ode, there is still more evidence that the West Wind is simultaneously a trope for the natural world and its antithesis, the self-sufficient self. That evidence is what might be called the failure of the poem. By this I mean its failure to succeed in its avowed goal of tapping awesome and seemingly eternal natural force or even of becoming the lyre of this power that "chariotest" seeds "to their dark and wintry bed," this "Wild Spirit, which art moving everywhere; / Destroyer and preserver." Immediately after commanding the wind to "hear, oh hear" his invocation in the last line of stanza 1, Shelley gives us two stanzas which could hardly be more mythopoeic, further removed from "a wood that skirts the Arno, near Florence," and a "day when that tempestuous wind, whose temperature is at once mild and animating, was collecting the vapours which pour down the autumnal rains.

In the second stanza Shelley pictures the wind as one whose clouds, "Angels of rain and lightning," are "Shook from the tangled boughs of Heaven and Ocean" and spread

> On the blue surface of thine aëry surge,
> Like the bright hair uplifted from the head
>
> Of some fierce Maenad.
>
> (lines 17–21)

In the third stanza the poet seems to go even further from his subject, the "wild West Wind" and "breath of Autumn's being." He speaks of

> Thou who didst waken from his summer dreams
> The blue Mediterranean, where he lay,
> Lulled by the coil of his crystàlline streams,

> Beside a pumice isle in Baiae's bay,
> And saw in sleep old palaces and towers
> Quivering within the wave's intenser day,
>
> All overgrown with azure moss and flowers
> So sweet, the sense faints picturing them!
> (lines 29–36)

Our sense that Shelley's address to the West Wind is really a plea to the self to inspire the self, that the commanding tone the poet uses to address nature is symptomatic of the poet's mortal fear of chaotic external reality and his desire not to be driven by it but rather to drive it (and thus live and write apart from its exciting and despoiling powers), seems to be borne out by the poem that gets written, the kind of inspiration that follows the invocation. This is a lyric in which figures do not even seem to grow out of subject and setting but, rather, out of other figures. The image of the Maenad's hair is suggested by an image of clouds as hair which, in turn, seems to be generated by simultaneous images of the environment as a tree and of tree boughs as hair. The picture of "old palaces and towers" is the vision of what "The blue Mediterranean . . . saw in sleep" *before* he was "waken[ed] from his summer dreams" by wind. This is a poem in which the achievement of the state requested in the invocator's petition—in this case, identification with the wind—takes place only in conditional syntax. Immediately after the two myth-making stanzas which follow the petition at the end of stanza 1, Shelley says, in stanza 4, that *if* he were a leaf or a cloud or a wave and "share[d] / The impulse of" the wind's strength, he "would ne'er have striven / As thus with thee in prayer in my sore need."

In the fifth stanza and shortest sentence of the poem, Shelley commands:

> Be thou, Spirit fierce,
> My spirit. Be thou me . . . !

Coming to the text after Lawrence, who suggests that in times past there has been a profound dissociation of the artistic sensibility and the world's chaos, the modern reader can almost hear the stanza speak two commands. There is the one that calls out for full identification of self and world, and there is another one that D. H. Lawrence has developed, a windy message in which the poet first tells the "Spirit fierce" simply to "Be," then tells himself to "Be" himself—and to be apart from that with which he supposedly wishes to be identified. To hear this latter call is, of course, to hear Shelley verging towards the kinds of self-analysis that

Lawrence will practice, to hear the kind of criticism of the dream-instinct that, Lawrence hopes, will eventually free us to move in the new direction.

The last utterance of Shelley's ode is even more interesting than the fifth stanza:

> Be through my lips to unawakened earth
>
> The trumpet of a prophecy! O Wind,
> If Winter comes, can Spring be far behind?

Why does a master of language such as Shelley end one of his most powerful poems with an eye rhyme? Convention is no adequate answer, for this is the only eye rhyme in the "Ode to the West Wind," and its position at what should be that of a trumpeting, apocalyptic call is surely puzzling. If one reads the poem as I have been suggesting it can be read, then the concluding couplet almost has the effect of turning the last stanza into a cry of despair. The poet is sinking, desperate, failing in his powers on one hand while on the other remaining utterly uninspired by the wind. It has not become him, borne him afar, empowered him. The poet, through the last stanza, ever so faintly suggests the paradox that Lawrence will find, the one that will stun Lawrence into a search for the new direction by bending Shelleyan breath. The attempt to avoid agency and to find originality through self-motivation is a route which leads to failure and, ultimately, to that state of acquiescent submission to the chaotic power of the world which is far less powerful than agency itself.

It is important to remember that Lawrence sees his own originality manifesting itself in the development of paradox, in the sensing of a profound problem in a predecessor's epistemology, and in the treacherously difficult attempt to throw it into relief. To heighten the visibility of a paradox in sensibility is, for Lawrence, the only way a man can begin to overturn values, to push off in new directions of time. That kind of heightening goes on as surely in "Song of a Man Who Has Come Through" as it does in "Lightning." It can be seen in the way the poet shows us how easy it is to do as Shelley does, that is, to confuse himself with the wind, to believe the very subject of his search is something different from what it really is. "If only, most lovely of all, I yield myself and am borrowed," he writes,

> By the fine, fine wind that takes its course through the chaos of
> the world
> Like a fine, an exquisite chisel, a wedge-blade inserted;
> If only I am keen and hard like the sheer tip of a wedge
> Driven by invisible blows,
> The rock will split, we shall come at the wonder, we shall find
> the Hesperides.

Here is a moment of danger, a moment of being pointed in that old direction where *world* (here called wind like "an exquisite chisel, a wedge-blade") is just another name for "self" ("keen and hard like . . . a wedge / Driven"). Until the line in which Lawrence says "Driven by invisible blows," it is impossible to separate the poet from his subject by his image. But with that ninth line of the poem, the shortest and penultimate line of the stanza, we can make the separation. The line is a triumphant recall of Shelley, for it powerfully amplifies what in Shelley's poem is—even for the modern reader—a barely audible and well-hidden admission. It asserts the primacy of any cosmic force over any agent; it declares that the existence of any chisel is inevitable evidence for the hammer, however invisible that greater reality or force may be to one yet lost in summer dreams of self. Once that line has been written, once that assertion has been made, Lawrence can conclude the ten-line stanza with trumpeting prophecy:

> The rock will split, we shall come at the wonder, we shall find
> the Hesperides.

That the line is an assertion is fitting, of course, since the opening out of Shelley's poem took the form of a question. Lawrence sees himself as the Spring Shelley hoped would follow Winter, the coming true of Shelley's prophecy of his own influence. But what Lawrence foresees or prophesies is not an inspired or influenced new poet or even new direction but, rather, the very world itself—the wonder—the place he has never seen but the existence of which his central self or soul passionately believes in.

The word "Hesperides" is, of course, maddening, its tone treacherous. Is it a joke? Or could a final allusion to myth and the Romantic Tennyson amount to a retraction Lawrence offers Shelley, the poet who dreamed of a dreaming Mediterranean and fierce Maenads? Is the word a moment of doubt, doubt that the rock of our grandparents' dreams can ever truly be split, or doubt that, even if it can, the wonder come by will be anything like the one that Lawrence believes in? Certainly, doubts of this kind pervade the other poems by Lawrence which converse with Shelley's ode. There are quite a few of these, and although space permits a lengthy discussion only of the "Song of a Man Who Has Come Through," it may be worth noting that a lyric like "Craving for Spring," a poem published in the same volume as "Song," is every bit as interested in recalling Shelley but a good bit less certain that the project is imminently feasible.

Lawrence addresses spring (rather than the wind) in a decidedly Shelleyan mode, perhaps so that he can agree with the need to be borne into a new era and at the same time minimize the importance of inspiration in the sense of breath or voice:

> Ah come, come quickly, spring!
> Come and lift us towards our culmination, we myriads;
> we who have never flowered, like patient cactuses.
> Come and lift us to our end, to blossom, bring us to our summer,
> we who are winter-weary in the winter of the world.

Elsewhere in the poem Lawrence seems wittily to call upon Shelley, only to end his stanza by telling us that Shelley is not really what he meant at all. The passage in "Ode to the West Wind" that Lawrence directs us towards is this one:

> Drive my dead thoughts over the universe
> Like withered leaves to quicken a new birth!
> And, by the incantation of this verse,
>
> Scatter, as from an unextinguished hearth
> Ashes and sparks, my words among mankind!
> (lines 63–67)

Lawrence writes:

> I wish it were spring
> cunningly blowing on the fallen sparks, odds and ends of the old,
> scattered fire,
> and kindling shapely little conflagrations
> curious long-legged foals, and wide-eared calves, and naked sparrow-bubs.
> I wish that spring
> would start the thundering traffic of feet
> new feet on the earth, beating with impatience.

The "fallen sparks, odds and ends of the old scattered fire" that Lawrence wishes would be kindled into new conflagrations do not turn out to be Shelleyan "words" and "thoughts," what the elder poet referred to as the "sparks" he wished to be "Scatter[ed]." They are not ideas at all. Rather, they are the sperm of winter becoming the summer's thundering traffic of feet.

The idea of a purely biological reawakening is probably offered with Whitman as much in mind as Shelley. In one of his most sensual effusions, entitled "From Pent Up Aching Rivers" (1860), Whitman hymns the reproductive power of the world in spring, "Singing the song of procreation, / Singing the need of superb children," chanting

> Of the smell of apples and lemons, of the pairing of birds,
> Of the wet of woods, of the lapping of waves.
> (lines 5–6, 17–18)

Read with Whitman in mind, the end of "Craving for Spring" seems a doubtful proclamation of competence in being free of old ashes, of the old, idealistic, Shelleyan fires. The last line of Lawrence's poem, indeed, seems to hint at the author's deep doubts that he can see the world in its pristine sensuality. "If you catch a whiff of violets from the darkness of the shadow of man," the poet says,

> it will be spring in the world,
> it will be spring in the world of the living;
> wonderment organising itself, heralding itself with the violets,
> stirring of new seasons.
>
> Ah, do not let me die on the brink of such anticipation!
> Worse, let me not deceive myself.

Lawrence, if he is here doubting his own personal and poetic liberation, his readiness to come at the world's physical wonder, is certainly unlike his bardic American predecessor. That does not mean, however, that Whitman offers the kind of significant challenge to Lawrence of the first lustre that Hardy sometimes poses and that Shelley consistently provides throughout the early years of the poet's development. Lawrence senses—and shows he senses—that Whitman does not really sing the world's rough chaos so much as he deceives himself while performing a late version of the Shelleyan song of self. Through the title of the "Song of a Man Who Has Come Through" and the line that begins "Not I, not I, but the wind" and never leads to the verb "sing," Lawrence directs us towards Whitman only to have us see how different his own poetic enterprise is. The American Romantic seeks to utter the words of the collective self that he believes to be the sum of the world's reality. He writes a poem entitled "Spontaneous Me, Nature" and begins another lyric with the words:

> One's-Self I sing, a simple, separate person,
> Yet utter the word Democratic, the word En-Masse.
> (lines 1–2)

Lawrence seeks a distinctness, a liberty, from men that will cause the self to be entirely effaced in pure apprehension of "the rock" of the world.

Whether or not Lawrence finds that distinction, that liberty, in his 1914 "Song" is as debatable as is the success of his struggle with his Shelleyan "instinct." But I believe that he thinks he does, for the poem does not communicate anywhere near the depth of doubt communicated by the phrase "deceive myself" at the very end of an otherwise ebullient "Craving for Spring." The word "Hesperides" may imply self-deception, but only barely, and anyway it is not placed at the end of the "Song."

Rather, the word "Hesperides" immediately precedes an ending that may be heard speaking with a measure of self-confidence:

> Oh, for the wonder that bubbles into my soul,
> I would be a good fountain, a good well-head,
> Would blur no whisper, spoil no expression.
>
> What is the knocking?
> What is the knocking at the door in the night?
> It is somebody wants to do us harm.
>
> No, no, it is the three strange angels.
> Admit them, admit them.

The first three of these eight lines are least troublesome; they confirm the reading of the poem that believes Lawrence seeks to be only the agent of creation's wonder, to become its human (but undistorting) voice. The lines that follow, though, introduce angels that are somewhat harder to interpret. A highly speculative reading might see them as those presiding angels of the past (Shelley, perhaps Whitman and Tennyson) who have been recalled in the double sense and rendered not only harmless but useful. The strange angels of Lawrence's wonder-ful ending may perhaps be better interpreted as beings akin to "the angel of reality" who, speaking in Wallace Stevens' "Angel Surrounded by Paysans" without "wing" or "tepid aureole," says:

> I am one of you and being one of you
> Is being and knowing what I am and know.
>
> Yet I am the necessary angel of earth,
> Since, in my sight, you see the earth again,
>
> Cleared of its stiff and stubborn, man-locked set.

The ambivalence towards the Shelleyan dream that can be found in the poems Lawrence wrote between 1906 and 1917, the ambivalence that we detect in the speaker's attitude in "Lightning" or in the last line of "Craving for Spring" or in the temptation, however fleeting, to use the chisel image to define both wind and self in "Song of a Man Who Has Come Through," is scarcely to be found in the poems that Lawrence wrote after publishing his 1917 volume. Many of these later works were brought out in 1923, in *Birds, Beasts and Flowers*; most of them use rather comfortably Shelley's poem "To a Skylark"; and all of them offer an excellent example of what Shelley meant to Lawrence after he had come through his first lustre.

The poem Lawrence wrote in Florence, in 1921, on the "Bat"

never precisely echoes the poem "To a Skylark." Indeed, it wants always to call the swallow the bat's opposite. And yet it is surely a fascinating and worthy companion poem to one of Shelley's greater Italian lyrics. Shelley imagines his aviary subject singing its way upward "In the golden lightning / Of the sunken sun," away "From the earth" from which it "springest" and toward "Heaven, or near it." Lawrence's picture of himself "sitting on this terrace, / When the sun from the west . . . / Departs" and watching "serrated wings against the sky," wings "Like . . . a black glove" when thrown up against "the light, / And falling back," recalls Shelley's antithetically. For Lawrence's subject (of which he, like and unlike Shelley, could say "Bird thou never wert") is opposite to Shelley's in every way. Unlike the bird that melts like a star of Heaven in the broad daylight, the bats are seen "sewing the shadows together." Unlike the lark that goes on ascending and ascending into the unseen, as if giving the lie to gravity, the bat's true mode is descent; bats are, Lawrence reminds us, creatures that even "hang . . . themselves . . . upside down" to sleep.

In "Bat," but perhaps more so in its textual neighbor, "Man and Bat," Lawrence emphasizes these downward (and inward) proclivities ("grinning in their sleep") in order to make the creature symbolic of the demon within. Bats are made to represent the little bit of uneducable self, the dark, primitive, grossly creaturely essence which even Lawrence, because he has heard the idealistic voices like everyone else, occasionally fears, abhors, and wishes to exorcise. The poet describes his attempt to get a bat "*out from my room!*" The room, however, occasionally seems to take on dimensions of the self. "I would not let him rest," Lawrence says, "Not one instant . . . cling like a blot with his breast to the wall / In an obscure corner":

> He *could* not go out . . .
> It was the light of day which he could not enter,
> Any more than I could enter the white-hot door of a blast furnace.

Lawrence, as if with Shelley in mind, comes to identify with a nonbird seeking shelter from the bright light of heaven that would always turn, in "quick parabola," back from the transcendental quest for the "intense lamp . . . / In the white down clear."

"Bat," "Man and Bat," and "To a Skylark" come together convincingly in "St. Matthew," one of the four poems on "Evangelistic Beasts" that Lawrence published, together with the poems on bats, in *Birds, Beasts and Flowers*. Shelley's role in "St. Matthew" is clearer than it is in "Bat," for whereas in the latter poem the swallow was the bat's antitype, in "St. Matthew" Lawrence specifically identifies the skylark with the ascent from dark reality. As does "Man and Bat," the poem speaks of a man's coming to terms with his own imperfectible nature; its speaker accepts the fact that the dark blood-consciousness has its undeniable place in human life. "St. Matthew" is a monologue in which the gospel writer, who was traditionally portrayed in Christian iconography as a winged man, uses the figures of lark and bat to portray himself as someone pulled in both directions, away from the earth and towards it, out of the dark denizens of the earthy blood-self and back into them with a joyous vengeance.

"I have been lifted up," the speaker reminds his Shelleyan Christ. "But even Thou, Son of Man, canst not quaff out the dregs of terrestrial manhood!" Consequently, as "evening" comes, Matthew explains, "I must leave off my wings of the spirit" and put on "Membraned, blood-veined wings" that "thread and thrill and flicker ever downward / To the dark zenith of Thine antipodes":

> Afterwards, afterwards
> Morning comes, and I shake the dews of night from the wings of my spirit
> And mount like a lark, Beloved.
>
> But remember, Saviour,
> That my heart which like a lark at heaven's gate singing, hovers
>   morning-bright to Thee,
> Throws still the dark blood back and forth
> In the avenues where the bat hangs sleeping, upside-down
> And to me undeniable, Jesus.

Lawrence's Matthew, to be sure, presents himself as having a Shelleyan side. But his recognition and acceptance of his inevitable, "terrestrial manhood" is without ambivalence, even confident-sounding.

In yet another bold poem about a winged creature as unlike a skylark as it can be, Lawrence asks, "Turkey-cock, turkey-cock / Are you the bird of the next dawn?" In spite of the evening setting of Shelley's poem, we can't help suspecting that the Romantic poet's blithe Spirit is among the present morning singers. The first paragraphs Lawrence had written in 1919 by way of introducing the American edition of *New Poems*, moreover, add some credibility to our suspicion:

> It seems when we hear a skylark singing as if sound were running forward into the future, running so fast and utterly without consideration, straight on into futurity. And when we hear a nightingale, we hear the pause and the rich, piercing rhythm of recollection, the perfected past. The lark may sound sad, but with the lovely lapsing sadness that is almost a swoon of hope. The nightingale's triumph is a paean, but a death paean.

> So it is with poetry. Poetry is, as a rule, either the voice of the far future, exquisite and ethereal, or it is the voice of the past, rich, magnificent. . . .
>
> With us it is the same. Our birds sing on the horizons. They sing out of the blue, beyond us, or out of the quenched night. They sing at dawn and sunset. . . . Our poets sit by the gateways, some by the east, some by the west. As we arrive and as we go out our hearts surge with response. But whilst we are in the midst of life, we do not hear them.
>
> The poetry of the beginning and the poetry of the end must have that exquisite finality, perfection which belongs to all that is far off. It is in the realm of all that is perfect. It is of the nature of all that is complete and consummate. This completeness, this consummateness, the finality and the perfection are conveyed in exquisite form: the perfect symmetry, the rhythm which returns upon itself like a dance where the hands link and loosen and link for the supreme moment of the end. Perfected bygone moments, perfected moments in the glimmering futurity, these are the treasured gem-like lyrics of Shelley and Keats.

Shelley and Keats are poets of the skylark and nightingale (and of the finality, perfection, and exquisite form the birds symbolize). They are also characterized by Lawrence *as* skylarks and nightingale; they "sing on the horizons, . . . out of the blue, beyond us, . . . at dawn and sunset." When Lawrence refers, in "Turkey-Cock," to the bird of dawn, he probably refers both to the skylark and to its Romantic hymnist. When he foresees the new day of the sensual, strutting turkey-cock, he foresees an era in which, rather than being obsessed with perfection and futurity and all that is far off—exquisite but in life unattainable—man will live and desire to live fully "in the midst of life." Lawrence also, by implication, foresees a poetry and poet that can take even the turkey-cock as subject.

A close examination of the poem confirms the hypothesis that "Turkey-Cock" is yet another poem about birds that Lawrence wrote with the skylark poet in mind. Shelley's bird had been virtually invisible ("Bird thou never wert," "we hardly see—we feel that it is there") and bodiless ("Thou art unseen" and "Like an unembodied joy"). It was known, rather, by its vocal artistry ("yet I hear thy shrill delight," "In profuse strains of unpremeditated art," "Like a poet hidden / In the light of thought, / Singing hymns unbidden"). Lawrence specifically avoids identifying with his object. To do so would cause his turkey to become a figure for himself or for poets in general. (Here the desire to avoid all reflexivity, all songs of self, threatens to become a joke.) Indeed, Lawrence writes three pages on the cock without mentioning sound or voice. Lawrence's thoroughly grounded, un-skylark is no hidden poet singing but rather an all-too-visible, all-too-embodied joy:

Your sort of gorgeousness,
Dark and lustrous
And skinny repulsive
And poppy-glossy,
Is the gorgeousness that evokes my most puzzled admiration.

Your wattles are the colour of steel-slag which has been red-hot
And is going cold,
Cooling to a powdery, pale-oxydised sky-blue.

The anti-Shelleyan physicality or bestiality of the cock virtually leaps from the evocative lines of this work, many of which afford an instructive comparison between the figurative languages used by the two poets. Shelley's similes direct the reader's mind towards the ideal or the abstract, either towards a faerieland vision of nature ("Like a glow-worm golden / In a dell of dew," "Like a rose embowered / In its own green leaves") or towards an idealized human realm ("Like a Poet hidden / In the light of thought," "Like a high-born maiden / In a palace tower"). And always Shelley reminds us that no simile can truly characterize the bird, which is divine, for "What thou art we know not." Lawrence's striking similes, on the other hand, point in the opposite direction ("Your wattles are the colour of steel-slag"), referring the turkey to "obscenely" bestial forms and finding its hot earthiness almost literal by comparison:

The vulture is bald, so is the condor, obscenely,
But only you have thrown this amazing mantilla of oxidised sky-blue
And hot red over you.
This queer dross shawl of blue and vermillion,
Whereas the peacock has a diadem.

Lawrence's figurative language is thus about as different as it can be from that of "To a Skylark." It tries to tell us, in Shelley's words, "What is most like thee" and then balks, not at comparing a bird to a high-born maiden but at comparing a bright-colored bird with a brighter one.

Shelley's skylark seems to stand as the symbol of what Shelley often wishes he could be. He never can know what the greater, transcendent poet speaks of, but he can imagine that if he could understand the bird's "sweet thoughts" he would learn "ignorance of pain":

With thy clear keen joyance
    Languor cannot be:
Shadow of annoyance
    Never came near thee:
Thou lovest—but ne'er knew love's sad satiety.

The turkey-cock, on the other hand, escapes knowledge of love's sad satiety by virtue of the fact that he is a supersexual force, an insatiable being. The turkey wattles are "The over-drip of a great passion." Lawrence speaks of the bird's "super-sensual arrogance," and the effect of almost every one of the poem's amazing descriptions is that we see the cock's entire body as an erection:

> You contract yourself,
> You arch yourself as an archer's bow
> Which quivers indrawn as you clench your spine
> Until your veiled head almost touches backward
> To the root-rising of your erected tail.

As for transcendental powers, the turkey has none. Far from seeking escape, or representing escape, from those fearful contraries that Shelley speaks of in his lyric (joyance and annoyance, desire and satiety, sleep and death, before and after, laughter and pain, sweetness and sadness, what is and what cannot be), the turkey-cock lives in and almost seems to embody a chaos of contradictions. Lawrence speaks of an ugliness and ostentation that can only be called "raw contradictoriness." He sees in the arch of the ruffling fowl's back

> a declaration of such tension in will
> As time has not dared to avouch, nor eternity been able to unbend
> Do what it may.

Thus if the bird can be said to live free of earthly care, it does so as differently from Shelley's skylark as can be imagined.

Lawrence's recurrent use of "To a Skylark" in these poems written during the twenties is fairly general and rather comfortable when compared to the difficult struggle with Shelley that is evident in such earlier lyrics as "Song of a Man Who Has Come Through." The various poems on birds offer arresting images of poetic objects, but they are not difficult, liberating acts of understanding a precursor. Rather, they are what the poet writes after he has settled in his mind what was wrong with the precursor, after he has left behind one stage of his life and poetic development for another.

MARTIN PRICE

Levels of Consciousness

STAGES OF CONSCIOUSNESS: "THE RAINBOW"

The Rainbow is a novel about three generations, but it is, even more, a novel about stages or states of consciousness. From the initial "drowse of blood-intimacy," the "heated, blind intercourse of farm life" we follow Tom Brangwen to his all-but-wordless courtship of Lydia Lensky, and at last to the freedom she gives him from himself. The second stage recounts the wedding of Lydia's daughter Anna to her cousin Will Brangwen; it has greater complexity and conflict, and it concludes with a division in their lives between a secret sensual intensity and a conventional, unachieved existence in the world outside. Finally, their daughter Ursula reveals the strain of the "modern," its loss of traditional beliefs and refusal of traditional roles, both its yearning and its arrogance. Like Conrad, Lawrence is aware of the painfulness of consciousness. He trusts it more, I think, because he has a stronger sense of the other dimensions of self.

At each of these stages Lawrence makes us aware of "the felt but unknown flame" that "stands behind all the characters." This is sometimes achieved by rhetorical intensity, in large part a method of repetition and parataxis, which is the author's own "struggle for verbal consciousness," the "passionate struggle into conscious being" that Lawrence speaks of in his foreword to *Women in Love*. This emergence into consciousness is

---

at once painful and strange; it keeps experience from seeming "too personal, too human." While the "flame" is felt in the energy of language, it is more fundamentally the energy of metaphysical thought which finds expression in the rhetoric. This is not to say that experience is used simply to demonstrate principles or cosmic truths. The concrete experience, dragged into living speech, coming to expression through the "pulsing, frictional to-and-fro" of words, is at once instance and archetype. Its metaphysical dimension is not caught in conceptual categories but rather in the revelation it affords—in its clarity and energy—of an awareness until now indescribable because unrecognized. There are occasions when, through biblical diction or religious allusion, Lawrence brings to that experience suggestions of traditional mystery and overtones of sanctity. But these do not commit Lawrence to an ultimate system or to "higher" meanings. His metaphysics shifts too often in idiom and image—accommodated to one realm or another, biological, theological, moral, whatever—to provide any finality. Lawrence has no interest in substance, but only in process.

The sense of process is nicely caught in Tom Brangwen's vision at the time of his daughter's wedding:

> He felt himself tiny, a little upright figure on a plain circled round with the immense, roaring sky; he and his wife . . . walking across the plain, whilst the heavens shimmered and roared about them. . . . There was no end, no finish, only this roaring vast space. . . . What was sure but the endless sky? But that was so sure, so boundless.

The title of the book suggests the relations between generations, each providing a doorway or an opening for the next. We see this in Anna as she lapses "into vague content": "If she were not the wayfarer to the unknown, if she were arrived now, settled in her builded house, a rich woman, still her doors opened under the arch of the rainbow, her threshold reflecting the passing of the sun and moon, the great travellers, her house was full of the echo of journeying." The flame behind the characters is suggested at other times by an idiom which hovers between traditional metaphor and the language—the jargon, one might call it—of "doctrine." As Tom falls in love with Lydia Lensky, it is as if he has "another centre of consciousness," as if somewhere in his body a strong light were burning. Tom goes about without seeing what he does, "drifting, quiescent," in a "state of metamorphosis." At a deeper level he is "letting go his will, suffering the loss of himself, dormant always on the brink of ecstasy, like a creature evolving to a new birth." And that theme is given complex statement through landscape images which enact the endless movement, the harsh discontinuities of loss and death, and the brilliant uncovering of new depths of reality:

> He could not bear to be near her, and know the utter foreignness between them, know how entirely they were strangers to each other. He went out into the wind. Big holes were blown into the sky, the moonlight blew about. Sometimes a high moon, liquid-brilliant, scudded across a hollow space and took cover under electric, brown-iridescent cloud-edges. Then there was a blot of cloud, and shadow. Then somewhere in the night a radiance again, like a vapour. And all the sky was teeming and tearing along, a vast disorder of flying shapes and darkness and ragged fumes of light and a great brown circling halo, then the terror of a moon running liquid-brilliant into the open for a moment, hurting the eyes before she plunged under cover of cloud again.

In the next generation, Anna and Will are more conscious, more free to accept experience. We see them in their marriage-bed like the lovers of John Donne's "The Good-Morrow." Their room is a "core of living eternity": "Here was a poised, unflawed stillness that was beyond time, because it remained the same, inexhaustible, unchanging, unexhausted." But they must waken into the world of time, where it is already midday; and Will begins to feel "furtive and guilty," drawing up the blind "so people should know they were not in bed any later." Will's "orderly, conventional mind" is where he lives in the ordinary daylight. But in church as in marriage he wants "a dark, nameless emotion, the emotion of all the great mysteries of passion." He attaches no "vital importance" to his everyday world nor does he "care about himself as a human being." His only reality lies in "his dark emotional experience of the Infinite, of the Absolute." For Anna, in contrast, the "thought of her soul" is "intimately mixed up with"—perhaps simply identical with—"the thought of her own self." She envies Will's "dark freedom and jubilation of the soul," but she hates it too. She rebuffs the claim of all mystery and mysticism; she mocks the symbols he adores until, under the pressure of her will, he becomes ashamed of his religious ecstasy.

Will and Anna do battle in defense of themselves, she of her conscious self and powerful will, he of his dark subterranean self. In their visit to Lincoln Cathedral, Will enters as if he were "to pass within to the perfect womb." The interior becomes a dark scene of ecstasy for him: "the perfect, swooning consummation, the timeless ecstasy. There his soul remained, at the apex of the arch, clenched in the timeless ecstasy, consummated." Anna is stirred by his rapture but adamantly defiant. She thinks of the open sky above the cathedral, and she cannot see it as a blue vault—not as a closed architectural form—but as "a space where stars were wheeling in freedom, with freedom above them, always higher." She spurns the sanctity of the altar and claims "the right to freedom above her, higher than the roof." As she frees herself of the enclosing unity of the cathedral, she insists upon the diversity and contrariness it includes—the grotesques, "little imps that retorted on man's own illusion." They "winked and leered" and denied that the Gothic structure was absolute; they offered "separate wills, separate motions, separate powers." And so she succeeds in divesting the cathedral of its power over herself and over Will. For Will, too, it now seems "too narrow" to contain life, and he thinks of the "whole blue rotunda of the day." He comes to see that "a temple was never perfectly a temple, till it was ruined and mixed up with the winds and the sky and the herbs." So that, at last, while he still loves the Church, it is only as a symbol; and for that very reason it exacts all the more devotion. "He was like a lover who knows he is betrayed, but who still loves, whose love is only the more intense. The church was false, but he served it the more intensely." And this is a dead end, a cessation of growth: "Something undeveloped in him limited him, there was a darkness which he could not unfold, which would never unfold in him." So, too, in place of the "great adventure in consciousness," Anna has accepted "the rich drowse of physical heat," an absolute of sensuality. She is content with the "heat and swelter of fecundity," but her daughter Ursula, in passionate opposition, craves for "some spirituality and stateliness."

Lawrence makes the story of Ursula essentially her attempt to become herself. By the close of the novel, her adventure in consciousness is hardly complete, but she has eluded the nets that might bind her movement. Unlike her mother, who will have "nothing extra-human," Ursula is "all for the ultimate." The church seems to her "a shell that still spoke the language of creation." She sees herself as one of the daughters of men to whom the sons of God will descend—"one of the unhistoried, unaccountable Sons of God." She rejects the natural and merely human, demanding some union with the mysterious and inexplicable "Absolute World." She learns to dissociate the spiritual from the ascetic. "The Resurrection is to life, not to death." Yet, while she comes more and more to accept the everyday world, there is still "some puzzling, tormenting residue of the Sunday world within her, some persistent Sunday self, which insisted upon a relationship with the now shed-away vision world." Her religious sense survives outworn doctrine and requires its new observances and its new sanctities; that remains a central part of the problem of how to become herself.

The inevitable interpenetration of spirit and sense, of visionary thought and physical desire, leads into Ursula's first attachment to Anton

Skrebensky. He seems to her a worldly embodiment of spiritual energy, perhaps one of the Sons of God. He represents for Ursula all the freedom she wants for herself: an aristocratic scorn for convention, bold irreverence, the achievement of one's "maximum self." It is in fact her own maximum self that Ursula seeks in what she thinks is her love for him. As they make love, the moon becomes a symbol of that maximum self gaining freedom: "Oh, for the cold liberty to be herself, to do entirely as she liked." If one hears echoes of Gwendolen Harleth, they are not inappropriate, even to the fear of the self she seeks to realize. Skrebensky serves her will but hardly seems otherwise to exist, and the "burning, corrosive self" she has become now terrifies her.

Before Ursula encounters Skrebensky again, she has tried several paths that prove to be culs-de-sac. The first is her love for her teacher, Winifred Inger. Lawrence presents something of what he will more fully realize in Gerald Crich and Gudrun later. Winifred Inger and young Tom Brangwen, Ursula's homosexual uncle, become lovers and at last are married, to live in the hideous Yorkshire colliery town where Tom's managerial career allows him to escape his self-hatred by serving the great machine. Winifred, too, finds an escape from "the degradation of human feeling" in the "impure abstraction, the mechanisms of matter." It is an escape from the self that is tempting to Ursula. She must make "a great, passionate effort of will" before she rejects the industrial machine as "meaningless." She is "miserable and desolate," but she will never give way to serving "such a Moloch as this."

A second false path comes in teaching school, where she becomes part of a machine of another sort, a "hard, malevolent system," unexamined, unquestioned, demanding of the teachers that they suppress their humanity. Ursula must lend herself to the "unclean system of authority," where power alone matters, and which can work only if one resorts to force. When she finds herself caning a pupil, Ursula feels that she is "in the hands of some bigger, stronger, coarser will." Lawrence is, I think, quite explicitly seeing in this "will" of the system a parody of that inhuman will that for him is an authentic depth of self. Ursula feels herself brutalized rather than caught up in vital impulse.

The third false path is an offer of marriage from Anthony Schofield, the brother of a fellow teacher. He is the chief gardener of a country house, and he lives in a beautiful park. Ursula feels guilty in refusing him but frightened at how close she has come to acceptance. "Her soul was an infant crying in the night. He had no soul. Oh, and why had she? He was the cleaner." He lacks a "soul" precisely in being so much one with the land he works, and it is her standing apart and seeing that beauty from the outside that has "separated them infinitely." He lacks the kind of consciousness with which she is burdened; he is a pastoral figure. "The true self is not aware that it is a self. A bird as it sings, sings itself. But not according to a picture. It has no idea of itself." Yet this nostalgia for simplicity, like the Tolstoyan hero's yearning for the reality of the peasants, cannot suffice. She is "a traveller on the face of the earth" and he "an isolated creature living in the fulfillment of his senses." Ursula's history is like a pilgrimage made up of encounters with those who fall along the way or seek to detain her in their own accommodations with life.

Ursula must learn again upon Skrebensky's return that she cannot achieve fullness of self through someone who has not enough self of his own. The limits of Skrebensky are his conventional desire to be an unthinking part of a system, "just a brick in the whole great social fabric." Time and military service in Africa have not changed his nullity. When he escapes from his social self, it can only be as a holiday, since he believes utterly in that self. Ursula, on the other hand, is becoming more and more sure of her "permanent self," and she is ready to let her social self survive as it can. The world exists only in a secondary sense, but "she existed supremely." For an interval "he and she stood together, dark, fluid, infinitely potent, giving the living lie to the dead whole which contained them." They feel assured, once again like Donne's lovers: "They were perfect. Therefore nothing else existed." They feel "absolute and beyond all limitations," the only ones to inhabit "the world of reality."

It is too much to sustain, for it is only a temporary escape from that other reality they try to persuade themselves they have annulled. She cannot supply him with the being he lacks. She must throw off his heavy need for her, for he feels like a corpse—one of "those spectral, unliving beings which we call people in our dead language." At last he becomes an incubus, weeping at the thought of losing her, pressing his need upon her "like a fate she did not want." He seems to her "added up, finished. She knew him all round, not on any side did he lead into the unknown." They make love for the last time on the shore under a fiercely bright moon. "The moon was incandescent as a round furnace door, out of which came the high blast of moonlight." In this scorching brilliance Ursula speaks in "a ringing, metallic voice," kisses him with "a hard, rending, ever-increasing kiss." Their struggle for consummation becomes an ordeal and agonizing failure for him.

Later, Ursula recognizes that "Skrebensky had never become finally real." She had "created him for the time being, but in the end he had failed and broken down." She remembers him with liking, "as she liked a memory, some bygone self." He was perhaps too much a projection of her own desire, and need, readily destroyed under the cold brilliance of desire become will. Ursula's destructive self-assertion has been savage in part because it was defensive. She has found herself about to marry Anton "out of fear of herself," unable to "rouse herself to deny" what he and everyone else has taken for granted. She veers between contempt for him and humiliating self-reproach as she considers a "bondaged sort of peace" in which she will become his wife and bear his child.

Ursula needs at last to be free of her history, to become "unhistoried, unaccountable" like the Sons of God. "The kernel was the only reality: the rest was cast off into oblivion." Like the religion which refuses enclosure by a cathedral roof, the self must refuse the limits of a personality, a "stable ego," a social role. It is the madness induced by self-betrayal that drives Ursula out into the rain. She feels threatened by the tree-trunks in the storm; they "might turn and shut her in as she went through . . . their grave, booming ranks." Finally, she encounters a wheeling herd of wild horses that block her way. They are "maddened like her, their breasts clenched . . . in a hold that never relaxed . . . running against the walls of time, and never bursting free." Their frustrate and tortured motion, eddying and uncontrolled, so much like the motions of her thought, threatens to crush her. Instead, it induces a last frantic effort that saves her life and loses the child she is bearing. Her final vision of the rainbow, like a covenant of new life, sees the "horny covering of disintegration" (the image is insectile) cast off so that "new, clean, naked bodies," like kernels free of their husk, "would issue to a new germination."

THE ACCESSION INTO BEING: "WOMEN IN LOVE"

The feelings of the characters in *Women in Love* find symbolic occasions for their expression. That Anna and Will conduct their conflict in Lincoln Cathedral is plausible enough and powerfully imagined. But in *Women in Love*, we might say, the characters are almost always in Lincoln Cathedral. From the first chapter the imagery of glistening northern whiteness is associated with Gerald Crich, and it recurs as a metaphor in different matrices or contexts, only to emerge as the literal setting of the final chapters. So, too, in a reverse pattern, the vast industrial system Gerald Crich creates is by the end encapsulated in the granite factory frieze Loerke has designed. The "glamour of blackness" that Gudrun finds, with an unstable mixture of attraction and repulsion, in the colliery landscape and the mines themselves is comparable to the disturbing power of Halliday's

African sculpture. These movements in and out of narrative surface, with their curious fusions and reversals of figure and ground, have a part in generalizing event and character, of drawing connections between private feelings and social structures, between the state of one's mind and the state of a culture.

The industrialist Thomas Crich makes clear the problems of consciousness that reach new intensity in *Women in Love*. He has caged his wife in his unrelenting kindness. "With unbroken will he had stood by this position with regard to her, he had substituted pity for all his hostility, pity had been his shield and his safeguard, and his infallible weapon. And still, in his consciousness, he was sorry for her, her nature was so violent and so impatient." Even as he dreads her scorn he thinks of her—or he wills himself to think of her—as a "white flower of snow." Crich brings the same enabling self-deception to his career as a mine-owner, profiting from the use of his workers while he seeks their love, "trapped between two half-truths and broken":

> He wanted to be a pure Christian, one and equal with all men. He even wanted to give away all he had, to the poor. Yet he was a great promoter of industry, and he knew perfectly that he must keep his goods and keep his authority. This was as divine a necessity in him, as the need to give away all he possessed—more divine even, since this was the necessity he acted upon. Yet because he did *not* act on the other ideal, it dominated him, he was dying of chagrin because he must forfeit it. He wanted to be a father of loving kindness and sacrificial benevolence. The colliers shouted to him about his thousands a year. They would not be deceived.

Since the characters in *Women in Love* tend to be more self-aware than those in *The Rainbow*, they must find more devious and complex ways of eluding that awareness. We can call this repression, as when Lawrence describes Gudrun's cheek as "flushed with repressed emotion." Lawrence does not, I think, mean by the term all that Freud does, but his sense of "repression" goes well beyond deliberate suppression. Gerald and Gudrun show the strain of denying feelings that sometimes escape them and are then seen with a somewhat prurient intensity or furtive self-distrust. They veer rather violently between rigid ordering and a sense of blind self-abandon.

The chapter called "Rabbit" is the most brilliant instance of this release from repression. There is preparation for the release in small, limited gestures whose import is all the greater for their obliquity. As Gudrun walks in the garden with Gerald, "her reverential, almost ecstatic admiration of the flowers caressed his nerves. She stooped down, and touched the trumpets, with infinitely fine and delicate-touching finger-tips." But when Gudrun tries to hold the rabbit Bismarck, it lashes out and scores her wrists with its claws. A "heavy cruelty" wells up in Gudrun, and Gerald observes it "with subtle recognition." As the rabbit eludes him, his own rage is excited, and he brings his hand down "like a hawk" on the neck of the rabbit. It screams with terror and submits. As he looks at Gudrun, she seems "almost unearthly": the scream of the rabbit has "torn the veil of her consciousness." The complex feelings they betray and recognize in each other are brilliantly caught:

> Gudrun looked at Gerald with strange, darkened eyes, strained with underworld knowledge, almost supplicating, like those of a creature which is at his mercy, yet which is his ultimate victor. He did not know what to say to her. He felt the mutual recognition. And he felt he ought to say something, to cover it. He had the power of lightning in his nerves, she seemed like a soft recipient of his magical, hideous white fire. He was unconfident, he had qualms of fear.

She adopts a note of "vindictive mockery" to cover her shame, but the shame is evident enough. There was a "league between them, abhorrent to them both. They were implicated in abhorrent mysteries." Later they exchange smiles of "obscene recognition" as fellow initiates. They share the desire both for cruel domination and for painful surrender, and they are drawn together by their fascination with power. One of the sources of power—power to use against Gerald—that Gudrun eventually finds is her verbal play with Loerke; with him Gudrun can bring to consciousness what Gerald cannot face. "From their verbal and physical nuances they got the highest satisfaction in the nerves, from a queer interchange of half-suggested ideas, looks, expressions, and gestures, which were quite intolerable, though incomprehensible to Gerald. He had no terms in which to think of their commerce, his terms were much too gross."

Gerald's nerves are caressed by Gudrun; Gudrun and Loerke later achieve satisfaction in the nerves. The nerves are channels of feeling, clearly; but they are also the source of consciousness and thought. As we have seen, Lawrence stresses the levels of self. At the upper reaches of consciousness are intellectual activity and the play of ideas; and, with a saturation of feeling, often aggressive, the play of wit and irony. Perhaps above, perhaps below, but closely related is the assertion of will. Further below is the play of sensation, of color, taste, touch. Further yet is the more fully sensual or sexual life. And as one descends below consciousness, beyond the ego and its defenses, one moves toward the loss or dissolution of self that becomes an experience of the timeless or immortal. One can speak of that experience as an intensity so great as to obliterate all awareness of limits, whether of self or time or place. It is timelessness in that intensity displaces duration. (Lawrence wrote of the Russian writer Rozanov that he was "the first to see that immortality is in the vividness of life, not the loss of life.") As we see in the chapter "Excurse" this intensity is not only the "marvellous fullness of immediate gratification, overwhelming, out-flooding from the deepest source," but, at the same time, "the most intolerable accession into being." One can speak of a descent into the undifferentiated stream of Being, the river of life itself; it must be followed in turn by a resumption of the self (perhaps on new terms) and a return to the limits of singleness and consciousness. This descent and return is, clearly, a sacramental occasion in Lawrence's religion, and it has its mystery; "the immemorial magnificence of mystic, palpable, real otherness." The adjectives are not otiose: "real" is defined by the conjunction of the "mystic" and the "palpable."

In contrast to this full experience of otherness is the partial descent, stopping short of the pain of a new reality, finding only a satisfaction of the nerves in its failure to be free of self like Ursula's tortured encounters with Anton Skrebensky under the brilliant moon in *The Rainbow*. As Lawrence wrote in a letter to Catherine Carswell (16 July 1916): "So that act of love which is a pure thrill, is a kind of friction between opposites, interdestructive, an act of death. There is an extreme *self-realization*, *self-sensation* in this friction against the really hostile opposite." Sensuality itself can be a premature destination, as we see in the African statuette. With the "dark involuntary being" denied or unrealized, the frustrated energies ascend into will, seemingly conscious and in the control of mind. Birkin charges Hermione Roddice with this. Her passion is a lie. "It isn't passion at all, it is your *will*. It's your bullying will." When Hermione boasts of her power of will, Ursula is struck by the "strangely tense voice," and responds with a "curious thrill," only in part of repulsion, to the "strange, dark, convulsive power" Hermione reveals. Birkin's response is less equivocal: "Such a will is an obscenity." We see the same will in Gerald Crich's relations with Minette: "her inchoate look of a violated slave, whose fulfillment lies in her further and further violation, made his nerves quiver with acutely desirable sensation. After all, his was the only will, she was the passive substance of his will. He tingled with the subtle, biting sensation."

Hermione Roddice is perhaps the clearest instance of radical fluctuation between the pleasure in receiving pain and the satisfaction in causing it. We first see her, extravagantly dressed, moving "as if scarcely conscious," walking with "a peculiar fixity of the hips, a strange unwilling motion"—seeming "almost drugged, as if a strange mass of thought coiled in the darkness within her, and she was never allowed to escape." She is "full of intellectuality," and "nerve-worn with consciousness." She seems to assert invulnerability through her rank and wealth and power, but under the show of pride she feels "exposed to wounds and to mockery and to despite." For she lacks a "robust self." Instead, she is at home with all that is "highest" in thought or art; she trusts in her "higher" knowledge, she wants to believe that Birkin will see "how she was, for him the 'highest,' " his "highest fate."

When Hermione visits Ursula's classroom, she praises Gudrun's little sculptures: "The little things seem more subtle to her." But Ursula resists the love of subtlety: "A mouse isn't any more subtle than a lion, is it?" Hermione goes on to fear that the children may learn too much: "Hadn't they better be animals, simple animals, crude, violent, *anything* rather than this self-consciousness, this incapacity to be spontaneous?" It is an important issue, placed early in the novel to distinguish between willed oblivion and true spontaneity. Hermione is, in fact, giving voice to her own torture, at the same time taunting Birkin with the withering effect of consciousness. The young, she says, may be "really dead before they have a chance to live." Birkin cuts across this: "Not because they have too much mind, but too little." And Birkin goes on to strip away Hermione's self-deception: "You don't want to be an animal, you want to observe your own animal functions, to get a mental thrill out of them. . . . Passion and the instincts—you want them hard enough, but through your head, in your consciousness." It is a cruel and humiliating charge, and it expresses, whatever more, Birkin's desire to escape her and, with her, some part of himself. When the break finally comes, her mind is a chaos and she struggles "to gain control with her will, as a swimmer struggles with the swirling water." Hermione's will gives way in an act of convulsive release, "unconscious in ecstasy" when she brings a ball of lapis lazuli down on Birkin's head—or seeks to, for he throws up an arm to save himself. Hermione, once she has lost Birkin, is a "priestess without belief," her "desecrated sanctities" leaving "only devastating cynicism" where the beliefs had been.

Gerald Crich and Gudrun Brangwen carry the contradictions we see in Hermione much further. Both of them are curiously guarded and vigilant. Birkin observes of Gudrun's sculpture that "she must never be too serious, she feels she might give herself away. And she won't give herself away—she's always on the defensive." So, too, Gerald, when he talks with Birkin, "would never openly admit what he felt." This finally bores Birkin: "Gerald could never fly away from himself in real indifferent gaiety." Instead, he has a passion for talk and especially for metaphysical discussion. But he does not take it very seriously. It is words he loves. For all his genitality and seeming strength, Gerald seems "always to be at bay against everybody." Especially, one can say, against himself. We learn early in the novel that he shot and killed his brother when as children they played with a gun. Was it a pure accident? Can there be a pure accident? Ursula can't believe that there was not an "unconscious will" behind it, but Gudrun is outraged by the suggestion. Birkin earlier has spoken about a crime's needing both a murderer and a murderee. A murderee is "a man who in a profound if hidden lust desires to be murdered." Gerald, in a sense, is both; he expects violence because he both dreads and wants it so much.

Halliday's African statues, and particularly one of a woman in childbirth, disturb Gerald, for they suggest "the extreme of physical sensation, beyond the limits of mental consciousness." Anything which represents a loss of control seems to him obscene. The next day he asks Birkin about the statue; he has spent the night with Minette, and the statue's face makes him think of hers. He hates the explicitness of its barbarity, but Birkin sees in the statue a "complete truth," the work of a culture that has carried pure physical sensation to its utmost. "It is so sensual as to be final, supreme." Like all art, it hurts. Gerald wants, however, "to keep certain illusions," just as he wants to leave money for Minette so as to separate that experience from the rest of his life.

Gudrun has a bolder mind than Gerald, and she allows herself to move freely and provocatively among the miners. She finds the "glamourous thickness of labour and maleness" exciting, both "potent and half-repulsive":

> This was the world of powerful, underworld men who spent most of their time in the darkness. In their voices she could hear the voluptuous resonance of darkness, the strong, dangerous underworld, mindless, inhuman. They sounded also like strange machines, heavy, oiled. The voluptuousness was like that of machinery, cold and iron.

Sometimes Gudrun feels this "hideous and sickeningly mindless." Sometimes she imagines herself pursued like a "new Daphne, turning not into a tree but a machine." The miners arouse in her "a strange, nostalgic ache of desire, something almost demoniacal, never to be fulfilled." The nostalgic ache is clearly not a yearning for the past but for a reduction to a simpler level of being, less conscious, a retreat from the difficulties of being fully human. It is the organism yearning to be reduced to mechanism or the mental to the more purely instinctive.

Gerald is first awakened to Gudrun's capacities by her cold, cutting indifference to Hermione's malicious dropping of her sketchbook in the water.

> Gerald watched Gudrun closely, whilst she repulsed Hermione. There was a body of cold power in her. . . . He saw her a dangerous, hostile spirit. . . . In her tone she made the understanding clear—they were of the same kind, he and she, a sort of diabolic freemasonry subsisted between them. Henceforward, she knew she had her power over him.

We see her flaunting of power when she dances provocatively before the castle at Shortlands. She ignores Gerald's warning of danger, and, when she sees a "faint domineering smile on his face," she strikes it. She feels "unconquerable desire for deep violence against him." But her will controls this. "She shut off the fear and discovery that filled her conscious mind. . . . She was not going to be afraid." When Gerald says, "You have struck the first blow," she replies, "I shall strike the last." A few minutes he tells her he loves her and grasps her arm "as if his hand were iron." She is afraid, and she responds "as if drugged, her voice crooning and witch-like."

Lawrence provides Gerald Crich with a history, and he defended his deployment of it in the book. Of the chapter to be called "The Industrial Magnate," Lawrence wrote to Catherine Carswell: "I want it to come where it does: you meet a man, you get an impression of him, you find out *afterwards* what he has done. If you have, in your arrogance, writ him down a nobody, then there is a slap in the eye for you when you find he has done more than you have done." But Lawrence provides no surprises; instead, we are interested in the ways in which his symbols expand to contain more and more of experience, unpredictably relating distinct realms to each other within the structure of a single temperament. Gerald, we learn, has "feared and despised his father," and the father, characteristically, has disliked his son without allowing himself to know it. Thomas Crich's long illness and slow death are torture for Gerald. With "something of the terror of a destructive child," he sees himself "on the point of inheriting his own destruction." He has in his youth refused to see or believe in the colliery; after Oxford he traveled in savage regions. But finally comes his chance to control the Crich industrial power. All that he ignores now becomes "subjugate to his will," and he rejects the specious humanitarianism his father tried halfheartedly to live by. Gerald sees the industry as a great machine obeying the will and mind of a single man. He introduces a brisk and heartless efficiency, planned by experts, reducing the workers to "mere mechanical instruments." At first the miners hate him; but they come to discover that participation in a "great and perfect system" is the kind of freedom they really want. It is, again, freedom from consciousness, the reduction of the organic to the mechanical, of work to something self-sufficient and depersonalized. Gerald finds himself reduced by the machine he has created; he tries to escape a feeling of emptiness that leads to near-madness.

The torture of watching his father's refusal to accept death and of seeing the slow extinction of a stubborn will (Gudrun admires the self-possession and control of the dying man) leads Gerald to the "subterranean desire to let go." When the death finally comes, he goes to the Brangwen house and slips up to Gudrun's room. She accepts his love; he gains strength from her and sinks to sleep on her breast like a child. It is the "sleep of complete exhaustion and restoration." But Gudrun has been "destroyed into perfect consciousness." She feels the "awful, inhuman distance which would always be interposed between her and the other being." She lies in an "exhausting super consciousness" until Gerald leaves in the morning; she is resentful of his power over her, her inability to withstand it, her submission to an ecstasy of subjection."

This scene is matched by a later one in the Alps. As Gudrun stands at night brushing her hair, she sees Gerald's face in the mirror as he stands behind her. She feels the pressure of his stare, "not consciously seeing her, and yet watching, with fine-pupilled eyes that *seemed* to smile, and which were not really smiling." She tries to bring him back with a question, but fails. There ensues a "strange battle between her ordinary consciousness and his uncanny, black-art consciousness." She is terrified by the force of his presence: "she felt she could not bear it any more, in a few minutes she would fall down at his feet, grovelling at his feet, and letting him destroy her." At last she finds a solution. She asks him to look in her bag for a small box. As he does so, she knows she has broken the spell, distracted him, freed herself of vulnerability. He has not perceived her panic, and now she has control again. Lawrence does not make the states of mind very determinate. She seems to fear something unconscious and murderous in him. And her escape from him is one instance of the seesaw of power that marks the last stages of their life together. Once more she lies awake as he sleeps, and she thinks about his power to organize industry. He is a splendid instrument: he could become a "Napoleon of peace, or a Bismarck." As she allows herself this dream of power, something snaps, and a "terrible cynicism" overcomes her. "Everything turned to irony with her. . . . When she felt her pang of undeniable reality, this was when she knew the hard irony of hopes and ideas." He seems a "superhuman instrument" ready to be used. But then the irony returns: "What for?"

As Gudrun lies awake thinking of all that might be achieved, each goal is stripped of promise: "one outside show instead of another." There is nothing to wish for. "Everything was intrinsically a piece of irony to her." At least there could be isolated, discrete "perfect moments." She awakens Gerald, thinking, "Oh, convince me, I need it." He reflects her "mocking, enigmatic smile" with his own. After they have made love, Gudrun hears a song from outside: "Gudrun knew that that song would sound through her eternity, sung in a manly, reckless, mocking voice. It marked one of her supreme moments, the supreme pangs of her nervous gratification. There it was, fixed in eternity for her."

I have dealt with the scene at some length because it marks both Gudrun's ascendancy and the cynicism which leaves her without purpose or belief. She turns increasingly to the small, sardonic Loerke. He is an artist, and he intrigues her by his "old man's look" and "uncanny singleness"—a king of stability and self-subsistency that Gerald lacks and that Gudrun, who lacks them, too, thinks the mark of an artist. Loerke has a photograph of a granite frieze he made for a "great granite factory in Cologne": "It was a representation of a fair, with peasants and artisans in an orgy of enjoyment, drunk and absurd in their modern dress, whirling ridiculously in roundabouts, gaping at shows, kissing and staggering and rolling in knots, swinging in swing-boats, and firing down shooting-galleries, a frenzy of chaotic motion." For Gudrun, Loerke represents the "rock bottom of all life." He has dispensed with all illusions; he is a "pure, unconnected will," the "very stuff of the underworld." Birkin sees him as a "little obscene monster of the darkness," who "hates the ideal utterly." A "gnawing little negation," he appeals to all who "hate the ideal also in themselves."

Ursula resists Loerke's appeal. She is outraged by the photograph of his statuette of a massive, rigid stallion on whose back sits sideways a naked girl "as if in shame and grief." Gudrun admires the work with "a certain dark homage," but Ursula blasts it with the kind of direct attack on its moral assumptions that Lawrence often makes in his criticism. Loerke condescendingly tells Ursula that the work of art is autonomous and has "no relation with the everyday world." They are, he says, "two different and distinct planes of existence, and to translate one into the other is worse than foolish." Gudrun joins him: "*I* and my art," she exclaims, "they have *nothing* to do with each other." Lawrence has, of course, shown us otherwise. Ursula will have none of this, and she is dealing as well with the repression we have seen throughout:

> "As for your world of art and your world of reality . . . you have to separate them because you can't bear to know what you are. You can't bear to realise what a stock, still, hide-bound brutality you are really, so you say 'it's the world of art.' The world of art is only the truth about the real world, that's all—but you are too far gone to see it."

Ursula has been accurate enough in supposing the girl to be one whom Loerke treated brutally. She has caught the perversity in Loerke's conception of the girl and of the horse in relation to her. If Ursula makes the method of moral criticism too easy, she is at any rate taking Loerke's work more seriously than the others. And she is making a claim for consciousness against the narcosis of aestheticism. However philistine she seems, she stands for the awareness which Gudrun and Gerald cannot endure. What makes Loerke appeal to Gudrun most of all in his ability to make her cynicism explicit and unashamed. He provides a form of play in which the intolerable can be made amusing.

Gudrun and Loerke play a game of "infinite suggestivity, strange and leering, as if they had some esoteric understanding of life . . . that the world dared not know." It is a game of "subtle inter-suggestivity," a "satisfaction in the nerves," a cultivation of the "inner mysteries of sensation." One can see the point in Lawrence's remarks on Poe: "For him the vital world is the sensational world. He is not sensual, he is sensational. The difference between the two is the difference between growth and decay." In Gudrun and Loerke there is a displacement of the sensual into the sensuous; it is eroticism without passion, "the subtle thrills of extreme sensation in reduction." At a deeper level Gudrun sees through this; she is not, at moments, so abandoned to cynicism as Loerke. She knows, however, that there is "no escape." She must "always see and know and never escape." She must always be "watching the fingers twitch across the eternal, mechanical, monotonous clock-face of time." More than Gerald, she cannot escape consciousness, barren and despairing as hers is; she can no longer achieve the sleep that is freedom from self.

In the final conflict of Gerald and Gudrun, each gains power in turn, "one destroyed that the other might exist, one ratified because the other was nulled." Gerald cannot bear to "stand by himself, in sheer nothingness." When he finally tries to strangle her, he is persuaded that her struggling is "her reciprocal lustful passion in this embrace." Roused to consciousness by Loerke's intervention, he feels only disgust and goes off into the snow, believing himself doomed to be murdered, and at last stumbling into the sleep of death.

Loerke has provided only a catalyst in the relation of Gerald and Gudrun. In providing Gudrun with an absolute of sensation, he is a counterpart of Halliday's African statuette, especially as Birkin describes it. The statue embodies thousands of years of onward movement into pure sensuality, long after the desire for creation has lapsed and all the other powers of the self have atrophied. It represents a "knowledge arrested and ending in the senses, mystic knowledge in disintegration and dissolution." But if this is the African process, its parallel and counterpart in the north is "the vast abstraction of ice and snow," "ice-destructive knowledge, snow-abstract annihilation." In Loerke we find a northern version of dissolution, full of sensual ideas but playing with them within the ego, turning them to knowledge. Each of the extremities is a false end; each is a stage of consciousness that has become an absolute, a stopping place, arresting the movement into the unknown and toward new creation. Gudrun voices this sense of entrapment in a cul-de-sac, the belief in endless repetitive continuity rather than the discontinuity of a new life. To Ursula, who wants to free herself entirely of the old world, Gudrun asks, "But isn't it really an illusion to think you can get out of it?" Gudrun is skeptical about getting beyond love to something, as Ursula puts it, that "isn't so merely *human*." And Ursula thinks, "Because you never *have* loved, you can't get beyond it."

Birkin's is the fullest consciousness in the novel. Lawrence achieves a nicer precision in his novels than in his other prose; and he achieves it in part by a mockery of Birkin's limitations. Birkin is an instance of the "last man," the prophet of a new order who must still live in the old, making his ascent of Pisgah but with no expectation of knowing directly the world he wishes to bring into being. There are dangerous temptations for such a figure, as we see in Shaw's hero in *Man and Superman*: self-pity and self-dramatization, particularly in the role of a prophet or Salvator Mundi. Related to this is the danger of allowing the negations one must insist upon to become an end in themselves, to become so absorbed in the process of dissolution as to lose a sense of its transitional function.

In the discarded "Prologue to *Women in Love*," Birkin reacts vindictively and jeeringly against Hermione's adoration of him and her cultivation of an "ecstasy of beauty." Interestingly, Birkin's attitude toward her recalls Paul's toward Miriam in *Sons and Lovers* ("He hated her, for her incapacity for love, for her lack of desire for him. . . . Her desire was all spiritual, all in the consciousness"). It recalls to a degree Ursula with Skrebensky ("all the soul was caught up in the universal chill-blazing bonfire of the moonlit night . . . the silver-cold night of death, lovely and perfect"). And it shows radical "vibration between two poles," between Hermione, "the centre of social virtue," and a "prostitute, anti-social, almost criminal." Birkin's homosexual impulse, strong, perhaps shared unconsciously by Gerald Crich, remains a secret kept by Birkin "to himself" and even "from himself." He "knew what he felt, but he always kept the knowledge at bay"—perhaps the closest we get to Lawrence's conception of repression. "It was in the other world of the subconsciousness that the interplay took place . . . the relieving of physical and spiritual poverty, without any intrinsic change of state in either man." In all of this we sense the frustration most of all:

> Never to be able to love spontaneously, never to be moved by a power greater than oneself, but always to be within one's own control, deliberate, having the choice, this was horrifying, more deadly than death. Yet how was one to escape? How could a man escape from being deliberate and unloving, except a greater power, an impersonal, imperative love should take hold of him?

Birkin is enduring the winter, but he is skeptical of the spring. There can at present be "only submission to death of this nature" and—if one can attain it—a "cherishing of the unknown that is unknown for many a day yet, buds that may not open till a far off season comes, when the season of death has passed away.

Colin Clarke has written eloquently about Lawrence's use of the Romantic theme of dissolution as necessary to rebirth, the paradox of finding birth through death, a paradox that can be expanded into the phases of a cycle. But Lawrence stresses most of all the temptation to rest in death, to lose oneself in those absolutes of spirit or sense that relinquish movement for stablity. Both Birkin and Ursula are tempted by such surrender, but each exposes the fallacies of the other; and in a sense they exacerbate themselves into passion and life. The effect is often somewhat comic, and the book gains power from that ironic stretch of consciousness in Lawrence. Ursula finds Birkin's despair "too picturesque and final," implicitly insincere or self-indulgent. She wants him as a lover, but he seems in love with his role; it is a disease he doesn't "want to be cured of." She admires his vitality and despises this "ridiculous, mean effacement" into a prig and a preacher. As she says later, "I don't trust you when you drag in the stars. . . . If you were quite true, it wouldn't be necessary to be so far-fetched." And she goes deeper: "You don't fully believe yourself what you are saying." He has set a goal, of a "pure balance of two single beings" as "the stars balance each other." If no actual experience can be expected to attain it, it may be only a cynical way of avoiding actual love. She makes him call her "my love" at last and accept the limited and immediate.

While Ursula seems to deny the flame that stands behind the

person, she is insisting upon the need to give oneself to another rather than avoiding life with interminable theory. When Birkin speaks of the dark river of dissolution, the long process of death that we mistake for life, Ursula is enraged again. Birkin insists upon discontinuity; the new beginning doesn't come "out of the end" but "after it." There will be a new cycle of creation, but not for them. Ursula is bitter: "You are a devil, you know, really. . . . You *want* us to be deathly." He gives in to love and scorns his "other self" as a "word-bag," but "still somewhere far off and small, the other hovered." Birkin wants something more than love, but he accepts the love that is offered him, whimpering to himself, "Not this, not this."

Ursula, however, has her own times of loving death. They come when she despairs of Birkin's love; she neither expects nor wants a new birth. In the chapter called "Moony" she has her own "profound grudge against the human being." (It is characteristic of Ursula to have a grudge rather than a theory). What seems her "marvellous radiance of intrinsic vitality" is in fact a "luminousness of supreme repudiation"; and she sits in shadows watching her counterpart in the "white and deathly smile" of the moon. When Birkin comes cursing Cybele, the pagan goddess whose priests were unmanned, casting stones into the water to smash the floating image, he is clearly attacking with ferocity what he imagines Ursula (and, earlier, Hermione) to stand for, an image of the threatening female will. But of course the image reforms, the flakes of light regathered, like a rose calling back its scattered petals.

Birkin asks Ursula for the "golden light" in her, and he turns off her suspicion of his wish to dominate by asking her in turn to drop her "assertive *will*," her "frightened apprehensive self-insistence." And he in turn acknowledges that he loves her. But he tries to distinguish the sensual fulfillment they will have from the "profound yearning" for something more. He thinks of the African statuette and its remarkable progression along a path of sensual understanding, but he thinks also of Gerald Crich and the "white demons of the north," of the alternative dissolution into whiteness and snow. And he comes at last to a third way, a "way of freedom":

> The individual soul taking precedence over love and desire for union . . . a lovely state of free proud singleness, which accepted the obligation of the permanent connection with others, and with the other, submits to the yoke and leash of love, but never forfeits its own proud individual singleness, even while it loves and yields.

Once Birkin and Ursula achieve the resolution of their love, they decide to resign from the "world of work" (the world in which Gerald finds so much of his fulfillment). They are going away, but to nowhere in particular. "It isn't really a locality," Birkin says. "It's a perfected relation." It is in fact "transit."

They can no longer endure the "tyranny of a fixed milieu." They must be rid of the past and of possessions. They believe that they must, like a statue of Rodin or Michelangelo, "leave a piece of raw rock unfinished to your figure. You must leave your surroundings sketchy, unfinished, so that you are never contained, never confined, never dominated from the outside." (For Gerald life is "artificially held *together* by the social mechanism.") They give away a handsome old chair they have bought. (Gudrun in contrast thinks of the "wonderful stability of marriage," a "rosy room, with herself in a beautiful gown, and a handsome man in evening dress who . . . kissed her.") As they cross the channel to Ostend, Birkin feels "overcome by the trajectory," the "wonder of transit," the "utter and absolute peace . . . in this final transit out of life." But Ursula is filled with a sense of "the unrealized world ahead," the "unknown paradise," a "sweetness of habitation, a delight of living quite unknown, but hers infallibly." She leaves behind her old identity, that "creature of history" who is "not really herself." She belongs now only "to the oneness with Birkin, a oneness that struck deeper notes, sounding into the heart of the universe, the heart of reality, where she had never existed before."

It is a movement without destination, and Lawrence deliberately ends with Birkin's reluctance to be content in this one relationship. "You are enough for me, as far as a woman is concerned. . . . But I wanted a man friend, as eternal as you and I are eternal." Ursula rejects the idea; it's "an obstinacy, a theory, a perversity." But Birkin remains unpersuaded. It is not an ominous close but a calculated anticlimax. Nothing ends, nothing stops. There is not the ironic juxtaposition of Conrad's versions of Jim, nor Linda Viola's cry of unrequited passion as it fills the dark gulf with the voice of illusion and pronounces Dr. Monygham the enviable and sinister triumph of Nostromo. Lawrence's ending does not preclude difficulty and difference, but the openness of the debate, the freedom of quarrel and banter, seems to presume a confidence in process and becoming that Conrad neither has nor wants to have.

DANIEL J. SCHNEIDER

Psychology and Art in "The White Peacock" and "The Trespasser"

The White Peacock . . . is in a sense a typical young man's novel. The very first paragraph of the novel establishes the conflict that informs the entire action. The gray, shadowy fish that "slide through the gloom of the mill-pond" are "descendants of the silvery things that had darted from the monks, in the young days when the valley was lusty"; but now "the whole place was gathered in the musing of old age." Life stagnates, bemused, incapable of developing. The rural community of Nethermere, with its symbolic overtones of submergence in the dark waters, is "the hollow which held us all," says the narrator, Cyril; and as Lettie says to the "primitive man," George Saxton, in an early choral passage:

> You are blind; you are only half-born; you are gross with good living and heavy sleeping. . . . You never grow up, like bulbs which spend all summer getting fat and fleshy, but never wakening the germ of a flower. As for me, the flower is born in me, but it wants bringing forth. Things don't flower if they're overfed. You have to suffer before you blossom in this life. When death is just touching a plant, it forces it into a passion of flowering.

But the characters of the novel do not flower. All are trapped. All desire to "break free," want something "fresh," want to come alive. But all are

---

victims of life's blind momentum, which sweeps them into relationships that condemn them to destruction, either psychic or physical.

Early in the novel, Cyril's father dies, destroyed in part by his wife's cruelty. Annable, the gamekeeper, dies in the quarry; and Lawrence suggests obliquely that Annable's effort to defy society and to live his own life as an "honest animal" has been thwarted by nature itself. Trying to climb out of the quarry, he is thrown back by the wall: " 'He'd be about half way up—ay—and the whole wall would come down on him.' " George Saxton, awakened to the possibilities of a new life by Cyril and Lettie, turns, after Lettie has married Leslie Tempest, to the sensual Meg, a sort of earth goddess; and as Meg becomes "mistress and sole authority," "a beautiful, unassailable tower of strength," George becomes her servant and, deeply frustrated, unable to make himself "whole and complete," drinks himself toward certain death. As for Lettie—the white peacock, the independent woman who has wished over and over again to "break free"—she allows herself to be married off to Leslie and is condemned to live "a small indoor existence with artificial light and padded upholstery." The volatile, restless Alice marries a clerk, and "all her little crackling fires were sodded down with the sods of British respectability." Emily, who has sought to free herself through her relationship with Cyril, marries a stolid Englishman and retreats into the "shadows" and "ease" of traditional life: "Emily had at last found her place, and had escaped from the torture of strange, complex modern life." As the coal miners of the district are "imprisoned underground," so the middle-class men and women are all imprisoned and "netted" by life. All become servants of the Schopenhauerian or Hardyan will. Their potentialities as individuals are drowned in the great ocean of life. The Great Will, the Life Force, fulfills its blind purposes. Beauty and cruelty, life and death, generation and destruction—all are intertwined; and all men become the servants, the slaves, of this Force—all, that is, except the narrator, Cyril, who removes himself from the battle, contemplates the spectacle, and is left, at the end, in an ambiguous position, not subservient to the Magna Mater, but isolated, detached, and apparently still yearning to escape his "rooted loneliness." He alone is not the mere victim and pawn of the Immanent Will. But the unresolved questions that hover over the novel are these: Can anyone escape bondage to the Great Force? Can one "flower"? If so, how?

These questions Lawrence was to explore for the rest of his life. What are the roads to freedom? Can man escape his servitude to the blind Life Force? Or is man—seen in the context of Nature, as Lawrence sees him throughout this novel—destined to carry out the Great Will from which he derives? Is he but the instrument, the agent, of the underlying reality? If so, has nature given him the power to act purposively as a free agent, not directed but the director, not lived by nature but the living, active creator?

The questions took the form, in Lawrence's formative years, of the great debates between mechanists and vitalists, between Schopenhauerian pessimism and Bergsonian or Shavian optimism, between the reductive monism of the naturalists and materialists and an idealistic liberalism that affirmed "progress." The youthful Lawrence, who sees man as divided within himself, is impressed by both sides of the debate.

As naturalist, Lawrence contemplates the great impersonal rhythms of nature. Again and again he carefully juxtaposes creative and destructive energies, life and death. A plum tree "which had been crucified to the wall, and which had broken away and leaned forward from bondage," produces "great mist-bloomed, crimson treasures, splendid globes"; but in the next paragraph Cyril looks at a "dead pool" which is "moving with rats." In chapter 4 there is a fair "in full swing," with active, vigorous life; then the church bell sounds "through the din": Cyril's father is dead. Flowers yearn "for the sun," in a Blakean desire for fulfillment; but, three paragraphs later, Cyril hears "the scream of a rabbit caught by a weasel." Over and over Lawrence reminds us of the admixture of sunlight and shadow, of creative and destructive force. Lapwings offer "a glistening white breast to the sunlight, to deny it in black shadow." Cyril and his friends trail their "shadows across the fields, extinguishing the sunshine on the flowers as [they] went." In Nottingham "the castle on its high rock stood in the dazzling dry sunlight; the fountain stood shadowy in the green glimmer of the lime trees"; in London the Life Guards march in scarlet and silver, "like a slightly wavering spark of red life blown along." But "the whole of the city seems a heaving, shuddering struggle of black-mudded objects deprived of the elements of life." At Christmastide a cart passes "gay with oranges" and "scarlet intrusion of apples, and wild confusion of cold, dead poultry." Thus, throughout the novel, descriptive passages suggest an allegorical world of light and darkness, fire and water:

> It was a windy, sunny day. In shelter the heat was passionate, but in the open the wind scattered its fire. Every now and then a white cloud, broad-based, blue-shadowed, travelled slowly along the sky-road after the fore-runner small in the distance, and trailing over us a chill shade, a gloom which we watched creep on over the water, over the wood and the hill.

A page later, the chicken that Mrs. Saxton has placed "on the warm hob to coax it into life" toddles into the fire and "there was a smell of cooked meat."

In developing his allegorical language, Lawrence everywhere focuses not only on light and darkness but also on the antithesis of heights and depressions. In Nethermere, Cyril says, "we felt ourselves the centre of the waters and the woods that spread down the rainy valley." The valley is opposed to the hills, the quarry to the land above, the earth to the heavens. Presenting a natural world of creation (the upward impulse toward maximum of being) and of destruction (the impulse to return to the bosom of nature), Lawrence very carefully makes human life a part of the natural Heraclitean rhythm. Men, too, bloom and are cut down by the scythe of time; men, too, make love—and kill. And women join in the cruelty, the *bellum omnium:* Emily kills a dog, and Lettie digs her nails into George's thumb; women, says Leslie, are also "cruel," like "Napoleon." If men are likened to bulls, savages, Indians, or wild beasts, women are like spiders (in their parlors); women, too, become "wild," and the beautiful Meg is, as we have seen, "a beautiful, unassailable tower of strength that may in its turn stand quietly dealing death."

In a world presented throughout as a remorseless process of creation and destruction, there would seem to be no room for free will. Yet Lawrence, as he beholds the great process, does not endorse blind submission to the laws of nature. On the contrary, he makes clear that the plight of all of these people is owing to their failure to assume responsibility. The central choral passage on this theme deals with Lettie's submission to Leslie:

> Having reached that point in a woman's career when most, perhaps all of the things in life seem worthless and insipid, she had determined to put up with it, to ignore her own self, to empty her own potentialities into the vessel of another or others, and to live her life at second hand. This peculiar abnegation of self is the resource of a woman for the escaping of the responsibilities of her own development. Like a nun, she puts over her living face a veil, as a sign that the woman no longer exists for herself: she is the servant of God, of some man, of her children, or may be of some cause. As a servant, she is no longer responsible for her self, which would make her terrified and lonely. Service is light and easy. To be responsible for the good progress of one's life is terrifying. It is the most insufferable form of loneliness, and the heaviest of responsibilities.

And if Lettie has failed to assume responsibility for her own life and has ignored her own "potentialities," the same comment is made implicitly on George Saxton and Leslie. Lettie, in her "seething confusion of emotion," turns to George repeatedly, waiting for him to make a decision. They are not, she tells him, "trees with ivy" but rather "fine humans with free active life"; so it is insane to act simply as nature's instrument: " 'You, for instance—fancy *your* sacrificing yourself—for the next generation—that reminds you of Schopenhauer, doesn't it?—for the next generation, or love, or anything!' " But George is too weak to act in his own right. Pathetically he begs Lettie, " 'Tell me what to do.' " "With terror and humility," he pleads: " 'No, Lettie; don't go. What should I do with my life?' " Thus, like Tom Brangwen, George remains immersed in the marsh, unable to assume responsibility for his life. Like Tom, he looks to marriage to make him "whole and complete," and once cut off from Lettie, who is "like the light" to him, he is "dark and aimless." He has "nothing to be proud of" in his life.

The same mistake is made by Leslie, who functions as a sort of Edgar Linton, contrasted with the Heathcliff of George. Leslie, too, is like a "moth" fluttering about the light of Lettie. Like George, Leslie too is "a child"; and he ends by serving Lettie, just as George serves Meg and as Tom Renshaw serves Emily as "the rejoiced husband and servant." Only Annable and Cyril, among the males in this book, escape servitude. But Annable is killed, and Lawrence makes it clear that Annable's determination to rear his children as healthy animals has disastrous results: Annable's wife, Proserpine, is desperate, and Annable's son, Sam, becomes a thief. Thus Lawrence implicitly condemns the man whose motto is "Be a good animal." At the end, only Cyril remains to exhibit the "right" way—the way of developing one's "potentialities" and of assuming responsibility for one's own life. Cyril, however, does not act; he stands outside of life and contemplates it in a spirit of detachment.

What, then, is the way to "flower"? Submission to the will of nature means death of the soul; acceptance of one's total animality brings disaster, and submission to social conventions is equally stifling. Is there a way to avert disaster?

The answer to this last question is implicit in the structure of the novel, and it is the answer that became central in Lawrence's thinking to the end of his career. There must, obviously, be some balance. The animal man is incomplete, only half-developed. As George Saxton comes to realize, it is not enough to be a "fixed bit of a mosaic," "a toad in a hole." Somehow the sensual man must emerge from unconsciousness—the dark waters in which the gray fish glide—and must connect himself with the "light" of consciousness and of spiritual development. At the same time, it is not enough to be a conscious being. Creatures like Emily and Lettie have lost the "meaning" of the snowdrops, which "belong to some old wild lost religion." The snowdrops, Lettie realizes, " 'belong to some knowledge we have lost, that I have lost and that I need. I feel afraid. They seem like something in fate. Do you think, Cyril, we can lose things off the earth—like mastodons, and those old monstrosities—but things that matter—wisdom?' " As she recognizes later, it is not just her independence or her having her own way that she wants: " 'When I've had my way, I do *want* somebody to take it back from me.' " It is her personal deficiency that prompts her to turn to George Saxton, to seek in the animal man the sensuality, or the connection with nature, that she has lost. Balance is needed. George and Lettie should complement each other.

We can see, in the light of this discussion, why Lawrence included Annable in the final version of his novel. Annable, as spokesman for animality, is the polar opposite of Cyril, the man of the spirit, the artist, the detached observer. Neither Annable nor Cyril finds an acceptable answer to the "strange complex problem of modern life." Annable's reversion to animality looks healthy when compared with Leslie's submission to society and to the white peacock; but as in *The Scarlet Letter* Hester's defense of "nature" ends in lawlessness, so Annable's way ends in animality. Cyril's detachment looks attractive when compared with the bondage of the others, but his isolation is a negative freedom *from* the world, not freedom *for* anything. The novel implies that spirit and flesh must be balanced in a new "responsible" way of life. But Lawrence cannot define this healthy alternative. Perhaps the greatest deficiency of the novel, then, is that in the last analysis Cyril remains unevaluated. While Lettie, George, Leslie, and the others are condemned for failing to assume life responsibility and while Annable's choice of animality is disastrous, we do not know how we are to judge Cyril's life. Lawrence does not wrestle with the question of whether Cyril can connect himself with another person without sacrificing himself; nor does Lawrence have a clear idea of what is entailed in the assumption of responsibility.

Yet Lawrence has already found the premises of his philosophy and of his psychology. The motive forces in *The White Peacock* are two: the sexual desire to connect with another person, thus carrying out the will of nature; and the desire to break free from the great process of nature, to realize one's potentialities for progress in one's own life. Lawrence sees clearly that these desires conflict. Although he is not able as yet to invent scenes in which these motive forces are exhibited in direct conflict, he does show in several scenes the attraction and withdrawal of lovers. Again and again Lettie teases George and then, having roused him, puts him off. Generally, the contrary impulses of the psyche are presented in dialogues in which the characters speak in symbolic equations that define the contending forces—the desire for spiritual development versus the desire for sexual connection; the desire for freedom versus the desire to surrender oneself to another person; the desire for "art" or culture versus the desire for nature. The language is philosophical, though *Geist* and *Natur* are presented, as in Hawthorne, in psychological terms. The following passage is representative:

> "This Atalanta," [Leslie] replied, looking lovingly upon [Lettie], "this Atalanta—I believe she just lagged at last on purpose."
>
> "You have it," she cried, laughing, submitting to his caresses. "It was you—the apples of your firm heels—the apples of your eyes—the apple Eve bit—that won me—hein!"
>
> "That was it—you are clever, you are rare. And I've won, won the ripe apples of your cheeks, and your breasts, and your very fists—they can't stop me—and—and—all your roundness and warmness and softness—I've won you, Lettie."
>
> She nodded wickedly saying:
>
> "All those—those—yes."
>
> "All—she admits it—everything!"
>
> "Oh!—But let me breathe. Did you claim everything?"
>
> "Yes, and you gave it me."
>
> "Not yet. Everything though?"

Lettie next asks Leslie to suppose that she is an angel, "like the 'Blessed Damosel,' " to whom he would pray; he answers:

> "Hang thin souls, Lettie! I'm not one of your souly sort. I can't stand Pre-Raphaelites. You—You're not a Burne-Jones—you're an Albert Moore. I think there's more in the warm touch of a soft body than in a prayer. I'll pray with kisses."
>
> "And when you can't?"
>
> "I'll wait till prayer-time again. By Jove, I'd rather feel my arms full of you; I'd rather touch that red mouth—you grudger! —than sing hymns with you in any heaven."
>
> "I'm afraid you'll never sing hymns with me in heaven."
>
> "Well, I have you here—yes, I have you now."

The language, as in Hawthorne, is pictorial: paintings or mythological figures are woven into the dialogue so that the split between spirit and flesh may be contemplated. At the same time, a psychological conflict is developed, the contest for supremacy between the spiritual woman and the sexually aroused man. If Leslie thinks he has "won," Lettie promptly puts him "below" her, as worshiper. She simultaneously offers herself to him, teasingly, and withdraws herself in a struggle to preserve her independence. But to present psychological conflict in allegorical language is to place a distance between the reader and the characters, the sort of distance between the reader and the characters, the sort of distance that a writer like Hawthorne, given his didactic intentions, wanted to maintain.

Lawrence, however, obviously more interested in felt life than is Hawthorne, runs a grave risk: that his readers will condemn his characters as being hopelessly artificial.

One of the great problems Lawrence does not solve is that of blending didactic allegory and real life. Sometimes the language is persuasively mimetic—as in Lettie's outburst " 'Oh!—but let me breathe.' " But in the next breath, Lawrence returns to the factitious Hawthornese. What he needs is a symbolic language to present the philosophical and psychological problem even as he presents felt life with intensity. He needs symbolic correspondences, not allegorical counters.

The wedding of felt life and allegory is so difficult that it continued to be a problem throughout Lawrence's career. The difficulties are suggested by *The Marble Faun*, in which we see Hawthorne working now with deliberate allegory, now with a symbolism that preserves our sense of a solid reality. In *The White Peacock*, Lawrence is as awkward as Hawthorne. In creating dialogue, Lawrence is often forced to ignore normal reticences or normal inarticulateness. The contrast between the conventions of allegory and those of realism is jarring:

> "Look!" [Lettie] said, "it's a palace, with the ash-trunks smooth like a girl's arm, and the elm-columns, ribbed and bossed and fretted, with the great steel shafts of beech, all rising up to hold an embroidered care-cloth over us; and every thread of the care-cloth vibrates with music for us."

With this one may compare her remark on the next page: " 'I can't tell you—so let me go.' " Even if Lettie must be seen as "the white peacock," preferring her dreams to the brutal reality, the symbolic passages seem intolerably affected. It took time for Lawrence to learn how to blend the two voices. Before arriving at a synthesis, he tries first to drive out the realistic in *The Trespasser* (to invent an almost purely symbolic world) and then to drive out the allegorical in *Sons and Lovers*. Neither of these strategies is quite what he was looking for. Yet each novel, in its own way, lays bare the laws of psychology that preoccupied Lawrence before the great period of his "coming through." And a coherent vision of life is exhibited in the action and characterization of both. When one sets the flaws of these novels against the power of their plots, negative criticism dwindles into unimportance.

"THE TRESPASSER"

The Trespasser is a stronger novel than it has generally been taken to be. Its power derives from the boldness and classic simplicity to its strong allegorical structure. The form Lawrence creates is designed to exhibit the clash of male and female impulses; and the plot, moving with peripeteia to the moral failure and suicide of the hero, exhibits the hero's defeat as an instance of a remorseless pattern in nature that he is not strong enough to overcome. The novel is impersonal; the author is detached. The *pattern* of the conflict and the inevitability of the outcome are what Lawrence wishes us to contemplate.

Freudian critics have tended to reduce the novel's content to an Oedipal problem; the Jungian critic Samuel Eisenstein views the novel as a portrait of the male condemned to "uroboric incest" with the Magna Mater, who controls and destroys him because he lacks the strength to "fight his way back up out of this 'heart of darkness' of the womb." According to John E. Stoll, "the tale of Helena and Siegmund illustrates what the passive male should not do to retain his masculine identity and survive." But Lawrence's symbolism and his psychology in *The Trespasser* are complex, and the pattern of male/female interaction is part of a general vision that these interpretations do not quite imply.

In truth, the novel presents, in a fairly well developed form, many of the major insights that Lawrence articulated later in "Study of Thomas Hardy," in "The Crown," and in his mature fiction and psychological writings. Moreover, the symbolism of light and dark, sun and moon, day and night, spirit and flesh, sky and sea, and fire and water is subtly employed to dramatize the central question of the novel—can the relationship between the antagonistic male and female result in fulfillment or only in destruction? The symbolism isolates for contemplation the elemental fears and desires of the psyche, and the relationship between man and woman is evaluated with such precision as is made possible only by a symbolic language. Certainly some of the negative criticism of *The Trespasser* is justified: sometimes the novel becomes pretentious, and from time to time it is difficult to take Helena seriously, because she seems childish. But once we accept, with Stoll, that the novel is essentially allegorical psychomachia, we can scarcely object that it lacks the mimetic density of a realistic novel or that the prose is "ostentatious" or "written to impress." That's like expecting the character of *The Marble Faun* to step out of their allegorical framework and to act like the characters in Henry James; and it's like complaining, as some do complain, that Hawthorne's symbolic descriptions, which project psychic duality into the natural world, are just padding. Like much of Hawthorne's fiction, *The Trespasser* is a psychological romance in which our attention is focused on elemental motive forces and on elemental patterns of psychic interaction. It lays bare these forces and interactions with a didactic, even a "scientific," clarity. That clarity is the strength of the novel. The many harsh evaluations of the novel generally fail to recognize its uniqueness and the complexity of the psychic interaction of Helena and Siegmund as revealed in the symbolism.

I had better begin by setting down the psychological and metaphysical principles that inform the novel:

1. The first principle is Schopenhauerian: the Life Force, or the Will to Live, is impersonal, implacable, and cruel; and the female, as the instrument of this force, does not hesitate to use the male for the realization of life's ends. This principle, at least, is Lawrence's starting point; but the Schopenhauerian insight was modified by Lawrence in the light of his personal experience. Unlike Schopenhauer, Lawrence wished to deal, not just with the elemental female, but also with the sensitive spiritual female of his own time and society. As Stoll and others have pointed out, such a female, as Lawrence sees her, sublimates her primal sexual energy by creating a world of fantasy in which she can ignore the brutal realities of the male's animal being and can transform him into a godlike spirit that alone can satisfy her craving for completion.

2. The male, like the female, is incomplete in himself, "derivative," "an outcast" who is without support until he can wed himself to the female. Hence he is driven by a blind desire to make the female everything, his raison d'être. At the same time, however, Lawrence accepts the Nietzschean idea that the male fiercely desires to strive "beyond himself," to become a heroic soul, proud and brave in his manhood, able to act independently against public opinion and conventions. Failure to follow this creative, purposive prompting entails psychic destruction; the inability to resist conventional opinion results in psychic death.

3. In their striving for wholeness of being, both male and female become antagonists. Each strives to triumph over the other, and when one triumphs, the other is nullified. The relationship becomes that of dominance and submission, "pride and subservience," rather than a healthy relationship of independent individuals in conjunction, neither being "nullified" by the other.

4. Life and death are inseparable. Life flowers into magnificence like the poppy, then falls back into the great source from which it derives. But life is also a creative striving toward individuation and light, an effort to escape the bonds of matter and death by adventuring "into the unknown" and by achieving "maximum of being." Schopenhauer's pessi-

mism is thus modified in Lawrence by a Bergsonian emphasis on creative evolution; and the man fails who gives up his struggle to achieve maximum of being, who denies "the strain of God" in him, or who accepts fatalistically his helplessness and insignificance in the cosmos.

In tracing Lawrence's dramatization of these principles, the critic must be particularly sensitive to the meaning of the dominant symbols, for the pattern of psychic conflict is presented in a pattern of symbolic oppositions. Stoll argues that for Lawrence the female is light and the male is dark. But this contention forces Stoll repeatedly to argue that the symbolism is employed ironically. For example, after quoting Helena's remark " 'I saw the sunshine in you,' " Stoll writes: "Let the reader tentatively accept 'sunshine' as one of the metaphors used to signify her all-consuming possessiveness, and seeing the sunshine in Siegmund will immediately suggest Helena's success in molding him to her own desire." Such a reading must ignore, first, the context of Helena's remark, which plainly indicates that Helena is, at this point in the action, battling "with her new subjugation to Siegmund." Second, Stoll must ignore the fact that sunshine, when introduced in the second chapter of the novel, is clearly associated with Siegmund's coming to life and selfhood after his long submission to duty, and that Helena repeatedly wishes to get out of the sun, to shade herself from it and to shade Siegmund from it. Third, the sun is almost explicitly identified with the male spirit [in that part] of the novel where Helena wishes to see "God at home in his white incandescence." Fourth, Lawrence associates the male with the sun in *The Rainbow* and in his explicit formulations of his symbolism in *Fantasia of the Unconscious*. The female he invariably associates with the moon and the sea.

As for the sea, its meaning is complex. R. E. Pritchard, in his *D. H. Lawrence: Body of Darkness*, points out that the sea is "akin to the underground cold, the great 'brute force' that is the unliving source and destroyer of life." I agree with this interpretation; but it is important to note that the attributes of the sea that are singled out for attention are also reflections of the state of mind of the observer: both Siegmund and Helena view each other as being "like the sea"; both yearn for but fear the sea. On one level, the sea is identified with the female origin or source and with Helena. On another, it is identified with the brute power that Helena associates with Siegmund's animality. The common denominator, however, is the brute primal energy of the undifferentiated (neither male nor female) Schopenhauerian will, which is both creative and destructive. When Siegmund bathes in the sea, he bathes symbolically in Helena, in the primal energy; Helena also bathes in Siegmund. Such bathing may be either rejuvenative or destructive, just as coition, in Lawrence's fiction generally, may issue either in rebirth, after death of the old self, or in death (the self obliterated by love, by the unconscious). As "the unconscious," the sea is contrasted with the sky and the sun. The female water is opposed to the male light or spirit. Life, originating in the darkness of the water, struggles to climb, or rise, into consciousness; but it is always pulled back by the destructive forces of nature, and the adventurous male spirit undergoes "death by water." We shall see, as we proceed, how carefully Lawrence works with these oppositions as he contemplates the "frictional to-and-fro" of his lovers.

At the beginning of the action, after the framing chapter in which we see Helena after Siegmund's death, Lawrence raises the question that became recurrent in his fiction: can a nullified or imprisoned individual find freedom and rebirth through sexual union? Siegmund, who "for years . . . had suppressed his soul, in a kind of mechanical despair doing his duty and enduring the rest," is in the grip of the life urge toward freedom and "maximum of being." He turns instinctively for fulfillment to Helena, who is associated symbolically with the moon and the sea. Siegmund "lifted his face to the moon," the moonlight enters his drawing room, "and he thought the whiteness was Helena." It is she who lies "at the core of the glamour" of the night, "like the moon"; and she is also associated with the sea: "Helena, with her blue eyes so full of storm, like the sea, but, also like the sea, so eternally self-sufficient, solitary."

Thus the first note of warning is sounded: Siegmund, the imagery suggests, may find this female sea uncaring. Nevertheless, the prospect of seeing Helena fills him with joy, and in chapter 3, as he journeys to the Isle of Wight, the key phrase becomes "morning sunshine." Lawrence works very delicately in this chapter with a buried metaphor that will become explicit: the sunshine, the glitter, and the morning are the world of life and the individuation of living creatures who, in their innocence, are unaware of the unliving, undifferentiated darkness beneath the outward forms (the maya of the world). "Siegmund's shadows" vanish in the glittering sunshine, and as he journeys toward the sea, "All his body radiated amid the large, magnificent sea noon like a piece of colour." At this point he has forgotten the dangers of the warlike-earth, dangers suggested by the "grim and wicked battleships" near Helena's island. But presently clouds "cast over him the shadows of their bulk, and he shivered in the chill wind." It begins to rain, and the rain puts out the sun. The symbolism, which associates "the blue sea" and "the blue haze" with Helena's "blue eyes," fuses the ideas of a destructive watery principle and of a destructive spirituality that Lawrence associates with "blue-eyed" or "northern" people. Helena is not warm or receptive. When Siegmund encounters her, she is "shivering with cold" and her arms are "blue." She becomes the cold female water and the cold female spirituality threatening his male flame and sunshine: "He only knew her blue eyes were rather awful to him." Although he senses immediately that "she was blind to him," his passion impels him to believe that he can "blind himself with her" and "blaze up all his past and future in a passion worth years of living." But Lawrence suggests ironically that the male fire will not prevail: Siegmund is "in her charge," and, again ironically, he is grateful for the mist that shuts out the harsh realities of his situation as husband and father.

Elated, he tells Helena, "There is nothing else but you, and for you there is nothing else but me—look!" But because this remark implies a limitation of her freedom and a loss of her self-sufficiency and because she is "quite alone with the man, in a world of mist," she flings herself suddenly "sobbing against his breast." Fearing to lose herself to him, she also resents his separateness from her. When Siegmund "dreamed by himself," Lawrence observes, "this displeased her. She wanted him for herself. How could he leave her alone while he watched the sky!" As the male turns his face to the sky and the creative sun, the female wants him to be earthbound.

The situation is familiar to readers of the later novels. Male and female are attracted to but fear each other. A to-and-fro of attraction and withdrawal defines their relationship; this is an oscillation, in the language of *Fantasia of the Unconscious*, between sympathetic and voluntary urges. Each wants total possession of the other and resents the other's separateness and self-sufficiency; each fears his or her own obliteration in love. The lion and the unicorn fight for the crown, not knowing that the victory of one over the other means death.

The problem is bound up with Helena's spirituality, her sexual fears. When, in chapter 4, Siegmund is aroused until he becomes "hot blood . . . without a mind; his blood, alive and conscious, running towards her," Helena's "heart leaped away in revulsion." For a moment the lovers seem to "melt and fuse together," but Helena wants only the dream of Siegmund, not the actuality, and "she sank away from his caresses, passively, subtly drew back from him." Her withdrawal, her fear of his blood lust, immediately makes his heart sink and his blood grow "sullen." Then she seeks to mollify him, justifying her withdrawal by telling him that she is cold. On a symbolic level, this coldness—like the coldness of the moon and sea—again threatens his male fire.

In chapter 5 the fire rises: Siegmund's eyes, we learn, "sought her swiftly, as sparks lighting on the tinder. But her eyes were only moist." Fire and water contend. Her "white dress . . . showed her throat gathering like a fountain-jet of solid foam to balance her head," her lace is "dripping spume," and it is only by degrees that the flame of his love and the firelight induce her to offer "him herself to sacrifice." There commences then the first phase of their love, in which Helena is "subjugated" to Siegmund.

Given peace by Helena's abandonment of herself to him, Siegmund now feels completed. As we might expect, the imagery suggests completion in the union of the female water and the male "morning": Siegmund becomes "like the sea, blue and hazy in the morning, musing by itself." " 'I feel at home here,' " he tells her, " 'as if I had come home, where I was bred.' " He is no longer "an outcast" but has returned to the female Source, has become one with the female, "like the sea." Yet Helena, "very hot, feverish and restless" in his arms, resents his possessiveness and turns "to look at the night. The cool, dark, watery sea called to her." She longs to be restored to her solitary female self-sufficiency and is pained because he, sated, "was beyond her now and did not need her." The two are incapable of creating a relationship that is not threatening to one of them, and the scene anticipates Lawrence's later treatment of this dilemma: for example, in *Women in Love*, where Gudrun envies Gerald's peace after she has yielded to him. Like Gudrun, Helena feels left out; and when Siegmund tells her that " 'the darkness is a sort of mother, and the moon a sister, and the stars children, and sometimes the sea is a brother: and there's a family in one house, you see,' " Helena's immediate response is to ask: " 'And I, Siegmund?' " She, he says, is " 'the key to the castle' "; but he feels on his cheek "the smart of her tears."

A general law of psychic life in Lawrence's fiction is that love, under the right conditions, transforms the individual: the old self dies in the darkness of the unconscious, and a new self may be born, eager to adventure into the unknown and to achieve maximum of being. That Lawrence had this law in mind as early as 1911 becomes clear when we follow the next stages of Siegmund's relationship with Helena. Having thrown all the dead mechanical nullity of his old life and having been completed by Helena's love, Siegmund wakes "with wonder in the morning," "transported to a new life, to realise my dream." It is again morning, the time for the flowering of the male spirit, or the light; and Siegmund, transformed, looks at "the poppies . . . blown out like red flame"—the symbols used in "The Crown" to represent the individual's maximum of being. Laughing, Siegmund swims in the sea, only to catch his thigh "on a sharp, submerged point." The "sudden cruelty of the sea" surprises the male, but he puts it out of his mind and, "delighted in himself," feels a new pride, though he is troubled that Helena "rejects me as if I were a baboon, under my clothing."

The conflict, muted, continues as Helena goes down to the sea and, alone, feels a complete "sense of satisfaction" as she creates her private world of dream and fancy, trying to wash away "the soiling of the last night's passion" and, like the sea, feeling "self-sufficient and careless of the rest." Siegmund, however, still rejoicing in his completeness ("with Helena, in this large sea-morning, he was whole and perfect as the day,") now wants the male sun: " 'I like the sunshine on me, real and manifest and tangible. I feel like a seed that has been frozen for ages. I want to be bitten by the sunshine.' " He seems about to take the Lawrencian course from rebirth in sexual union to purposive, creative activity in the sunlight of the public world. But Helena shrinks from the extreme of heat and turns again to the sea, approaching so close to the edge of the cliff that she frightens Siegmund. Her counterassertion of the female principle against his male triumph is short-lived, however. At the end of this chapter she is "frightened" by the thudding of Siegmund's heart, which she associates with that of "a great God thudding out waves of life, . . . unconscious." Siegmund has become for her the unconscious heart of the cosmos, the blind will, and she, the spiritual woman, is threatened by the tyrannical God.

In chapter 7 Lawrence extends the symbolism of the sea as a brutal principle in nature. Siegmund's peace is shattered when "the muffled firing of guns on the sea" suggests the brutality and cruelty of a world in which men must fight to survive. He is like Kubla Khan in Xanadu. Proceeding along the shore with Helena, he is suddenly afraid of becoming "trapped and helpless" as the sea moves in. Yet he is also "elated" by the danger, the threat of the "brute sea," "the great battle of action." But Helena sees the danger in this male lust for power. Seeing him "smiling brutally," she hates "the brute in him" and, "turning suddenly," leaves him. Later, when he catches up with her and kisses her, he again feels completed: he is "sea and sunlight mixed" and Helena is "moulded to him in pure passion." But she, having lured him away from the scene of male battle, having won him back to her, feels a "strange elation and satisfaction" and says, " 'It might as well have been the sea as any other way, dear.' " It is a queer speech in which she seems to subscribe, fatalistically, to a romantic *Liebestod*; but death-by-water is death in the female element, so that her speech says in effect: "If you must die, better to die in me, not in male battle." Whatever the motivation for her speech—and she herself does not understand why she speaks those words—she is at least half in love with a death that can release her from the tyranny of the brutal world; and her words again foreshadow Siegmund's death. After they have given a light bulb that they have found on the shore to some children, the chapter ends ominously with a reminder of his family: "he was thinking of his own youngest child." The symbolism is fairly obvious: As Siegmund watches Helena "lifting her fingers from off the glass, then gently stroking it, his blood ran hot." The bulb is the penis and is associated with male light and fire. Helena gives the bulb away, indifferently. The symbolism repeats that of chapter 3, where Siegmund's light is threatened by cold, rain, and mist.

Siegmund's dominance over Helena continues into chapter 8, where she, feeling "destroyed," her soul "blasted," sees all things as "made of sunshine more or less soiled." Apparently the male sun has triumphed, and her "pride battled with her new subjugation to Siegmund." But Siegmund, now full of life, ventures "recklessly in his new pride" and swims again in the sea, which ominously drinks "with its cold lips deeply of his warmth." He turns "his face to the sun," becoming the "happy priest of the sun"; and though he is dimly aware that "under all, was this deep mass of cold, that the softness and warmth merely floated upon," he feels "like Adam when he opened the first eyes in the world." Helena, too, sees "the sunshine in [him]," and the chapter is indeed all sun. But the darkness of hostile reality cannot be forgotten. When Siegmund asks Helena whether she does not " 'feel as if it were right—you and me, Helena,' " he finds "her eyes full of tears."

So the oscillations continue beneath the surface of the relationship. In chapter 9 a brief interlude of tranquillity occurs. A late-afternoon lethargy, a "large, fruitful inertia," falls upon the lovers, and in a "twilight of sleep," their passion "softly shed," they are liberated in dreams. "New buds were urged in their souls as they lay in a shadowed twilight, at the porch of death." But of course they are unaware of death; it is the narrator who reminds us that the poppies bloom, that their seeds falls "into the hand of God," that then "new splendid blooms of beauty" are born. The lovers are part of the great process of life and death. Sleeping "at the porch of death," they are mysteriously renewed, revived; but the process is impersonal, and the lovers do not comprehend the strange rhythms of life and death and life resurgence in which they act out their lives. It is not until chapter 10 that Siegmund shows uneasiness about being a helpless part of the great process. As the sun sets, he asks Helena, " 'Don't you think we had better be mounting the cliffs?' "—a remark that in the symbolic context bespeaks his desire to free himself from the tyranny of matter and the great impersonal will. And when Helena, "smiling with irresponsible eyes," answers him, " 'Why should we?' " he feels again "the distance between them," her "child-like indifference to consequences," which he contrasts with his own awareness of "the relentless mass of cold" beneath the "delicious warm surface of life," "the mass which has no sympathy with the individual, no cognisance of him." Siegmund, prompted to act purposively against nature's blind processes, is at the same time in love with his enemy. He knows he must act purposively, but he is unable to assert his male will.

Night follows day in this poem of psychic conflict, and after the "sun chapters," chapter 11 is a "night chapter," in which the roles of Siegmund and Helena are dramatically reversed. The lovers walk through the meadows and wild lands and copses until it is late at night and they are lost. Helena is naturally pleased by the immersion in darkness: "She asked for the full black night, that would obliterate everything save Siegmund." And Siegmund also feels joy in the oneness provided by the night. " 'You seem to have knit all things in a piece for me,' " he declares. " 'Things are not separate: they are all in a symphony.' " Whereupon Helena feels "triumphant and restored." In her possessiveness, she creates her dream lover and her Zauberland under the moon, uttering phrases of "whispered ecstasy," her soul moving "beyond life," "a little way into death." Siegmund has relinquished himself to her and to the night; but her gloating over him in this ecstasy of possessiveness poisons the relationship. "Suddenly she became aware that she must be slowly weighing down the life of Siegmund." "Stunned, half-conscious," he murmurs, " 'Hawwa,—Eve—Mother!' " And he becomes the child, her child, under the moon and the sway of the female night. Indeed, he is almost destroyed as a self-responsible individual: he feels "rather deathly," "half gone away," and Helena's "strange ecstasy over him" has been "like a pure poison scathing him." She walks on "in triumph" under the moon, "pleased with her fancy of wayward little dreams." But Siegmund, demolished as a man, associates himself with the crucified Christ and thinks: "Let me get under cover. . . . Let me hide in . . . the sudden intense darkness. I am small and futile: my small, futile tragedy . . ." The life and pride he has felt in the sunlight have been smashed, and he is now small and insignificant, swallowed by the devouring Mother.

At this point, Lawrence, having exhibited Siegmund's failure to act purposively after the rejuvenating passion, inserts the chapter in which Siegmund meets his Doppelgänger, Hampson. The purpose of the chapter is to objectify Siegmund's problem, the problem of a man who cannot go beyond sympathetic union with women to achieve full manhood in purposeful activity but must seek his raison d'être in destructive passion, or in "vivid soul-experience." Hampson defines the error of making woman the be-all and end-all of life. Men attracted to " 'supersensitive' " women, he argues, become " 'their instruments' "; the supersensitive woman " 'can't live without us, but she destroys us. These deep, interesting women don't want *us*: they want the flowers of the spirit they can gather of us. . . . they destroy the natural man in us—that is, us altogether.' " The frustration of the male's sexual pride causes destruction of his capacity to flower in purposive striving. Hampson suggests the way to achieve freedom and fulfillment: he says that he strives beyond himself; and the remark is so penetrating that it prompts Siegmund to reflect: " 'You make me feel—as if I were loose, and a long way off from myself.' " A short time later, when Siegmund encounters Helena, he defines his problem: " 'I know I'm a moral coward,' " he says, and asks, " 'What is myself?' " Having failed to strive beyond himself, he confesses weakly that he cannot throw off public opinion, which hovers about them in the form of the conventional landlady.

Now, as if desperate, Siegmund turns again to the sun, declaring that he wants a "sun-soaking," though Helena, who longs for shade, wants him to put on a hat. Still casting about for a release from his problem, Siegmund yearns for the simple animal life of a farmer and takes satisfaction in the intense sun, a "furnace" that causes his hands to become "full of blood" and "swollen with heat." But Helena, seeing his satisfaction, feels "very lonely" and resents having "to play to his buoyant happiness, so as not to . . . spoil one minute of his consummate hour." His happiness leaves her "unnecessary to him," and she turns to her fancy of a Mist Spirit that shuts out "the outside." Then, as Siegmund continues to brood on his moral cowardice, Helena is unable to contain any longer her revulsion from his animality. Seeing him as "a stooping man . . . something of the 'clothed animal on end,' like the rest of men," she suffers a sudden "agony of disillusion." Her repugnance toward his "brute embrace" and her feeling that she is imprisoned by him drive her into a sudden wild sobbing that stuns him, so that "a death [takes] place in his soul." Even as he enfolds her in his arms, he is "quite alone" and cannot be helped by the woman who would save "him from searching the unknown." It is, of course, her very effort to keep him from searching the unknown that is destroying him.

At this point, seeing his withdrawal from her, Helena suddenly dreads losing him and determines to "get him back." Once again she becomes the mother, soothing him "till he was child to her Madonna." But he recognizes clearly now that he has not the courage to "compel anything, for fear of hurting it." He will not be able to defy convention;

and Helena, aware of his wife and his children, cannot help him. Dimly aware at this point that she has "done wrong" by rejecting his animal desire, she tries to take refuge in him "as a child does when it . . . hides in the mother's bosom." Thus *she* becomes the child to *him*, as he had earlier become the child to her. Both, like Gudrun and Gerald, seek to discard their responsibility as adults; but they can find no mature way to love, and "the sense of the oneness and unity of their fates was gone."

The movement of their relationship, from illusion to disillusion, is recapitulated in the symbolism of chapter 17, where Siegmund first finds the morning kind and tender and then, after injuring himself again on the rocks of the sea, recognizes that the kindness is an illusion. The morning, too, with its bright sunshine, is an illusion: the warm flowers of life rest upon the coldness of the sea with its "sea-women . . . striving to climb up out of the darkness into the morning." Nature remains cruel and impersonal; and Siegmund, looking at the sea, reflects: " 'I am nothing. I do not count. I am inconsiderable'." To him the sea is destructive, impersonal, female. To Helena, however, it is "a great deal like Siegmund. . . . the sea as it flung over her filled her with the same uncontrollable terror as did Siegmund when he, sometimes, grew silent and strange in a tide of passion." Only when the sea is "blazing with white fire, . . . transfused with white burning, while over it hung the blue sky in a glory, like the blue smoke of the fire of God," only when she can see "God at home in his white incandescence, his fire settling on her like the Holy Spirit," can she worship and adore. The fire of the Spirit must burn "among the waves." She rejects the brute nature of the sea, just as she rejects Siegmund's flesh and blood.

Unaware of how deeply she has injured him in his pride and self-esteem, she is "happy" as the time for her departure draws near. Siegmund, his illusions gone, sees sharply that " 'she is sufficient to herself—she doesn't want me.' " " 'She is alone and a law unto herself: she only wants me to explore me, like a rock-pool, and to bathe in me. After a while, when I am gone, she will see I was not indispensable.' " He no longer believes in the "strain of God" in him. The sun, burning into him, is, he thinks, "certainly consuming some part of me." Now it is as if, unable to identify himself with the creative, purposive flame of God, he can only submit himself to God's destructive fire. When Helena reminds him that it is time to leave, he almost hates her.

The journey homeward intensifies the pathos of Siegmund's condition. Ironically, he, who most needs help, gives help to Helena. When she, tormented by "the heat of her neighbour's body" in the train, turns to Siegmund for "his strength of nerve to support her," he submits "at once, his one aim being to give her out of himself whatever she wanted." As his last strength is sucked up by her, he contrasts himself with a gentleman who acts bravely and quickly to save his launch from disaster. And he sees again "the shadow" through the petals of the day:

> I can see death urging itself into life, the shadow supporting the substance. For my life is burning an invisible flame. The glare of the light of myself, as I burn on the fuel of death, is not enough to hide from me the source and the issue. For what is a life but a flame that bursts off the surface of darkness and tapers into the darkness again.

Thus in language that strongly anticipates that of "The Crown," Siegmund realizes that he will return to the undifferentiated source in which individual identity is abolished, the source of death and of life, the female darkness. His sole consolation is that "the death that issues differs from the death that was the source"; he can "enrich death with a potent shadow, if I do not enrich life." So he sees himself in the context of the universal process, as one of the bees, rushing "out of the hive . . . into the dark meadows of night." And he consoles himself: "If the spark goes out, the essence of the fire is there in the darkness." After returning to Beatrice and his children, he arrives at the knowledge that life is "implacable in its kindness," beyond human pity. As life's child, he is glad to have parents stronger than himself.

On the last morning of his life, he witnesses the conflict of sun and moon. The sun, a cat, stalks the mouse-moon and destroys it. The passage is typical of the "descriptive writing" that readers often condemn in the novel. But the imagery is of course symbolic and is designed to heighten the pathos. Throughout the night Siegmund has lain in bed, his body sweating, "a terrible, heavy, hot thing over which he had slight control." His "outrage" at the horrible heat of his body "and the exquisite torture of the drops of sweat" reflects his disgust with the tyranny of matter, the animal body and passion that have driven him into helplessness. Then, when he sees lightning in the sky, he watches "with wonder and delight," as if he were witnessing the advent of the spirit, of that light which can triumph over the darkness. The day destroys the night, and the moon becomes "a dead mouse which floats on water." He has witnessed a cosmic triumph over the female night, the body, the sea, the unconscious. But that one brief vision of triumph only underscores his own desperation and helplessness; once day has prevailed, it proves to be "unreal" to him: "Everything out of doors was unreal, like a show, like a peep-show. Helena was an actress somewhere in the brightness of this view. He alone was out of the piece." In the end he can see only the shadow, not the substance—death, not life. He commits suicide.

Helen, as he predicted, has not found him indispensable. Though she grieves for a year after his death, she turns at last to Cecil Byrne, and Lawrence suggests that this new relationship will be, in one way or another, a remorseless repetition of her relationship with Siegmund. " 'I might as well not exist,' " Byrne reflects bitterly, " 'for all she is aware of me'." As the scar of Helena's sunburn wears off—token of her forgetting of Siegmund—she seeks "rest and warmth" in Byrne; but, at the same time she makes "a small, moaning noise, as if of weariness and helplessness." Condemned by the Life Force to seek out the male, she resists to the end her total subjugation to his passion. She does not want to be burned by Byrne. Thus Lawrence's allegory of the conflict of elemental male and female forces concludes—not anticlimactically, as Stoll and Eisenstein argue, but rather with a scene that underscores the pathos of Siegmund's defeat and the remorselessness of the will, which urges male and female into connections that threaten the "integral selfhood" of each. The synthesizing principle of the novel is this: whatever is included is for the sake of exhibiting with maximum clarity and pathos the remorselessness of the great impersonal process that urges male and female into destructive union.

The cosmic to-and-fro goes on. Lawrence's vision is almost purely Schopenhauerian. The will, that great elemental sea, casts up a world of living creatures, fair appearances in the sunshine, and it calls them back to itself, implacable. It creates, moreover, a war of each against the other—the war of sun and moon, day and night, sky and sea, male and female. Lawrence sees that in this cosmic war there are no winners. If darkness triumphs over light, or light over darkness, destruction occurs. Each principle needs the other for its completion. The female darkness calls to the male light, and the light to the darkness. A vital harmony and reconciliation is needed. But polar opposites cannot *fuse*, for fusion means annihilation. The two principles can be connected only when established in their separateness; in Birkin's language, they can become separate but in conjunction. Only in such a relationship are they free to realize "maximum of being." Siegmund is destroyed because he seeks maximum of being in the woman, at the expense of his male selfhood. Identifying with the darkness, he denies the "strain of God" in him; and a moral coward, he surrenders all life responsibility. The only solution for Siegmund—the only solution for any of Lawrence's male heroes—is to affirm a proud integral selfhood, to fight against the dead world of convention and the blind forces of nature, and to adventure into the unknown. At the same time, this adventure must be based on a healthy connection with the female, on healthy sexual fulfillment in the great Source. Once that fulfillment is achieved, the male can acquire the courage to "trespass."

This analysis reveals that Lawrence had thought through, in 1912, several of the basic articles of his philosophy. In *The Trespasser* he daringly created a prose poem in which the to-and-fro of antagonistic forces is exhibited and analyzed in carefully wrought symbolic language. Far from indulging in "fine writing" in this book, Lawrence everywhere works intelligently to define the psychological dilemma of modern man and woman. *The Trespasser* is not a turgid outpouring of melancholy youth but the early experimental work of an intelligence in full command of a metaphysic and a psychology that, for many readers, define accurately the realities of their inner lives.

MARGOT NORRIS

The Ontology of D.H. Lawrence's "St. Mawr"

In a sense, D. H. Lawrence's novella *St. Mawr* is a Romantic allegory of the salvation of the dark, wild, true, animal self by retreat from modern culture, technology, and enlightenment. Like other "savage pilgrimages" in Lawrence's fiction, its conceptual movement appears to be a simple switch from one axis of a traditional binary system (nature / culture, body / mind, spirit / ideal, Dionysus / Apollo, and so on) to the other. But this naïve interpretation, even when conducted on both thematic and tropological levels, obscures the radicalness of Lawrence's enterprise, which is nothing less than the dismantling of an anthropocentric ontology. In *St. Mawr*, Lawrence does battle with the most fundamental premise of the Western humanistic tradition: that human being is superior to animal being because man thinks, speaks, and differentiates between good and evil.

The savage pilgrimage of *St. Mawr* is an ontological journey into what Lawrence calls "the fourth dimension," the "heaven of existence" where each creature "attains to its own fullness of being, its own *living* self." Insofar as this displacement is symbolized by the traditional narrative device of mythic journey into a sacral region, *St. Mawr* is allegory. But the term inadequately reflects the ironic relationship between the quester and her object. Since becoming the animal is becoming what one is, the quest has the ironic circularity of Nietzsche's eternal recurrence. But neither is the quest tautological. One can be an animal without *being* an

---

From *Beasts of the Modern Imagination: Darwin, Nietzsche, Kafka, Ernst, and Lawrence.*

animal, and it is precisely the wedge of difference between these two statements (and the ontological conditions they represent) that is the philosophical object of the novella. The epistemological ramifications of this enterprise constitute the perceptual shift of a Copernican revolution: we must forego our anthropocentric vantage, and seeing "as the animal," from the point of view of our human *animal* being, situates us in the paradoxical realm of knowledge Lawrence oxymoronically calls "blood consciousness." The savage pilgrimage therefore becomes a critical adventure rife with philosophical paradox, an intellectual recapture of noncognitive experience, a representation of "unseen presences," a mimetic critique of mimesis. The biocentric universe Lawrence substitutes for the anthropocentric one is, finally, silent and unconscious, an ontology founded on the negation of the self-conscious subject and therefore inaccessible to literary inscription. Lawrence develops devious strategies to outflank these paradoxes: a complex figurative language to adumbrate states of being that are usually expressed in the negative, and the development of the kind of negative polemic found in Nietzsche's *Zarathustra*, which teaches that one cannot be taught. One cannot learn to live as the animal by reading books (like *St. Mawr*); one can only surrender to the tacit knowledge of the body, the instincts, the blood. Learning to be the animal is surrender to biological fate. . . .

The marital, psychological, and cultural conflicts in *St. Mawr* are . . . mere symptoms of the greater ontological collision of alien dimensions, "a battle between two worlds. She realized that St. Mawr drew his hot breaths in another world from Rico's, from our world." Since the value systems of the two worlds are totally inverted, or rather, since conceptual categories like value are meaningless in the biocentric universe, each confrontation between them produces the "breaks" or ruptures that constitute the central dramatic events of the plot: St. Mawr's murderous "breaks" in riding, and the women's break with European culture. The clash of a moral (valorized) and an amoral universe also has generic implications for the novella: the misunderstandings, ironies, and incongruities it generates produce comic effects and grotesqueries like those of the Shropshire tea. The Vyners can hardly believe their ears when they realize that Lou and her mother do not value Rico, husband and son-in-law, more than they do their horse. They respond with baffled outrage to this shattering of their self-evident anthropocentric truth. The comedy ceases once civilization is left behind. The work's dissonances, which should be neither discounted nor deplored, are actually felicitous consequences of the novella's philosophic matter.

In attempting to dismantle the anthropocentric ontology, Lawrence confronts the interpretive dilemma that ensues whenever the essential premises of the Western system of thought are challenged. Critical analysis as a rational tool is a specifically human capability belonging to the stock of anthropomorphic resources that are the target of the challenge. The circular dilemma of Lawrence's critical writings (conducting a rational critique of reason) is replicated in the corresponding literary works (where he conducts a mimetic critique of mimesis). How can Lawrence argue, in the conventional rhetoric of argumentation, that being is not subject to argumentation? How can Lawrence represent, in fiction, the falsity of the representation of being produced by conventional fictional technique? Lawrence's problem, like Nietzsche's, is to make his writing constitute an act, a verb rather than a noun, a gesture rather than an object. Lawrence can be the animal, but he cannot speak being the animal except through the duplicity of an experiential fiction that becomes the pretext or "true origin" of the text: the killing of the porcupine that inspires the Nietzschean thoughts of "Reflections on the Death of a Porcupine," the touch of the stallion that awakens the animal self prior o the secondary activity of the discursive critique in *St. Mawr*. . . .

The tropology of St. Mawr, the stallion, is likewise circular and self-negating. Reading St. Mawr as an archetype, as the fixed and universal symbol of an unconscious meaning (such as the dark god, phallic potency, the life force) obscures his paradoxical function as a self-referential metaphor. The wild animal, or the domestic animal that retains its wildness, already *is* in the fourth dimension without any special dispensation. Lawrence must drive a wedge of difference between our anthropomorphic and a biomorphic perception of the animal by transforming it into a metaphor of itself, by giving it "glamour," by casting over it a spell of enchantment. As metaphor, the familiar horse, the domestic hackney, becomes *unheimlich* (untamed, unhomely, alien) to us as his wildness and potency, the fullness of animal being that is ordinarily hidden (*heimlich*), becomes apparent, because it is seen from his own perspective rather than ours. The truth of the metaphor of St. Mawr is its own literal residue, the wild animality of the horse, the fullness of equine being. "Just think of St. Mawr! . . . We call him an animal, but we never know what it means. He seems a far greater mystery to me than a clever man. He's a horse. Why can't one say in the same way, of a man: *He's a man*?"

Reading St. Mawr, the stallion, merely as a Freudian totem of the absent father, a symbolic displacement of all the phallic potency lacking in the modern young men, risks distorting his circular symbolic function by giving him a specifically anthropocentric reference. Lawrence deliberately introduces a shift from metaphor to metonymy in the tropology of St. Mawr, describing the horse in zoomorphic similes, an allotropic practice widely found in the poetry. Lawrence actually negates St. Mawr's totemic function by stripping him of his patriarchal role as the repository of meaning, authority, and law. It is precisely the discursive, social world, the Lacanian Symbolic, that is dismantled in the novella, in order to restore the preverbal, preinfantile, prehuman, presexual universe of the origin, where even the Lacanian Imaginary, with its specular images, is dissolved. "Even the illusion of the beautiful St. Mawr was gone," thinks Lou in the last reference to the stallion in the novella. St. Mawr's metaphoric and metonymic functions are ultimately self-referential and self-negating, serving as clew to the real, and inserting into our anthropocentric apprehension of it a wedge of difference. Once the fourth dimension is reclaimed, St. Mawr, horse and novella, may be lost and forgotten. . . . The ontological status of *St. Mawr*, the work of fiction, is that of a text crossed out, a text we are meant to read and forget, a text that is inscribed, then cancelled, in our conscious mind, so that it may return to haunt us like a dream, to move our affective being, to kindle our nostalgia for wildness and wilderness, to stimulate our instincts and passions from within.

The movement of the *Heimkehr* [or metaphysical homecoming] in *St. Mawr* is inscribed within the narrative and philosophical trajectory that spans Lou's homelessness at the beginning of the story ("She didn't 'belong' anywhere") and her homecoming announcement ("*This is the place*") upon her arrival at Las Chivas. The quotation marks bracketing "belong" alert us to the registers of metaphysical meaning Lawrence will tap in exploring the question of home and origin. Lawrence obviates the more superficial interpretations of Lou's rootlessness, as American maladaptation to the European cultural ethos or as temperamental uncongeniality, by generalizing her malaise to the other major figures as well. These figures share a common feature of origin in coming (St. Mawr and Lewis from Wales, Rico and the Manbys from Australia, and Mrs. Witt and Phoenix from America) from lands in which the decadence of civilization is not yet far enough advanced to extinguish their racial capability for vitality. By displacing these figures to fashionable London, Lawrence is able to measure their latent potential for life by the degree of alienation their cicurated environment generates in them. By this criterion, St. Mawr inevitably leads, for the formula inverts the cultural equation of home with domestication. Instead, an implicit definition emerges of home as the site that enables a fullness of life and an intrinsic perfection of being: a site, necessarily, of ferity.

Lou's failure to "belong" anywhere develops an epistemological character as soon as the narration moves more closely into her thoughts and feelings. Yet Lawrence uses the plot to undermine a purely existential interpretation of her alienation. Although Lou's sensation of watching her social world become increasingly oneiric and wraithlike ("Everything just conjured up, and nothing real" suggests a phenomenological awakening. Lawrence is careful to make its source external to her consciousness. By a skillful interweaving of the symptoms of magic and psychosis, he allows Lou to develop a reality disturbance that is beyond her volition or control. . . .

Lou initially conceals her irrational impulses by cloaking them in socially acceptable motives, pretending (even to herself) to buy St. Mawr for Rico. In the course of the story, the instinctive is revaluated, and the ability to experience magical and psychotic symptoms and to act impulsively becomes accepted as a healthy sign of unextinguished animal life. The intuitive tropism toward the wilderness (and its correlative, the transmogrification of Europe) is replicated in each of the pilgrims. But to preserve the authenticity of experience, to guarantee that it is not mimetic, copied, passed from one to the other, Lawrence limits communication among the figures (except for Lou and her mother) to assure their independent development. He also carefully individualizes their symptoms and tailors them to the peculiarities of each figure: Phoenix, the desert dweller, apprehends London as a nightmarish mirage; Lewis shares the feral vantage of St. Mawr and therefore perceives "the presence of people . . . as a prison around him"; Mrs. Witt the improbable society matron, suffers funny hallucinations of grotesque tea ceremonies. At the last, Lou rationalizes her motives only for the sake of successful dispatch ("You and I are supposed to have important business connected with our estates in Texas") while allowing her intuitive, biocentric "knowledge" to direct her decisions and actions. . . .

By making the mannikin of automaton synonymous with the eunuch in the figure of Rico, Lawrence suggests the psychological equivalence of supplements (representations, mimetic figures, effigies) and partial objects (fetishes, metonymies). Both are founded on a lack and therefore constitute a mediation between presence and absence, part and whole. Rico's poses, attitudes, handsome figure, and meticulous dressing and elaborate costume changes ("He has had a couple of marvellous invalid's bed-jackets sent from London: one a pinkish yellow, with rose-arabesque facings. . . . The other is a lovely silvery and blue and green soft brocade") are supplements for a lack that is defined, and becomes apparent to Lou, in contrast with the animal, St. Mawr. Lawrence alludes to it almost immediately when he describes Rico with a qualified animal trope. He is "the animal . . . gone queer and wrong," tamed and domesticated, the horse "edging away from its master," the horse that dares not make a break, the dog that "daren't quite bite." Rico's lack or deficiency is a purely Nietzschean lack of power, of which his sexual dysfunction or disinclination is merely a symptom. In order to avoid confounding this power with its anthropomorphic supplements (money, social importance, bureaucratic control, and so forth) he has Lou recognize its lack in Rico's eyes by contrast with the eyes of St. Mawr. "At the middle of his eyes was a central powerlessness, that left him anxious. . . . But now, since she had seen the full, dark, passionate blaze of power and of different life in the eyes of the thwarted horse, the anxious powerlessness of the man drove her mad."

Lawrence constructs a pathology for Rico that makes his vocation as artist the figure of his ontological castration. In Rico, Lawrence assimilates to the artist Nietzsche's "dangerous concept of the artiste," equating artist and actor as creators of simulacra that supplement their lack of animal vitality and potency. "But now she realized that, with men and women, everything was an attitude only when something else is lacking. Something is lacking and they are thrown back on their own devices. That black fiery flow in the eyes of the horse was not 'attitude.' It was something much more terrifying, and real, the only thing that was real." Rico belongs also to the uncanny version of the artist as vampire or ghoul who must appropriate the living animal vitality in order to nourish his deadness, like Hoffmann's Sand Man, the object of Freud's analysis in "The Uncanny," who plucks out the eyes of the living in order to make the wooden doll more lifelike. Rico appropriates St. Mawr in this way, using the powerful animal as a prop for the handsome figure he cuts in the Row, apprehending him two-dimensionally, as an aesthetic object, a still life or "composition" together with Lewis: "They'd be *so* amusing to paint: such an extraordinary contrast!" Lou, on the other hand, apprehends St. Mawr without mediation and without ulterior motive: directly, experientially, through a touch sensitive to the texture, temperature, and pulse of life. "She was startled to feel the vivid heat of his life come through to her, through the lacquer of red-gold gloss. So slippery with vivid, hot life!"

The sexual analogue of Rico's artist is the castrating eunuch, a figure that emphasizes the artist's negative and spectral function as reproducer of his own lack, progenitor of his own sterility. . . . Lawrence recognizes that the artistic function is inherently fetishistic, that art is inevitably a secondary creation of the object in a reduced dimension, miniaturized, like the Priapus on Rico's intaglio; reduced to two-dimensionality, like Rico's portraits; and trivialized, like the gods appropriated from the realm of religion and faith in order to serve decorative functions. "The world always was a queer place. It's a very queer one when Rico is the god Priapus. He would go round the orchard painting lifelike apples on the trees, and inviting nymphs to come and eat them." Lou's interpretive function does not reverse the fetishism of art and restore the object to wholeness; her interpretation of Rico as a painted / painting phallic god, a perpetually regenerating effigy, only recognizes the fetish as fetish, the object as partial, by situating it contextually in relation to its lack. Nowhere is the structural complication of Lawrence's ontological rhetoric more brilliantly in evidence than when he resorts to a metonymic metaphor for Rico. "If his head had been cut off, like John the Baptist's, it would have been a thing complete in itself, would not have missed the body in the least. . . . The head was one of the famous 'talking heads' of modern youth."

. . . But what of St. Mawr? Lawrence establishes the distinction between two kinds of aggressiveness as the ethical crux of the novella. "But St. Mawr? Was it the natural wild thing in him which caused these disasters? Or was it the slave, asserting himself for vengeance?" The difference between the two is precisely one of mediation. The wild thing's aggressiveness is autotelic, referring only to itself, to the potency of its life flowing forth unchecked and dangerously. The slave's aggressiveness is social, intersubjective, self-conscious, and devious. The slave's vengeance is not active but reactive, its source is not in the self but in the perception of the "other," its motive is extrinsic (aggressiveness not for its own sake but for an ulterior, self-conscious motive), and, because it is born of weakness, its tactic is one of inflicting secret harm in order to maintain itself in safety. This is the doubled psychology of Lou's apocalyptic nightmare vision of evil with its obsessional theme of betrayal.

> But she thought with horror, a colder horror, of Rico's face as he snarled *Fool*! His fear, his impotence as a master, as a rider, his presumption. And she thought with horror of those other people, so glib, so glibly evil.
>
> What did they want to do, those Manby girls? Undermine, undermine, undermine. They wanted to undermine Rico, just as that fair young man would have liked to undermine her. . . .
>
> Mankind no longer its own master. Ridden by this pseudo-handsome ghoul of outward loyalty, inward treachery, in a game of betrayal, betrayal, betrayal. The last of the gods of our era, Judas supreme!

In Rico, Lawrence combines the doll, the mannikin, with its emotional correlative of secondary, reactive aggressiveness (anger) to produce the automaton. "Rico's anger was wound up tight at the bottom of him, like a steel spring that kept his works going, while he himself was 'charming,' like a bomb-clock with Sèvres paintings or Dresden figures on the outside." The metaphorics of mechanized and remote-control violence (bombs, dynamite, guns) serve to distinguish the various kinds of mediated, human aggressiveness from the spontaneous, autotelic power of wild animals. "I always felt guns very repugnant: sinister, mean," Lawrence writes in "The Death of a Porcupine." The meanness refers, no doubt, to the instrumental function of weapons that spare their users all risk except that of reciprocal fire. Lawrence's military pacifism and existential militancy are in no way self-contradictory; he believes in the right and duty to kill but mocks the Italian hunters (*l'uomo è cacciatore*) training their rifles on tiny songbirds. Wild things possess courage commensurate with their intrinsic power ("the wild thing's courage to maintain itself alone and living in the midst of a diverse universe,") while Rico, like the Italian hunters, like a terrorist, conspires "to live in absolute physical safety, whilst willing the minor disintegration of all positive living."

Lawrence uses Mrs. Witt as a version of Rico in order to establish subtle differences in the causality of fetishism. She shares Rico's mechanical aggressiveness ("Mrs. Witt was *so* like a smooth, levelled gun-metal pistol") although its source is not a lack but an intellectual displacement, a misunderstanding. She devalues and represses her own real power ("In her strong limbs there was far more electric power than in the limbs of any man she had met") in favor of Mind, an instrument and supplement in Lawrencian ontology, a fiction compensating for a lack. In Mrs. Witt's fetishism, her mania for trimming shrubbery, her voluptuous response to hair, her fondness for shoes ("She was a demon in shoes. . . . Yes, she had brought ten pairs of shoes from New York. She knew her daughter's foot as she knew her own") we see not only the castrating tendency, the need to "cut up" the body because it cannot be apprehended whole, but also the possibility of vitality kept alive and unextinguished, however misdirected and cathected. Mrs. Witt's pathology is not ontological, like Rico's, but purely epistemological. As a "pure psychologist, a fiendish psychologist" she knows only analysis and vivisection, the ability to apprehend the Lawrencian body in fragments, in its dead parts ("If you cut a thing up, of course it will smell"). The apprehension of wholeness, of structures in their proper relations of presence and absence, eludes her precisely because it must be found in the instinctual subject (the body electric as perceptual organ) rather than in the object of contemplation or analysis. . . .

Since the Lawrencian body "knows," holistic vision, predicated upon power and fullness of life, is possible only for the strong: Mrs. Witt is capable of it; Rico is not. Mrs. Witt's first signs of recuperation are expressed in epistemological terms, as a revision (re-vision) of her thinking, a seeing of things not from a different angle but in a different structural relationship. This recuperation is therefore also rhetorical or poetical, as when she dissolves the metonymic organization of the figure of the body. "But—do you know?—it hadn't occurred to me that a man's beard was really part of him. It always seemed to me that men wore their beards, like they wear their neckties, for show. I shall always remember Lewis for saying his beard was part of him. Isn't it curious, the way he rides? He seems to sink himself in the horse. When I speak to him, I'm not sure whether I'm speaking to a man or to a horse." Her second observation, abolishing the discontinuity between the human and the animal, is clearly intended to serve as an analogue to her first observation abolishing the fetish. The implication is that the fetish, even when it is a part of the body, or the body itself, is always a cultural object (the beard as a necktie), and that a holistic vision therefore depends upon seeing the human (generic "man") as a natural rather than a cultural entity, namely, as an animal.

In order to give his concept of holistic vision a prerational heritage, and to define instinctive or irrational perception as a visionary plenum to which rationality represents an occlusion, Lawrence borrows from early Greek mythology the ocular metaphor of the "third eye." "Pan was the hidden mystery—the hidden cause. That's how it was a Great God. Pan wasn't *he* at all: not even a Great God. He was Pan. All: what you see when you see in full. In the daytime you see the thing. But if your third eye is open, which sees only the things that can't be seen, you may see Pan within the thing, hidden: you may see with your third eye, which is darkness." . . .

The irony of having the mythology of the "third eye" imparted to the company of arch and gay young Edwardians ("Our late King Edward" is invoked in the company that includes an "Eddy Edwards") by the goatish artist and philologist Cartwright, serves to draw a sharp distinction between knowledge and recognition. "Isn't it extraordinary that young man Cartwright talks about Pan, but he knows nothing of it all?" Recognition (re-cognition) implies the repetition of an earlier cognitive experience, in Lou's case the experiential knowledge acquired through St. Mawr. Lou knows what Cartwright is talking about because she has already seen through her "third eye." Mrs. Witt has not, but she could. " 'But what do you know of the unfallen Pan, mother?' 'Don't ask me, Louise! I feel all of a tremble, as if I was just on the verge.' " The unconscious basis of knowledge is also evident in its relation to wit rather than erudition. When Lou blurts out that she just sees a sort of "pancake" in contemporary young men, the pun on Pan identifies, with the unconscious quickness, accuracy, and wit of a free association, the source of the young men's corruption in domestication and harmlessness. . . .

The fall of St. Mawr, a brilliant moment of poetic compression, is structured like a palimpsest that inscribes in the contemporary moment of a prosaic riding accident a perverse version of classical, medieval, and apocalyptic emblems of the Manichean struggle of man with the animal and with his own animal nature. Foreshadowed by an earlier allusion, Hippolytus appears to be there, the horse tamer and devotee of the virginal Artemis punished for his denial of life by the hippocampine Poseidon, god of the sea and god of horses. The reptilian St. Mawr also conjures up the dualistic dragon of Lawrence's *Apocalypse* ("the grand divine dragon of his superhuman potency, or the great demonish dragon of his inward destruction"), the dragon of aboriginal life in contest with the St. George of civilized and christianized England.

Allotropism, a version of wholeness in Lawrencian morphology, functions as an antidote to the fetish because it describes a metonymy without a lack: relatedness and contiguity without substitution. The Lawrencian cosmos (Nature) is a plenum full of interrelated creatures and things that are neither equal nor fixed as a result of differences in degree and kind of power. Lawrence's political theories are firmly grounded in the natural politics of Nietzsche and must therefore be read without anthropomorphic distortion. Although Lawrence's great chain of being sounds deceptively progressionist ("And man is the highest, most developed, most conscious, most *alive* of the mammals: master of them all") it does not have an anthropocentric teleology or eschatology. In Lawrence's cosmology man is neither the end of creation nor the measure of all things ("One would think, to read modern books, that the life of any tuppenny bankclerk was more important than sun, and stars"), and although as a species, a creatural form, the human is more vivid than other species, individual humans may be deader than dandelions. Since for Lawrence, as for Nietzsche, strength and weakness are vitalistic concepts emptied of their anthropomorphic residue, the cardinal distinction between the human and the animal is erased and replaced by the transgeneric distinction of the wild and the domesticated. The master / slave relationship between Rico and St. Mawr becomes reversed on these grounds, with the stallion,

"Lord St. Mawr," as the master not by preordination but by default. "St. Mawr, that bright horse, one of the kings of creation in the order below man, it had been a fulfilment for him to serve the brave, reckless, perhaps cruel men of the past, who had a flickering, rising flame of nobility in them."

The long denouement following the fall of St. Mawr is designed precisely to demonstrate that the opposite of social hierarchy is not democracy but natural hierarchy. Lawrencian aristocracy is founded on neither birth nor money but on vitalism and a kind of "soul"—the nonideational, nonidealistic "flame" of a deanthropomorphized theology in which God is the sum of all quickness. The conceptual pairing of upper-class women and lower-class men does indeed obliterate the old social barriers as the ladies and their grooms head for America, but their new relationship does not constitute a new democratic social realignment. Phoenix, a servant in England, remains a servant in America, although on the entirely different grounds and criteria of the natural order. Although he is more potent than Rico (Lord Carrington) since he subdues St. Mawr after the first trouble in the Row, and more vitally connected to Nature, he traffics in mediated objects and is too materialistic. According to Lawrence, "the providing of food, money, and amusement belongs, truly, to the servant class. The providing of *life* belongs to the aristocrat." Phoenix, offering Lou an implied prostitution more degrading than her marriage to Rico ("He was ready to trade his sex, which, in his opinion, every white woman was secretly pining for, for the white woman's money and social privileges") is rejected and relegated to the function of groom and chauffeur.

To describe his hierarchical Nature rife with inequalities, Lawrence uses a vocabulary redolent of the emotional connotations of social class. The polarity of Lawrencian Nature at its best and at its worst is inscribed in the antonymy of the words *glamour* and *squalor*, both pertaining to the wilderness and marking the subtle distinction between its soul and its matter. *Glamour* resides in the deanthropomorphized fourth dimension. "The flying-fishes burst out of the sea in clouds of silvery, transparent motion. Blue above and below, the Gulf seemed a silent, empty, timeless place where man did not really teach. And was again fascinated by the glamour of the universe." By penetrating to its etymological root in Scottish and Welsh usage, Lawrence strips the word *glamour* of its resonances of meretricious beauty and restores it to the realm of magic and enchantment. Glamour, then, once more connotes an animistic universe where power radiates from natural things and exerts itself on the irrational and intuitive sensibility of the human.

Squalor and *sordidness*, also attributes of the savage wilderness, refer to the materiality of nature, particularly to the excess of inert and lifeless matter best characterized by the filth that accretes to the overcrowded welter of indiscriminate life. Excessive fecundity resulting in the herding, lumping, and cohesion of living things overwhelms their vitality with materiality. Lawrence shares Nietzsche's repulsion by the herd, recapitulating the mildly nightmarish welter of babies in the Brangwen household in the sordid infestations of goats and pack rats on Las Chivas. But whereas the violence of the natural competitive struggle restores ecological balance to the wilderness, the democracy of civilization produces the evil of Lou's nightmare. "Creation destroys as it goes, throws down one tree for the rise of another. But ideal mankind would abolish death, multiply itself million upon million, rear up city upon city, save every parasite alive, until the accumulation of mere existence is swollen to a horror."

The *Heimkehr* in *St. Mawr* entails the return to an ontological ferity: not just a return to the wilderness, but a virtual, if practicable, abolition of the social. The result is a curious paradox that resonates to Freud's unhomely home, a community that is not a community but a misanthropic ménage of people and animals marked by mutual indifference, separation, and solitude, but related in quickness and power. Lou's misanthropy betrays its ferity in her analogy: "A sort of hatred for people has come over me . . . and I feel like kicking them in the face, as St. Mawr did that young man." Indifference is not predicated upon a lack (a "human" deficiency) in this new order of relationships. Humans now relate to each other as animals do, without social consciousness of each other, without intersubjectivity, without concern for impressions or prestige, without concern for each other's conscious response, without malice, seduction, envy, supplication, or love. Lewis all along relates in this way to humans and animals alike. Lou, whose relationship to St. Mawr has been pulsating, instinctive, and mystical from the first, only later recognizes this as the natural order of things. "He knew her and did not resent her. But he took no notice of her. He would never 'respond.' At first she had resented it. Now she was glad. He would never be intimate, thank heaven."

Orignality, getting life straight from the source, is also possible only in the wild state in which the mediation of the social, the cultural, the intersubjective, the rational, and the communicative are abolished. Lawrence uses a distaff metaphor, "knitting the same pattern over and over again," to describe rational thought as divorced from feral origins and from natural power. Because it is submitted to convention, tradition, and influence, that is, to synthetic and man-made structures and laws, rational thought is mechanical, repetitive, and artificial. The "thought" of feral humans like Lewis is the paradoxical process of animal instinct: "He has a good intuitive mind, he knows things without thinking them." To Lawrence, artistic imagination is subject to the same limitations and cultural conditioning as reason and is therefore as incapable of originality. "Every possible daub that can be daubed has already been done, so people ought to leave off." Like Nietzsche, Lawrence would subscribe to a notion of aesthetics as "applied physiology," to an art whose function vis-à-vis life is to serve as a stimulant rather than a simulacrum.

Lawrence likewise views language as a cultural entity with the power to appropriate life and assimilate it to culture. The self consequently becomes victimized by idle talk and transformed into a purely social (that is, meditated) object, as Mrs. Witt recognizes to her sorrow. "I seem to have been a daily sequence of newspaper remarks, myself. . . . I never had any motherhood, except in newspaper fact. I never was a wife, except in newspaper notices. I never was a young girl, except in newspaper remarks. Bury everything I ever said or that was said about me, and you've buried *me*." The self's natural residue, the creatural animality or vitality of its body, is ejected from the ontological sphere by language. But Lawrence does not intend to privilege literary or fictional language over journalistic writing either. Bad novels merely multiply a language that does not speak vitality and consequently succeeds only in camouflaging its own void: "I feel as if the sky was a big cracked bell and a million clappers were hammering human speech out of it." Lawrence used the bell image elsewhere to contrast with human speech the sound of wild and unmediated animal life in the neighing of St. Mawr: "the powerful, splendid sound . . . like bells made of living membrane."

As we know from the experience of Alexander Selkirk (though hardly from the anthropomorphic fantasies of Defoe) the wilderness can rob human beings of their speech and restore ("reduce," from an anthropocentric perspective) them to ferity. The recuperative power of the wilderness is precisely its ability to extract and reclaim wild, natural life from socialized, acculturated human beings. On Las Chivas this power takes the form of the ability to induce aphasia in the New England woman who is Lou's predecessor. "At the same time, the invisible attack was being made upon her . . . she could not keep even her speech. When she was saying something, suddenly the next word would be gone out of her, as if a pack-rat had carried it off. And she sat blank, stuttering, staring in the empty cupboard of her mind, like Mother Hubbard, and seeing the cupboard bare." America is not, geographically, an originary site, and where civilization has made inroads, originality is no longer possible. "*Plus ça change, plus c'est la même chose,*" Mrs. Witt says, watching the American tourists in Havana. Lou echoes the phrase in Santa Fe, another tourist haven. Civilized America easily replicates European mediations and produces some of its own, replacing horses with motor cars, for example. The "more absolute silence of America" is possible only in a brutal wilderness, like that of Las Chivas, which can repel the social and cultural imperialism of its human invaders and thereby preserve a feral ethos for Lou's misanthropic ménage.

Lou's *Heimkehr* is possible only upon completing her abdication of the social, the domestic, the homely, a process begun upon her first meeting with St. Mawr and concluding when, with the overcoming of her last temptation (Phoenix) she renounces all sexual intercourse that could implicate her in an interpersonal or social relationship. " 'I am not a marrying woman,' she said to herself. 'I am not a lover nor a mistress nor a wife'." Lou ultimately forecloses the human, social world as she does her home in Westminster, shutting it down like a museum, separating herself with finality from cultural artifacts that are extruded from life, salvaged from fate and time, immobilized in the stasis of death. "She felt like fastening little labels on the furniture: *Lady Louise Carrington Lounge Chair, Last used August, 1923.* Not for the benefit of posterity: but to remove her own self into another world, another realm of existence."

The concluding description of the wilderness, one of the most splendid pieces of Lawrencian topography, is analogous in its epistemological and ontological functions to the visions earlier induced in Lou by St. Mawr. Before producing forms or images, these visions produce an affect. The first "split some rock in her" and released a torrent of tears; in another, Lou "breathes" St. Mawr's great animal sadness like a terrible sigh. The first sight of Las Chivas likewise triggers a desire ("Yet it was the place Lou wanted") and an emotional response ("Her heart sprang to it"). Her vision is also preceded by a recognition; her "*this is the place*" carries the conviction of one who knows because she has been there before, as though Lou were the atavist or reincarnation of the defeated little New England woman whose heart had nonetheless absorbed the magic of the monstrous land. This accounts for the narrational rupture represented by the description: although its narrator exhibits the extreme omniscience of prehistoric knowledge (the miserable pioneering failures scarcely merit record or attention), Lou (who does not know the history of the place) responds *as though* she knew, as though the ominsciently narrated description displayed her unconscious knowledge. She echoes the prosopopeia of the topography in alluding to the spirit of the place ("I can't tell you what it is. It's a spirit. And it's here, on this ranch. It's here, in this landscape"), and she predicts for herself an experience like that of the New England woman, who is unknown to her ("I don't know what it is, definitely. It's something wild, that will hurt me sometimes and will wear me down sometimes. I know it"). Lou's instinctive fullness of knowledge gains discursive expression only at the price of logical fracture and inconsistency: "I don't know . . . I know it."

Born experientially of Lawrence's Kiowa Ranch, this remarkable description of Las Chivas subverts the traditional rhetorical function of description, which is allied to that of the musuem (to erect monuments, to fix grandeur for posterity, to submit Nature to the conditions of the Institution). His enargia (and Lawrence might have approved the metaphysical propriety of this allusion to "vividness" of style) is above all devoted to the kinetic landscape, the vivid and destructive firmament, the vegetation as sensitive and protean and dangerous as a wild animal. "Strange, those pine-trees! In some lights all their needles glistened like polished steel, all subtly glittering with a whitish glitter among darkness, like real needles. Then again, at evening, the trunks would flare up orange-red, and the tufts would be dark, alert tufts like a wolf's tail touching the air." This landscape is unlike the pastoral or Romantic landscape in that humans with their consciousness and their aesthetic sensibility are excluded from this wilderness unless they are assimilated to its ferity. "The great circling landscape lived its own life, sumptuous and uncaring. Man did not exist for it." The little New England woman is seen from the vantage of the grey squirrel "as if she were the alien" and feels herself a trespasser on her own land, which negates all concept of property. "The berries grew for the bears, and the little New England woman, with her uncanny sensitiveness to underlying influences, felt all the time she was stealing." The description represents the settlers' failure to domesticate the wilderness (even their plumbing is described in the metaphors of cicuration, "the wild water of the hills caught, tricked into the narrow iron pipes, and led tamely to her kitchen"), as a grateful repulsion of cultural achievement in favor of the living feral world. Lou has no plans to imitate the pioneer endeavor: "I was rather hoping, mother, to escape achievement."

The dialogue between Lou and Mrs. Witt that concludes *St. Mawr* shares the function of other Lawrencian endings: to frustrate faith in communication and rational discourse, to confirm that the quest for the origin must be original (singular and inimitable) and that the text must be negated as a didactic instrument since it can do no more than stimulate an affect, kindle a latent desire, trigger a memory or a nostalgia. But the interlocution also has a certain psychoanalytic significance because the two women are mother and daughter, and Mrs. Witt (not the individual, the social entity, but the body, the animal) constitutes Lou's own vital origin. The *Heimkehr* is also the reconciliation with the mother, in their special relatedness that survives the paradoxes of their situation ("I want to be alone, mother: with you here") and of their figural language (the disjunction of sexual and religious metaphors in their dialogue) to coincide in a commonality of desire. Their end is a Nietzschean *amor fati*, and Lou's submission to the God that is the sum of all quickness, the spirit of the wilderness, the secret, feral home of her animal self, is no more than Mrs. Witt's desire to surrender to a positive death, to die into the unconsciousness of the pulse of life, "to be folded then at last into throbbing wings of mystery, like a hawk that goes to sleep."

Chronology

1885 David Herbert Lawrence is born on September 11 in Eastwood, a Nottingham mining village, the fourth child of Arthur Lawrence, a coal miner, and Lydia Beardsall Lawrence, a former schoolteacher of lower-middle-class background.

1898–1901 Attends Nottingham High School on a County Council Scholarship.

1901 Meets Jessie Chambers, who becomes his childhood amour and the model for "Miriam Leivers" of *Sons and Lovers*; goes to work for a dealer in artificial limbs.

1902–06 Becomes pupil-teacher at British School at Eastwood; begins writing *The White Peacock* and poems. Engaged to Jessie Chambers.

1906–08 Attends Nottingham University College, taking the teacher's certificate course.

1908–11 Teaches at the Davidson Road Boy's School; Jessie Chambers sends some of his poems to Ford Madox Hueffer's *English Review*, where Lawrence's poetry is first published in the November, 1909 issue of *English Review*. Friendship with Helen Corke, a schoolteacher.

1910 Starts writing *The Trespasser*; engagement with Jessie broken off; starts writing *Paul Morel* (to become *Sons and Lovers*). His mother dies of cancer, December 10.

1911 His first novel, *The White Peacock*, is published by Heinemann in January.

1912 Falls ill, and gives up teaching. Introduced to Frieda von Richthofen Weekley, the thirty-two-year-old wife of his former French professor at University College, Nottingham. *The Trespasser* published in May. Lawrence and Frieda elope, travelling together in Germany and Italy. Finishes *Sons and Lovers*; writes plays, stories and poems.

1913 *Sons and Lovers* published in May. *The Insurrection of Miss Houghton* (to become *The Lost Girl*) begun. Works on draft of *The Sisters* (to become *Women in Love* and *The Rainbow*); writes tales published as *The Prussian Officer* (1914). Meets John Middleton Murry

1914 Frieda divorces Weekley and marries Lawrence. *Study of Thomas Hardy* written, and work continues on *The Sisters*.

1915 *The Rainbow* published in September, suppressed for "indecency" in November. Writes *The Crown*.

1916 Lives in Cornwall, finishes writing *Women in Love*.

1917 Denied passport to U.S.; rejected as medically unfit for military service; expelled by military from Cornwall on suspicion of spying.

1918 Drafts *Movements in European Literature*, the play *Touch and Go* and *The Fox*.

1919 Writes tales published as *England, My England*; drafts *Aaron's Rod*; returns to Continent: Florence, Capri, Taormina.

1920 *Women in Love* is privately printed in New York. Completes and publishes *The Lost Girl*; writes *Birds, Beasts and Flowers*, *Psychoanalysis and the Unconscious* (1921) and a novel, *Mr. Noon*.

1921 Writes *Fantasia of the Unconscious* (1922), *The Captain's Doll* and *The Ladybird*.

1922 Visits Ceylon and Australia, where he writes most of *Kangaroo*. *Aaron's Rod* published in April. Takes up residence in Taos, New Mexico.

1923 Completes and publishes *Birds, Beasts and Flowers; Kangaroo* published; begins work on *The Plumed Serpent*. Visits Mexico and Europe.

1924 Writes *Mornings in Mexico* (1927), *St. Mawr* (1925) and the tales, *The Princess* and *The Woman Who Rode Away*.

1925 Completes *The Plumed Serpent* and the play, *David*. *St. Mawr* published.

1926 *The Plumed Serpent* published in January. Takes up residence near Florence. Begins writing *Lady Chatterley's Lover*.

1927 Begins work on *Escaped Cock* (published as *The Man Who Died* and *Etruscan Places* (1932).

1928 Completes *Lady Chatterley's Lover*, published first in Florence, though numerous pirated editions appear in England. Resides in South of France. Postal authorities seize manuscript of *Pansies*. Completes *The Man Who Died* (1929).

1929 Police raid exhibition (July) of Lawrence's paintings at the Warren Gallery, London. Writes *More Pansies*, *Pornography and Obscenity*, *Apocalypse* and *Nettles*.

1930 Dies of tuberculosis at a sanatorium near Antibes, France, on March 2.

1960 Penguin Books publishes unexpurgated *Lady Chatterley's Lover* in England, and is prosecuted under the Obscene Publications Act. After a celebrated trial, Penguin wins.

Contributors

HAROLD BLOOM, is the recipient of the 1985 MacArthur Foundation Award and Sterling Professor of the Humanities at Yale University. He is the author of *The Anxiety of Influence, Poetry and Repression* and many other volumes of literary criticism. His forthcoming study, *Freud: Transference and Authority*, attempts a full-scale reading of all of Freud's major writings. He is the general editor of *The Chelsea House Library of Literary Criticism*.

DAVID J. GORDON, Professor of English at Hunter College, is the author of *D. H. Lawrence as a Literary Critic* (1966) and *Literary Art and the Unconscious* (1976).

PHILIP RIEFF, Franklin Professor of Sociology at the University of Pennsylvania, is the author of *Freud: The Mind of the Moralist* (1959) and *The Triumph of the Therapeutic: Uses of Faith after Freud* (1966).

FRANK KERMODE's books include *Romantic Image* (1957), *The Sense of an Ending: Studies in the Theory of Fiction* (1967), *Continuities* (1968), *The Classic* (1975) and *The Art of Telling: Essays on Fiction* (1983). He is currently a member of the English Department at Columbia University.

LOUIS L. MARTZ, Sterling Professor Emeritus of English at Yale University, is the author of *The Poetry of Meditation* (1962), *The Paradise Within* (1964), *The Poem of the Mind* (1966), *The Wit of Love* (1969) and *Poet of Exile* (1980).

COLIN CLARKE is the author of *Romantic Paradox: An Essay on the Poetry of Wordsworth* (1962) and *River of Dissolution: D. H. Lawrence and English Romanticism* (1969).

DAVID CAVITCH, the author of *D. H. Lawrence and the New World*, is Professor of English at Tufts University.

SANDRA M. GILBERT, Professor of English at Princeton University, is the author of *Acts of Attention: The Poems of D. H. Lawrence* (1972) and co-author (with Susan Gubar) of *The Madwoman in the Attic: The Woman Writer and the Nineteenth-Century Literary Imagination* (1979).

BARBARA HARDY, Professor of English Literature, Birbeck College, University of London, is the author of *The Appropriate Form: An Essay on the Novel* (1970), *The Advantage of Lyric* (1976) and *Forms of Feeling in Victorian Fiction* (1985).

F. R. LEAVIS was a Fellow of Downing College, Cambridge and the author of *Revaluation: Tradition and Development in English Poetry* (1936), *The Great Tradition: George Eliot, James and Conrad* (1948), *D. H. Lawrence, Novelist* (1955) and *Nor Shall My Sword* (1972).

GARRETT STEWART, Professor of English at the University of California at Santa Barbara, is the author of *Dickens and the Trial of the Imagination* (1974) and *Death Sentences: Styles of Dying in British Fiction* (1984).

LEO BERSANI is Professor of French at the University of California at Berkeley and the author of *Marcel Proust, Balzac* and *A Future of Astyanax: Character and Desire in Literature*.

ELIZABETH BRODY TENENBAUM is Associate Professor of English at Herbert H. Lehman College in the City University of New York. She is the author of *The Problematic Self*.

H. M. DALESKI, Professor of English Literature at the Hebrew University of Jerusalem, is the author of *The Forked Flame: A Study of D. H. Lawrence* (1965), *Dickens and the Art of Analogy* and *Joseph Conrad: The Way of Dispossession* (1977).

JOYCE CAROL OATES has taught at the University of Detroit and the University of Windsor, in Ontario; since 1978, she has been a member of the Creative Writing Program at Princeton University. She is the author of over forty books of fiction, poetry and criticism.

GEORGE LEVINE is Professor of English at Rutgers University and author of *Boundaries of Fiction: Carlyle, Macaulay, Newman* and *The Realistic Imagination: English Fiction from Frankenstein to Lady Chatterley*.

ROSS C. MURFIN is Professor of English at the University of Miami and the author of *Swinburne, Hardy, Lawrence, and the Burden of Belief* (1978) and *The Poetry of D. H. Lawrence: Texts and Contexts* (1983).

MARTIN PRICE, Sterling Professor of English at Yale University, is the author of *Swift's Rhetorical Art: A Study in Structure and Meaning* (1953), *To the Palace of Wisdom: Studies of Order and Energy from Dryden to Blake* (1964) and *Forms of Life: Character and Moral Imagination in the Novel* (1983).

DANIEL J. SCHNEIDER, Professor of English at the University of Tennessee, is the author of *The Crystal Cage: Adventures of the Imagination in the Fiction of*

Henry James, Symbolism: The Manichean Vision and *D. H. Lawrence: The Artist as Psychologist.*

MARGOT NORRIS is Professor of English at the University of Michigan and the author of *The Decentered Universe of "Finnegans Wake"* and *Beasts of the Modern Imagination.*

Bibliography

Albright, Daniel. *Personality and Impersonality: Lawrence, Woolf, and Mann*. Chicago: The University of Chicago Press, 1978.

Alvarez, Alfred. "D. H. Lawrence: The Single State of Mind." In *A D.H. Lawrence Miscellany*. Edited by Harry T. Moore. Carbondale: Southern Illinois University Press, 1961.

Balbert, Peter. *D.H. Lawrence and the Psychology of Rhythm: The Meaning of Form in "The Rainbow."* The Hague: Mouton, 1974.

Bedient, Calvin. *Architects of the Self: George Eliot, D. H. Lawrence, and E. M. Forster*. Berkeley: University of California Press, 1972.

Ben-Ephraim, Gavriel. *The Moon's Dominion: Narrative Dichotomy and Female Dominance in Lawrence's Earlier Novels*. London: Associated University Presses, 1981.

Bersani, Leo. "Lawrentian Stillness." In *A Future for Astyanax*. Boston: Little, Brown & Co., 1976.

Blackmur, R. P. "D. H. Lawrence and Expressive Form." In *The Double Agent*. New York: Arrow Editions, 1935.

Blanchard, Lydia. "Love and Power: A Reconsideration of Sexual Politics in D. H. Lawrence." *Modern Fiction Studies* 21 (1975): 431–43.

Bloom, Harold. "Lawrence, Blackmur, Eliot, and the Tortoise." In *The Ringers in the Tower: Studies in Romantic Tradition*. Chicago: The University of Chicago Press, 1971.

Booth, Wayne C. *The Rhetoric of Fiction*. Chicago: The University of Chicago Press, 1961.

Burns, Aidan. *Nature and Culture in D. H. Lawrence*. Totowa, N.J.: Barnes and Noble Books, 1980.

Cavitch, David. *D. H. Lawrence and the New World*. Oxford: Oxford University Press, 1969.

Clarke, Colin. *River of Dissolution: D. H. Lawrence and English Romanticism*. New York: Barnes and Noble, 1969.

Daleski, H. M. *The Forked Flame: A Study of D. H. Lawrence*. Evanston: Northwestern University Press, 1965.

Dervin, Daniel. A "Strange Sapience": The Creative Imagination of D. H. Lawrence. Amherst: The University of Massachusetts Press, 1984.

Dix, Carol, ed. *D. H. Lawrence and Women*. Totowa, N.J.: Littlefield, 1980.

Draper, R. P. "Authority and the Individual: A Study of D. H. Lawrence's *Kangaroo*." *Critical Quarterly* 1 (1959): 208–15.

Ebbatson, Roger. *The Evolutionary Self: Hardy, Foster, Lawrence*. Totowa, N.J.: Barnes and Noble, 1982.

Empson, William. "Lady Chatterley Again." *Essays in Criticism* 13 (1963): 101–04.

Engel, Monroe. "The Continuity of Lawrence's Short Novels." *Hudson Review* 11 (1958): 210–19.

Ford, George H. *Double Measure: A Study of the Novels and Stories of D. H. Lawrence*. New York: Holt, Rinehart and Winston, 1965.

Gilbert, Sandra M. *Acts of Attention: The Poems of D. H. Lawrence*. Ithaca: Cornell University Press, 1972.

Goodheart, Eugene. *The Utopian Vision of D. H. Lawrence*. Chicago: The University of Chicago Press, 1963.

Gordon, David J. "Sex and Language in D. H. Lawrence." *Twentieth Century Literature* 4, vol. 27 (Winter 1981).

Gutierrez, Donald. *Lapsing Out: Embodiments of Death and Rebirth in the Last Writings of D. H. Lawrence*. Rutherford, N.J.: Fairleigh Dickinson University Press, 1980.

Hardy, Barbara. *The Appropriate Form: An Essay on the Novel*. London: Athlone Press, 1964.

Hartman, Geoffrey H. "Symbolism Versus Character in Lawrence's First Play." In *Easy Pieces*. New York: Columbia University Press, 1985.

Hinz, Evelyn H. "The Paradoxical Fall: Eternal Recurrence in D. H. Lawrence's *The Rainbow*." *English Studies of Canada* 3: 466–81.

Hochman, Baruch. *Another Ego: The Changing Views of Self and Society in the Works of D. H. Lawrence*. Columbia, S.C.: University of South Carolina Press, 1970.

Hough, Graham. *The Dark Sun*. London: Duckworth, 1956.

Howe, Marguerite Beede. *The Art of the Self in D. H. Lawrence*. Athens, Ohio: Ohio University Press, 1977.

Humma, John. "The Imagery of the *Plumed Serpent*: The Going Under of Organicism." *The D. H. Lawrence Review* 3, vol. 5 (Fall 1982).

Kazin, Alfred. "Sons, Lovers and Mothers." *Partisan Review* 29 (1962): 373–85.

Kermode, Frank. *D. H. Lawrence*. New York: Viking Press, 1973.

———. "Lawrence and the Apocalyptic Types." *Critical Quarterly* 10 (Spring 1968): 14–38.

Kinkead-Weekes, Mark. "The Marble and the Statue: The Exploratory Imagination of D. H. Lawrence." In *Imagined Worlds: Essays on Some English Novels and Novelists in Honour of John Butt*. Edited by Maynard Mack and Ian Gregor. London: Methuen, 1968.

Knight, G. Wilson. "Lawrence, Joyce, and Powys." *Essays in Criticism* 11 (1961): 403–17.

Langbaum, Robert. *Mysteries of Identity: A Theme in Modern Literature*. New York: Oxford University Press, 1977.

———. "Lords of Life, Kings in Exile: Identity and Sexuality in D. H. Lawrence." *American Scholar* 4 (1975): 807–15.

Leavis, F. R. *D. H. Lawrence, Novelist*. New York: Alfred A. Knopf, Inc., 1956.

———. *Thought, Words and Creativity: Art and Thought in Lawrence*. New York: Oxford University Press, 1976.

Meyers, Jeffrey. "D. H. Lawrence and Homosexuality." *London Magazine* 13 (1973): 68–98.

———."*The Rainbow* and Fra Angelico." *D. H. Lawrence Review* 7 (Summer 1974): 139–56.

Miko, Stephen J. *Toward "Women in Love": The Emergence of a Lawrentian Aesthetic*. New Haven: Yale University Press, 1971.

Miller, J. Hillis. "D. H. Lawrence: *The Fox* and the Perspective Glass." *Harvard Advocate* (1952): 137.

Moore, Harry T., ed. *A D.H. Lawrence Miscellany*. Carbondale: Southern Illinois University Press, 1959.

Moynahan, Julian. *The Deed of Life: The Novels and the Tales of D. H. Lawrence*. Princeton, N.J.: Princeton University Press, 1963.

Murfin, Ross C. *The Poetry of D. H. Lawrence: Texts and Contexts*. Lincoln: University of Nebraska Press, 1983.

Oates, Joyce Carol. "Lawrence's Götterdämmerung: The Tragic Vision of *Women in Love*." *Critical Inquiry* 3, vol. 4 (Spring 1978).

Partlow, Robert B., Jr. and Moore, Harry T., eds. *D. H. Lawrence: The Man Who Lived*. Carbondale: Southern Illinois University Press, 1980.

Presley, John. "D. H. Lawrence and the Resources of Poetry." *Language and Style*, vol. 12: 3–12.

Ragussis, Michael. *The Subterfuge of Art: Language and the Romantic Tradition*. Baltimore: The Johns Hopkins University Press, 1978.

Rieff, Philip. *The Triumph of the Therapeutic: Uses of Faith after Freud*. New York: Harper and Row, 1966.

———. Introduction to "*Fantasia of the Unconscious*" and "*Psychoanalysis and the Unconscious*" by D. H. Lawrence. Harmondsworth, Eng.: Penguin Books, 1977.

Ruderman, Judith. *D. H. Lawrence and the Devouring Mother: The Search for a Patriarchal Ideal of Leadership*. Durham, N.C.: Duke University Press, 1984.

Sagar, Keith. *The Art of D. H. Lawrence*. Cambridge: Cambridge University Press, 1966.

Sale, Roger. *Modern Heroism: Essays on D. H. Lawrence, William Empson, and J. R. R. Tolkien*. Berkeley: University of California Press, 1973.

Schwartz, Daniel R. "Lawrence's Quest in *The Rainbow*." *Ariel: A Review of English Literature* 3, vol. 2: 43–66.

———. "Speaking of Paul Morel: Voice, Unity, and Meaning in *Sons and Lovers*." *Studies in the Novel*, vol. 8: 255–77.

Simpson, Hilary. *D. H. Lawrence and Feminism*. London and Canberra: Croom Helm, 1982.

Spender, Stephen, ed. *D. H. Lawrence: Novelist, Poet, Prophet*. London: Weidenfeld & Nicolson, 1973.

Spilka, Mark. *The Love Ethic of D. H. Lawrence*. Bloomington: Indiana University Press, 1955.

Stoll, John E. *The Novels of D. H. Lawrence: A Search for Integration*. Columbia, Mo: University of Missiouri Press, 1971.

Tenenbaum, Elizabeth Brody. *The Problematic Self: Approaches to Identity in Stendhal, D. H. Lawrence, and Malraux*. Cambridge, Mass: Harvard University Press, 1977.

Trilling, Diana. "A Letter of Introduction." In *The Selected Letters of D. H. Lawrence*. Edited by Diana Trilling. New York: Farrar, Straus & Cudahy, 1958.

———. "D. H. Lawrence and the Movements of Modern Culture." In *We Must March, My Darlings: A Critical Decade*. New York: Harcourt Brace Jovanovich, 1977.

Urang, Sarah. *Kindled in the Flame: The Apocalyptic Scene in D. H. Lawrence*. Ann Arbor, Mich: U.M.I. Research Press, 1983.

Vickery, John B. "Myth and Ritual in the Shorter Fictions of D. H. Lawrence." *Modern Fiction Studies* 5 (1959): 65–82.

Widmer, Kingsley. *The Art of Perversity: D. H. Lawrence's Shorter Fiction*. Seattle: University of Washington Press, 1963.

———. "Lawrence as Abnormal Novelist." *The D. H. Lawrence Review*, vol. 8: 220–32.

Worthen, John. *D. H. Lawrence and the Idea of the Novel*. London: Macmillan Press, 1979.

Acknowledgments

"Lawrence as Literary Critic" by David J. Gordon from *D. H. Lawrence as a Literary Critic* by David J. Gordon, copyright © 1966 by Yale University. Reprinted by permission.

"The Therapeutic as Mythmaker" by Philip Rieff from *The Triumph of the Therapeutic: Uses of Faith after Freud* by Philip Rieff, copyright © 1966 by Philip Rieff. Reprinted by permission.

"Lawrence and the Apocalyptic Type" by Frank Kermode from *Modern Essays* by Frank Kermode, copyright © 1970 by Frank Kermode. Reprinted by permission.

"Portrait of Miriam" by Louis L. Martz from *Imagined Worlds: Essays on Some English Novels and Novelists in Honor of John Butt* edited by Maynard Mack and Ian Gregor, copyright © 1968 by Methuen & Co., Ltd. Reprinted by permission.

"Reductive Energy in *The Rainbow*" by Colin Clarke from *River of Dissolution: D. H. Lawrence and English Romanticism* by Colin Clarke, copyright © 1969 by Colin Clarke. Reprinted by permission.

"*Aaron's Rod; The Plumed Serpent*" by David Cavitch from *D. H. Lawrence and the New World* by David Cavitch, copyright © 1969 by David Cavitch. Reprinted by permission.

"The Longest Journey: Lawrence's Ship of Death" by Sandra M. Gilbert from *Acts of Attention: The Poems of D. H. Lawrence* by Sandra M. Gilbert, copyright © 1972 by Cornell University. Reprinted by permission.

"Women in D. H. Lawrence's Works" by Barbara Hardy from *D. H. Lawrence: Novelist, Poet, Prophet* edited by Stephen Spender, copyright © 1973 by George Weidenfeld and Nicolson, Ltd. Reprinted by permission.

"*The Rainbow*" by F. R. Leavis from *Thought, Words and Creativity* by F. R. Leavis, copyright © 1976 by F. R. Leavis. Reprinted by permission.

"Lawrence, 'Being,' and the Allotropic Style" by Garrett Stewart from *Towards a*

Poetics of Fiction edited by Mark Spilka, copyright © 1977 by The Indiana University Press. Reprinted by permission.

"Lawrentian Stillness" by Leo Bersani from *The Yale Review* 1, vol. 65 (October 1975), copyright © 1975 by Yale University. Reprinted by permission.

"The Problematic Self" by Elizabeth Brody Tenenbaum from *The Problematic Self* by Elizabeth Brody Tenenbaum, copyright © 1977 by the President and Fellows of Harvard College. Reprinted by permission.

"Aphrodite of the Foam and *The Ladybird Tales*" by H. M. Daleski from *D. H. Lawrence: A Critical Study of the Major Novels and Other Writings* edited by A. H. Gomme, copyright © 1978 by A. H. Gomme. Reprinted by permission.

"Lawrence's Götterdämmerung: The Apocalyptic Vision of *Women in Love*" by Joyce Carol Oates from *Contraries: Essays* by Joyce Carol Oates, copyright © 1981 by Joyce Carol Oates, Inc. Reprinted by permission.

"*Lady Chatterley's Lover*" by George Levine from *The Realistic Imagination: English Fiction from Frankenstein to Lady Chatterley* by George Levine, copyright © 1981 by The University of Chicago. Reprinted by permission.

"Lawrence and Shelley" by Ross C. Murfin from *The Poetry of D. H. Lawrence: Texts and Contexts* by Ross C. Murfin, copyright © 1983 by The University of Nebraska Press. Reprinted by permission.

"Levels of Consciousness" by Martin Price from *Forms of Life: Character and Moral Imagination in the Novel* by Martin Price, copyright © 1983 by Yale University. Reprinted by permission.

"Psychology and Art in *The White Peacock* and *The Trespasser*" by Daniel J. Schneider from *D. H. Lawrence: The Artist as Psychologist* by Daniel J. Schneider, copyright © 1984 by The University Press of Kansas. Reprinted by permission.

"The Ontology of D. H. Lawrence's *St. Mawr*" by Margot Norris from *Beasts of the Modern Imagination: Darwin, Nietzsche, Kafka, Ernst, and Lawrence* by Margot Norris, copyright © 1985 by The Johns Hopkins University Press. Reprinted by permission.

Index